Child Victims and Restorative Justice

INTERPERSONAL *VIOLENCE*

SERIES EDITORS

Claire Renzetti, Ph.D.
Jeffrey L. Edleson, Ph.D.

Parenting by Men Who Batter: New Directions for Assessment and Intervention
Edited by Jeffrey L. Edleson and Oliver J. Williams

Coercive Control: How Men Entrap Women in Personal Life
Evan Stark

Childhood Victimization: Violence, Crime, and Abuse in the Lives of Young People
David Finkelhor

Restorative Justice and Violence Against Women
Edited by James Ptacek

Familicidal Hearts: The Emotional Styles of 211 Killers
Neil Websdale

Violence in Context: Current Evidence on Risk, Protection, and Prevention
Edited by Todd I. Herrenkohl, Eugene Aisenberg,
James Herbert Williams, and Jeffrey M. Jenson

Poverty, Battered Women, and Work in U.S. Public Policy
Lisa D. Brush

Child Victims and Restorative Justice: A Needs-Rights Model
Tali Gal

Child Victims and Restorative Justice

A Needs-Rights Model

TALI GAL

Oxford University Press, Inc. publishes works that further Oxford University's objective of excellence in research, scholarship, and education

Oxford is a registered trademark of Oxford University Press in the UK and in certain other countries

Published in the United States of America by Oxford University Press, Inc.,
198 Madison Avenue, New York, NY, 10016
United States of America
www.oup.com

Library of Congress Cataloging-in-Publication Data

Gal, Tali.
Child victims and restorative justice : a needs-rights model / Tali Gal.
p. cm. – (Interpersonal violence)
Includes bibliographical references and index.
ISBN 978-0-19-974471-8 (hbk. : alk. paper)
1. Children–Crimes against. 2. Restorative justice. 3. Children's rights.
4. Child welfare. I. Title. II. Series.
HV6250.4.C48G35 2011
362.88083–dc22 2011008732

1 3 5 7 9 10 8 6 4 2

Typeset in Arno Pro

Printed on acid-free paper

Printed in the United States of America

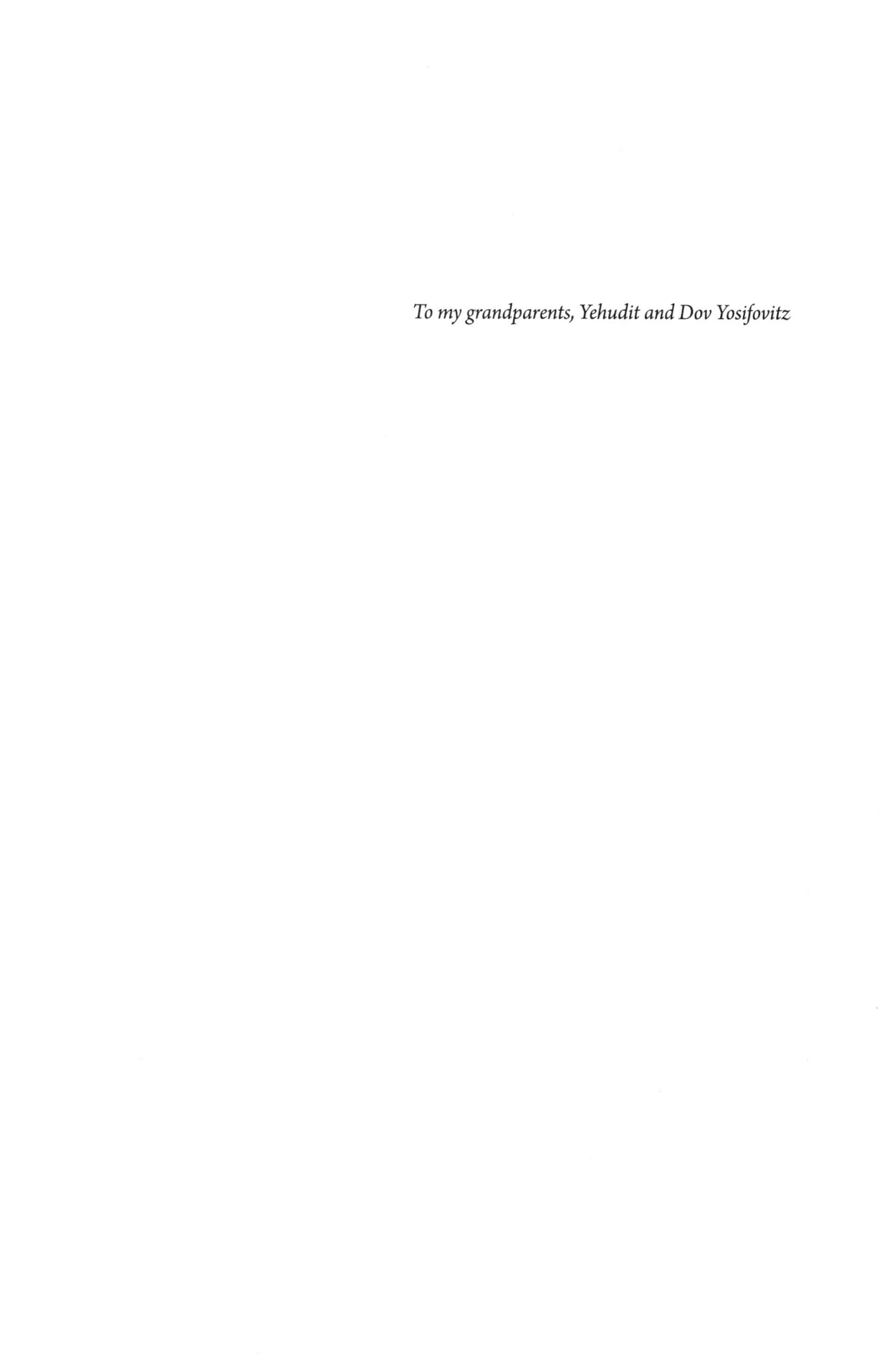

To my grandparents, Yehudit and Dov Yosifovitz

PREFACE

I had been a children's rights lawyer, working regularly with victimized children, when I decided to examine the appropriateness of restorative justice as an alternative to the criminal process for child victims. I was led by frustration with the formal court process and its inability to address the needs and views of my young clients. These victims, and often their families, felt they were being unheard, disrespected, and lost in the system—despite some far-reaching laws protecting child victims and witnesses from the hassles of the court process. Victims I represented and their families did not experience closure, nor did they feel that "justice was done." It was not revenge they wanted, but rather the opportunity to tell their story and to let their offenders know what harm they had caused. They also wanted professionals to take them seriously and consider their views. Lacking any real solutions, I often could only comfort them and refer them to treatment.

Beyond my frustration with the criminal process, my work as a children's advocate also taught me the degree to which children of all ages want and are able to take part in decision-making processes in matters regarding their lives. Parents and professionals are so focused on protecting children from harm (a novel goal in itself) that they sometimes forget to treat them as individuals with distinct wishes, strengths, and viewpoints. At the same time I often encountered the limitations of a strictly rights-based approach, which might suit lawyers but does not necessarily promote the interests of children. I was searching for something more complete than rights terminology but stronger than children's needs.

After having spent months reading through the psychology and sociology literature, I realized that there were many links between the needs of victimized children and their human rights, and I began making these links more explicit. One of the major problems in the field of childhood victimization is the fact that different professions do not really communicate with each other. For instance, the psychological literature on control is invaluably rich, and so is the legal and criminological literature on victims' participation rights. However, it is very difficult to find studies on the effects of participation in the criminal process on children's sense of control.

Another problem is that whereas children's rights have penetrated into the majority of children's policies, and similarly victims' rights have deeply affected criminal justice systems internationally, those who fall into the dual definition of being a victim *and* being a child are unable to benefit from these modern revolutions: victimized children are typically still regarded as objects of protection.

It was a long and varied journey, geographically as well as chronologically, writing this book. It started while I was doing research work in RegNet—the Regulatory Institutions Network located at the Australian National University in Canberra, Australia—and ended while I was at the Institute of Criminology at the Hebrew University in Jerusalem. Institutionally, I am grateful to RegNet and the ANU as well as to the Institute of Criminology and the Hebrew University for funding my research during the two phases of this project. I have been particularly fortunate to work among the brilliant academics at RegNet and have benefited from their wisdom. First and foremost, I am exceedingly indebted to John Braithwaite for being an inspiring mentor and for his generosity in sharing his experience, insight, and knowledge. Heather Strang was extremely influential in the development of this book and provided many thoughtful observations and constant encouragement. I am also grateful for many excellent scholars who read earlier drafts and provided helpful comments: John Seymour, Joan Pennell, Eliza Ahmed, Hilary Charlesworth, Nathan Harris, Lyn Hinds, and Brenda Morrison. Valerie Braithwaite was the first to suggest that I publish my research as a book, and I am eternally grateful for her advice. At the Hebrew University, David Weisburd provided invaluable assistance and guidance toward the publication of the book, as did David Levi Faur. The Oxford team were tremendously skillful, and I particularly appreciate the work of Nicholas Liu, Antonio Orrantia, and Aparna Shankar. It was an honor working with the Interpersonal Violence series editors, Claire Renzetti and Jeff Edleson, and they provided many helpful suggestions and ongoing support for this project. The anonymous readers were exceptionally generous in reading the manuscript and providing excellent comments, which I tried to address (even if I was unable to meet all of their concerns). I am particularly grateful for one anonymous reader who insisted I become more familiar with the connection between domestic violence and child abuse; this has significantly influenced the final manuscript.

On a more personal level, I have been blessed with a support system that is rich with experts in fields relevant to this book. I would especially like to thank Sharon Bessell, Tamar Morag, Mary Schwartz, Herman Schwartz, and my father Reuven Gal, who contributed their time and thoughts through reading chapters and early drafts and commenting on them, in addition to providing their encouragement and support. And, of course, this project would have not been published without the ongoing kindness, love, and encouragement of my family. My greatest thanks go to my husband, Omri Guttman, for being my anchor in stormy days, and to my children, Guy and Maya, for giving me daily reminders of the important things in life.

I hope this book will make a difference in some child's life, as even one child is a whole world.

CONTENTS

Child Victims and Restorative Justice

1

Introduction

The Victimization of Children

Children are arguably the population group most vulnerable to crime. The overall risk of being victimized before reaching the age of 18 years is higher than for an adult (Finkelhor, 2008). In a national sample of over 2,000 American children, aged 2 to 17 years, 71% of the children reported that they had been victimized in the previous year (Finkelhor, 2008, pp. 34–35). Over half of the participants experienced some kind of assault during the study year, with higher rates for boys than for girls; 1 in 10 experienced injury as a result. About one-fifth also experienced bullying. One in four children experienced property victimization and one in eight a form of child maltreatment (Finkelhor, Ormrod, Turner, & Hamby 2005). One of the most serious consequences of victimization is that it significantly increases the risk for further victimization. These "poly-victims" (Finkelhor, 2008, pp. 35–36) are particularly distressed and vulnerable. Sexually assaulted children are most likely (97%) to become poly-victims, experiencing additional victimizations such as assault, maltreatment, and property crime (Finkelhor et al., 2005). Due to their dependency on adults, children have very little control over their environments and, therefore, often cannot escape harmful situations. Children witnessing domestic violence provide a stark example of childhood victimization due to abusive environments. It is known today that roughly half of the children who witness domestic violence in their homes are also victims of abuse themselves (Edleson, 1999).

At the same time, only a small portion of child victims report the crimes against them, especially when they have been sexually assaulted or abused within their families (Fortin, 2003, p. 519). Moreover, children who find the courage and disclose their victimization are often further traumatized by the criminal justice system (Fortin, 2003; Herman, 2003; Morgan & Zedner, 1992; Zedner, 2004). Even when stress-reducing techniques are used, children of various ages are excluded from the process, are not consulted, and are treated, at best, as objects of protection rather than as stakeholders. Furthermore, child victims are often left without emotional healing, because their specific needs and the developmental consequences of their victimization are not considered. Only very rarely do they experience a sense of justice and closure following their involvement in the criminal justice process (Groenhuijsen, 2004; Herman, 2003).

In the research arena, childhood victimology (Finkelhor & Dzuiba-Leatherman, 1994) is a neglected field of victimology. While much attention has been given in recent years to child abuse—both physical and sexual—other types of crime against children and youths, such as physical assaults, property crimes, emotional abuse and neglect, have been studied to a much lesser extent. Moreover, the phenomenon of childhood victimization has not been studied as a whole, with only a few exceptions (Finkelhor, 2008; Morgan & Zedner, 1992). Following the work of David Finkelhor and his colleagues (Finkelhor, 2008; Finkelhor et al., 2005; Finkelhor & Kendall-Tackett, 1997), this book looks at childhood victimization holistically, addressing the full range of crimes against children. At the same time, because of its complexity and severity, child abuse (including the witnessing of domestic violence) is afforded some specific discussions. It is important to remember, however, that the various forms of child abuse and intrafamilial violence occur much less frequently than other (though, admittedly, often less complex and damaging) crimes against children such as physical assault, property crimes, and sexual harassment (Finkelhor, 2008, pp. 30–32, 44).

One reason for the lack of adequate solutions for children's needs once victimization has occurred is the failure to regard child victims as human rights holders. Efforts to punish those who harm children, and to minimize the process-related side effects, are based on assumptions regarding the vulnerability of children and their special needs for care and protection; those efforts do not address children's wishes and their need to practice their evolving capacities (Freeman, 1983, p. 105). Similarly, in the academic arena, studies on childhood victimization typically focus on issues such as children's revictimization and their status as witnesses, while neglecting others such as children's understandings of the process and their ability to engage in decision-making processes (Melton & Limber, 1992, pp. 181–182). There is, then, a need for a broader perspective through which to examine existing and developing practices addressing childhood victimization, one that might expand the horizons of related research as well.

Accordingly, the aim of this book is to explore ways to address the difficulties faced by victimized children, using an integrated needs-rights approach. In addition to a critical analysis of the criminal justice process, this book examines the appropriateness of restorative justice as a means to address the needs and rights of child victims and proposes some principles for action in restorative justice that might increase the likelihood of meeting the needs, as well as human rights, of child victims.

Following this introductory chapter, Chapters 2 and 3 set the stage for the central analytic instrument I use in this book—the needs-rights model, introduced toward the end of Chapter 3. These two chapters might be seen as creating the glossaries of the two fields, namely human rights and psychosocial needs, that are used in the rest of the book. Chapter 2 introduces the rights discourse, with the competing arguments for and against its use in the context of children. Two approaches to rights—Martha Minow's relational rights and Katherine Hunt Federle's empowerment rights—provide strong justifications for, as well as more fine-tuned definitions of, the kind of rights discourse that I employ throughout this book.

Indeed, this text brings into play a rights discourse in which *rights* are seen in their broad meaning and are intertwined with *needs*. These rights include self-determination of children (through participation) as well as protection and development. They include respect for the child as an individual, as well as the right to family and community support. Accordingly, theories linking children's rights and their needs are discussed.

Once the case for a rights discourse has been established, Chapter 2 moves on to introduce the main international human rights instrument that mirrors such a broad rights approach—the 1989 United Nations Convention on the Rights of the Child. It particularly discusses six of its provisions that best represent the rights of child victims in the needs-rights model, namely the four guiding principles of the Convention of best interests, participation, nondiscrimination, and development, and the two victimization-related provisions of protection and rehabilitation.

A strict rights-oriented approach, however, as broad as it may be, does not provide a rounded solution for what child victims face following their victimization. Accordingly, Chapter 3 moves to a different arena, that of sociology and psychology. Using psychosocial literature, this chapter reviews theories and empirical findings regarding the effects of crimes on children and their needs in the healing process. Toward the end of the chapter, an integrated model of children's human rights and their psychosocial needs is introduced. Because the needs-rights model explicated in Chapter 3 is the basic framework on which the following chapters build, Figure 1.1 is presented here as a matter of a preview. As elaborated in Chapter 3, the needs-rights model links each human rights principle to empirical findings on children's needs following victimization.

Chapter 4 describes the status of child victims in criminal justice processes in adversarial legal systems. It provides a detailed review of the particular difficulties that they face, as well as some recent reforms and their levels of success. In its second part, the chapter deploys the needs-rights model to evaluate the criminal justice system, adding another layer to the model. Once again, Figure 1.2 presented here is a preview for the more elaborate discussion included in Chapter 4 on each of the four parts, or clusters, of the model.

The chapter concludes with some thoughts about the contribution of the model as an evaluation tool and in uncovering the limited ability of the criminal process to address the full scope of the needs and rights of child victims.

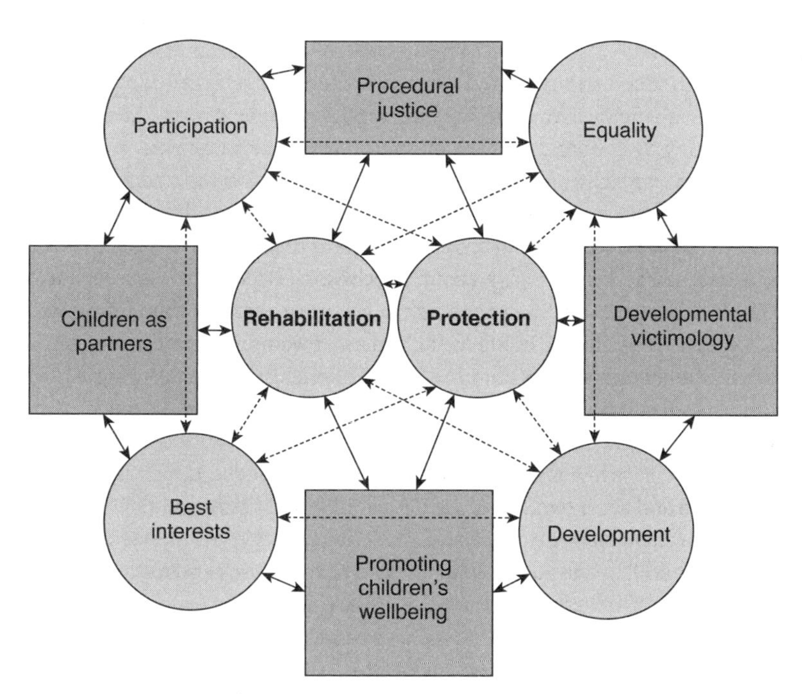

Figure 1.1 Integrating psychosocial and legal discourses: a needs-rights model for child victims.

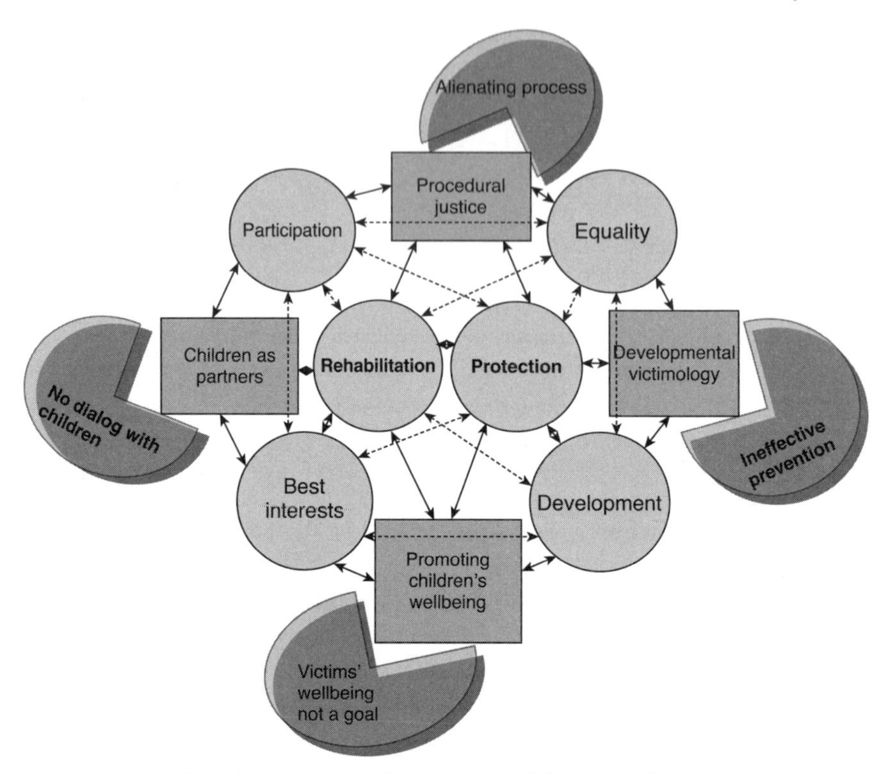

Figure 1.2 A needs-rights evaluation: shortcomings of the criminal justice process.

Chapter 5 provides a description of empirical evidence about what works in the field of restorative justice and child victims. The chapter reviews five case studies in which child victims have been involved in restorative settings, and discusses the central concerns and challenges that emerge from these cases and their evaluation studies. There is also a separate discussion on the unique concerns and challenges appearing in the application of restorative justice in cases of family violence. The case studies presented in Chapter 5 demonstrate, however, the great potential of restorative justice in meeting the needs and rights of child victims while maintaining their safety and wellbeing, even when dealing with the most complex forms of victimization. Considering the potential, as well as the risks, regarding the involvement of child victims in restorative justice settings, the lessons learned from these case studies are used in the following chapter in constructing recommendations for practice.

Accordingly, Chapter 6 returns to the needs-rights model, this time as a template for deriving subsidiary principles for action in restorative settings.

Similar to the methodology used in Chapter 4 regarding the criminal justice process, here too, the model's elements are grouped into four clusters, and each of them is analyzed to suggest such subsidiary principles. At the risk of being overly repetitive, I present Figure 1.3 to prepare the readers for this last layer of the needs-rights model. The somewhat cluttered description of this final layer of the model is followed toward the end of Chapter 6 by a more practical section, where eight heuristics are proposed for practitioners who want to conduct child-inclusive restorative justice.

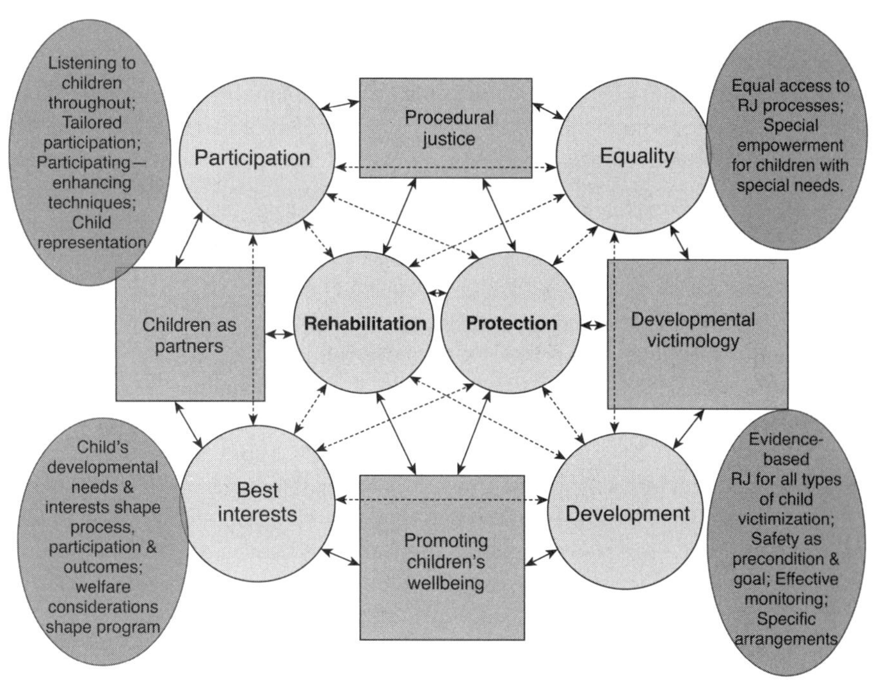

Figure 1.3 A needs-rights framework for a child-inclusive restorative justice: subsidiary principles for action (RJ = restorative justice).

The concluding chapter summarizes the central arguments of the book, recognizes the limitations of the suggested needs-rights model and its value, and finishes with some ideas for broader implications.

SOME BASIC DEFINITIONS

While children of various ages face different challenges that may require very different responses, this book refers to all children aged from 3 to 18 years. This age threshold is based on Selman's (1980) findings that at around the age of 3, children are able to recognize that other people may have different viewpoints.[1] Although children aged 0 to 2 years are also human rights holders, their capacity to implement their rights in the terms developed in this text is limited. The upper limit of age 18 years is guided by the internationally accepted definition, as appears in the United Nations Convention on the Rights of the Child.

This broad definition of childhood reflects the notion that all children are entitled to equal human rights. It is acknowledged, however, that there are vast differences in children's capacities to exercise their human rights, resulting not only from their age but also from the different worlds they live in, their families, and their own characteristics. Clearly, very young children cannot articulate their views in a way similar to that of school-aged children and adolescents. Their capacity to make decisions is also very limited. Nevertheless, this book shows that even young children are able to form their views and express them in many ways. Therefore, the relevant question that I ask here is not *whether* young children are rights holders, but rather, *how* they can practice their rights in justice processes that follow their victimization.

Similarly, while different types of crime pose different problems and varying levels of physical, emotional, and financial consequences, this book is not limited to a certain type of crime. Rather, it looks at the full scope of childhood victimization. Following Finkelhor's typology of crimes against children (2008, pp. 23–24), I refer in this text to (1) conventional crimes such as physical assaults, robbery, and theft; (2) crimes violating children's welfare such as abuse and neglect and the witnessing of domestic violence (see Finkelhor, 2008, p. 26); and finally, (3) noncrimes—actions involving coercion and force that would have been considered crimes if committed between adults, such as peer and sibling assaults. Corporal punishment, although considered violent and criminal if committed between adults, is on the boundary of the definition of crime because many jurisdictions do not consider it a crime (Finkelhor & Kendall-Tackett, 1997). Over 20 countries, however, have enacted laws prohibiting corporal punishment of children in the past three decades, with Sweden taking the lead in 1979).[2] While this book addresses the full range of childhood victimization, it also includes some more specific discussions about the unique challenges and concerns emerging from what is generally considered the most serious category of crimes against children, namely sexual and physical violence within the family.

While broad in the target population and definition of crime, the scope of this book is limited in other ways. First, it looks at *criminal* responses to child victimization, not child protection proceedings or social work services that typically follow child abuse cases. The forms of restorative justice that are discussed in this book all include an encounter (either direct or indirect) between an offender who had admitted of committing a crime and the victim, and all aim at finding ways to repair the harm done to the victim and the community. There are, however, close ties between such processes and child protection restorative justice processes, particularly family group conferences. These are conducted largely in cases of child abuse and neglect and family violence and are aimed at finding ways to secure the safety of the child (and sometimes the mother) while maintaining, as much as possible, family ties.[3] Further explanation regarding the differences and similarities between child protection and criminal justice family group conferences is provided in Chapter 5, including some discussion about the theory and practice of child protection family group conferences. The differentiation between the two contexts is often vague. Indeed, criminal child abuse and neglect cases where a restorative process takes place instead of the criminal process can potentially address child protection issues, such as a safety plan for the child, as well as domestic violence concerns. In other words, while this book discusses the feasibility of restorative justice as an alternative to the criminal process, it assumes that in cases where the crime has occurred within the family, restorative justice might also act as an alternative to child protective processes. Indeed, this might be a first step toward the centralization and unification of criminal, protective, and compensation-related processes into one institution confronting crimes against children (Finkelhor, 2008, pp. 164–165).

Second, this text is not located in any particular jurisdiction. It uses an international set of human rights norms as well as general psychosocial theories. Clearly, jurisdictions vary in their laws and procedures as well as existing practices, and I typically refer to specific legal systems only as examples. While Chapters 4 (discussing the criminal justice process) and 5 (reviewing restorative justice programs) do refer to national and local practices, they are limited to Western, adversarial legal systems only. These are, mainly, the United States, Canada, the United Kingdom, Australia, and New Zealand. Findings on the practices and approaches toward child victims in inquisitorial and non-Western jurisdictions are not included.

Finally, although this book discusses strategies to respect the needs, rights, and wishes of child victims, it does not suggest that the needs, rights, and wishes of other stakeholders are unimportant or should be given less weight. The emphasis on empowering children, listening to their views, and including them in the process is intended to fill a gap in the literature and in practice, not to negate such approaches toward the other involved parties. In fact, the needs-rights perspective I describe in this book would often promote, rather than jeopardize, the rights of other participants. For example, the needs and rights of abused children would typically require to ensure not only their own safety but also that of their nonabusive parents, while maintaining (as much as this is possible and desirable) their family ties (Pennell & Anderson, 2005; Pennell & Burford, 2000b).

Two comments on the vocabulary I use in this book are needed as well. First, the words *offender* and *perpetrator*, which are used frequently throughout the text, have a broader meaning than their legalistic one. In the legal sphere, there are important differences between *suspects* (those investigated by the police for alleged crimes), *defendants* (those prosecuted in court), and *offenders* (those who have been found guilty in a criminal court). In this book, *offenders* includes all three meanings, but this does not mean that the presumption of innocence is dismissed. This is for two reasons. First, at least in the restorative context, offenders are typically required to take responsibility for the crime as a precondition for taking part in the processes, and as a result their criminal conduct is indisputable. Second, this book focuses on victims' experiences, and from their perspectives, there is an offender whether or not he or she has been identified, prosecuted, and found guilty. It is acknowledged, however, that many offenders do not meet the legal definition, and that they are entitled to be regarded innocent in the criminal process until (and if) they are found guilty.

Similarly, while the words *victim* and *child victim* are used regularly, it is noted that from a legal perspective, victims are regarded only as *alleged* victims in the preliminary stages of investigation, since it is assumed that nothing is established until proved in court. Here too, however, I use a more inclusive meaning of the term, one that respects the personal perspectives of those who have experienced victimization (whether or not there is an identified perpetrator who has been found guilty). It is important to remember, however, that not all victims meet the legal definition of the word.

Since restorative justice plays such a central role in the second part of this book, the following section provides a general introduction to the concept (much more on restorative justice will appear in Chapters 5 and 6).

RESTORATIVE JUSTICE: DEFINITION AND CENTRAL PRINCIPLES

Born out of disappointment with both the retributive and rehabilitative justice paradigms, restorative justice has emerged as a "third lens" (Strang 2002, p. 43; Zehr, 1990). According to Howard Zehr, one of the architects of the restorative justice paradigm, restorative justice differs from retributive justice in that it regards crime not as an act against the state, but an act against people and relationships; reactions to crime need not impose pain for the pain inflicted, but heal and restore whatever was damaged. To make the reaction address the true needs of those who have been affected by the crime, the direct stakeholders are the ones who ought to sit together and decide on the appropriate ways to "right the wrongs" (Zehr, 1990). This is the translation of the lens into action—the process that applies it:

> Crime is a violation of people and relationships. It creates obligations to make things right. Justice involves the victim, the offender, and the community in a search for solutions which promote repair, reconciliation, and reassurance (Zehr, 1990, p. 181).

Restorative justice, then, is both a theory encompassing values and principles, and a process implementing them (Braithwaite & Strang, 2001). Focusing on the process, Tony Marshall provided the most widely accepted definition, according to which a restorative justice process is:

> a process whereby parties with a stake in a specific offence collectively resolve how to deal with the aftermath of the offence and its implications for the future (1999, p. 5).

The parties with a stake in the offense are typically victims, offenders, and the affected community; the damage to be restored is whatever the stakeholders see as needing to be restored (Braithwaite, 1999, p. 6).

The United Nations' *Basic Principles on the Use of Restorative Justice Programmes in Criminal Matters* (2002) provide a similar definition. A "restorative process" is defined as:

> any process in which the victim, the offender and/or any other individuals or community members affected by a crime actively participate together in the resolution of matters arising from the crime, often with the help of a fair and impartial third party. Examples of restorative justice process include mediation, conferencing and sentencing circles (Article I (3)).

Van Ness and Strong (1997) claim that a number of movements have contributed to the development of restorative justice theory. First, the informal justice movement called for the return of the conflict from professionals (in particular lawyers) back to individuals, as had been the case in ancient legal systems (1997, pp. 16–17). Nils Christie (1977), in particular, defined *conflict* as a property that had been stolen by the state from the direct parties, who lost the opportunity to resolve it in their own terms.

A second ideology that contributed to the development of restorative justice is that of restitution as a preferred way of sanctioning offenders. Restitution as a sanction acknowledges the victim's harm, provides a less intrusive alternative to incarceration, has rehabilitative potential for offenders, is relatively easy to implement and enforce, and might reduce revengeful crimes (Van Ness & Strong, 1977, p. 18).

The victims' rights movement has been another important force in the development of restorative justice theory (Van Ness & Strong, 1997). The victims movement advocated increasing services and financial restitution for victims (mainly in Europe), and for more participation and other procedural rights in the criminal process (particularly in the United States) (Strang, 2002, pp. 26–33; Van Ness & Strong, 1997, pp. 19–20). The inability of the criminal justice system to make victims parties in the process led to a cry for "a new justice paradigm" (Fattah, 1997, p. 264).

A fourth critical movement in the development of restorative justice was the emergence of reconciliation and conferencing (Van Ness & Strong, 1997, pp. 21–22)—two informal justice practices that developed and gained popularity since the 1980s. Victim–offender reconciliation or mediation programs emerged principally in the United States and involved direct encounters between victims and offenders, with the aid of a facilitator or a mediator. These victim–offender mediation or reconciliation programs typically included both restitution and some forms of reconciliation and were received with considerable levels of satisfaction by both offenders and victims (Poulson, 2003; Umbreit, Coats, & Voss, 2001). Conferences, or family group conferences, emerged in 1989, in New Zealand, and were influenced by traditional Maori practices. Conferences involve not only the offender and the victim, but also their family members and other supporters, as well as community representatives. Conferencing has shown considerable success in addressing the interests of both victims and offenders, including in cases of serious crimes, although it has also been subject to criticism (Burford & Pennell, 1998; Immarigeon, 1999; Kurki, 2003; Maxwell, Kingi, Robertson, Morris, & Cunningham, 2004; Merkel-Holguin, 2000). A third strand, that of sentencing circles and healing circles, has also emerged, particularly in Aboriginal communities in Canada.[4]

A final movement that contributed to the development of restorative justice is what Van Ness and Strong (1997) call "social justice" (1997, p. 22). This includes abolitionists and feminists who emphasized the structural injustice inherent to the criminal justice approach, and in particular to prisons, and called for alternative responses to crime and a broader understanding of justice (see, for instance, Bianchi & van Swaaningen, 1990; de Haan, 1990; Gordon West & Morris, 2000; and Hudson, 2003).

John Braithwaite's seminal book *Crime, Shame, and Reintegration* (1989) was instrumental in conceptualizing restorative justice and explicating its power. The three fundamental arguments of the reintegrative shaming theory are that, first, tolerance of crime makes things worse; second, that stigmatization makes crime worse still; and, third, that reintegrative shaming—whereby the actions of offenders are being condemned but at the same time offenders themselves are being acknowledged as accepted members of the community—prevents crime (Braithwaite, 2002a, p. 74).

Another theory that has been influential in the development of restorative justice is Tom Tyler's *procedural justice* theory (Tyler, 1990). Tyler suggests that offenders who perceive their case as being dealt with fairly are less likely to reoffend; accordingly, it is argued that victims and offenders perceive restorative justice as fairer than criminal court processes because it involves people who support them rather than people whose role is to stigmatize them. Therefore, restorative justice might be more effective in reducing crime (Braithwaite, 2002a, pp. 78–79).

Indeed, it might be argued that restorative justice theory includes elements from each of these ideological backgrounds: (1) It promotes individual participation and empowerment and a shift from professional decision making; (2) It emphasizes the importance of material reparation to the victim; (3) It treats victims' needs and wishes as central; (4) It promotes a shift away from the punitive to a more restitutive approach.

While restorative justice programs vary significantly in different jurisdictions, cultures, and contexts, some values emerge as common to all of them. Morris and Maxwell argue that the critical values of restorative justice are:

> the primacy of victims, offenders and communities of care through their inclusion in decision-making processes about how to deal with the offending and its aftermath; acceptance by victims, offenders and communities of some community or collective as well as individual responsibility for the offending and/or the reasons underlying it; an increased understanding on the part of victims, offenders and communities of care of the reasons for the offending and its impact on others; respect for all the parties involved in the process and the avoidance of stigmatic shaming; acknowledgment of responsibility for the offending through making amends; the reduction of reoffending; the reintegration of offenders and victims within their communities of care; and healing victims' hurt (Morris & Maxwell, 2001, pp. 267–268).

Other critical restorative justice values identified in the literature are: (1) participation (Marshall, 1999, p. 5; Moore & McDonald, 2000; Roche, 2003, p. 25); (2) reparation (Roche, 2003, p. 25; Sherman, 2000); (3) community involvement (Marshall, 1999, p. 5; Sherman, 2000); (4) crime as belonging to individuals (Morris & Maxwell, 2001; Roche, 2003, p. 25); (5) deliberation (Moore & McDonald, 2000; Sherman, 2000); (6) flexibility of practice (Marshall, 1999, p. 5); (7) equality (Braithwaite, 2003b; Moore & McDonald, 2000; Sherman, 2000); (8) forward-looking approach (Marshall, 1999, p. 5); and (9) victims' involvement (Sherman, 2000).

Restorative justice, then, puts the stakeholders—the victim, the offender, and the relevant community—at the center of the decision-making process, thereby empowering them to take an active role in repairing the harm that resulted from the crime. The recurring notions of empowerment, active participation, and nondomination apply to all participants, but importantly, in the current context, they apply to victims, including vulnerable ones. Child victims represent one such special population that calls for special treatment in both practice and theory of restorative justice. Very little has been achieved in this direction, and this book aims to fill this gap.

The first step, however, will be to set the theoretical basis for a needs-rights perspective in the context of child victims, and in particular to examine the appropriateness of a rights rhetoric in the case of children. Accordingly, Chapter 2 discusses the human rights of children, and those of child victims in particular.

2

Children's Rights

A Theoretical Analysis

INTRODUCTION

The goal of this chapter is to explain why a needs-rights model is an effective method for analyzing existing criminal justice systems and for designing new, alternative mechanisms to confront crimes against children. First, this chapter explains why we are using rights as the lens through which to look at existing and potential reactions to crimes against children. Admittedly, children's rights present a particularly difficult case for rights theorists, mainly due to children's limited capacities, greater vulnerabilities, and dependency on others. Especially in the context of childhood victimization, where clearly the protection of children and the prevention of further harm are central issues, one may reasonably ask: Why talk about children's rights when it is more realistic to talk, for instance, about obligations toward children or simply children's needs?

A practical reply is that children's rights rhetoric has already been adopted worldwide in international treaties and statements and is acknowledged as an important way of promoting children's welfare and interests. Most recently, for instance, the *World Report on Violence against Children* (Pinheiro, 2006, p. 34) recommended, among other things, to educate children and adults on children's rights and to fully respect the rights of the child, including the participation right (Covell & How, 2009, p. 229). But beyond the fact that rights rhetoric is already being used, this chapter shows that (1) rights can structurally empower children, and (2) rights can strengthen relationships. Both of these benefits are particularly attractive for child victims, who by their very victimization need (and deserve) to be empowered and connected to their supportive communities.

Only a certain rights framework, however, provides these benefits and overcomes the conceptual difficulties of attaching rights to children. This is a human-rights framework that links children's needs with their rights. Therefore, the second task of this chapter is to explain the special relationship between children's rights and children's needs. The leading rights theory that regards children as rights bearers is the interest theory, which defines rights as any needs, or interests, that are considered basic and universal. The interest theory has been suggested as an alternative to the will theory, which draws a necessary connection between rights and an autonomous will (Dwyer, 2006, p. 292), and therefore excludes all those viewed as lacking the capability of making independent, rational choices such as children and people with mental health problems.

Following an interest-based, or a needs-based rights theory, numerous scholars propose varying categorizations of children's rights, presenting a complex net of welfare, protection, and self-determination rights. While different authors make somewhat different categorizations, the interrelationship between children's needs and their rights is a reoccurring theme in their arguments. The needs-rights model used in this book is, therefore, a reflection, or a practical translation, of existing theoretical constructions of children's rights.

Once the theoretical basis for a needs-based rights framework is set, this chapter discusses the 1989 United Nations Convention on the Rights of the Child (hereafter, the Convention, or CRC), the single most widely ratified treaty (Price-Cohen, 1992). The Convention sets up a comprehensive bill of children's rights that includes both self-determination and protective rights. While their application varies across nations, it seems that there is no dispute about the importance of these rights, at least as political aspirations. In light of the nearly consensual nature of the Convention and its comprehensiveness, the needs-rights model described in this book draws its "rights" component from the CRC.

The chapter has two parts. The first conducts an inconclusive review of the debate around children's rights. This review demonstrates that needs-based rights frameworks are less vulnerable to criticism and can effectively address the conceptual, practical, and moral difficulties that a children's rights regime presents. The second part of this chapter reviews some international human rights documents relating to children and discusses in detail the Convention and the specific rights relating to child victims, which will later be imported into the needs-rights model.

As promised, however, the chapter begins with a discussion on the arguments for and against the rights discourse—both in general and in the case of children in particular.

THE RIGHTS DISCOURSE: CRITICS AND PROPONENTS

The choice of using a rights-based perspective to discuss childhood victimization may seem obvious to many. The political power of a rights-based discourse to address existing social problems and the international consensus on the importance of children's rights make it almost a necessity to turn to this terminology when discussing reactions to childhood victimization. Nevertheless, other readers might suspect the relevance, efficacy, or legitimacy of a rights-based terminology. Indeed, the most prominent literature on child victims does not use a rights terminology (see, for instance, Finkelhor, 2008, and Morgan & Zedner, 1992). Moreover, similar to feminism's skepticism and ambivalence toward rights talk,[5] children's rights proponents have acknowledged the limitations of a rights-based discourse. Rights in general and children's rights in particular raise concerns from various directions. Cass Sunstein (1995) identified six types of claims against rights. The following paragraphs unfold these concerns and link them with equivalent arguments that have been expressed with regard to children. The responses to these claims are not presented side by side to them. Rather, they are embedded in the discussion on the distinctive rights discourse I use in this book.

A first type of critique against the rights discourse is that it disguises the fact that rights are dependent upon communal support and are social in their nature (Sunstein, 1995). For example, a right to free speech has no meaning without a community of listeners, but the existence of such community is not part of the right. Feminist critics of the children's rights discourse follow this direction claiming that children's rights ignore the interdependence between children and mothers and between men and women. The emergence of children's rights terminology threatens women's independence and may be used to further control and marginalize women, in the "best interests" of children (Lim & Roche, 2000; Olsen, 1992). For example, children's rights rhetoric might lead to the insistence on regular contact between a "safe" father and a child despite ongoing violence toward the mother by the father.[6]

A second line of argument is that since rights are often presented in absolute terms, a rights discourse leaves no room for compromise and competing considerations and, therefore, is not suitable for complex issues (Sunstein, 1995). Some feminists argue that the simplistic language that characterizes the rights discourse fails to address the complex experiences and concerns of women (Charlesworth & Chinkin, 2000, p. 208). With regard to children, and referring largely to a simplistic rights terminology granting children full privacy and autonomy rights, some critics argue that this would "abandon" them to adultlike rights and expose them to adult-world dangers (Hafen & Hafen, 1996; Small & Limber, 2002, p. 56).

A third claim against rights is that they are general and indeterminate, and therefore unhelpful in resolving concrete conflicts and meeting human needs. The abstract language of rights leaves so much space for political considerations and manipulations when balancing competing rights, the argument goes, that there is hardly any meaning to the rights discourse in difficult situations (Charlesworth & Chinkin, 2000, p. 209; Higgins, 1999). A clear example of this difficulty in the children's rights field is the right of children that their best interests would be a primary consideration in decisions affecting them. As I argue later in more detail, the best interests right can be interpreted and implemented in numerous ways in each case and, therefore, is criticized for providing no real guidance as to the way children's matters should be dealt with.

A fourth critique is that critics argue that rights foster selfishness and individualism and neglect connections and social dimensions (Minow, 1990). A needs terminology, it has been argued, is, at least ostensibly, more compassionate, responsive, and "feminine" than rights talk (Waldron, 2000, p. 123). This concern is particularly salient in the children's rights arena, where an "ethic of care" (Gilligan, 1982) is arguably the most appropriate framework because of their inherent dependency on others (Lim & Roche 2000). Onora O'Neill (1992, pp. 25–29), for instance, argues that a rights discourse does not recognize the importance of kindness and involvement toward children, which are central to the child's wellbeing. Hence, to include these important obligations toward children, O'Neill proposes using an obligations-based perspective (O'Neill, 1992).

A fifth concern regarding rights is that they protect existing, unjust distributions of power through the protection of the private sphere. Specifically in the context of women's rights, it is argued that rights often focus on autonomy, privacy, and liberty—values that might be relevant to male, autonomic individuals—while at the same time neglecting the needs of women and the abuse of private power within the home and the workplace (Higgins, 1999). More generally, rights discourse has been criticized for its lack of ability to change race, class, gender, and sexual preferences discrimination and subordination, as the rights that have traditionally been included leave the private spheres intact (Klare, 1991). This argument is closely related to Martha Minow's "dilemma of difference" (Minow, 1986, 1990, p. 146). Rights rhetoric offers only two separate tracks—one track of freedoms and civil rights, granted only for those who are identified as autonomous, rational, and capable of making independent decisions; and the second of protections and social provisions, at the price of exclusion and disempowerment, for those who are labeled dependent, incompetent, and irrational.

People belonging to the latter group can find themselves in a worse situation than they were without having used the rights discourse:

> Thus, to this day, many fields of law divide society into persons who are mentally competent and persons who are not. The competent have responsibilities and rights; the incompetent have disabilities and, perhaps, protections. The competent can advance claims based on principles of autonomy; the incompetent are subject to restrains that enforce relationships of dependence. (Minow, 1990, p. 126)

Finally, critics argue that the rights discourse emphasizes entitlements and neglects personal responsibilities and obligations (Minow, 1986; Waldron, 2000). Children's rights, it is argued accordingly, fail to acknowledge the importance of children's responsibilities and duties that, in fact, promote their rights and interests in the long run. This is the case, for instance, regarding children's duty to attend school and follow teachers' instructions in order to gain education (Hafen & Hafen, 1996, pp. 476–477).

In addition to these general concerns, children's rights present particular theoretical and practical difficulties (Ezer, 2004; Minow, 1995a). First, the traditional liberal theory of rights assumes independent, rational individuals who are capable of making choices and expect freedoms from governmental interference. Children do not fit into this theoretical framework (Minow, 1995a, p. 1579). Indeed it has been argued that children cannot be rights holders, as they are incapable of making choices and exercising, or waiving, their rights (Hart, 1982). As John Stuart Mill stated in his influential text *On Liberty*:

> It is, perhaps, hardly necessary to say that this doctrine is meant to apply only to human beings in the maturity of their faculty. We are not speaking of children, or of young persons below the age which the law may fix as that of manhood or womanhood. Those who are still in a state to require being taken care of by others, must be protected against their own actions as well as against external injury. (Mill, 1859, pp. 22–23)

As a result, children have been largely denied the freedoms that are part of liberal society. Minow (1990, p. 288) uses children's rights as an illustration of her "dilemma of difference": Children are either granted rights as equal to adults, or protections which deprive them from their autonomy and relies on their incompetence and dependence upon adults. The rights approach, Minow argues, while aiming to challenge the exclusion of discriminated populations, still allows the different treatment of those whose difference is regarded justified or relevant, such as children. This difference-based denial of rights to children, according to Minow (1990, p. 285), is not based on value-neutral, scientific knowledge regarding children's capacities, but reflects societal beliefs about what children need and how to control risks to the community. In other words, the provision and denial of rights to children are based on social constructions of childhood, which differ across time and cultures (Bridgeman & Monk 2000, p. 3).

Children's rights, then, present serious challenges to the liberal notion of negative rights (protecting people against actions by the state). To give an example, even though the right to privacy is indisputable with regard to adults (no one would support the state's interference with a law-abiding adult's decision regarding their domicile), the state regularly removes children from their homes and makes placement decisions on their behalf. But children's rights are, at least ostensibly, compatible with a notion of positive rights obliging states to *act*, especially for protection (Ezer, 2004, p. 3). Nevertheless, children's positive rights are subject to critique as well (Minow, 1995a, pp. 1579–1580). First, many positive rights remained unrecognized, and without enforcement it has been argued that using the rights rhetoric is futile (Ezer, 2004). Talking about moral or natural rights in relation to children, it is argued, is merely a political standpoint, not a descriptive one; that since children's welfare rights are being constantly violated, it is pointless to adhere to them (O'Neill, 1992). Finally, welfare or positive rights are typically linked with paternalism toward the subjects of these rights and their further exclusion from society (Minow, 1990, p. 288).

On the political level, the children's rights terminology creates strong objections and controversy. It has been criticized for creating conflict between children and their parents (Brennan & Noggle, 1997, p. 14), limiting the authority of parents (Hafen & Hafen, 1996, p. 472), interfering in the private sphere of the family (Glennon & Schwartz 1995, p. 1563), and competing with parents' rights (Ezer, 2004). Another related critique is that children's rights discourse creates regression from traditional child-rearing disciplines toward "laissez-faire" permissiveness (King, 1994).

The critique against children's rights terminology, however, has not remained unanswered. Similar to the case of rights in general, most of the arguments against children's rights can be explained largely by the different meanings this concept bears for different critics. Sunstein's claim that "the real question is not whether we should have rights, but what rights we should have" (Sunstein, 1995, p. 757) applies to children as well. Many of the objections, for example, relate to the children's liberation movement, which advocated for equal rights and freedoms to all children in the 1970s (Fortin, 2003, p. 591). With John Holt and Richard Farson as their most prominent advocates, the liberationists argued that children should be seen as a minority group that deserves to have adult freedoms and self determination rights, similar to other discriminated-against minorities such as African Americans and women (Farson, 1974; Holt, 1974). Not surprisingly, this approach faced strong objections. In particular, this approach signaled the dichotomy related to Minow's difference dilemma, between "self-determination rights"—freedoms and legal rights—on the one hand, commonly associated with adults and teenagers approaching adulthood, and "child welfare" discourse on the other, which focuses on the state's obligation to nurture and protect all children against abuse, neglect, and other forms of child victimization (Rogers & Wrightsman, 1978, pp. 4–6). As suggested earlier, many of the objections relate to children's self-determination rights, although some critics attack the welfare-needs approach as well.

Rights proponents, then, insist on a more nuanced discourse that differentiates between different types of rights. Replying to critiques regarding the excessive individualism associated with rights discourse, for instance, Sunstein (1995) claims that many rights in fact help in constructing communal life and are dependent on the existence of community and social institutions. This is certainly true regarding the right to participate in decision-making processes granted to children in the Convention, because participation can only occur in the presence of others involved in making a decision affecting the child.[9]

For many rights proponents, therefore, rights rhetoric needs to be fine-tuned not deserted (Klare, 1991, p. 97). Needs-based rights and international human rights are two specific paradigms that are considered particularly immune to criticism and that maximize the benefits of a rights talk, and they are the subject of the following discussion.

From Needs versus Rights to Needs-Based Rights

Traditionally rights were regarded as creating duties of omission, rather than of action, whereas needs were regarded to create obligations to assist, help, and provide. This dichotomous categorization is not prevalent today (Waldron, 2000, p. 124). For Jeremy Waldron, rights and needs complement each other. Rights can be used to promote assistance and positive action, but they do it in a different way than needs-talk does (2000, p. 128). The language of needs is an objective, neutral assessment of the needs of a certain subject, based on others' expertise or understanding of someone else's human needs. Rights, in contrast, are typically (although not always, such as in the case of young children) expressed in one's own voice (2000, pp. 129–130). Thus rights reflect not only respect for the person but self respect as well:

> Both rights and needs amount to a demand that certain interests be attended to; but only rights-talk presents those interests in the voice of one who would be a full-fledged *member* of society, who is not going to go away, and who expects to be taken seriously as a enduring source of continuing demands (Waldron, 2000, p. 131).

So the needs discourse has its own faults: It assumes passiveness. It focuses on someone else's needs. Rights-talk in contrast, Waldron claims, has traditionally been expressed by rights bearers or has reflected the wishes of such rights bearers, as independent agents (2000, p. 123). Moreover, needs-talk has not proved to be effective, and politicians have not been quick in responding to claims about needs. African Americans in the United States, for example, have been describing their needs for generations, without any improvement in their situation (Waldron, 2000, p. 122).

Waldron, however, does not call for the abandonment of needs-talk, only that the rights-talk can provide an important framework to discuss human needs while addressing ideas of self-respect and dignity. Moreover, he suggests that placing needs *within* the rights-talk framework creates links to duties and responsibilities. For Waldron, to identify a need is to give a diagnosis, but using this diagnosis to claim a right makes a claim that creates duties on others (2000, pp. 131–132).

Waldron's description of the reciprocal relationship between needs and rights is an important building block in the needs-rights model this book proposes and will be revisited later on.

An International Human Rights Discourse

Another recurring (and related) theme raised by advocates of the rights rhetoric is the need to differentiate between an Americanized, legalistic rights rhetoric and the broader human rights terminology presented in the international arena (Charlesworth & Chinkin, 2000; Higgins, 1999; Minow, 1995b). A central difference between the two is that the narrower rights framework is generally associated with negative rights or freedoms only, whereas the international body of human rights includes positive rights that address welfare needs as well (Minow, 1995b).

In contrast with the narrow rights discourse, the international human rights framework is less vulnerable to criticism (Higgins, 1999, p. 226). For example, the vagueness of rights can be seen as a feature rather than a vice within an international human rights framework, allowing human rights to be used as aspirations, measures to evaluate societies and encourage mobilization. Moreover, human rights are often regarded as independent of a social contract or the existence of legal remedy when they are not addressed. In other words, although they are somewhat abstract and often lack remedial measures, they are broader and have political power (Charlesworth & Chinkin, 2000, pp. 210–212). International human rights have also been used to transform whole societies and create communal dialog—thus encouraging collective mobilization rather than individual claims. An international human rights discourse is defensible, therefore, against many of the critiques against rights talk. One of the greatest challenges for the human rights framework, however, is to address diversity in identities and cultures; this can be achieved if human rights are ready to meet the "personhood" and the associated needs of various types of individuals, with the full range of cultural, gender, and geographic differences (Higgins, 1999, p. 245). In our current context, an international human rights perspective to children would strive to offer standards that can be relevant for victimized children of different countries and whose realities are vastly different.

Whether or not one agrees with critiques of rights, the prevalence of rights-talk in politics and civil deliberation demonstrates its popularity, if not its effectiveness, notwithstanding its possible existing shortcomings. It seems, however, that a special kind of rights discourse, one that is based on international human rights principles and that addresses human needs as well, can potentially overcome much of the critique against rights.

When the subject in question is children's rights, however, and in particular the rights of victimized children, there is a need for further persuasion. After all, it seems beyond dispute that society owes its victimized children some basic obligations such as safety, rehabilitation, and protection from further harm. Why then insist on a rights-based framework, with all of its associated controversies? Two particular approaches to children's rights emphasize the strengths of a rights-based approach to children and effectively address many of the concerns. The first is Minow's relationship-based approach to rights.

Minow's Relational Model of Rights

Concerned with the dilemma of difference, Minow envisions a broad meaning of *rights*, which actually reflects both the differences between children and adults (through protection rights) and the equality of children as human beings (through legal, autonomy rights) (Minow, 1990, p. 288). For Minow, rights-talk can include three types of children's rights (1995b, p. 296): children's liberation, child protection, and social welfare and redistribution. While each one of these rights groups might be vulnerable to various critiques, when combined together into a broad framework, children's rights discourse presents a more robust template. The human rights approach, according to Minow, deploys this broader understanding of children's rights, based on children's entitlement to dignity, respect, and freedom from arbitrary treatment (Minow, 1995b, p. 296).

Minow (1995b, pp. 299–303) further replies to critiques regarding children's autonomy rights. These objections are based on a contention that children lack the capacity to know their own interests and to engage in an adversarial exchange. To argue that children are different than adults because they lack power, Minow contends, obscures the fact that it is the *relationship* that creates the power differences, and these can be changed. Autonomy, she argues, is not a precondition for having rights. Rather, being a rights holder depends on a community willing for the individual to make claims and participate in the ongoing definitions of personal and social boundaries. Self-determination rights, therefore, express the interconnections between the right holders and others who carry obligations toward them.

Addressing the concerns regarding rights as creating conflicts and weakening relationships, Minow (1990) claims that under this broader understanding of the rights framework, legal rights language translates, rather than initiates, conflict. Conflict already exists when legal remedy is sought. Moreover, Minow argues that rights can affirm community, as they acknowledge the claimants' membership and participation in the larger society. Rights discourse creates dialog in the community and a process of understanding, in which community ties are strengthened. Through a rights discourse, community members negotiate the relationships between them—such as between children and adults. The discourse of rights therefore not only is not inflammatory, as some of its objectors think, but rather it enhances equality among the members of the community, at least equality of attention; it urges the powerful to listen to the weak and their claims:

> The use of rights discourse affirms community, but it affirms a particular kind of community: A community dedicated to invigorating words with power to restrain, so that even the powerless can appeal to those words.... Committed to making available a rhetoric of rights where it has not been heard before, this community uses rights language to make conflict audible and unavoidable, even if it is limited to words, and certain other forms of expressions (Minow, 1990, p. 299).

Therefore, while acknowledging the faults of the rights language, Minow appreciates the power rights rhetoric has in attending power differences within relationships (1990, p. 269). Accordingly she suggests, instead of rejecting the rights rhetoric, to use it to challenge suppression and power imbalances (Minow, 1990, p. 307). Seeing rights as a language that can bring about change responds to claims against rights—both regarding their indeterminacy and those that question their objective foundations:

> The language of rights helps people to articulate standards for judging conduct without pretending to have found the ultimate and unalterable truth... children no less than adults can participate in the legal conversation that uses rights to gain the community's attention (Minow, 1990, p. 308).

To address the difference dilemma (the dichotomy between competent, rational people who are granted rights on the one hand, and dependent, incompetent, and irrational people who are subject to paternalistic protections on the other), Minow suggests unraveling the presumptions that create these differentiations and taking the perspective of the other. From that new perspective, people might become aware of injuries or features that were not considered earlier (Minow, 1990, p. 375). She provides three examples of policies that consider the experience of "others" without excluding them: The shift to sidewalks accessible for handicapped (this can result in improving the lives of the "majority" as well, such as parents with prams and cyclers);

the adoption of "universal isolation" procedures in hospitals to protect everybody from HIV/AIDS instead of only those who are diagnosed as sick; and teaching all school children sign language (Minow, 1990, p. 377). Taking someone else's perspective and using rights to address relationships is not a solution, however, but a first step. The next step, Minow suggests, is to work on the problem of differences in specific contexts and try to communicate with those others and address their perspectives. The focus on relationships contributes to the identification of institutions that create differences and adjusts them according to the various needs of diverse actors (Minow, 1990, pp. 383–384):

> The way things are is not the only way things could be. By aligning ourselves with the "different" person, for example, we could make difference mean something new; we could make *all* the difference (Minow, 1990, p. 377).

In the context of children, Minow's theory promotes a complete reevaluation of previous assumptions regarding children's incapacities and exclusion, through a change of perspective to that of children themselves. It might mean, for example, talking with children to evaluate their own beliefs about their capacities in various fields and a joint reconstruction of rules regarding their participation in civil life. It might also mean that instead of excluding children from decision-making processes altogether, such processes need to be adjusted to become clear to children and to make their participation feasible in ways that fit their different mental, cognitive, and emotional capabilities.

Federle's Empowerment Rights Model

Another helpful conceptual approach toward children's rights is what Katherine Hunt Federle calls the *empowerment rights perspective* (1995). She argues that it is necessary to recognize the centrality of power (and lack of it) in interpersonal interactions. Children are a powerless group, as their rights depend on the good will of adults, and elites in particular. Rights, in this context, are a valuable commodity as they are able to remedy powerlessness. Rights can provide the powerless with access to political and legal hierarchies and with means of challenging their oppression and subordination. Therefore, from an empowerment rights perspective, granting children rights may empower them—in other words, make adults treat children with respect. For example, under an empowerment rights perspective children in divorce proceedings would be accorded the same legal status as their parents through representation, equal opportunities to state their opinions, and their consent as a condition for any agreement. Similarly, in child protection procedures, an empowerment rights perspective would require legal representation of children, and their rights would be central in the process and its outcomes.

Federle rejects Minow's theory with regard to children; she argues that giving centrality to relationships in fact strengthens their hierarchical nature where children are powerless (Federle, 1994). Minow, however, does not claim that the relationships between children and their parents and other adults are based on equality. Rather, she aims to expose the imposition of assumptions regarding children's incapacities through an examination of the relationships within which these assumptions have been made.

There are power imbalances in Minow's relational analysis, which, she argues, rights-talk might transform. It seems, therefore, that both writers regard rights as an important political instrument, with the potential to empower the powerless through negotiating the inequalities within the community, while maintaining (and even strengthening) community ties, including families. Similar to "general" human rights advocates, then, both Minow and Federle, while acknowledging the limitations of the rights discourse, support its use for its political power in changing realities and promoting children's issues. As Minow argues, rights discourse is the "coin of the realm in national, and increasingly in international law and politics," and children's rights advocates should follow women and African American movements in putting children's issues "on the map" (1995b, p. 297).

The Advantages of a Children's Rights Discourse

While children's rights terminology raises theoretical and practical concerns, it also offers advantages to both children and society in general.

First, the normative, declarative function of rights language is considered important. Rights discourse can shape people's beliefs and evoke a process of adopting these rights in people's behavior as well as through legislation (Ezer, 2004, p. 48). A prominent example in support of this argument is the legal ban, enacted in Sweden in 1979, on corporal punishment against children and the significant reduction in public support of corporal punishment that followed what was then regarded as a revolution (Durrant, 2000).

Second, from a deontological perspective, rights rhetoric is associated with respecting children as individual human beings. It does not depend on competence or capacity, but on dignity and decency. As Michael Freeman argues, children may have rights simply "by virtue of being children" (1998, p. 140). Similarly, John Eekelaar (1992) emphasizes the importance of attributing rights to children in order to respect their growing capacities to make decisions. Rights terminology, therefore, is a reminder for adults to refrain from unneeded paternalism and to respect the child's present or future wishes always.

Third, a needs language might be sufficient in normal situations, but not all children enjoy a normal environment. Often in reality children are vulnerable, and their best interests are not always the primary consideration of their parents or caretakers; the rights-talk becomes critical when the initial assumptions of parental love and care and children's general wellbeing collapse (Fortin, 2003, p. 592; Freeman, 1992, p. 55). Indeed, the prevalence of child abuse shows the price of nonintervention. As Minow (1990, pp. 303–304) argues, to leave the private sphere untouched by law is to desert children to their own destiny, with high risk of being abused.

Fourth, children can have rights even when those rights are not implemented in reality. Michael Freeman turns to Dworkin's "rights as trumps," according to which rights are not dependent on state legislation. A right exists when it will be "wrong" or unfair of the state to act against it, even when that action benefits the general public or the majority (Dworkin, 1981, p. 139). Considering children's rights, Michael Freeman believes that rights terminology can be at the visionary, not the descriptive sphere; therefore, the lack of a statute protecting a right or creating an enforcement mechanism for it does not mean that it does not exist (1983, p. 35). Joel Feinberg too acknowledges that there are some "manifesto rights" that are not necessarily correlated with someone else's duty:

> Natural needs are real claims if only upon hypothetical future beings not yet in existence. I accept the moral principle that to have an unfulfilled need is to have a kind of claim against the world, even if against no one in particular (1980, p. 153).

Therefore, he is willing to be forgiving to "manifesto writers":

> for this is but a powerful way of expressing the conviction that they ought to be recognized by states here and now as potential rights and consequently as determinants of present aspirations and guides to present policies. This usage, I think, is a valid exercise of rhetorical license (Feinberg, 1980).

Finally, a key value of rights rhetoric it its political power (Kennedy, 1997): Rights discourse grants claims a status stronger than mere "value judgments" and, at the same time, are different from factual political claims. "A claim based on rights and incorporated into law is more compelling than a claim based simply on needs" (Covell & How, 2009, p. 24). Claiming a right means that the claimer is correct in making a certain judgment. In other words, "rights are mediators between the domain of pure value judgments and the domain of factual judgments" (Kennedy, 1997, p. 305).

RIGHTS THEORIES IN RELATION TO CHILDREN: THE NEEDS-RIGHTS CONNECTION

If the rights discourse is a valid framework for discussing issues concerning children, then the next step is to identify rights theories that explain and define children's rights. Of particular interest are those theories that suggest solutions to the needs–rights dichotomy (or, in Minow's words, the difference dilemma)—the difficulty in granting rights (rather than needs) to those that are considered "different" or "incompetent," such as children and people with disabilities.

However before describing child-inclusive rights theories, it is important to first discuss the most central rights theory that, among other reasons, has been criticized for excluding children, as well as other incompetent people, from the realm of rights. This is the will, or the choice theory (Hart, 1982). According to the will theory, as a precondition for having rights one must have the ability to make rational choices that lead to either waiving or claiming them from those who hold an obligation against him or her. Hence, the existence of an obligation toward a person and the ability of that person to activate this obligation constitute a right toward that person (Bandman, 1973; Marmor, 1997).

The natural conclusion that follows the will theory is that children (at least young ones) cannot have rights, as they lack the capacity to claim or waive them (Campbell, 1992). But is this outcome unavoidable? Hart claims that the will theory does not necessarily exclude children from having rights: Children are rights holders under the will theory, albeit represented by others such as their parents or other guardians until they reach maturity (Hart, 1982, p. 184, fn. 86). Another proposition is that the will theory can be applied to children if we consider them as having the potential for being capable of making decisions in the future (Coady, 1992). Like Hart, Coady believes it is sufficient that the child is represented by a proxy (such as the child's parent) who exercises the child's rights.

These propositions are problematic, however, as they raise questions about the appropriate representative for the child and the extent to which such a representative can be true to the child's own interests when conflict arises. In many child custody cases, for example, both parents claim to represent the child's interests and yet each of them argues for conflicting arrangements. An additional difficulty is related to the way such a representative is to decide what the child's true wish is (and not the child's interest, need, or welfare), without letting that adult's own views affect his or her decision (Archard, 2002). It is easy to see how, when represented by proxy, not the actual choice of the child but other elements may activate or waive the child's right; this contradicts the very notion of the will theory, which bases itself on free will. It is not surprising, then, that most children's rights theorists reject the will theory and search for other, child-inclusive, rights theories.

Neil MacCormick uses children as a "case study" to criticize the will theory as a whole (1982, pp. 157–165): The duty to care for children, he argues, is not discretionary; nobody—not the child, nor the parents, nor any other adult as representing the child—can waive it. Therefore, the choice aspect is missing, and yet there is no question that children are entitled to such nurture, care, and love. Even when a child is abandoned or neglected, the child's right does not cease to exist. Rather, those who fail to fulfill it (the parents in most cases) may face sanctions, and the state takes over, at least temporarily, to ensure that someone else fulfills the child's right to care, protection, and nurture. MacCormick concludes that children do have rights, irrespective of their ability to waive or claim them and even when their rights are not fulfilled in practice. The will theory, therefore, cannot be applied to children and is thus inappropriate.

The interest, or welfare theory (Campbell, 1992; MacCormick, 1982; Marmor, 1997; Raz, 1986), has been suggested as an alternative to the will theory, chiefly in order to overcome the conceptual difficulty of including children and other incompetent (or simply different) populations. Under the interest theory, a precondition for holding rights is the existence of such basic and important needs or interests that deserve to be protected by a duty imposed on others. Such a duty does not create the right—rather, it is the outcome of having a right (MacCormick, 1982, p. 158). Needs, then, are not contradictory to rights, but in fact define rights; needs-based rights exist independently of the existence of a duty to address them.

The existence of rights irrespective of existing corresponding obligations is demonstrated by Feinberg (1980, p. 140):

> Imagine a hungry, sickly, fatherless infant, one of a dozen of children of a desperately impoverished and illiterate mother in a squalid Mexican slum. Doesn't this child have a claim to be fed, to be given medical care, to be taught to read? Can't we know this before we have any idea where correlative duties lie? Won't we still believe it even if we despair of finding anyone whose duty is to provide these things? Indeed, if we do finally assign the duty to someone, I suspect we would do so because there is a prior claim, looking, so to speak, for a duty to go with it.

An interest-based theory of rights, then, regards all children as rights holders, notwithstanding their capacity to claim these rights nor the existence of an identified entity obliged to fulfill them. It is important, however, to acknowledge the difficulties that the interest theory presents in this context. Tom Campbell (1992) comments that the decision as to what children's interests are, which ideally is based on psychological empirical knowledge, but in reality is often unclear, may result in paternalism. On the same vein, Federle (1994) argues that the interest theory defines the rights of children based on their *incapacities*. Children have rights because they are vulnerable and, therefore, need protection. It seems then, that whether children's interests are defined as needs or as rights, both terminologies might lead to overpaternalism and dependency upon the views of others rather than the rights holders themselves.

The following paragraphs provide a review of some typologies that attempt to categorize children's rights while trying to avoid the risk of over-paternalism. All are based on the foundations of the interest theory: Rights are basic, universal interests and depend on neither individual capability to claim them nor on an identified party whose duty is to provide them. Table 2.1 summarizes these typologies and captures the unique contribution of each as well as the similarities between them.

Hilde Bojer's (2000, pp. 30–36) revised Rawlsian "social contract" is an attempt to address the overpaternalism concern through an integration of welfare interests with free will. In his well-known book *A Theory of Justice*, John Rawls (1999) suggests a notion of *primary goods*, which are normally rights and liberties, powers and opportunities, income and wealth. He proposes that under a *veil of ignorance,* any rational, knowledgeable person (only without knowledge on his or her own position in society) would choose a social contract that provides equal rights to the primary goods, with the exception of inequality in favor of the most disadvantaged people in society as long as it is in everyone's advantage.[8] Referring to children's rights as resulting from the veil of ignorance, Bojer argues that since the primary goods are common to all humanity, in any circumstances, there is no need to try and reveal what a given child would choose for himself or herself. Despite the fact that Rawls does not suggest a detailed list of primary goods, Bojer claims that there are some assumptions that can be made regarding children's basic needs based on general knowledge, without failing to treat them with overpaternalism. These universal basic needs are love and security, material resources, and opportunities to grow and develop. Through these general assumptions, Bojer claims to overcome the concern regarding overpaternalism, raised by Campbell (1992). For Bojer (2000), the participants in Rawls's "original position," acting under the "veil of ignorance" and thus not knowing their own position in society, may reasonably assume that there are 50% chances for each of them to be a woman, and no less than a 100% chance to be born as a child—and therefore need care, protection, and nurture. She further argues that since any participant in the original position may be a child, and since children can be considered as the "least advantaged group," it is reasonable to assume that rational participants would agree to distribute society's resources in the benefit of children to provide them protection, nutrition, and minimal living conditions. This would be important for the participants in two aspects: First, for the time of their childhood itself, and second, their childhood being a condition and the foundation for their development into successful adults. Thus, any participant in the original position would want to ensure nutrition, preventive health care, education, and emotional care for all children by distributing enough of society's income into childhood.

Bojer's theory addresses the overpaternalism concern through imposing general assumptions as to children's basic interests—similar to the general assumptions Rawls

Table 2.1. Children's Rights Typologies

Children's rights theories	Method	General categorization	Types of rights	Contribution
Bojer (2000)	An extended Rawlsian social contract	Protection, nutrition, and minimal living conditions	Love and security, material resources, opportunities to develop	No need to make individual assumptions
Wolfson (1992)	Capability as a continuum	Constant move from "project interests" rights to "welfare interests" rights	Emphasis changes according to individual's situation	A general theory applicable to children
Feinberg (1980)	Three types of rights	A rights—liberties; A+C rights—welfare; C rights—special protections and anticipatory autonomy	C rights include education and developing decision-making skills	All have welfare rights; a right to develop decision making skills
Campbell (1992)	Four types of rights	1. Universal human rights, 2. special protections, 3. rights as future adults, 4. specific rights for adolescents	1. Life, health care, non-discrimination; 2. protection and care; 3. development (including autonomy); 4. special provision	Adolescence as a special group
Eekelaar (1992)	Three types of interests	1. Basic interests, 2. developmental interests, 3. autonomy interests		Autonomy interests here and now

A = adults' rights; A+C = adults' and children's rights; C = children-only rights.

makes in regard to adults' primary goods. Her model then is vulnerable to the same criticism that Rawls' theory is, regarding the appropriateness of these general assumptions. Bojer's analysis, however, is vulnerable in another way. The contention that people in the original position will unanimously prefer a distribution of goods that takes care of children is problematic, as Minow (1990, p. 154) points out. To assume that requires us to assume that all people in Rawls's theory are risk-haters. There may be, however, many others who prefer taking risks in favor of more goods for those who are better off in this imaginary state. These risk-prone people would vote differently and would not want to ensure children's primary goods at the expense of goods for capable adults. To include children in a general theory of rights based on other people's decisions, then, is similar to depending on proxies to represent children's rights and is equally problematic.

In contrast with the dichotomous division between the will and interest theories—or between rights and needs—Wolfson (1992) proposes a model of rights that regards capability as a continuum and, accordingly, generates a gradual shift from welfare rights to freedoms. People's rights are identified according to two types of interests—project interests, requiring free will and ability to make choice, and welfare interests, which do not depend on free will. As the individual becomes autonomous, fewer positive welfare rights are required and the state is expected to step away and provide more freedoms and negative rights. At the same time, if a person becomes unable to assert his or her own project interests (such as in the case of comatose people), then the state steps in and provides positive welfare rights. Therefore, under Wolfson's theory, *all* people hold both project and welfare interests. This dual understanding of rights within each individual might eliminate the clear-cut differentiation between the competent and the incompetent. Applying Wolfson's theory to children, a continual pendulum between protections and freedoms can be envisioned. Whenever a child is able to act independently, he or she should be granted autonomy and freedoms. Whenever a child needs assistance and support, the relevant positive rights should be granted, but without depriving the child's autonomy unnecessarily. Indeed, capturing capability as a continuum is particularly appropriate in the case of children, since their gradual development and growing autonomy is a natural, universal process.[9]

Another effort to capture the rights-needs equilibrium in a nondichotomous way is Joel Feinberg's (1980) distinction between adults' rights (or A rights, which are liberties); rights provided both to adults and children (A–C rights, which are welfare rights); and rights provided exclusively to children (C rights). Children-only rights, according to Feinberg, include food, shelter, and love; protection against abuse and neglect; and, importantly, the "anticipatory autonomy rights" that ensure that future adults can later exercise both their liberties (adults' rights) and their welfare rights (adults' and children's rights). These "rights in trust" are primarily the right to adequate education and the right to develop decision-making skills. Feinberg's analysis is valuable in overcoming some of the conceptual obstacles raised earlier in three ways. First, similar to Minow and Wolfson, Feinberg too regards welfare interests as part of the rights discourse, not a contradiction to it. Second, his analysis demonstrates that those considered incapable, such as children, have not only welfare interests (or rights) but "developmental" rights as well. Such developmental, or "rights in trust" include participation. Third, Feinberg's account indicates that adult, "capable" people are also subjects of welfare rights, thus diminishing the sharp dichotomy between the capable and the incapable.

Tom Campbell (1992) categorizes children's rights into the following four rights categories: universal human rights that children hold simply by being human beings, such as the rights to life and health care, and the right against torture and discrimination; specific rights for children such as protection against abuse, to nurture, and the right not to be illicitly transferred abroad (similar to the protection elements of Feinberg's children-only rights); rights as future adults (particularly the right for development); and specific rights for adolescents, such as the Convention's provision of adequate standard of living according to the child's development. Similarly, John Eekelaar (1992) divides children's rights into three groups: basic interests to physical, emotional, and intellectual care; developmental interests to fulfill the child's potential; and autonomy interests—freedom to choose a lifestyle.

Campbell and Eekelaar demonstrate additional efforts to avoid the needs-rights trap. Eekelaar specifically includes the autonomy interest separately from the development interest. That means, according to Eekelaar, that children have a right to practice their autonomy as much as they can, not in order to ensure their full development into productive adults in the future, but because they are entitled to it, here and now. Campbell's theory is somewhat broader, as it includes general human rights as well as a specific rights group for adolescents. Both scholars, however, treat children as having specific rights in addition to, and not instead of, the rights they share with the rest of humanity.

DEFINING CHILDREN'S NEEDS: SOME EXEMPLARY ATTEMPTS

The previous section reviewed some theoretical efforts to categorize different types of rights for children. It highlighted the idea that children have a range of rights, from those considered most protective, based on assumptions regarding children's basic needs, through universal welfare rights granted to every human being, to the most "liberal" rights associated with self-determination and autonomy. It also identified the interrelationship between children's needs and children's rights: Any rights discourse cannot be robust against criticism if it is not based on some theory of needs, but a theory of needs relies on a rights discourse to give it its political and normative force. The following discussion therefore reviews some projects aiming to define a list of universal needs, whether of people in general or of children. Table 2.2 provides a brief summary of the different needs typologies.

Flekkøy and Kaufman (1997) identify a distinction between basic needs and mere wishes or desires, based on Abraham Maslow's hierarchy of needs (1954).[10] Flekkøy and Kaufman (1997) claim that Maslow's theory is instructive as it offers an inclusive list that leaves out other "needs" claimed to be merely wishes and desires, not common to humanity in general. Furthermore, Maslow's model is important in making the connection between rights and responsibilities and in highlighting the societal benefit when people's needs are fulfilled. People reach the fourth level of the ladder (self-esteem) through having their rights respected by others; at the same time, people who reach that stage are better able to respect others (Flekkøy & Kaufman, 1997, pp. 10–11). Finally, Flekkøy and Kaufman (1997, p. 29) emphasize that the varying needs in Maslow's ladder are not organized according to their importance, but rather their urgency: Physical needs, for instance, are no more important than the need to self-actualization; they are just more immediate.

Doyal and Gough's (1991) project is to identify a universal list of human needs, while respecting cultural differences. For them, needs are those goals that are

Table 2.2. CHILDREN'S NEEDS TYPOLOGIES

Children's needs theories	Method	General categorization	Contribution
Flekkøy and Kaufman (1997)	Maslow's needs of children	1. Physical, 2. safety, 3. social, 4. esteem and autonomy, 5. self-actualization	Hierarchy in timing, not importance; excludes mere wishes
Doyal and Gough (1991) (adults' needs)	Universal needs-avoidance of serious harm	1. Physical survival; 2. personal autonomy, mental health, opportunities	USC: nutrition, housing, safe work and physical environment, health care, secured childhood, significant relationships, economic security; education
Ochaíta and Espinosa (2001)	USC for children	Same basic needs, different satisfiers for children	Includes active participation
Nussbaum (2000)	Capabilities approach	Life, health, safety, senses, imagination, emotions, reason, affiliation, other species, play, control	Children's basic needs secured for their future capabilities
Freeman (1983)	Liberal paternalism	What would we wish for in order to mature into rationally autonomous adults	A procedural search tool; allows some paternalism (forced education)

USC = universal satisfier characteristics.

"instrumentally and universally linked to the avoidance of serious harm" (Doyal & Gough, 1991, p. 42). But is there a consensus as to what serious harm is—or in other words, what is a normal, unharmed condition? Doyal and Gough assume that there is an objective, scientific "truth" about what people need in order to avoid serious harm: The two basic human needs are *physical survival* and *personal autonomy*, because these are the preconditions for any individual action.

Autonomy includes three basic elements: the ability to make informed choices (and hence children must be educated); mental health (a certain level of minimal rationality); and opportunities (certain level of freedoms). *Physical survival* means physical health. People may face serious harm when their health is in such condition that it limits their active participation in social life.

While Doyal and Gough's basic needs are universal, they acknowledge that cultures vary in the ways they satisfy them. In adding the "characteristics" component, they argue that it is possible to identify *universal satisfier characteristics* (USC): those characteristics of satisfiers that apply to all cultures. For example, it is possible to define a certain number of calories a day, or "protection from disease-carrying vectors" as a universal measurement. These intermediate needs (bridging between the general, universal basic needs and the specific, local satisfiers) are grouped as follows: nutritious food and clean water; protective housing; a nonhazardous work environment; a nonhazardous physical environment; appropriate health care; security in childhood; significant primary relationships; physical security; economic security; appropriate education; safe birth control and child-bearing (for women) (Doyal & Gough, 1991, pp. 155–158).

Applying this theory to the case of children, Ochaíta and Espinosa (2001, pp. 313–315) argue that while the manifestations of Doyal and Gough's list of needs and their satisfiers differ in accordance with children's stages of development, the needs themselves, categorized as physical health and autonomy, apply to children and adolescents as well. They propose an alternative list of satisfiers for the basic needs of children:

> **Satisfiers for the physical health of children:** Adequate nutrition; adequate housing; adequate clothing and hygiene; health care; sleep and rest; adequate exterior space; physical exercise; and protection from physical risks.
> **Satisfiers for children's autonomy:** Active participation and stable norms; primary affective bonds; interaction with adults; formal education; nonformal education, play, and recreation; protection from psychological risks; and acceptance of sexual needs (the latter being common for both basic needs) (Ochaíta & Espinosa, 2001, p. 315).

The inclusion of active participation in Ochaíta and Espinosa's account of satisfiers for children is particularly interesting as it creates a link between what has traditionally been associated with "self-determination rights" on the one hand, and children's basic needs on the other. Put differently, taking active participation in decision-making processes is, at least for these scholars, part of children's basic needs.

Doyal and Gough's theory is closely related to Martha Nussbaum's *capabilities approach* (2000). She proposes a feminist account of justice and rights that is committed to universal norms, and at the same time sensitive to local differences. Under her capabilities approach, rather than focusing on a person's satisfaction or even the person's material resources, one should ask what an individual *can* do and be. Seeing each individual as an end means that we need to secure for each and every individual the minimum level of capabilities that allow him or her to live in a truly humane way. Nussbaum's list of capabilities represents, she claims, a type of "overlapping consensus," as people from very different cultures would agree on them (2000, pp. 76–80): life; health; bodily integrity; senses, imagination, and thought; emotions; practical reason; affiliation; other species; play; and control over one's environment. The emphasis in her theory is on capabilities and not on actual functioning, because people must be able to *choose* whether to realize their capabilities or not. Nussbaum acknowledges that the list does not mean that society can fully guarantee all these capabilities. It does mean, however, that society can hope to guarantee the social basis for these goods, and that it should be seen as a list of political goals that can be used for aspiration and comparison. Similar to Doyal and Gough (1991), Nussbaum argues that in order to make the capabilities available to adults, society should require certain functions in childhood, such as education, health, emotional wellbeing, dignity, and bodily integrity. In other words, the state's interest in adult capabilities gives it a very strong interest to treat children appropriately. Thus, it is legitimate for the state to actively interfere to promote the provision of capabilities for those who lack them within the family. The state should interfere, for example, to promote and protect female children's capabilities in order to secure their equality in adulthood; to abolish child-marriage and child labor; and to provide compulsory education to all (Nussbaum, 2000, p. 282). Children, therefore, should be accorded basic rights as "future citizens." It is important to note, however, that as opposed to Ochaíta and Espinosa (2001), Nussbaum does not highlight the importance of ensuring children's rights *here and now*, for their present wellbeing. Ochaíta and Espinosa, in contrast, focus on the needs of children as such, and attach a normative status of rights to these needs without relying on the future adults children are expected to become.

As an alternative to empirical examination of children's needs, Michael Freeman proposes a "procedural search tool" of *liberal paternalism*. Under this methodology, to find out what children's rights are we should ask:

> What sort of action or conduct would we wish, as children, to be shielded against on the assumption that we would want to mature to a rationally autonomous adulthood and be capable of deciding on our own system of ends as free and rational beings (Freeman, 1983, p. 54–58).

This test ensures some freedom and space for making mistakes, but screens out decisions that would risk the life, or physical or mental health, of the child. Applying this test, Freeman argues that some form of compulsory education must be provided, as it is one of the most important conditions for securing the future of children.

CONCLUSIONS SO FAR

The first part of this chapter discussed the advantages and challenges of a rights-based discourse with regard to children and presented some theoretical frameworks that are more immune against criticism. A robust rights template is based on a human rights approach, which is in turn interlinked with needs. The interest theory is the general framework under which children are right holders, as it does not require, in contrast with the will theory, capability as a condition for having rights. Rather, it is the universality of certain needs, or interests, that justifies their normative anchoring as rights. The interest theory broadens both the scope of "rights" (to include welfare as well as self-determination rights) and the target populations (to include the "incapable" as well as the "capable"). Following this basic notion that children are rights holders simply by being human, and that their rights derive from their interests, different writers suggest various typologies for children's rights. Table 2.1 and its accompanying text reviewed some of these typologies, suggesting that while children hold a mix of self-determination, welfare, and developmental rights, any children's rights discourse is inherently intertwined with a needs discourse (Bojer, 2000; Campbell, 1992; Eekelaar, 1992; Feinberg, 1980; Minow, 1995b; Wolfson, 1992). Accordingly, basic needs are not only the justification of having rights; they also identify the nature of many of children's rights. Indeed the dispute around children's rights demonstrates that needs and rights do not necessarily collide. In fact, in this context, they complement each other. As Waldron (2000) argues, rights-talk can provide an important framework to discuss human needs while addressing ideas of self-respect and dignity (2000, p. 131). In other words, needs should be placed within the rights-talk. Once a need has been diagnosed, the rights-talk takes over to create an associated claim, which in turn creates an obligation by others (2000, pp. 131–132).

It seems then that whichever approach one takes, any theory of interests necessitates some kind of empirical investigation to define the scope and nature of children's rights. Omission to conduct such an empirical investigation is problematic not only due to the imposition of other people's views regarding children's needs and wishes (the overpaternalism problem), but it also leads to uncertainty as to the nature of children's interests. As Table 2.2 and its accompanying text demonstrated, empirical and theoretical efforts have resulted in similar, yet nonidentical conclusions (see Doyal & Gough, 1991; Maslow, 1954; Nussbaum, 2000; Ochaíta & Espinosa, 2001).

The combined reviews of the rights and needs typologies, when put together, reveal that there is no real dichotomy between the rights of "younger" and "older" children, as children of all ages need a certain level of protection as well as a certain level of autonomy. Teenagers might need protection, support, and provision of special services to secure their safety from adult or peer violence. Concurrently, even very young children need adults to respect their autonomy and provide them with opportunities to practice their negotiation and decision-making skills, in measures that fit their age. Therefore, it would be artificial and inaccurate to claim that *autonomy* should be (if at all) granted only to adolescents and adults whereas *protection* is what society owes to its young children. Children of all ages deserve—and need—respect for their liberties as well as protection against harm.

In any case, and despite the concerns raised, a theory based on basic interests is still preferable over the alternative will theory, which excludes children by definition. Further, as Jane Fortin argues, the vagueness around the definition of children's interests is not that detrimental in a practical sense, since the CRC, with its immense popularity, sets a comprehensive list of children's interests presented as rights (Fortin, 2003, p. 18).

If children's rights, and more so needs-compatible international human rights, is a viable discourse, then the next step is to explore the international arena. Accordingly, the second part of this chapter includes a brief review of international children's rights documents and a detailed discussion of the CRC with particular focus on rights directly related to child victims.

INTERNATIONAL CHILDREN'S RIGHTS DOCUMENTS

With the emergence of child development as a distinct social science field in the 20th century, it became widely accepted that children are entitled to human rights just as any other human being (Flekkøy & Kaufman, 1997, pp. 22–23). International attention grew and was expressed in several international documents.

The 1924 *Declaration of Geneva* (hereafter: Geneva Declaration) is the document regarded to be the first human-rights instrument that deals specifically with children's rights, although it regarded children as "objects" that need protection, rather than individuals with personal rights. For example, the fourth principle of the Geneva Declaration provides that:

> The child must be put in a position to earn a livelihood and must be protected against every form of exploitation (*Declaration of Geneva,* 1924).

The next significant United Nations document addressing the rights of children was the 1959 *Declaration of the Rights of the Child* (UN, 1959; hereafter: 1959 Declaration). This Declaration was more detailed and regarded children as subjects to their own legal rights, but still addressed only the protective aspect of children's rights. Additionally, it is unclear who is obligated under the 1959 Declaration to provide the rights enumerated in it, and to this extent this document is vague (Freeman, 1983, p. 19).

Both the Geneva and the 1959 Declarations were predominantly of a declarative nature and did not include any enforcement or follow-up mechanisms.

The first binding international provisions regarding children were included in two general human rights covenants, both adopted by the United Nations on the same day in 1966. Both provisions, however, focused again on the rights of children to special measures of protection and thus dealt, in fact, with children's welfare. Children's freedoms and autonomy had not been specifically acknowledged yet. The *International Covenant on Civil and Political Rights* provided in Article 24(1) that:

> Every child shall have, without any discrimination as to race, color, language, religion, national or social origin, property or birth, the right to such measures of protection as are required by his status as a minor, on the part of his family, society and the State (UN, 1966a).

The *International Covenant on Economic, Social and Cultural Rights* provided, in Article 10, that:

> Special measures of protection and assistance should be taken on behalf of all children and young persons without any discrimination for reasons of parentage or other conditions (UN, 1966b).

In addition to general human rights and specific children's rights documents, the international community has also acknowledged the special status of crime victims, as specified in the *Basic Principles of Justice for Victims of Crime and Abuse of Power* (1985; hereafter: the Principles). Adopted by consensus in the General Assembly of the United Nations, the Principles are based on the philosophy that victims of crime should be adequately recognized and treated with respect for their dignity. Accordingly, the Principles state the importance of access to fair and respectful judicial mechanisms, prompt redress, adequate assistance and other services, state compensation, restitution, information, participation, and informal alternatives of conflict resolution instruments, including restorative justice, for victims. Victims' privacy and safety are also stated as crucial.

Another relevant UN document is the *Guidelines on Justice in Matters Involving Child Victims and Witnesses of Crime* (2005), adopted by the Economic and Social Council. While this UN resolution holds a weaker status than treaties and declarations accepted by the UN General Assembly, its exclusive focus on the rights of child victims makes it an important source of information regarding agreed-upon standards in the area. Following the general principles stated by the CRC, the guidelines stipulate that professionals should treat child victims and witnesses of crime according to the following principles: dignity, nondiscrimination, best interests, protection, harmonious development, and participation.[11] The document then moves on to translate these general principles into more specific guidelines. Importantly, the guidelines provide that age should not be a barrier to a child's right to participate in the justice process; that children have a right to be protected from hardships during the justice process; and that reparation should be combined with any criminal, informal, or community justice procedure such as restorative justice. These guidelines will be discussed in further detail in Chapter 4, where the needs-rights of child victims within the criminal process are discussed.

The most recent international document on child victims, and the most comprehensive attempt to address the special needs and rights of child victims is the model law: Justice in Matters Involving Child Victims and Witnesses of Crime (UNODC & UNICEF, 2009; hereafter: model law). The model law, based on the 2005 guidelines, was developed by the United Nations Office on Drugs and Crime in cooperation with the United Nations Children's Fund (UNICEF) and the International Bureau for Children's Rights. While not binding, the model law is designed to assist governments in drafting relevant national legislation in conformity with the guidelines and the CRC.

The model law emphasizes the importance of the best interests of the child (Article 1) and among its main principles it states that:

> A child victim or witness of crime shall be treated in a caring and sensitive manner that is respectful of his or her dignity throughout the legal proceedings, taking into account his or her personal situation and immediate and special needs, age, gender, disabilities if any and level of maturity (Article 2 (2)).

The model law also states that child privacy should be protected as well as the victim's right to express his or her views, opinions, and beliefs freely, and the right to contribute to decisions affecting his or her life, including those taken in the course of the justice process (Article 2(6)). The model law also protects child victims within the criminal process from contact with offenders (Article 4). The model law further specifies special protections and provisions that address the varying obstacles a child victim may face during each of the criminal process stages. During the investigation stage, for instance, the model law secures specially trained investigators that are familiar with a child-sensitive approach and are guided to avoid repetition of the interview to prevent secondary victimization of the child. During the trial phase, the model law requires separate waiting areas for child victims and appropriate courtroom facilities. Another safeguard in this stage is a prohibition from prosecuting child victims for giving false testimony (Article 22). The model law allows the judge, when applicable, and with due regard for the rights of the accused, to prohibit cross-examination of a child victim or witness by the accused. A cross-examination may be undertaken by the defense lawyer under the supervision of the judge, who will have the duty to prevent questions that may expose the child to intimidation, hardship, or undue distress. The model law also permits other measures to protect the privacy and physical and mental wellbeing of the child and to prevent undue distress and secondary victimization (Article 28). In the post-trial period, the model law addresses the child victims' right to restitution and compensation (Article 29) as well as their right to information on the release of the convicted person (Article 33). Article 30 of the model law requires informing the child of available restorative justice programs and how to access them.

THE UN CONVENTION ON THE RIGHTS OF THE CHILD

By far the most comprehensive international binding document with regard to children's rights is the 1989 Convention on the Rights of the Child. This Convention, for the first time, acknowledged children as individuals fully entitled to human rights—civil, political, economic, social, and cultural—without neglecting their special needs for protection (Detrick, Doek, & Cantwell, 1992, p. 27).

Small and Limber (2002, pp. 61–63) argue that the uniqueness of the Convention lies in the following characteristics:

First, the Convention enjoys worldwide consensus as it has been ratified by almost all countries in the world, with only Somalia and the United States as exceptions. Although the United States has not ratified the Convention, the common view is that it enjoys such wide international consensus that in fact the Convention reflects customary international law, to which the United States is subject (Flekkøy & Kaufman, 1997, p. 1).[12] At the same time, the Convention is flexible and sensitive to cultural differences more than any other human rights instrument (Alston, 1994). The unprecedented popularity of the Convention combined with its flexibility made it a powerful political instrument that has affected internal legal and constitutional debates as well as professional education within nations (Van Bueren, 1999b).

Second, the Convention includes the widest variety of rights for children—social, legal, cultural, civil, and human rights—and therefore represents a new, broader approach to children's rights. Children are no longer regarded as merely objects of protection (although the right to be protected is a central principle); they are human beings, part of the world's community, and thus deserve to be treated with respect for their human rights and freedoms. Most importantly, the Convention provides a broad framework of citizenship for children through the introduction of the *participation principle* for the first time (Roche, 1999).

Third, the Convention is unique in its coherent nature and indivisible articles, with children's dignity as its central theme that should be read into each one of its articles (Melton, 1991; Van Bueren, 1999a).

Finally, the Convention created for the first time, with the founding of the United Nations Committee on the Rights of the Child (hereafter, the Committee), a mechanism for evaluation and follow-up for state-members, thus making it an effective, dynamic document. Not only did the monitoring mechanism create a system of "naming and shaming" of states that do not comply with the Convention's words and spirit (Covell & How, 2009, p. 22), it has also established a unique source of guidance and interpretation to the meaning of the various articles of the CRC and of children's rights in general, a sort of international resource center for both theoreticians and activists (Small & Limber, 2002).

An additional advantage of the Convention is that it proposes a relatively pragmatic agenda compared with the disputable liberationist approach. The Convention does not include any provision that aims at treating children as adults, nor does it state that even "mature minors" should be entitled to complete autonomy and freedom in decision making. The Convention focuses, in this area, on the right of children to *participate* in the decision-making processes that precede any decision affecting their lives, giving gradually more weight to children's views as they mature and develop their capacities—not the right of children to make their own decisions. Children are envisioned, then, by the Convention not as independent individuals making their own choices, but rather as interdependent (yet active) partners in shared decision-making processes regarding their lives.

A related aspect of the CRC is what Barbara Bennet Woodhouse (1998) calls the "fiduciary model" of parents' rights reflected in the Convention. Under this view, the

CRC regards children as individual, separable persons, though depending on their parents for love, nurture, and authority structures necessary for their growth to autonomy. The Convention grants parents authority that they must use as *trustees* for the protection of rights and interests of their children and in guidance for their adulthood. Rather than limiting parents' autonomy, then, the Convention actively protects the family and the parent–child relationship, albeit as one of trust, not of ownership. Acknowledging that children have human rights serves thus to strengthen, rather than diminish, the human rights of their parents. This particular trait of the Convention will be revisited later in this book in relation to the importance of empowering the family, and particularly non-offending parents, to become partners in decision-making processes following child victimization.

The Convention, however, has its limitations and should not be seen as a panacea for all children's problems (Martineau, 1997, p. 233). It has been argued that it imposes Western values on non-Western nations, with only the "reservations" option for states to practice cultural norms.[13] As a result, there has been an excessive use of the reservation mechanism that causes a demarcation of the Convention itself (Freeman, 2002). Further, the Convention has been criticized for falling short of addressing systemic poverty and for its failure to impose responsibilities on children as active members of civil society (Martineau, 1997, pp. 240–241). From a feminist perspective, concerns have been made regarding the various ways in which the CRC might actually harm women, making them "hostages" of the best interests of their children (Olsen, 1992). Moreover, it has been argued that the "bill of rights" embedded in the Convention is not inclusive, and at the same time is too broad or vague (Todres, 1998). Finally, it has been suggested that the rights included in the convention do not have equal value, that some are more worthy of protection than others, and that some are merely "manifesto rights" (King, 1994).

Despite these shortcomings, however, the Convention can be understood in a way that meets the central concerns of both protective and liberationist approaches. The Convention is a vibrant, effective instrument on which states report regularly and on which much has been written. Most importantly, the CRC is considered to be the most comprehensive international document addressing the rights of children worldwide. This is the first document that refers to children as individuals entitled to rights of their own, which they may exercise in a gradual manner according to their evolving capacities, without neglecting the welfare of children and the importance of their family and community ties. For these reasons, and provided that an international human rights approach is the preferred framework to address children's victimization, then there is no better document than the Convention to be used as a template for constructing a rights-based child victims model. The following sections, accordingly, discuss the central provisions of the Convention, while exploring their possible consequences when applied to child victims.

THE GENERAL PRINCIPLES OF THE CONVENTION

The Convention represents a holistic approach according to which its various articles should be implemented interdependently (Van Bueren, 1999a). The official UN blueprint for the implementation of the Convention identified four "general principles" as having a guiding status, and which therefore should be applied to each one of the other Convention's articles (Hodgkin & Newell, 2002, p. 42). Accordingly, the Committee requires reporting states to demonstrate how the general principles are reflected in the implementation of each one of the Convention's specific rights.[14] Thus, it is important to start with a description of the four guiding principles of the Convention, by the order of their appearance.

First Guiding Principle: Equality (Nondiscrimination)

1. States Parties shall respect and ensure the rights set forth in the present Convention to each child within their jurisdiction without discrimination of any kind, irrespective of the child's or his or her parent's or legal guardian's race, color, sex, language, religion, political or other opinion, national, ethnic or social origin, property, disability, birth or other status.
2. States Parties shall take all appropriate measures to ensure that the child is protected against all forms of discrimination or punishment on the basis of the status, activities, expressed opinions, or beliefs of the child's parents, legal guardians, or family members (CRC, Article 2).

The nondiscrimination principle requires that all children are provided with the same rights, both *de jure* and *de facto*. The first and most obvious implication of the nondiscrimination principle is that states should treat equally all disadvantaged groups of children in their allocation of goods, including children belonging to minority groups; disabled children; children born out of wedlock; children who are nonnationals, migrants, refugees, displaced, or asylum-seekers; and children who work or live in the streets.[15]

It is important to note, however, that equality does not mean that children should receive exactly the same resources, protections, or freedoms. To achieve substantive equality, a legal system has to be sensitive to the *inequalities* of children and provide them with the required means to overcome these inequalities as much as possible in order to provide all children equal opportunities (Van Bueren, 1999a).

Martha Nussbaum articulates this point eloquently:

> To treat A and B as equally well-off because they command the same amount of resources is, in a crucial way, to neglect A's separate and distinct life, to pretend that A's circumstances are interchangeable with B's, which may not be the case. To do justice to A's struggle, we must see them in their social context, aware of the obstacles that the context offers to the struggle for liberty, opportunity, and material wellbeing (Nussbaum, 2000, p. 69).

It seems, then, that the Convention sets a substantive equality principle under which each child should be treated with equal respect to his or her special circumstances, needs, and capabilities. This broad meaning of equality is similar to Minow's (1990, pp. 375–377) relational rights approach, under which she calls for taking the perspective of the "other" and changing institutions in order to enable the full inclusion of those who might be considered "different."[16]

Thus, in the context of this work, Article 2 creates an international obligation on states to ensure that all child victims have equal access to mechanisms of prevention and protection, reporting, investigating, and prosecuting, as well as rehabilitation and reintegration. This includes children who were victimized while being tourists or illegal residents in the country and children of minority groups. All available services should be adequately accessible for children with special needs, children in rural parts of the country, and poor children in the periphery or in urban ghettos. While the laws protecting child-victims are likely to apply to all children without discrimination, states are expected to ensure the equal *implementation* of these laws as well, which is significantly harder to achieve. In practice, to ensure meaningful equality to child victims, states need to be sensitive to the special needs of different children and meet these special needs through the provision of various aids: Some children are surrounded with violence in high-risk neighborhoods and need a secured shelter in which they can privately disclose their victimization. Some children need longer periods of therapy to recover from their victimization due to past traumas or individual traits. Others may need representation by an advocate who will speak on their behalf to overcome their own and their parents' inability to assert their rights (this may be the case with foreign residents, illiterate children and families, or children and parents with disabilities). Other children may have to receive physical support in order to participate in the process that follows their victimization: translators for hearing impaired children; ramps for children in wheelchairs; or specific intervention plans for different types of mentally disabled children.

Second Guiding Principle: The Best Interests of the Child

1. In all actions concerning children, whether undertaken by public or private social welfare institutions, courts of law, administrative authorities or legislative bodies, the best interests of the child shall be a primary consideration.
2. States Parties undertake to ensure the child such protection and care as is necessary for his or her wellbeing, taking into account the rights and duties of his or her parents, legal guardians, or other individuals legally responsible for him or her, and, to this end, shall take all appropriate legislative and administrative measures.
3. States Parties shall ensure that the institutions, services and facilities responsible for the care or protection of children shall conform with the standards established by competent authorities, particularly in the areas of safety, health, in the number and suitability of their staff, as well as competent supervision (CRC, Article 3).

In many ways the best interests principle seems to be simple to grasp as it relates to the wellbeing of children—surely a consensual value, even among those who object to the children's rights terminology. However the Convention goes further than simply stressing the importance of the wellbeing of children; it creates an *obligation* for state members to always give *primacy* to the child's best interests. This creates a twofold difficulty. Not only is it challenging to identify the best interests of the child in specific situations (and this point will be discussed in further detail below), but state authorities are also expected to weigh these interests against other competing interests while giving primacy to the former interests. The "primacy" weight granted to the child's interests under Article 3 means that they should take precedence over other considerations external to the child. It does not, however, grant the child's interests an exclusive status, as would be the case if an alternative wording such as "the paramount consideration" had been chosen.[17] Perhaps most importantly, however, the best interests principle creates a duty to make an *individual* examination of the interests of the specific child, instead of relying on general assumptions regarding children in different situations. Put differently, the Convention provides that children have a right that their best interests would be assessed individually whenever a decision is made affecting their lives, and that their assessed interests would be a primary consideration in that decision.

The best interests principle is relevant to child victims in two ways. First, Article 3(2) creates a duty upon states to allocate financial and human resources to the *prevention* of child victimization.[18] This obligation is based on an assumption that the safety and well-being of children is always in their best interest, and there is no need to make individual enquiries as to each child's interests in this regard. Second, Article 3(1) means that after victimization has occurred and during the process following the offense, the victimized child's best interests must be a primary consideration. The duty to give primacy to the interests of child victims during the process following their victimization is not without problems. Other interests might be paramount in these circumstances, such as the right of the offender to due process, the interest of the prosecution to efficiently and quickly handle cases, and the general public interest to prevent crime.[19] The conflict may be even greater when the perpetrator is also a minor, and thus deserves a "best interests primacy" approach as well. For example, existing provisions regarding the use of screens, video links, and pretrial testimony are aimed at securing the child's wellbeing and best interests, but they must be balanced against the competing rights of the defendant to confrontation, cross-examination, and the rule against hearsay evidence (Hodgkin & Newell, 2002, p. 252). Such balance may lead legislators to provide children with special procedural protections while requiring special evidentiary and procedural safeguards to protect the competing interests.

Additionally, there may be a conflict between the best interests of the specific victimized child and the general interest of *all children* for protection and safety (Alston, 1994, p. 14). For example, even when the child victim's best interest is to be diverted from the court process to an alternative, restorative justice gathering, still in order to protect other children, a criminal justice procedure might be preferred if it is expected to be more effective both in preventing the specific perpetrator from recidivating and in deterring others from crime.

Therefore, giving primacy to the child's interests is not always as simple as it seems in theory, even for those who work in various aspects of children's safety and protection. It seems that the Convention's contribution is to add guidance for hard cases, where such guidance is really needed. Therefore, when treating child victims, special attention should be given to their interests even when competing with other legitimate, important interests. In other words, the balance should be tilted in favor of the child's interests even in cases where if it were an adult instead of the child other interests would have received priority.

Given the notion that the child's best interests should prevail, other contentious questions arise, such as who is to decide what the child's best interest is and how such judgment should be made (Todres, 1998). In many cases, the question is not an easy one. Decision-makers may find themselves struggling to reach the right decision as to the best interests of the child, with several competing views. Often the child's wishes are in contrast with what others regard as his or her best interests; there are cases in which the parents' view of what is best for their child contradicts the child's views, the views of the social workers, or of other state authorities. When, then, should the parents' view of the child's interest overcome the child's own view and when should the parents' views be overruled by the state authorities?

Flekkøy and Kaufman (1997, p. 45) suggest that a decision should refer to a specific question, depend on the child's current needs and stage of development, reflect the child's culture, and preferably take into account not only the immediate interests of the child but the long-term interests of the future adult. Freeman (1983, pp. 51–52) suggests a liberal paternalism approach based on the promotion of "primary social goods" in Rawls's words.[20] He suggests that as a rule, parents should take into account their children's views, but eventually parents are expected to make a decision that best promotes the child's interests in achieving those primary goods: liberty, health, opportunity. These can be neutrally examined, Freeman argues, at least to some extent. This test implies that whenever parents do not follow the "child's primary goods" rule (with the future of the child in mind), the court, or other third party, should have the authority to intervene and make a decision.

It is questionable, however, how neutral this test really is. Let us take an example of a 12-year-old boy who has been assaulted, and whose parents object to his participation in a restorative justice process following his victimization, arguing that this will be a damaging experience for him. The child, on the other hand, wishes to participate. Let us also assume that in this particular system, a special committee decides on matters that relate to children in restorative justice settings. How should this committee decide? Should it follow the child's or the parents' wishes? Following Freeman's test, they can assert that the child's recovery (which undoubtedly will affect his future conceptions of justice, trust in people, self-image, and so forth) depends on the opportunity he is given to face his assailant, ask questions, and receive answers. At the same time, the committee can hold that the parents are making a choice within the scope of their authority to promote the boy's primary goods, as they are concerned that the process will revictimize the child. The unquestionable values of "future opportunity" or "health" for children, therefore, become debatable when translated into specific real-life dilemmas.

Brennan and Noggle (1997) propose a formula for balancing the child's wellbeing and the child's wishes. According to their argument, parents carry the following three types of duties toward their children: They are obliged not to violate the rights of the child, to prevent others from violating these rights, and to promote the interests of the child. The third duty, which concerns the child's interests, may be in conflict with the other two duties that concern the child's rights. It is the parents' responsibility to find the balance in these situations between protecting the child's rights and promoting the child's interests. Further, Brennan and Noggle argue that the equal moral status of children requires parents to take their rights seriously, even when conflicting with the child's wellbeing. Thus, parents should infringe their child's rights (for instance, act against their wishes, violate their privacy) only when such infringement is absolutely necessary to protect the child's interests, and only to the level necessary. Taking children's rights seriously means that parents (and more broadly, decision-makers), should respect the wishes of the child as much as possible, as long as it is not in conflict with the child's interests. Even then, adults should make an effort to respect those wishes to the maximum extent possible.

However, Brennan and Noggle (1997) do not manage to address the concern about adults making their own judgments regarding the child's best interests. Indeed, it seems that the problem of value-biased decisions by adults will linger whatever the test is.[21] How, then, is it possible to create an objective mechanism that respects the child's wishes but at the same time secures the child's primary goods?

Brennan and Noggle's formula relates to the relationship between the best interests principle and other children's rights, with the underlying presumption that these are separate, sometimes competing, spheres. In other words, the wellbeing of the child is not considered by them as part of the bill of rights of children, in contrast with the right to self-determination. The Convention, however, reflects a more holistic view under which the best interests interpretation must be consistent:

> with the spirit of the entire Convention, and in particular with its emphasis on the child as an individual, with views and feelings of his or her own . . . (Hodgkin & Newell, 2002, p. 42).

Thus, the best interests principle, as it appears in the Convention, gives a significant role to the child's wishes and should be interpreted in a way that most faithfully reflects the child's views and feelings. Hence, it is possible to argue that the best interests of the child should have primacy over other interests *external* to the child. As far as the child's own competing rights, the child's views should be given maximum weight in accordance with the age and maturity of the child, and as long as these wishes are not severely endangering the child's interests.

Therefore, turning back to the 12-year-old boy in the previous example, because nobody can predict what will happen at the restorative process and what the outcomes will be for the child, the parents (or the committee) should perhaps follow the child's wish and belief that it would be in his best interest to participate in it, unless they are positive that the restorative justice process will be an extremely harmful event that will worsen his emotional (or even physical) condition. This does not mean, however, that the adults involved hold no further responsibilities. They should, for instance, take measures to limit the risks of further traumatizing the child and help him participate in the process in a way that will promote his best interests.

The best interests principle indeed suffers from vagueness and implementation difficulties. It is, however, an important reminder of the centrality of the child and the need to consider the specific child's circumstances in every case.

Third Guiding Principle: Life, Survival, and Development

> 1. States Parties recognize that every child has the inherent right to life.
> 2. States Parties shall ensure to the maximum extent possible the survival and development of the child (CRC, Article 6).

The outcomes of child victimization may be devastating for children, especially when the perpetrator is a parent (Herman, 1992). Indeed, child victimization, and particularly physical and sexual abuse, not only threatens the right of children to life, it also jeopardizes their right to survival and development (Hodgkin & Newell, 2002, pp. 85, 94). Research shows that violence against children, including sexual abuse and exploitation, have a potentially serious short-term as well as long-term effects on the development of children (Hodgkin & Newell, 2002, p. 94). Indeed, Article 6 of the

Convention is closely related to Article 19 regarding protection against child abuse. The Committee related to the right to life, survival, and development when discussing violence against children. For example, in its concluding observations on the initial report of Guatemala, the Committee stated that it:

> is deeply alarmed at the persistence of violence against children.... The high number of child victims of violence raises serious concern, particularly in view of the ineffectiveness of investigations into crimes committed against children which paves the way for widespread impunity.[22]

The right to life, survival, and development highlights the close links between childhood victimization and childhood witnessing of domestic violence. The *World Report on Violence against Children* states that the adverse psychological and emotional effects of witnessing interpersonal violence at home are as severe and long lasting as those of direct victimization (Pinheiro, 2006, p. 70). Taking the right to survival and development seriously means then that domestic violence should be treated not only as a crime against the direct victim (typically the mother), but as a type of childhood victimization as well.

If victimization is such a danger to the child's safe development, society then carries an even heavier burden to ensure the healthy development, and healing, of a child who has been victimized. In other words, Article 6 creates yet another source of normative obligation on states to strive to repair harms caused to children by crime in order to maximize their chances for positive development. States should search for the best way to restore the child's development, even if that means putting aside other interests. Allowing children to participate in decision making, for example, might help them learn to use the "little power they actually have" and to develop their judgment (Rayner, 2002). Furthermore, reacting in a responsive, sensitive, and empowering way to children's loss may encourage their growth from their victimization (Murray, 1999).

Parents' Role and Children's Evolving Capacities

Article 5 is closely related to the development principle:

> States Parties shall respect the responsibilities, rights and duties of parents or, where applicable, the members of the extended family or community as provided for by local custom, legal guardians or other persons legally responsible for the child, to provide, in a manner consistent with the evolving capacities of the child, appropriate direction and guidance in the exercise by the child of the rights recognized in the present Convention.

This article introduces three important concepts central to the Convention: the centrality of the family (including the extended family, where this is part of the local culture); the conception of the child as a subject of rights on his or her own, rather than a mere recipient of protection; and finally, the duty of the family and the general society to help the child practice his or her rights in a gradual manner, according to the child's evolving capacities (Hodgkin & Newell, 2002).

These three concepts are interrelated. The family is the central societal group that carries not only rights, but duties and responsibilities toward the child. Family responsibilities are aimed at helping the child practice his or her rights according to the child's evolving capacities:

> The civil rights of the child begin within the family . . . The family is an essential agent for creating awareness and preservation of human rights, and respect for human values, cultural identity and heritage, and other civilizations. There is a need to consider appropriate ways of ensuring balance between parental authority and the realization of the rights of the child, including the right to freedom of expression.[23]

The notion of the child's "evolving capacities" is a key concept in the Convention (Hodgkin & Newell, 2002, p. 91) and, together with the development principle, provides guidance to the implementation of children's rights and freedoms. Instead of setting strict ages to regulate levels of autonomy and weight of the child's views, the Convention sets a flexible formula based on the individual child's capacities. The concept reflects the notion that children do not instantly become adults once they turn 18. Childhood is a process in which children gradually learn how to make decisions and practice their rights, and families should support children in gradually enhancing their autonomy. In practice, the evolving capacities concept means that when a child is able to practice any of the rights provided in the Convention, it is the parents' (as well as the state's) responsibility to allow the realization of that right, unless there are compelling reasons not to do so. Moreover, parents are expected to guide their children in *developing* their capacities through practice in order to promote their maturation into autonomous adults.

In the child victim context, this notion means that children should be encouraged to actively participate in the decision-making process whenever they are ready to do so and in a manner suitable for their capacities. The family, relatives (where appropriate), and state authorities are expected to provide guidance and support to the child and find ways to include him or her in the process in a way that fits the child's capabilities at that point.

Fourth Guiding Principle: Participation

Children's right to participate in decision-making processes affecting their lives is perhaps the acme of the Convention and its central contribution to the children's rights discourse. While several articles in the Convention set various aspects of children's rights to free expression and self-determination, Article 12 provides the general principle of respect for the child's views:

> 1. States Parties shall assure to the child who is capable of forming his or her own views the right to express those views freely in all matters affecting the child, the views of the child being given due weight in accordance with the age and maturity of the child.
> 2. For this purpose, the child shall in particular be provided the opportunity to be heard in any judicial and administrative proceedings affecting the child, either directly, or through a representative or an appropriate body, in a manner consistent with the procedural rules of national law.

The participation principle is a relatively new concept and perhaps the most controversial among the guiding principles, as it reflects an expansion of the rights rhetoric beyond those promoting the protection and welfare of children. The participation principle, however, is not necessarily a rival to welfare and protection. In fact it is arguable that the wellbeing of children depends, among other things, on their opportunities to be active participants in decision-making processes, as such opportunities develop their trust in others, self-esteem, and a sense of being respected (Flekkøy & Kaufman, 1997, pp. 62–63). Participation is also considered to have strong educational and developmental components and, accordingly, may be regarded as another basic *need* in a child's development (Ochaíta & Espinosa, 1997).

The participation principle is justified not only for its developmental and educational value in children's growth, but it is also claimed to be beneficial to democratic society in general. First, practice in shared decision-making processes helps children become future competent participants who are tolerant to other people's views and who respect themselves and others. These traits cannot be taught theoretically; they need to be gradually acquired through experiencing shared decision-making and problem-solving processes. Second, involving children in decision-making processes benefits the present surroundings of the children—the family, the school, and the community—through gaining more knowledge on the children's perspectives and strengthening democratic values within themselves (Flekkøy & Kaufman, 1997, pp. 56–57).

In a UNICEF publication, Gerison Lansdown (2001, pp. 5–6) argues that children's participation is important because children may have valid views about their best interests that are different from adults' views; children are typically less cynical, more optimistic, and more flexible in their approach to the future and, therefore, might offer fresh ideas and creative solutions. Furthermore, adult-based decisions that are aimed at promoting children's welfare based on assumptions rather than on actual children's views often turn out to be wrong.

Lansdown (2001) also claims that excluding children from the decision-making process actually includes a twofold discrimination against children. First, it represents a denial of their fundamental right to participate embedded in Article 12 of the Convention. Second, it prevents children from influencing and exercising whichever rights are relevant in the specific case (2001, p. 7). Thus, to take child victims as an example, excluding them from the discussion regarding the outcome of the process that follows their victimization would not only infringe their general right to participate, but would also prevent them from advocating for restoration that fits their needs, possibly resulting in less preferable outcomes for them.

Lansdown (2001) notes, however, that using children to promote an adult agenda is at best tokenistic and at worst exploitative. Therefore, age-appropriate, sufficient information must be provided to allow children to have meaningful input. Accordingly, and following the indivisibility concept (Van Bueren, Capelaere, Morris, Skelton, & Nielsen, 1999), the combination of the participation and the nondiscrimination principles suggests that all children should be treated with equal respect in any decision-making process regarding their lives, regardless of their age, situation, ethnicity, abilities, and other factors.[24] Accordingly, states committed to follow the Convention's standards are expected to make special efforts to empower disempowered children, thus ensuring a true and meaningful participation for all children. Children, in any case, cannot be required to participate—their attendance and participation must be voluntary (Lansdown, 2001, pp. 9–10).

The participation principle contains two aspects: first, it provides children who are capable of doing so with the right to *express* their opinions freely in all matters affecting them. This right has been stated both in the Universal Declaration of Human Rights (Article 19) and in the International Covenant on Civil and Political Rights (Article 9(1)). However, Article 12 of the Convention encompasses another aspect of participation, which has never been incorporated in a child-focused international document before (Detrick et al., 1992, p. 28). Beyond freedom of expression, Article 12 provides that children's opinions will be considered and given *due weight* according to their age and maturity (Hodgkin & Newell, 2002, p. 145).[25] Article 12(2) specifies the application of the participation principle with respect to judicial and administrative proceedings, where the child's views should particularly be heard either personally or by a representative.[26] Surely, the criminal process that follows the child's victimization is a "matter affecting the child," as Article 12(1) provides. Decisions regarding the nature of the process itself (should it be referred to court or to an alternative process?), the role that the child should take in it, and its outcomes (what kind of punishment, or restitution, should be inflicted on the offender?) affect the child directly and, therefore, require adults to consider the child's views. Sometimes these decisions concern even the safety of the child and his or her future life.

The participation principle does not mean that children have a veto right or that their opinions should always be determinative in the decision-making process (Hodgkin & Newell, 2002; Ochaíta & Espinosa, 1997). In other words, this principle is not the equivalent to the children's liberationists' claim that children should be able to make their own decisions as part of their rights to self-determination and autonomy. Rather, it indicates the right of children to have their capacity to autonomy promoted through participation and consultation (Fortin, 2003, p. 20). Moreover, it is arguable that the child's right *to be heard* and considered on matters concerning the child's life substitutes the right adults (and more mature children) hold to make their own choices (Archard, 2002). In fact, some argue that the Convention did not go far enough in securing children's right to meaningfully participate in decision-making processes, because of its failure to explicitly address power imbalance and other structural obstacles that hinder the ability of children to actually make a difference through their participation (Olsen, 1992, p. 210). Indeed even with regard to child-inclusive reforms that invest in creating opportunities for children to participate in decisions affecting them, concerns have been expressed regarding the effectiveness of children's participation. Ruth Sinclair, for instance, referring to child protection conferences in Britain, argues that children are, at best, listened to, and only seldom receive meaningful opportunities to actually influence decisions (2004, pp. 110–111). Nevertheless the limited participation might result not from the wording of the Convention (or national regulation reflecting the Convention's articles), but rather from the way it is understood and implemented. When following the Convention's blueprint, the participation right is envisioned to be practiced and shaped by the other guiding principles and emphasis on respect for children. Children's participation, therefore, should be understood not as mere consultation, in which children's views are sought, but the decision is made by others. In true participation that follows the words and spirit of the Convention, children take part in the actual decision making (Thomas, 2007).

In other words, it is possible to see the participation right as granting children more than a right to be heard, but less than a right to independent decision making. This makes sense, in light of the Convention's emphasis on the family and the community and their importance for children. Considering the fact that the participatory right is understood and implemented narrowly, however, the Convention is admittedly vulnerable to criticism for not clearly stating that children have a right, to the extent possible, to be partners in deliberative decision-making processes regarding issues affecting them.

The differentiation between the right to make one's own decisions and the right to take part in the decision-making process might make the participation principle presented in the Convention easier to accept, but at the same time, it raises the question whether there is a certain stage where participation is not enough, and full autonomy can be asserted. Gary Melton (1999), however, argues that too much emphasis has been put on the question of when children can make their own decisions. This question, he explains, creates an atmosphere of conflict between children and their parents or other adults. It puts too much weight on the question of capacity, which is problematic. First, many adults do not have ideal reasoning capacity, and it is unfair to expect children to have such capacity. Second, empirical studies show that at age 14, children have similar intellectual and social capacities as adults, allowing them to make decisions as adults would. Third, even younger children, who are not able to articulate their reasoning, will often follow adult models and eventually reach the same decisions adults would. Fourth, practicing decision making is important even before children reach full capacity. In fact, Melton holds that practice and experience in decision making, and not age, promote the development of such capacities; age is not the crucial question since the first time will always be problematic, even in mature age. Fifth, there are other, broader rationales for making decision making accessible for children notwithstanding their capacities, such as encouraging children to speak out and seek help even at young ages. This may be important, for example, with sexually transmitted diseases or abuse and neglect cases. Finally, even when a child has reached full capacity, when the parents are influenced by the decision, it is only fair to allow parental involvement. Thus, a gradual growth in autonomy through practice and guidance in the decision-making process until the child is ready for full autonomy is preferred. This, in Melton's view, is the essence of the participation principle of the CRC.

It may be surprising to realize, moreover, that children regard the opportunity to participate in the decision-making process—to be listened to, considered, and respected—as more important than having their opinion accepted (Morrow, 1999; Thomas & O'Kane, 1998). Accordingly, Melton (1999) argues that children feel that they are taken seriously if their views are listened to and considered with respect, even if the final decision is made by others.

Therefore, while not creating a right to make independent decisions, Article 12 does mean that the older and more mature the child is, the more weight should be given to his or her views, even when "adults" think differently. Whatever the child's age is, however, a comprehensive understanding of the Convention implies that adults should try to engage in a dialog with the child, to allow mutual exchanges of feelings and viewpoints. The difficult question is how to apply the participation principle in real-life situations. Different writers have tried to confront this challenge.

Moira Rayner (2002, p. 6) argues that the nature of the specific subject matter affects the weight that is given to the child's view. She holds that the greater the effect of the decision on the child's life is, the more important it is to consult with the child and to be influenced by the child's views, while ensuring that the child receives adequate explanation and information on the matter.

Flekkøy and Kaufman (1997, p. 65) emphasize the need to balance between overprotection and underprotection of children, leaving them just the right spaces for adequate participation in decision making. They argue that the best interests and the evolving capacities principles are sufficiently guiding in finding the middle way. In practice, Flekkøy and Kaufman suggest that it is important to consider, in each individual case, how much and what kind of protection the child needs, while:

> taking into consideration the maturity and experience of the child, the situation, the consequences of the decisions to be made and the benefits of increasing experience and autonomy. Perhaps it is necessary to consider whether the child, even if deemed incapable to make the entire decision on his or her own, could be capable of giving an opinion or making a "part" decision, as one step to the final decision. It is also important to consider the consequences of not letting the child voice an opinion, make a choice or share a decision making (1997, p. 67).

With reference to medical treatment, Nancy Walker (2002) proposes a model under which children progress from *assent* (the child is informed and cooperates with the adults' decision), through *dissent* (the child may have a different view that should be taken seriously, assuming he or she has a sufficient knowledge and understanding of the matter), to *consent* (when the child is appropriately informed and well aware of the circumstances and has the capacity to consent, there should be no coercion in treatment). Similar to the Convention, Walker's model focuses on children's evolving capacities in decision making, rather than on strict age classification. She further argues that this model should be applied in accordance with the "best interests of the child" standard, which in this context requires that the child: (1) receives developmentally appropriate information; (2) has all questions sufficiently answered; (3) expresses his or her opinions freely; (4) has those opinions heard and respected; and (5) participates as completely as possible considering the child's developmental level.

Walker integrates, as required by the Convention, the participation, best interests, and evolving capacities principles together. Surely, in many areas other than medical treatment, the question is not whether or not to conduct some procedure but rather an open-ended question. Walker's model, however, might be still useful in other contexts as well. For example, applying her model to the context of reactions to childhood victimization, a young child who has been victimized should be informed of a decision to refer the case to a restorative justice setting and should have an opportunity to express his or her feelings about it. A more mature child might be asked for a more detailed opinion regarding matters arising from that decision, such as the preferred outcomes of the process and the list of participants. The child can also decide whether or not to take part in the process. Older children should perhaps have, in addition, a veto right against the decision to have a restorative process itself.

Anne Smith (2002, pp. 82–85) points out that even very young children are capable of understanding their experiences and expressing themselves. Her review of empirical research suggests that babies, infants, and preschoolers are active participants in their environments, and that when approached appropriately, even 3- and 4-year-old children can communicate about their views, difficulties, and wishes. Thus, even very young children can participate in significant ways in decision making. She further argues that adults should be sensitive to the child's current level of understanding and allow gradual growth in the responsibilities and weight given to the child and the child's views. More specifically, a child's advocate may need to suggest the alternatives, but if the child is aware of such alternatives there is no need to be overpaternalistic. Moreover, parents and professionals should understand that children need to have the opportunities to express their views, initiate actions, and make decisions in order to mature into decision-making, involved citizens (Smith, 2002, pp. 82–85).

It is important to note that the scope of the participatory principle is very wide. It applies to all matters affecting the child, even those that are not specifically mentioned in the Convention (Pais, 1997). The participatory principle is not only broad in terms of the matters it applies to, but also in the *level* of participation provided to the child, according to the child's age and maturity:

> This article sets one of the fundamental values of the Convention and probably also one of its basic challenges. In essence it affirms that the child is a fully fledged person having the right to express views in all matters affecting him or her, and having those views heard and given due weight. Thus the child has the right to participate in the decision-making process affecting his or her life, as well as to influence decisions taken in his or her regard (Pais, 1997, p. 426).

Roger Hart's (1992) work on children's participation provides an important instrument for measuring child participation. Hart proposes a "ladder of participation" to help evaluate existing participatory projects and construct new ones. Hart's ladder has been most influential in both practice and research, although it was also criticized and revised (Thomas, 2007). The ladder has eight levels. The lower three levels represent different forms of using children in ways that may seem participatory but in fact do not allow children to have real input in decision-making processes. The five higher levels represent true participatory rungs. Hart emphasizes that different levels of participation are appropriate in different cultures, contexts, and ages. Levels 4 and 5 describe projects that are designed and run by adults but children understand their meaning; the decision-making process is transparent; and in the latter, children are consulted and their opinions are treated seriously. In Level 6, decisions are made in a shared manner between children and adults, as opposed to mere consultation where the decision-makers are the adults. The highest two levels describe projects that are initiated and managed by children themselves. Notwithstanding the controversy around the exact definition of the different rungs in Hart's ladder, the importance of his typology is in identifying "nonparticipation" practices and differentiating consultation with shared decision making (Thomas, 2007).

In the context of child victims, Levels 5 and 6 of Hart's ladder are particularly interesting. Level 5 describes processes where children are consulted and their views are seriously considered. Level 6, however, is significantly different as it describes situations in which children are partners in the decision-making process and have equal voice to that of the adults. Level 6 then presents a broader participatory model than that explicitly described by the Convention, one that is, however, implied in the Convention's spirit. While Article 12 of the CRC is closer to Hart's Level 5 (i.e., consultation, transparency, and full information), the integration of the Convention's guiding principles and its underlying values overall can in fact lead to a Level 6 understanding of children's participation, namely, being partners in a shared dialog. As Hart argues, different circumstances, the child's age, cultural considerations, and other aspects determine the appropriate level of participation in a particular case. As will be discussed later in this book, restorative justice creates spaces for Level 6 participation for those children who are ready to carry the responsibility of equal and shared decision making.

The Child's Participation Right and the Child's Family

Attention should be drawn to the implications the participation principle has on the role of the child's family. The Convention regards the family, and specifically the child's parents, as the central role players in the child's life, aiming at strengthening the status of the parents, not weakening it. Being the innermost circle of the child's caretakers, parents are provided with rights and responsibilities to promote their children's rights and interests. Thus with regard to participation, the Convention does not attempt to intervene between children and their parents (with the exception of protecting the child's wellbeing—see Article 3(2)), but rather to regulate the relationship between the *state* and the child directly. Article 12 focuses, then, on administrative and judicial decisions, not on internal family matters. The family's traditions and beliefs are respected as long as they are not harmful to the child. However, parents are expected to guide and support their children's participation in decision making, in accordance with their evolving capacities, as Article 5 provides. Additionally, being a child-focused document, the Convention does imply that when state intervention has already occurred, the child has a right to have his or her own opinion justly considered even in cases of conflict with the parents' views (Flekkøy & Kaufman, 1997, pp. 58–60).

CHILD-VICTIMS' RIGHTS UNDER THE CONVENTION

According to the Committee, the Convention's guiding principles—participation, best interests, equality, and development—should be integrated in the interpretation of each one of the specific provisions and guide their implementation (Hodgkin & Newell, 2002, p. 42). Therefore, these principles were reviewed here as they are necessarily relevant in the context of the rights of child victims. It is equally important, however, to explore the Convention's specific provisions relating to child victims. The following provisions could be relevant in some ways:

- The right of the child not to be unjustly separated from his or her family (Article 9): This right becomes relevant when an intrafamilial offense has been reported, such as in child abuse or domestic violence. In such cases the implementation of Article 9 means that the removal of the abuser, rather than the child, should be considered.
- Protection against arbitrary violation of the child's privacy (Article 16): This right is relevant whenever the child's personal matters become of interest to others, such as the case of a private journal being used as evidence or when the child's body is being intruded for forensic medical examination.
- Protection against abuse, neglect and violence, whether inflicted by family or others who care for the child (Article 19): This Article relates directly and explicitly to childhood victimization and will be discussed in more detail below.
- Special protection for out-of-home children (Article 20): This Article is relevant either when a child has been placed in an alternative placement

due to intrafamilial offense, or in relation to the protection of all children who reside in such alternative placements, against victimization.

- The right of children with disabilities to receive equal opportunities and services according to their needs (Article 23): This Article applies to child victims with special needs.
- The right to access to health services (Article 24): This provision becomes relevant to child victims when they need medical treatment or mental health services.
- Specific protections against abuse related to narcotic drugs (Article 33), sexual abuse (34), trafficking (35), and other sorts of exploitation (36): These specified obligations on states to protect children from practically all crimes emphasize the importance of the right of children to be safe and the positive duty upon states to ensure their safety.
- Protection against torture and other cruel, inhumane and degrading treatment or punishment (Article 37): Although this provision is usually associated with the rights of child offenders, it has direct relevance to the subject of this book, as it prohibits violence against children who are in state institutions. This includes protection against corporal punishment and other forms of violence against children in boarding schools, militias, and detention facilities (Hodgkin & Newell, 2002, pp. 545–547).
- The right to recovery and reintegration (Article 39): This right is also explicitly and directly related to child victims, and therefore will be discussed in detail below.

As this list demonstrates, several provisions articulate the right of children to be protected against the occurrence of victimization. Once a child has been victimized, a whole other set of rights is being activated. Two provisions, however, target exclusively the situation of childhood victimization, namely Articles 19 and 39. Article 19 focuses on prevention and protection, and Article 39 focuses on the recovery of children who have already been victimized. Article 19, however, relates only to violence by the child's caretakers, and should be read together with the other "preventive" provisions, namely Articles 33, 34, 35, and 36. The reactive measures specified in Article 39 apply on all forms of child victimization.

Protection Against Victimization by Caretakers

Article 19 provides:

1. States Parties shall take all appropriate legislative, administrative, social and educational measures to protect the child from all forms of physical or mental violence, injury or abuse, neglect or negligent treatment, maltreatment or exploitation, including sexual abuse, while in the care of parent(s), legal guardian(s) or any other person who has the care of the child.
2. Such protective measures should, as appropriate, include effective procedures for the establishment of social programmes to provide necessary support for the child and for those who have the care of

> the child, as well as for other forms of prevention and for identification, reporting, referral, investigation, treatment and follow-up of instances of child maltreatment described heretofore, and, as appropriate, for judicial involvement.

The first part of this Article focuses on the responsibility of states to protect children from all forms of maltreatment. Accordingly, children are entitled to be safe from being victimized by their caretakers, including their parents or other guardians, their teachers, foster families, or any other caretaker. The protection provided in the Article includes sexual, physical, and emotional abuse; neglect; negligent treatment; maltreatment; or exploitation—a wide array of actions and omissions. According to the Committee, corporal punishment—whether inflicted within the family, schools, or other institutions, as well as in the penal system—is also prohibited by the Convention (Hodgkin & Newell, 2002, pp. 259–274). Domestic violence has also been considered by the Committee as a form of child abuse, based on findings regarding the adverse emotional harms and the risks it causes to children. State parties are therefore expected to protect children not only against direct maltreatment and abuse but against witnessing domestic violence in their homes as well (Hodgkin & Newell, 2002, pp. 260–261).

The second part of this Article lists specific measures that governments are expected to take to ensure such protection and to assist child victims. The Guidelines for Periodic Reports specify that states should show legislative prohibitions of all forms of child abuse; the existence of complaint and reporting procedures, and remedies such as compensation; procedures for intervention by the authorities to protect child victims; and educational and other measures adopted to promote positive and nonviolent forms of discipline. The Guidelines further ask states to relate to existing programs for support and rehabilitation of child victims, confidential help lines, advice, or counseling (Hodgkin & Newell, 2002, p. 680).

Thus, not only does Article 19 oblige states to protect children from abuse and exploitation, but it also provides these children with remedial measures, an aspect that appears also in Article 39. However, the Article creates these duties only with relation to victimization by caretakers, which even when interpreted broadly does not include stranger-perpetrators. Therefore, it should be read with Articles 33–36, which expand the protection right to other contexts as well.

The Right to Rehabilitation

Article 39 states:

> States Parties shall take all appropriate measures to promote physical and psychological recovery and social reintegration of a child victim of: any form of neglect, exploitation, or abuse; torture or any other form of cruel, inhuman or degrading treatment or punishment; or armed conflicts. Such recovery and reintegration shall take place in an environment which fosters the health, self-respect and dignity of the child.

According to this provision, once victimization has occurred, an obligation is created toward the child to promote his or her emotional healing as well as their social reintegration. Therefore, punishing offenders is not enough; the responsibility of state members toward young victims continues until they are fully rehabilitated.

The 1996 *Declaration of the World Congress Against Commercial Sexual Exploitation of Children* (World Congress Against Commercial Sexual Exploitation of Children, 1996) provides an important account of what is expected from states with regard to rehabilitation and reintegration of child victims. It particularly demonstrates the connection between child-friendly processes and the rehabilitation of child victims. Article 5 of the Declaration, titled "Rehabilitation and Reintegration," provides that states:

> a) Adopt a non-punitive approach to child victims of commercial sexual exploitation . . . and establish a child-friendly judicial system, taking particular care that judicial procedures do not aggravate the trauma already experienced by the child and that the response of the system be coupled with legal aid assistance and provision of judicial remedies to the child victims;
> b) Provide medical, psychological and other support to child victims of commercial sexual exploitation . . . with a view to promoting the self-respect and dignity of the child with conformity with the Convention on the Rights of the Child;
> c) Train medical personnel, social workers, non-governmental organizations and others working to rehabilitate and reintegrate child victims of commercial sexual exploitation on the Convention on the Rights of the Child, other relevant human rights standards and child development;
> d) Take effective action to remove societal stigmatization . . . facilitate the rehabilitation and reintegration of child victims in community or family settings . . .

Apart from stressing the importance of child-friendly processes, this declaration requires states to do more than the provision of universal services to children at risk or families in crisis. Special services, with the child victims as their specific target population, should be established in order to ensure effective rehabilitation.

CONCLUSIONS: A FULLY CONNECTED WEB OF CHILDREN'S RIGHTS

This chapter presented the theoretical foundations for children's rights as the basis for any discussion on reactions to childhood victimization. The most fundamental justification for children's rights is that children belong to the human race, which entitles them to equal respect as any other members of society. The notion of children's dignity is also central in the Convention (Melton, 1991), as its preamble demonstrates:

> Considering that, in accordance with the principles proclaimed in the Charter of the United Nations, recognition of the inherent dignity and of the equal and inalienable rights of all members of the human family is the foundation of freedom, justice and peace in the world,
>
> Bearing in mind that the peoples of the United Nations have, in the Charter, reaffirmed their faith in fundamental human rights and in the dignity and worth

> of the human person, and have determined to promote social progress and better standards of life in larger freedom,
>
> . . .
>
> Considering that the child should be fully prepared to live an individual life in society, and brought up in the spirit of the ideals proclaimed in the Charter of the United Nations, and in particular in the spirit of peace, dignity, tolerance, freedom, equality and solidarity . . . (Extracts from the Convention's Preamble).

Despite criticism against the use of rights terminology with regard to children, it seems that a special type of rights discourse provides a more robust framework. This is a rights discourse based on the international human rights framework, one which acknowledges the importance of protection and family ties as well as self-determination and autonomy. A rights discourse that connects rights with needs is therefore more vital than one that excludes needs or is in competition with them.

Indeed, respect for children means respecting both their special vulnerabilities, or needs, and their evolving capacities by allowing them to exercise their rights increasingly as they mature (Flekkøy & Kaufman, 1997, p. 49). As the first part of this chapter showed, the interest theory grounds rights on people's basic needs and, therefore, avoids categorizing people according to their capabilities or lack of them.

Justifying rights on the basis of needs, however, does not mean that needs-based rights are necessarily weaker than choice- or will-based rights. The various models reviewed and summarized in Table 2.1 by Feinberg (1980), Campbell (1992), Eekelaar (1992), Wolfson (1992), Minow (1995b), and Bojer (2000) have demonstrated that children hold a complex mix of welfare, human, liberal, and protection rights. These rights typologies echo other efforts to identify children's universal needs, as described in Table 2.2 and its accompanying text. The international body of human rights reflects a similar holistic approach toward children's rights, combining liberal rights and protective needs. Children's positive right to protection, for example, was stated internationally as early as 1959, in the United Nations' *Declaration of the Rights of the Child*, linking the child's needs with the child's rights (Ezer, 2004, p. 23).

The CRC has gone the furthest in articulating a comprehensive, interrelated network of children's welfare and liberal rights, reflecting the multidimensional understanding of rights presented by the above-mentioned scholars. The Convention's guiding principles of equality, best interests, participation, and the right to life, survival, and development are indivisible and should be read into each one of the Convention's other provisions. This interlinking method offers a broad, flexible, and yet powerful network of rights that extends beyond the protection–autonomy dichotomy. For example, as Flekkøy and Kaufman (1997) suggest, the dilemma between overprotection and underprotection related to the participation principle can be adequately addressed through the deployment of the best interests and the development, or the evolving capacities principles in its implementation. In other words, the integrated use of the four guiding principles provides a tool for resolving internal dilemmas and ostensibly conflicting priorities in the application of children's rights.

The Convention also reflects an inclusive attitude toward children, similar to what Minow (1990, p. 375) calls "taking the perspective of the other." Indeed, the Convention requires society to make the needed adjustments to *include* children in public discourse while addressing their vulnerabilities, instead of excluding them from adult world due to their limited experience and lack of maturity. Accordingly, the Convention stipulates that children should be encouraged to develop their evolving capacities, receive any aids they need to overcome disabilities, and take part in decision-making processes according to their capabilities. In other words, the Convention creates a utopian framework in which the worlds surrounding children are being fitted according to their special needs, allowing them to be active actors in them. At the same time, and similar to Minow's emphasis on the importance of relationships, the Convention acknowledges the centrality of the child's family, relatives, culture, and nationality.

It seems, then, that the Convention is unique in its unprecedented holistic approach toward children, as well as in its (perhaps surprising) worldwide popularity. Therefore, while there are limitations to the rights discourse in general and to children's rights as reflected in the Convention in particular, its nearly universal ratification makes children's rights part of today's political reality. The question then that justice systems across the globe should ask is not whether children (or child victims, in the context of this work) have rights, but instead how the Convention should best be implemented to meet these rights. In other words, and in the context of this book, children's rights is, theoretically and practically, a valid instrument in evaluating current responses to childhood victimization, making the Convention an important international measurement for the achievements (and failures) in this field.

The next step of this chapter was, then, to map those rights in the Convention that relate to child victims. Although the Convention's 42 substantial articles are intertwined and affect each other, this chapter focused on the six most relevant provisions that apply to child victims. Four of them are the guiding principles of the Convention, namely the best interests; equality; the right to life, survival and development (termed here the development principle, for simplicity); and the participation principle. Additionally, two provisions relate exclusively to child victims: the right to be protected from all forms of violence, and the right of child victims for physical and psychological recovery and social reintegration. The interrelationship between these provisions is reflected in Figure 2.1. As the image demonstrates, while the four guiding principles affect each other and have direct application on policies regarding child

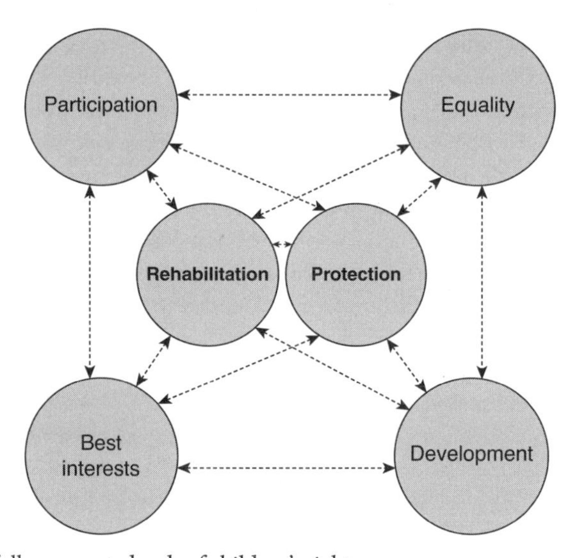

Figure 2.1 A fully connected web of children's rights.

victims, they also influence, or shape, the understanding and implementation of the two specific rights, namely the right to protection and to rehabilitation.

One could argue against this account that it fails to include other international norms that are relevant to the context of childhood victimization. For example, perhaps the right of crime victims to restitution from the offender stated in the Declaration should be included in this model. However, there is merit in keeping this account broad and open for specific interpretations in accordance with varying cultures, mechanisms, and circumstances. The right to restitution from the offender has a narrower nature and can be considered as part of the rehabilitation right or the best interests principle. Moreover, unlike the Convention, the Declaration is not a binding instrument, and therefore its provisions have a weaker status compared with that of the Convention's Articles.

Furthermore, each one of the six rights in this account (the four guiding principles and the two specific provisions) reflects, beyond its literal meaning, a complex body of understandings as discussed earlier. For example, *equality* means not only procedural, but substantive equality (Van Bueren, 1999a), which requires individual evaluation of the child's difficulties in having equal access to whichever institution is being considered and efforts to overcome these obstacles. *Participation* carries along Roger Hart's (1992) differentiation between meaningful and tokenistic participation and, accordingly, goes beyond the explicit wording of Article 12. *Development* indicates the importance of considering (and promoting) the evolving capacities of the child and, accordingly, a gradual expansion of children's autonomy dictated by the capabilities of each specific child. *Protection* refers not only to Article 19 (crimes by caretakers, including child abuse through exposure to domestic violence) but to the other specific provisions that create protections against extrafamilial exploitation. Finally, *best interests* should be understood in its broad meaning, which includes the child's wishes. Therefore, one should read this account of child victims' rights as a coded presentation of a much more complex network of interrelated values.

A recurring theme emerging is this chapter has been the interrelationship between an empirical investigation of children's needs, on the one hand, and a normative analysis of their basic rights, on the other. First, an examination of children's needs, or interests, provides the foundation for children's rights. In other words, at least some of the rights children have are based on their universally acknowledged needs, as the interest theory of rights suggests. Rights, in turn, provide these needs a certain power, a status strong enough (at least theoretically) to bring about political change. As Waldron (2000, pp. 131–132) argues, the needs discourse provides a diagnosis, and the rights discourse uses this diagnosis as claims to create duties upon others.

But this is not the full picture of the mutual relationship between needs and rights or of the empirical and the normative discourses in the context of child victims. An important feature of the Convention is the broad meaning of its provisions. This allows flexibility and adjustments for different cultures, children, and circumstances. This, however, also presents a difficulty in translating its provisions into action. Indeed, vagueness is one of the main critiques against rights discourse in general, and the Convention in particular. An empirical exploration might be helpful in uncovering the specific meanings of the Convention's provisions in the context of childhood victimization and overcome this concern. This is the underlying assumption of *psychological jurisprudence* (Melton & Limber, 1992), which calls for the cooperation of law and psychology to allow evidence-based judicial decisions. In other words, empirical findings of children's daily realities provide not only the general justifications for children's various rights, they also fill these rights in content regarding specific circumstances. If we are serious about treating children as individuals with subjective worldviews rather than mere objects of protection, then we need to make efforts to uncover their authentic perspectives and experiences (Melton & Wilcox, 2001, p. 12). This can only be done through the systematic study of children's views and needs. Chapter 3, therefore, aims to complete the needs-rights template through reviewing psychosocial findings regarding childhood victimization.

3

Child Victims' Needs

Empirical Findings

INTRODUCTION

This chapter uses a psychosocial prism to look at childhood victimization and its challenges. It presents findings regarding the effects of victimization on children and reviews what we know today about their needs in the healing process.

A pure needs terminology, however, has its own limitations. Just like a simplified rights terminology is vulnerable to criticism, so is a simplified needs talk. First, every child is different and every child victim is different yet. The specific needs of each victimized child will therefore be unique and will depend on the child's own strengths and vulnerabilities, the nature of the victimization, the support network around the child, and many other variables. More broadly, social factors such as gender, race, culture and socioeconomic status greatly affect the way children experience victimization and their ability to heal from it. The resilience of children who live in poor, minority-populated urban neighborhoods and face repeated exposure to violence is probably different than that of middle-class children who experience a singular violent or sexual victimization. Most importantly, perhaps, is that the wishes of individual children differ and accordingly shape their needs. The needs terminology can therefore identify only findings regarding what many, or some, children need in their healing process.

A second reservation is that expressed needs are, at least to some extent, culturally based, because victims' expectations and wishes depend on the existing remedies they are aware of. The identified needs may therefore depend on the information given to victims who participated in the studies reviewed here. Victims' expressed needs, therefore, may change with time and geography, and depend on the design of the study (Maguire, 1991; Shapland, 1984, p. 277). Other limitations of the needs talk are the risk of overpaternalism, lack of political power, and the centrality of value judgments (Maguire, 1985, pp. 539–540).

It is therefore important to remember throughout this chapter that the "needs" reviewed here are only a part of a combined needs-rights template, which is less vulnerable to criticism. Accordingly, in the second part of this chapter the identified needs are mapped and correlated with children's human rights. A needs-rights model is then introduced, visualizing the interrelationships between the "web" of child victims' rights and their empirically founded needs.

The first part of this chapter describes what victims—adults and children—face in the aftermath of their victimization. It then moves to talk about victims' needs in their healing process, explaining these needs through selected theories and findings relating to stress, coping, and trauma in childhood and adolescence. Since many of the theories in these areas have not been developed, nor tested, specifically around children, the literature pertaining to adult victimization is discussed as well. This inconclusive review of the literature is clustered into central themes of victims' needs for control, support from others, a safe encounter with the perpetrator, a sense of justice, social acknowledgment, and reparation.

The final part of this chapter synthesizes the findings and links them with the various child victims' rights identified in the previous chapter. The outcome is a combined empirical and normative framework of needs and rights—a template for evaluating responses to childhood victimization and for creating new ones.

CRIME AND ITS AFTERMATH

Victimization generates profound emotional distress, even trauma (Davis, Taylor, & Lurigio, 1996; Maguire, 1985, p. 549; Shapland, 1984). Serious emotional repercussions appear not only after violent or sexual crime; there is evidence of the psychological toll paid by victims of burglary, robbery, and assault as well (Maguire, 1985; Shapland, 1984). The pervasiveness of distress is striking, with symptoms appearing across socioeconomic status, gender, geography, and population groups (Norris, Kaniasty, & Thompson, 1997).

Being a victim of any crime changes the way people perceive the world and themselves (Norris et al., 1997). Victims of crime typically experience two devastating realizations (Zehr, 1990). The first is that the world is not an orderly place, with a reason for everything and logic behind actions. The second assumption shattered by crime is that of autonomy: when attacked, victims are involuntarily deprived of their power, therefore losing their control over their body, property, and actions. The results of these experiences translate into various elevated symptoms such as depression, anxiety, hostility, and alienation (Norris et al., 1997).

People react very differently to crime, however, and differ in the ways and pace in which they reconstitute their perceptions of the world (Cook, David, & Grant, 1999). Reactions to similar crimes can vary from minor, short-term stress reactions to long-lasting clinical symptoms. Furthermore, different individuals may respond with vastly different ways of coping, even to the same kind of assault. Differences in reactions to crime result from variations in the individual's internal and external resources, the crime itself, previous victimization, societal status, and other ecological circumstances (Cook et al., 1999, p. 18; Norris et al., 1997).

Despite the diversity in reactions, it is typically possible to identify three stages of crime reactions (Cook et al., 1999, p. 26; Zehr, 1990):

- The impact stage, during and immediately after the victimization
- The recoil or adjustment phase
- Reorganization or resolution.

In the initial impact phase many victims feel "overwhelmed by feelings of confusion, helplessness, terror, vulnerability" (Zehr, 1990, p. 20). Even victims of burglary report feeling angry, shocked, and frightened and suffer sleeplessness in reaction to the crime (Mawby & Kirchnoff, 1996). As they move on to the adjustment or recoil phase, victims try to cope with the new situation. The emotions experienced in the impact stage typically decline in intensity and are gradually replaced by anger, guilt, anxiety, wariness, shame, and self-doubt; many victims have wide mood swings, their senses of control and safety are shattered, and trust in others is damaged. Additionally, victimization can have a detrimental effect on victims' health, close relationships, and sex life. Another central issue is self-blame, where victims need to find answers to their questions about their own responsibility in order to heal (Zehr, 1990, pp. 20–23). The final phase of reorganization occurs if, and when, victims recover from the initial trauma, regain their sense of autonomy and power, and resume normal relationships with others (Zehr, 1990, p. 25). An important contribution to victims' healing is professional help, which, when provided promptly, effectively, and continually, can significantly reduce the crime-related symptoms (Norris et al., 1997, p. 156).

Most victims suffer from the aforementioned emotional difficulties during the days, weeks, or months that follow their victimization (Maguire, 1991). When victims do not have opportunities to move on in the healing process, they are more likely to suffer long-term consequences. Such effects might include post-traumatic stress disorder (PTSD), addictions, depression, suicidal behavior, and anxiety disorders (Cook et al., 1999, pp. 34–35). Even when emotional distress does not reach the level of PTSD, the persistence and consistency of the negative emotional effects are surprisingly high, lasting up to 2.5 years after the victimization (Norris et al., 1997; Shapland, 1984, p. 276).

Crime, then, challenges people's normal lives and can seriously affect them. When the victim is a child, the effects of the crime can be more serious and last longer due to the developmental nature of childhood. The next section focuses on the specific impacts of crime on children.

The Effects of Childhood Victimization

Most studies that explore childhood victimization and its consequences focus on abuse. Only a few look at other crimes against children or at the full spectrum of crimes, although children regularly become victims of other crimes such as assault, property theft, robbery, and sexual assault. Furthermore, notwithstanding the types of victimization examined, most findings refer to the negative repercussions of crimes against children rather than children's expressed needs: what children themselves perceive as important in their healing process. This section will therefore begin with a review of the literature focusing on the effects of victimization in general on children, with special attention to child abuse and post-trauma symptoms—two strands of the literature that have been the most salient in developing empirically based knowledge on the effects of victimization on children (Finkelhor, 2008, p. 65). A discussion on the expressed or implied needs of victimized children will follow.

Morgan and Zedner (1992) were the first to provide an extensive description of childhood victimization and its effects beyond the scope of sexual and physical abuse. The authors conducted a U.K.-based study that included 54 child victims of physical assaults, 19 victims of sexual assault or abuse, 19 children who witnessed suspicious behavior, 14 witnesses of indecent behavior, and 66 children who were victims of theft. Additionally, 40 children were indirect victims (burglary, mother's rape and assault, and racial attack) (1992, pp. 46–47). Some of Morgan and Zedner's data demonstrate the significant consequences children suffer even in crimes that are not typically associated with trauma and those that are not directed exclusively against them. For example, children whose houses were broken into reported feeling invaded and complained that their sense of safety in the home was shattered, and many shared the feelings of loss and shock with their adult family members. In some cases their own possessions were stolen, and the authors emphasized the relatively high value of these possessions for the children's budget. Children often saw the house immediately after the burglary and experienced the influx of police investigators, insurance agents, and repairmen that followed (Morgan & Zedner, 1992, p. 63). Bicycle theft emerged as a very distressing offense against children: it may be the most valuable possession they have and their only means of mobility. Some children also felt guilty and were afraid of their parents' reaction to the theft (1992, p. 65).

Morgan and Zedner found that the psychological effects of crime predominate among children. Children's distress may be enhanced by lack of understanding of what had happened or the meaning of the act. It may also be the child's first experience as a victim, and his or her lack of experience makes it more difficult to cope and to comprehend the crime. Children's dependency on adults to help them cope and prevent further harm is an additional factor contributing to their difficulties. When adults fail to protect the child, the shock is enhanced (Morgan & Zedner, 1992, pp. 53–54). In cases of physical assault, child victims admitted fearing going back to school, going out to town, or going outside at all—worrying that an assault could happen again. Violent crime, then, elevated fear and affected children's daily lives (1992, p. 61). The authors also found that because of children's greater vulnerability and physical weakness, incidents that may seem trivial to adults can be very threatening to young victims. Fear of further victimization and fear of the offender lasted up to months and years after the incident (1992, p. 66). Over 90% of children in the study were distressed immediately after the crime. Children who were more seriously hurt by physical and sexual assault, children who witnessed their parents being seriously victimized, and some of the children whose homes had been broken into were deeply affected in the longer term (1992, p. 73).

With regard to coping with crime, Morgan and Zedner's data indicated clearly that the most important help child victims get is from their families—just talking about the crime was reported as most helpful (1992, p. 169). However, three-quarters of the children and their families expressed the need for further support outside the family (1992, p. 170). Drawing from their findings, Morgan and Zedner claimed that parents are not always able to identify, and meet, the needs of their victimized children, even in nonsexual crimes. To better address children's needs, the authors claim, it is important to let them express their wishes and take them into consideration (1992, p. 183).

Moving to more recent literature, the most significant body of research today on child victimization is that of David Finkelhor's research group (Finkelhor, 2008). Based on existing data and developmental theories, Finkelhor and Kendall-Tackett (1997) propose a developmental perspective on reactions to crimes against children. Certain developmental dimensions contribute to the way crime affects children. The way the child understands the crime (appraisals), the specific developmental task the child faces, the available coping mechanisms, and the child's social environment all shape the way the child is affected by the crime (Finkelhor, 2008, pp. 72–73). With regard to appraisals, children's understanding of the crime varies in accordance with their age and cognitive development. Very young children, for instance, may not understand the full meaning of their sexual abuse as opposed to older children, although they might still suffer the physiological outcomes.

With regard to the developmental task the child is facing at the time of the crime, victimization can affect the child's development in three ways: delaying the mastering of a new developmental task, distorting the outcome of the tasks, and creating regression, so that a newly achieved task is lost. Young children who are facing the task of creating secure attachments, for instance, are harmed by neglectful and abusive mothers (Finkelhor & Kendall-Tackett, 1997, p. 17). Another task at early childhood is forming emotional regulation—learning to control and balance emotions. Children who are overwhelmed with fear and victimization may be unable to regulate their emotions and act permanently on highly emotional levels (Finkelhor & Kendall-Tackett, 1997). At preschool age, children's cooperative play and friendships may be disrupted by their victimization. At age 8 to 9, children learn to use dissociation methods to cope with stress. Accordingly, children who are victimized at this stage may be more prone to extreme problems of dissociation (Finkelhor, 2008, p. 81).

Not only internal characteristics change as children age—the availability and significance of different external factors vary as well (Finkelhor, 2008, pp. 84–87; Finkelhor & Kendall-Tackett, 1997). For example, while parents (in particular mothers) are the most important buffering factor in coping with stress in early childhood, peers become more central for adolescents. Similarly, peer and community reactions (such as discrimination, a sense of honor and shame) may be more influential on older children than on young ones (Finkelhor, 2008, p. 85). The authorities that typically intervene are also different in varying stages of childhood. In preschool years parents are most involved in resolving children's conflicts, while for school-aged children the school authorities may be dominant in intervening when conflict arises. Police and other justice-related authorities intervene only when adults are involved as well, or in extreme situations. For older teens, however, police are more ready to step in even in peer violence.

Another categorization regards the impact of childhood victimization. Some impacts are typical to all kinds of crimes ("generic" implications), such as a sense of powerlessness, betrayal, and injustice, while others are specific to some crimes, for example sexualized behavior following sexual abuse, and insecure attachment as an outcome of parental maltreatment (Finkelhor, 2008, p. 88; Finkelhor & Kendall-Tackett, 1997, pp. 22–23). There are further "local" impacts (temporary consequences such as anger, re-experiencing the event, self-blame) and developmental impacts that become integrated in the child's personality (such as adopting bullying behavior, sexualized behavior, drug abuse, or impairment of self-esteem) (Finkelhor, 2008, pp. 88–89). The developmental impacts are those that make childhood victimization distinct from adult victimization. Finally, childhood victimization identifies direct effects as well as indirect effects resulting from those developmental effects. For example, the inability to form peer relationships may cause further problems, such as depression (Finkelhor, 2008, p. 89).

Child Abuse

While child abuse in its various forms is not "pandemic" in its occurrence (Finkelhor, 2008, p. 33), the severity of its short- and long-term effects, combined with the richness of the literature describing them, justifies special attention within this review. It should be remembered, however, that from a comprehensive childhood victimization perspective child abuse is only one, relatively uncommon, type of victimization (Finkelhor, 2008, p. 44). The definition of child abuse varies among legal systems and scholars, but for the purposes of this chapter child abuse is defined as ongoing physical or sexual violence or neglect of children by their caretakers or other known adults. Domestic violence is a special case of child abuse. First, when there is ongoing abuse of one family member, others suffer victimization as well (Pennell & Burford, 2000a, p. 137).[27] This is particularly true when children are exposed to violence targeted at their mothers. The involvement of children in domestic violence incidents is common and varies in the ways children are exposed to it (Edleson, 1999). Children are often sent outside or are left alone during conflict periods to protect them from the abusive behavior. When children remain close to the violent outburst they are often in direct physical danger, and some actually get hurt either by mistake or while trying to protect their mothers. Whichever role or position children in abusive environments take, they are scarred by the recurring experience of seeing their mothers abused, hurt, and in imminent danger (Fantuzzo & Mohr, 1999). Studies consistently show that children who witness domestic violence are, on average, more likely to have behavioral, social, and emotional problems (Schechter & Edleson, 1999, p. 10). Indeed, the seriousness and pervasiveness of the consequences of children's exposure to domestic violence are comparable to those resulting from direct parental abuse (see, for instance, Fantuzzo & Mohr, 1999; Garner & Nishith, 1997, p. 74). Furthermore, there is extensive overlap between direct child abuse and domestic violence, with child abuse occurring in roughly half of the homes where the mother is victimized (Edleson, 1999). Finally, domestic violence is a major risk factor for various forms of child abuse and neglect (Zolotor, Theodore, Coyne-Beasley, & Runyan, 2007).

Judith Herman (1992) explains the reasons for the uniqueness of childhood abuse and the "developmental" nature of these consequences, to use Finkelhor's terminology: Abused children need, like other children, to develop trust, form primary attachments with their parents, develop a sense of self, regulate their bodily functioning, and develop a capacity for initiative and capability for intimacy. They also must preserve a sense of hope and meaning. To achieve all these normal developmental tasks, abused children will do everything they can to absolve their abusive parents of any blame. Accordingly, Herman argues, abused children develop great capacities of suppression and denial, which in turn shape (and distort) their development. The most powerful adaptation abused children mobilize is dissociation—a state where the mind travels away from the body. Another defense mechanism for abused children is to believe that they are to be blamed for their inner wickedness. Often, these deformed developmental achievements such as dissociation and a perception of inner badness remain with the child long after the abuse is gone. Moreover, children who grow up in abusing families are typically unable to develop an inner sense of safety, as children in normal situations do. They do not have inner representations of trustful, safe images since their parents are just the opposite of this. Therefore, they desperately cling to other (potentially abusive) people, while at the same time they keep looking for their parents' love and affection (Herman, 1992, p. 107).[28]

Briere and Elliott (1994) provide a detailed review of current empirical knowledge regarding the short- and long-term impacts of childhood sexual abuse, echoing Herman's explanations. They propose that the aggregated consistent findings of studies conducted in recent decades led many to conclude that childhood sexual abuse is a major risk factor for a variety of problems such as post-traumatic stress, cognitive disorders, emotional pain, avoidance, an impaired sense of self, and interpersonal difficulties. Based on the aggregated studies, the primary psychological impacts of sexual abuse of children seem to occur in at least three stages:

- Initial reactions to victimization, involving post-traumatic stress, disruptions of normal psychological development, painful emotions, and cognitive distortions

- Accommodation to ongoing abuse, involving coping behaviors intended to increase safety and/or decrease pain during victimization
- Longer-term consequences, reflecting the impacts of the initial reactions and abuse-related accommodations on the individual's ongoing psychological development and personality formation (Briere & Elliott, 1994, p. 55).

Among the *cognitive* distortions associated with the initial stage, the following have been documented most often in studies: chronic self-perception of helplessness and hopelessness, impaired trust, self-blame, and low self-esteem. This negative self-perception is typically related to assumptions that children make about their inherent badness, based on misinterpretation of maltreatment as, in fact, punishment for unknown transgressions (Briere & Elliott, 1994, p. 59). The documented symptoms of *emotional* distress that characterize the first stage are increased depression, anxiety, and anger (Briere & Elliott, 1994, p. 57). *Physical* expressions of anxiety that have been associated with child sexual abuse include headaches, stomach pain, bladder infections, and chronic pelvic pain (Briere & Elliott, 1994, p. 57). *Behaviorally*, anger may be expressed in chronic irritability, unexpected or uncontrollable feelings of anger, and difficulties in expressing anger. Children frequently express anger in behavioral problems, as well as in fighting, bullying, or attacking other children (Briere & Elliott, 1994, p. 58). In the *social* realm, interference with the child's sense of self may translate into a continuing inability to define one's own boundaries or reasonable rights when faced with the needs or demands of others in the interpersonal environment. Abused children also experience interpersonal difficulties such as distrust of others, anger at and/or fear of those with greater power, and perceptions of injustice. As a result, sexually abused children are found to be less socially competent, more aggressive, and more socially withdrawn (Briere & Elliott, 1994, pp. 59–61).

Post-Trauma Symptoms in Children

Some child victims of violent or sexual crimes develop post-trauma symptoms, which have been studied in the PTSD literature. In 1987, a definition of PTSD symptoms specific to children was added to the general definition in the *Diagnostic and Statistical Manual* (DSM) published by the American Psychiatric Association (Keppel-Benson & Ollendick, 1993, p. 30). Children who meet the clinical definition as a result of a traumatic event demonstrate symptoms drawn from the following three categories (Keppel-Benson & Ollendick, 1993, pp. 30–35; Spender & John, 2001, p. 72):

- Re-experiencing the event: children might have intrusive thoughts, nightmares, flashbacks and vivid memories, and might engage in repetitive play.
- Avoidance and numbness: traumatized children might avoid thinking of and experiencing aspects related to their trauma; might become uninterested in activities, become numb, or regress in their developmental skills; might develop trauma-related amnesia; or might become emotionally withdrawn.
- Increased arousal: sleep and concentration difficulties, irritability, and hyperarousal in trauma-related situations.

While this definition provides important information on possible sequelae of childhood violent or sexual victimization, it is important to consider its limitations in the context of child victims. The starting point of PTSD literature is not victimization as such, but rather traumatic events. It therefore neglects other, non-post-trauma (but still significant) behaviors, as well as the more common forms of child victimization such as bullying, sibling assault, and indecent acts by strangers (Finkelhor & Kendall-Tackett, 1997). Ongoing victimization conditions such as neglect also fly below the radar of PTSD literature (Finkelhor, 2008, p. 67). Additionally, PTSD literature focuses on emotional results of victimization (or trauma) that reach psychopathology and neglects other cognitive, behavioral, and attitudinal dimensions such as perceptions of justice and social skills (Caffo, Forresi, & Strik-Lievers, 2005; Finkelhor, 2008, p. 68).

Furthermore, because the clinical diagnosis appearing in the DSM is based on adults' symptoms, it fails to identify a variety of symptoms common among children and adolescents according to their developmental stage (Anderson, 2005). Indeed, empirical studies investigating children's reactions to trauma document other common symptoms not included in the DSM, in particular trauma-related fears, the experience of guilt, and behavioral disturbances (Keppel-Benson & Ollendick, 1993, pp. 35–36; Spender & John, 2001, p. 72). Another dimension of trauma not appearing in its clinical definition is that it affects the central nervous system in the victim's brain, and in particular can have a significant impact on the developing brain of children, something that typically does not happen among the fully developed brains of adults. As a result, traumatized children have their whole neural systems organized around their trauma, and are consequently dysregulated and poorly equipped to handle any form of subsequent stress (Finkelhor, 2008, p. 66). Finally, the comorbidity of PTSD with depression and anxiety disorders has also resulted in researchers questioning the validity of the PTSD definition in children and adolescents (Caffo et al., 2005).

Spender and John (2001) claim, based on their review of 45 studies on sexually abused children, that, beyond the PTSD official symptoms, other typical symptoms are fears, behavior problems, sexualized behaviors, and low self-esteem. No one symptom (including the formal PTSD ones) was found as characterizing the majority of these children. About one-third of the sexually abused children had no symptoms. Their review of findings suggests that symptoms vary among age groups:

- Preschool victims suffer mainly from anxiety, nightmares, general PTSD, internalizing, externalizing, and inappropriate sexual behaviors.
- School-aged children suffer most commonly from fear, neurotic and general mental problems, aggression, nightmares, school problems, hyperactivity, and regressive behavior.
- For adolescents, the most common problems are depression, withdrawal, suicidal or self-injurious behaviors, somatic complaints, illegal acts, running away, and substance abuse.

Greater levels of symptomatology are correlated with these factors: penetration, high duration and frequency of the abuse, use of force, parental abuse, and lack of maternal support. About two-thirds of the children included in the studies showed recovery within 12 to 18 months (Spender & John, 2001). Additional factors affecting reactions to trauma were documented in other studies, such as whether the trauma was acute (one-time occurrence) or chronic, the degree of exposure, the life threat involved and the physical injury caused, prior traumatic experiences, and prior emotional conditions (Keppel-Benson & Ollendick, 1993, pp. 36–39). The existence of a network of social support has been found to have a buffering effect in many studies (Caffo et al., 2005, p. 425), with maternal support emerging as the most important factor in determining children's reactions to abuse (Finkelhor, 2008, p. 84).

VICTIMS' NEEDS IN THE HEALING PROCESS

The previous section has shown that the effects of childhood victimization vary but are visible across the full range of victimization types, victims' developmental stages, and areas of functioning (such as emotional, cognitive, behavioral, and social) (Finkelhor, 2008, p. 70). Much less is known about victims' expressed *needs* in the process that follows their victimization. This is the focus of the following section.

With regard to adult victims, victimologists identify the following as victims' central needs in their healing process:

- Compensation for their losses: Beyond the practical need for financial aid, compensation is, perhaps more than anything, symbolic (Strang, 2002, p. 17; Zehr, 1990, p. 26). There is therefore special importance for direct restitution from the offender because this expresses, more than state compensation, the offender's accountability for the crime (Shapland, 1984, p. 278).
- Having their questions regarding the crime fully answered (Zehr, 1990, p. 26): To regain a sense of order in their lives, victims desperately need answers to certain pressing questions: Why did the crime happen? And more specifically, why did it happen *to me*? Finding answers to these questions may help them feel again that there is reason for everything in the world, and therefore future victimization can be avoided by certain behaviors (Zehr, 1990).
- Opportunities for their emotions to be expressed and validated (Ahmed, Harris, Braithwaite, & Braithwaite, 2001, p. 189; Herman, 2005; Zehr, 1990, p. 26), "someone to talk to" (Maguire, 1985).
- Having a sense of control and opportunities to participate in the resulting process, to regain their lost sense of power (Cook et al., 1999, p. 40; Shapland, 1984; Strang, 2002, p. 12; Zehr, 1990, p. 26).
- Safety—feeling that what happened to them will not happen again, to themselves or to others (Herman, 1992, p. 63; Zehr, 1990, p. 26)
- Experiencing justice as a fair and respectful process (Shapland, 1984; Strang, 2002, p. 17; Tyler, 1988; Zehr, 1990, p. 13).
- Having access to information about the process and its outcomes (Maguire, 1985, pp. 545–546; Shapland, 1984; Strang, 2002, p. 11).
- An apology, or symbolic restoration (Brook & Warshwski-Brook, 2009; Strang, 2002, pp. 18–23).

When these needs are examined in conjunction with the legal process that follows victimization, they can be clustered into the following process-related needs groups: empowerment and control, procedural justice, direct interaction with the perpetrator, supportive group discussion, support network, and reparation. This section explores each of these elements and reviews theories that explain how they can help victims cope with the aftermath of their victimization. Since the literature on the specific needs of child victims is much more limited, this section relies principally on data regarding adult victims, with indirect findings on children as complementaries. More research is needed before we can decisively point to the exact needs of child victims. Therefore, at least with regards to the needs that have not yet been identified as important for child victims, one should regard this analysis as tentative only. Some of the theories, however, have been tested with regard to young victims as well, and these studies are discussed here and used to construct a clearer understanding of the expressed needs of victimized children.

Empowerment and Control

Victims say that they want to take part in the process that follows their victimization. Although they do not necessarily want to be the ones who decide how their perpetrator should be punished within the criminal justice process (Wemmers, 2004), victims consistently express their need to be consulted and informed about its progress (Shapland, 1984; Strang, 2002, pp. 8–13). Why do victims want to be involved, considered, and updated regarding the progress of "their" file in the justice system? One of the reasons is their need for a sense of control, a feeling one has that he or she can have at least some impact on the process or its results. Indeed, psychosocial studies repeatedly emphasize the importance of regaining control following victimization and the need to be empowered. Control is associated with coping, rehabilitation, and positive appraisals. Several theories explain the importance of control for victims of trauma in their healing process, and some of them are supported with empirical findings. The following paragraphs discuss these theories as they pertain to the following questions: Why is control important to victims? What kind of control is effective, and to what extent does this need exist among child victims?

Lazarus and Folkman's Model of Coping

In Lazarus and Folkman's seminal work on stress and coping (1984), control can be understood both as an *appraisal* (a cognitive process in which a person judges or evaluates a situation and its controllability) and as a *coping mechanism* (when a person makes efforts to take control of a situation or of his or her emotions in order to manage a stressful situation). For example, it is an appraisal when a person believes that he or she can run away from a violent offender. It is a coping mechanism when the victimized—and now injured—person tries to calm down and not move until help arrives, to minimize further harm. Both meanings of control are intertwined and affect each other in an ongoing process of appraising and coping (Seiffge-Krenke, 1995).

In the case of the process that follows victimization, control indeed might be helpful both as an appraisal and a coping mechanism. First, talking about their victimization with supportive listeners may help victims understand how much control they actually had, or did not have, when the event took place, and therefore perceive the crime in a different way, one that makes more sense in their world (positive appraisal). Second, having some degree of control over the process and its outcomes may be a powerful coping tool for victims in their healing. Lazarus and Folkman (1984) warn, however, that control is not always a helpful coping mechanism, and that it may in some situations enhance stress if assuming control opposes one's preferred style of coping. With children in particular, one should be cautious about forcing victims to assume control when this is not what they wish (Murray, 1999).

Brickman's Four Models of Coping

Brickman and coworkers' (1982) extensively cited typology proposes four models of coping, differing in the level of control people are perceived as having over past events (i.e., they are blameworthy or not) and the level of control they presumably have in their treatment (i.e., they are either responsible for "getting better" or not).

Under the *moral model*, a person is considered responsible for both the origin of the problem (blame) and for the solution. It is interesting that already in 1982 Brickman and coworkers mentioned restitution mechanisms as reflecting the moral model, because they emphasize the offender's accountability and at the same time empower him or her to take part in "fixing" what he or she has done (Brickman et al., 1982, p. 380).

Under the *medical model*, people are held not responsible for either the problem or the solution. Due to their incapacity, they are expected to be passive and receive the help of others in resolving their problem. Arguably, the criminal justice process often treats child victims according to this model. While they are typically not blamed for their victimization, they are also excluded from taking any part in the solution.

The *enlightenment model* represents situations where people are held responsible for the problem they face, but at the same time are perceived as unable to solve it by themselves (Brickman et al., 1982, p. 374). The criminal justice system and its treatment of offenders arguably fits the enlightenment model, as it blames offenders for their actions but takes full control over the "solution" of the problem through a one-sided decision regarding the punishment.

Finally, under the *compensatory model*, people are not held responsible for the problem (they are not blamed for past events), but are regarded as responsible for the solution. Help is provided through encouragement to take control and make the necessary steps to solve the problem themselves. The authors state their preference for the compensatory model because it is the only one that allows people to maintain a sense of control over their lives (since they are considered capable of helping themselves) without being blamed for their situation (Brickman et al., 1982, p. 377). This fits Herman's (1992, p. 192) argument that an important step in therapy for trauma victims is empowering patients to take responsibility for their recovery, while absolving them of responsibility for the crime. As I show later in this book, restorative justice is arguably effective in helping victims because it treats them according to the compensatory model. Restorative justice processes ideally absolve victims from blame over their victimization and at the same time provide them with opportunities to affect the way the solution is shaped.

A small-scale empirical study (Rabinowitz, 1978, cited in Brickman et al., 1982, p. 375) supported the existence of these four models. Brickman and coworkers (1982, p. 375) further examine the compensatory and the moral models that both require people to take responsibility for the solution of their problems. Their review of empirical findings suggests that people who are encouraged to assume responsibility over the solution to their problems (as reflected in both models) demonstrate better results in addressing them compared with those who are treated as passive, incapable individuals depending on external help. The two models, however, differ in important ways. In the moral model, the person with the problem is blamed for it, while in the compensatory model there is no attribution of blame.

The authors suggest that absolving people from responsibility for the cause of their problem (the compensatory model) is more effective than blaming them (the moral model), although empirical evidence in this regard is less clear. They argue that their categorization might address what they call "the dilemma of helping" (1982, pp. 376–377): helpers regard people as either morally bad and therefore undeserving of receiving help (such as the case with the punitive response to criminals), or weak and dependent on others—using the moral model in the first instance or the medical model in the second. As the next chapter shows, the criminal justice system's treatment of child victims often falls into this trap. Victimized children are often considered innocent and vulnerable, incapable of making their own decisions and therefore excluded from any decision-making process. Awareness of the two other existing models—the compensatory and the enlightenment models—opens up more opportunities for both helpers and those being helped.

Frazier's Temporal Control Model

Patricia Frazier's model of *temporal control* (2003) is particularly interesting because it examines control specifically in the context of victimization. Frazier differentiates between various types of control perceptions according to their timing in relation to the offense committed against the victim. She claims that perceived past control (which translates into self-blame or blaming the offender for the victimization) is an ineffective adjustment mechanism. Perceived future control (believing that one can prevent future victimization) is also maladaptive, since the victim may refrain from any social activity or from going out altogether. The most effective type of perceived control for healing is "present control," where the victim's perception is of having control over what is happening at the present, in the recovery process, rather than on the past or future events. The temporal control model also differentiates between vicarious and personal control (the former means attributing control, or blame, to the perpetrator, while the latter refers to attributing control, or blame, to oneself), and the relations of those to post-trauma adjustment.

To test this model, Frazier conducted a study of 171 female sexual-assault survivors aged 16 and over. Questionnaires were filled in at 2 weeks, 2 months, 6 months, and a year after victimization. At all four times, self-blame (past personal control) was associated with more distress. Blaming the offender (vicarious past control) was also found to be correlated with greater distress, although to a lesser extent. Conversely, at all four periods, control over the recovery process (present personal control) was highly correlated with lower distress levels. Future control was somewhat helpful in healing, although to a much lesser extent, with some mixed results (2003, pp. 1261–1262). After controlling the effects of linear change over time, increased present control still had the strongest correlation with decreased distress. Furthermore, decreased past control (lower self-blame) was also found to be correlated with decreased distress. Frazier concluded that for successful healing, it is more helpful to focus on the present (e.g., focus on the recovery process) than to focus on the past (personal or vicarious control) or even the future.

Frazier's theory might be taken further to argue that victims can benefit from having a sense of control not only on the *healing* process, but also on the *legal* process that follows their victimization. Just like the psychological treatment, the legal process is directly related to the crime; similarly, it involves discussing the past event in retrospect;

and it *can* (at least to some extent) be controlled by the victim, unlike the crime itself or future crimes. Therefore, perhaps a significant positive effect can occur when victims feel that they have some control over the present legal situation that follows their victimization, in the same manner that having control over the psychological process helps them to recover. It is important to note, however, that Frazier's study was conducted on victims aged 16 and over. It is unclear whether its findings can be generalized to younger victims as well. Nevertheless, if control is important for victimized children as well, then it seems that Frazier's model might be helpful in identifying the specific type of control that can be most effective in cases of child victims. It would be interesting, therefore, to test Frazier's theory with young victims as well, with perhaps "present control" in referring to the legal process.

Maruna's Desistance Theory and Herman on Healing

Shadd Maruna's (2001) study of offenders' rehabilitation discovered a similar comparison between different types of control and responsibility taking. Maruna found that for offenders to rehabilitate, it was important to find a personal history that allowed desistance from crime. One fertile way, he found, was to see the past as something the offender had no control over (due to a bad childhood, alcohol and drugs, life circumstances, and other external reasons). At the same time, to desist from crime in the long run, offenders had to take responsibility for their present behavior and to actively refrain from crime.

Perhaps victims can benefit from a similar technique of "rewriting" their victimization as something that happened that was not their fault while taking active steps in recovering from it. This fits Herman's (1992, p. 192) argument that an important step in therapy for trauma victims is empowering patients to take responsibility for their recovery, while absolving them of responsibility for the crime. It is also easy to see how this assumption is closely related to the compensatory model described by Brickman and coworkers (1982). Without empirical validation, however, these ideas can be seen only as possible directions for future research.

Control: Common Themes

Various writers, then, emphasize the centrality of assuming control over the present events in coping with uncontrollable past life events. Some common themes emerge. As demonstrated in Table 3.1, past control is the equivalent to what Lazarus and Folkman (1984) consider as appraisal—looking at the past and understanding the responsibility that both the victim and the offender have had over the crime. Present control, in contrast, is what the authors describe as a coping mechanism, because it involves the victim taking actual control over a present situation in order to improve his or her life situation. It might be concluded, following Lazarus and Folkman (1984) and Frazier (2003), that using control as coping (present control) is more effective in moving on from the status of victim, than using control as appraisal (past control).

The enlightenment and the compensatory models proposed by Brickman and coworkers (1982) are also comparable with the hypotheses made by Lazarus and Folkman, Frazier, Maruna, and Herman. As Table 3.1 shows, while the enlightenment model places control over the past (blaming the individual) and denies any control over the resolution of the problem, the compensatory model does just the opposite: it frees the individual from having past control (blame) but requires full responsibility

Table 3.1. Theories on Control and Their Analysis of Past and Present Control

Theories of control	Past control: ineffective coping	Present/future control: effective coping
Lazarus and Folkman	Control as appraisal	Control as coping
Brickman et al.	Enlightenment model: blamed for problem, not responsible for solution	Compensatory model: not blamed for problem, responsible for solution
Frazier's temporal control	Past control (vicarious/ personal) as maladaptive	Present control for recovery
Maruna's desistance theory	Self-blame, no change	Not responsible for being down, responsible for getting up, change
Herman	Self-blame	Responsibility to recover

to resolve the problem. Indeed, Brickman and coworkers (1982) too seem to emphasize the importance of present and future control in the context of victimization.

Maruna (2001) similarly emphasizes the importance of empowering the individual to have control over the present while minimizing the attribution of blame for the past. While Maruna focuses on offenders trying to rehabilitate, Herman (1992) makes the same argument (relying on her extensive experience as a therapist) regarding victim healing. For her, too, victims need to be absolved from any blame for their past victimization, but at the same time assume control over their recovery.

Having a sense of control over the present situation is arguably effective, then, in coping with stress and healing from trauma according to various authors, relying on somewhat limited empirical evidence. It is yet to be asked whether and to what extent having a sense of control is beneficial for children in general, and child victims in particular. The following section reviews existing findings and points to questions that are yet to be addressed in future studies regarding control as a coping mechanism for child victims.

Children and Control

While some empirical studies have examined children's use of control as a coping mechanism in varying contexts, control has not been tested in the context of childhood victimization. This is not surprising, considering the dearth of strength-based literature on children in general and child victims in particular. Therefore, the following discussion reviews some theories on control and studies focusing on children's coping with stressors other than victimization, such as homesickness, family and school problems, divorce, and medical treatment. Further research is clearly needed to explore whether these findings can be extended to childhood victimization.

Developmental psychology defines control *cognitions* (or appraisals) in two dimensions (Weisz & Stipek, 1982): *outcome contingency*—the assessment whether and to what extent the outcome can be influenced by the behavior of people like the individual who assesses the situation, and *personal competence*—the assessment of the individual's own ability to change the outcome. To test this two-dimensional model on children's cognitions, Weisz (1986) conducted a study of 78 children aged 8 to 17 who were treated in public mental health clinics. Data supported this model, and a strong correlation was found between the combined assessments of contingency and competence and perceived control. Children who felt that problems at school or in the family could be changed through children's behaviors, and children who felt that they personally could improve their situation, perceived their situation as more controllable than those who had lower perceptions of either outcome contingencies or their personal competence. At the same time, these two dimensions were clearly independent of each other (Weisz, 1986, p. 791). Contingency beliefs significantly predicted the most positive treatment outcomes: children who believed that "what kids do" determines what happens at home and school showed the highest reduction in problem behaviors. Competence beliefs, in contrast, showed little predictive power. These findings suggest that children who believe that children in general have a say or can change a certain situation cope better with a related problem in comparison with those who believe that children's behavior or opinions are irrelevant to the subject.

With regard to control as *coping*, the psychological literature uses a two-process model of control (Rothbaum, Weisz, & Snyder, 1982, cited in Thurber & Weisz, 1997) to distinguish between *primary control* (changing the stressful environment in order to make it more comfortable for the individual) and *secondary control* (changing oneself to fit the environment). A third categorized way of coping is *relinquishing control*—simply giving up. A study by LaMontagne, Hepworth, Johnson, and Cohen (1996) of 90 children aged 8 to 17 years undergoing major elective surgery supported the assumption that as children age they use more active methods of coping, believing that they can address and change existing challenges (primary control strategies). Younger children, in contrast, perceive the world as uncontrollable and therefore turn to more avoidant, or secondary control, strategies.

In a study about coping with homesickness, 315 boys and 717 girls aged 8 to 16 who attended residential sports summer camps were interviewed regarding their homesickness levels and coping (Thurber & Weisz, 1997). Almost all children engaged in "layered coping"—a mix of secondary and primary control. The most common primary control strategy was seeking social support, and the most common secondary control coping was thinking about other things (Thurber & Weisz, 1997, p. 515). Consistent with the findings in the previous study of children in mental health clinics (Weisz, 1986), low controllability (perceiving the situation as uncontrollable) was associated with more severe homesickness and with more relinquished control. Among those who perceived high controllability, primary control coping was associated with highest levels of homesickness. This suggests that in relatively uncontrollable situations, asserting control might actually increase negative feelings (Thurber & Weisz, 1997, p. 516). Overall, however, the children who were most homesick were those who perceived low controllability and relinquished control (Thurber & Weisz, 1997, p. 516).

Langer, Chen, and Luhmann (2005) tested the three control-related coping strategies of primary, secondary, and relinquished control among children treated in an emergency department for minor lacerations. They interviewed 50 children aged 5 to 17 years before and after the treatment, and videotaped some of them during the procedure. Their findings support the hypothesis that in uncontrollable situations, asserting primary control (trying to change the situation) is maladaptive compared with asserting secondary control (trying to change one's own behavior and reactions). Children who predicted they would exert primary control over the situation showed greater signs of distress during the procedure compared with those who used secondary control or relinquished control. Moreover, children who exerted secondary control during the process reported less pain after the procedure. Twice as many children reported using secondary control after the procedure compared with the number of children who predicted using it before getting into the treatment room. The authors suggest that once children realized that the situation was uncontrollable, they switched into the more adaptive coping strategy of controlling their own behavior, emotions, and responses to the situation (Langer et al., 2005, p. 620).

Closer to the context of legal processes, Graham and Fitzgerald (2005) interviewed children of separating parents and asked them about their participation in matters regarding their residences. Children were clear about their wishes to be listened to and be taken seriously:

> ... when I am listened to, I don't have to say it ten thousand times and I have just to say it once and they will talk to me ... I guess I know what is going on and stuff (Graham & Fitzgerald, 2005, p. 6).

When asked about their particular cases, however, children said they were not included in the process, nor did they receive adequate information. While expressing belief in their ability to be involved in decisions regarding their lives, children also talked about their vulnerabilities, sadness, and loss. The authors suggest that excluding children from these subjects might further disempower them. In contrast, including them in related processes while acknowledging their vulnerabilities and special needs might promote their resilience.

These studies suggest that in various arenas, children want to and do better when they believe that they can influence the situation they are in. Furthermore, when they in fact try to change the situation or assert control, the outcomes depend on the objective reality: when their attempts are fertile (that is, when the situation can indeed be influenced by their actions), children's emotional state is improved significantly. If, however, the situation is uncontrollable, or is not dependent on their behavior, seeking to assert control is found to be maladaptive. This is a cautionary reminder that "control" is not always a good thing. If it is futile, it can be harmful.

Procedural Justice

Closely related to the psychological term *control*, victimology studies have found that crime victims want to feel that they are treated fairly—namely, that they are given an opportunity to express their views and to be accorded respect and listened to (Shapland, 1984; Strang, 2002, pp. 13–15; Wemmers, 2009). Furthermore, aggregated data from various studies suggest that victims who experience inclusion, choice, and empowerment in the process that follows their victimization have better mental health outcomes compared with those who are denied such experiences (Herman, 2003).

Psychological analyses of fairness perceptions suggest that people care as much, or more, about how they are treated in decision-making processes as they do about the outcome (Thibaut & Walker, 1975). Procedural fairness is linked to control over the process (ability to have a voice in the process) and to control over the outcome (ability to influence the final decision) (Thibaut & Walker, 1975; Tyler, 1988). Process control is considered the central or only element in people's judgments of procedural fairness

(Tyler, 1988). The importance of procedural fairness stems from the sense of respect, inclusion, and group membership that people achieve when they feel they are treated fairly and listened to, notwithstanding the process outcomes (Lind & Tyler, 1988; Tyler, 1990). Procedural justice is particularly important for those who feel excluded or marginalized (Gonzales & Tyler, 2008). Perhaps more importantly, procedural *injustice* is connected with feelings of anger and dissatisfaction (Folger, 1977; Greenberg, 1987) and may reduce self-esteem even when the outcome is considered positive (Koper, Knippenburg, Bouhuijs, Vermunt, & Wilke, 1993). Beyond process control, other aspects associated with procedural fairness are consistency, the ability to suppress bias (neutrality), decision accuracy, correctability (opportunities to correct mistakes), and ethicality (Leventhal, 1980).

Children and adolescents perceive procedural justice as no less important than adults. In a series of cross-cultural studies Melton and Limber (1992, p. 178) found strong preference for an adversarial procedure where due-process rights are protected (especially through participation) among both Norwegian and American children (Melton & Limber, 1992, p. 180).

Hicks and Lawrence (1993) tested different procedural justice elements and their importance for children. Interviewing 715 students of seventh and ninth grade from two different schools, they found that like adults, adolescents consider their representation by a lawyer as important, as well as judges making an effort to be fair, impartial, polite, and calm, and the process to be confidential (Hicks & Lawrence, 1993). Some process-related attributes, however, are distinctively important to children and adolescents. Process *outcomes* are least important for children, but parents' presence is crucial. Fathers are more often associated with the legal support area and mothers with emotional support. Younger children are more concerned with having their mothers present (needing their emotional support) while older children view their fathers' presence as critical, protecting their legal rights. Girls consider procedural justice as more important than boys (Hicks & Lawrence, 1993).

In a subsequent set of several studies, Lawrence (2003) collected data from 1116 children and young people aged 12 to 24 through a computer-based interactive program. Participants were asked about the importance of procedural justice criteria in three different types of disciplinary contexts involving adult authorities (mothers, schoolteachers, and magistrates). Overwhelmingly, and in contrast with Melton and Limber (1992), children of all ages and in all three scenarios considered procedural safeguards that relate to the authority figure—being consistent, fair, and neutral—as most important. In contrast, safeguards relating to the child, such as having a voice and being able to ask questions, were consistently regarded as less important (Lawrence, 2003, p. 30). Some age differences emerged: as children aged, explanations given by the decision-maker (especially mothers) became more important, as well as adults' calmness (2003, p. 32). Consistent with Lawrence (1993), older girls were more concerned about adults' behavior and fairness than older boys.

These findings suggest that for young people, being dealt with by a neutral, respecting adult is sufficient. Participating in the process, in contrast, is not considered central for a procedure to be fair. However, as the authors themselves claim, there can be several explanations for these findings. First, it is possible that child participation is unimportant as long as adults behave as they are expected to. When authority figures do not deliver a neutral, fair, and well-communicated justice, children's views regarding the importance of their participation might change (Lawrence, 2003, p. 35). Second, children perhaps are not aware of their participation opportunities. Processes regarding children's matters exclude them from discussions so regularly that they simply "don't know it could be done differently" (2003, p. 32). Indeed, the computer-based interview methodology makes it impossible to provide detailed explanations, encouragement, and persuasion regarding the seriousness of the participation opportunity, which are important to overcome children's inexperience in participation (Melton & Limber, 1992). Finally, it is possible that presenting the same questions to children who have had personal experiences with adult authorities (and more so to those who have encountered injustice) might lead to different reactions. In any case, these findings are an important reminder that "participation" is not a magic word that makes procedures fair in children's minds, nor is it a concept familiar in practice for all children.

Direct Interaction with the Perpetrator

A related subject to control and fairness is that of confronting the offender. Such a confrontation can be adversarial, hostile, and harmful from the victim's perspective, but it can also be a healing experience. Beyond the potential for emotional benefits, a direct interaction with the perpetrator provides an opportunity for the victim to receive restitution directly from the offender, based on his or her own actual wishes and financial needs, therefore offering a tangible, practical advantage (Shapland, 1984). Indeed, as early as in 1984, Joanna Shapland found that 18% of her victim sample were interested in some kind of a mediation process with their offenders (Shapland, 1984, p. 270).

There is very little empirical knowledge in the psychosocial literature about the possible outcomes of such face-to-face encounters, although it is widely acknowledged that restorative practices provide space for an exchange of emotions with healing as a goal (Cook, Daly, & Stubbs, 2006). First empirical evidence for the positive effect of a direct encounter with the perpetrator on victims' mental health was found in Caroline Angel's (2006) study of restorative justice experiments conducted in different places in the United Kingdom. Angel's hypothesis was that restorative justice victim–offender interactions are in many ways equivalent to cognitive behavioral therapy (CBT), because in both settings the victim faces, in a safe environment, trauma-related elements. Testing her hypothesis on a randomly assigned group comparison of burglary and robbery victims, Angel found that face-to-face restorative justice encounters were more effective in reducing traumatic symptoms among crime victims in comparison with court. Based on her findings she concluded that restorative justice has a therapeutic effect on victims, similar to that of one of the most effective therapy treatments to trauma victims known today.

While Angel's study provides the most significant contribution to the understanding of the therapeutic power of the legal process that follows victimization, other analyses of the derivative consequences of direct, positive interactions between victims and perpetrators are also useful.

Richard Lazarus' (1999) "positive reappraisal" emphasizes the emotional process that may happen in a successful, open confrontation. He claims that through positive reappraisal people change their emotions by looking at things differently, and therefore can move on from negative feelings to more positive ones (Lazarus, 1999, p. 116). Although positive reappraisal is an internal process, receiving explanations from the offender and learning more about him or her might be a significant external aid. Anger can be shifted into compassion or sympathy, or at least defused. For example, a 4-year-old child whose house had been broken into had been having nightmares about a giant monster breaking into her house and had problems recovering from the trauma. She then participated in a restorative justice process and saw the young offender for the first time. The offender, who was seemingly from a lower socioeconomic background, showed great remorse. On the way home the child suggested inviting him over for dinner. It seems that the encounter made the crime (and the criminal) look completely different in her eyes.[29]

Direct Interaction as an Opportunity for Apology and Forgiveness

More empirical evidence exists with regard to one possible outcome of direct interaction between victims and offenders: the exchange of apology and forgiveness between them. As mentioned earlier, victims want to receive a sincere apology and to have an opportunity (in contrast with being pressured) to grant forgiveness (Brook & Warshwski-Brook, 2009; Strang, 2002, pp. 18–23; Strang & Sherman, 2003).

Bibas and Bierschbach (2004, p. 113) argue that apology and remorse are important remedial social rituals in which the offender acknowledges social norms and vindicates the victim's harm, thus helping the victim heal. Apology also restores the moral balance as the offender takes responsibility, expresses remorse, and demonstrates an intention to refrain from future crime (Taft, 2000). Since apology is a relational act, to be effective and genuine it has to be given in a face-to-face discussion between the victim and offender, it has to include communication of emotion (such as sadness or shame), and it should happen with the right timing (Petrucci, 2002).

Carrie Petrucci (2002) presents findings that indicate the potential value of apology, both in decreasing crime and in enhancing victims' wellbeing. A face-to-face apology by the offender helps victims correct erroneous, negative self-attributions and at the same time to move on from anger to more positive feelings toward the offender as well, thereby reducing their aggression. Victims are empowered by the process of apology because they are given a choice whether to accept it and forgive the perpetrator, or reject the apology. Apology, as Brook and Warshwski-Brook (2009, p. 516) argue, "although it might only be a brief moment in time, may often be the magic turning point that permits the conflicting parties to reconcile."

Ohbuchi, Kameda, and Agarie (1989) conducted an experiment on 58 female Japanese undergraduate students who were verbally insulted. Supporting Petrucci's hypotheses, those who received an apology from the harm-doer had better impressions of their perpetrator than those who were not given an apology. They also felt better compared with those who were not apologized to, and their aggression levels toward the harm-doer were lower.

Darby and Schlenker (1982) demonstrated in an empirical study that even 3-year-old children appreciate apologies and make more positive attributions to those who apologize, especially when the apology is elaborated and includes an offer to help. All participants in their study of 221 kindergarten/first-grade, fourth-grade, and seventh-grade children showed less anger, a less retributive approach, more forgiveness, and more positive thoughts for perpetrators who apologized, with elaborated and compensative apologies being most accepted.

It is important to remember, however, that apologies are not always sincere or complete, nor are they a panacea for all crimes and all circumstances (Herman, 2005; Rogehr & Gutheil, 2002). For an apology to provide true symbolic reparation, it has to be perceived as sincere by the victim. A sincere apology means that the perpetrator, at the very least, authentically expresses his or her acknowledgment of his or her own responsibility for what happened as well as regret (Brook & Warshwski-Brook, 2009). For example, perpetrators might admit the facts but limit their responsibility for them for reasons such as "misjudgment" or some external powers that affected the outcome, or they might express an expectation to be freed from any sanction as a result of their apology. These "botched" apologies (Rogehr & Gutheil, 2002) may further hurt victims.

An important feature of apology is that it opens the door for victims to forgive, which is a way to overcome resentment (Taft, 2000). Notwithstanding the importance of forgiveness for the *wrongdoer*, receiving an apology and granting forgiveness are milestones in the healing process of the *victim* (Brook & Warshwski-Brook, 2009). As Zehr explains:

> Forgiveness is letting go of the power the offence and the offender have over a person. It means no longer letting that offence and offender dominate. Without the experience of forgiveness, without this closure, the wound festers, the violation takes over our consciousness, our lives. It, and the offender, are in control. Real forgiveness, then, is an act of empowerment and healing. It allows one to move on from victim to survivor (Zehr, 1990, p. 47).

The work of Robert Enright and his colleagues provides empirical basis for the claim that forgiveness helps those affected by unfair hurt to strengthen their self-esteem, reduce depression, anger, and anxiety, and promote hope. This was found true, for instance, with adult survivors of sexual abuse who forgave their abusers (Enright & Kittle, 2000). Moreover, based on their studies on various populations, Enright and Kittle (2000) speculate that survivors of severe trauma may benefit most from forgiveness.

What about children of various ages? To test the ability of young adolescents to understand and practice forgiveness, Park and Enright (1997) interviewed and gave questionnaires to 30 junior-high-school students aged 12 to 14 and 30 college students aged 20 to 22, all residing in Korea. All participants had experienced a serious, unfair conflict with a close friend in the previous 5 to 6 months. The researchers found that the older participants were, the greater their understanding of forgiveness was. The relationship between the understanding of forgiveness and the actual forgiveness was moderate, but there was a correlation between the degree of understanding forgiveness and willingness to take active steps to reconcile with the friend. The authors suggest that young adolescents who are more developed will seek reconciliation more often. They propose a categorization of three patterns of forgiveness that roughly characterize the different developmental stages of young people:

1. For children and young adolescents, forgiveness is typically intertwined with revenge or getting compensation from the offender, so aggression and "getting back" is considered. Hostility may remain even when forgiveness is expressed by words and gestures. Therefore, at this stage of development, physical or psychological revenge or compensation should typically occur before forgiveness is possible.
2. At a higher level of development (typically in mid-adolescent years), the individual feels pressured to forgive by peers and family, and

therefore expresses forgiveness while unrevealed feelings of anger might still prevail.

3. Typically by college age, internal forgiveness can take place. It occurs unconditionally and is an authentic process of understanding the actions of the other and of beneficence.

Park and Enright (1997) conclude that young adolescents are in transition between the first and second patterns described above. Peer support and encouragement to forgive can be influential for adolescents who fit into the second pattern (since in that pattern external influence is central), while these will not be as effective without some sort of symbolic or material compensation from the wrongdoer for those who forgive according to the first pattern. Peer support and guidance can also encourage more developed youth to engage in an internal process of forgiving (pattern 3). Since young adolescents (at least in Korea) are in transition from the first to the second pattern described above, Park and Enright emphasize the importance of evaluating the stage of development of an adolescent before engaging in any forgiveness-related process.

Cultural differences notwithstanding, it seems that forgiveness in itself can have a positive impact on victims' emotional health. What about younger children's forgiveness capacities? Enright and Fitzgibbons (2000) claim that children as young as 4 years are able to understand forgiveness if their parents model forgiveness, or if they are educated about forgiveness.

For example, Enright and his colleagues have been researching forgiveness patterns among 6-year-old children in Belfast by providing an educational program on forgiveness with the hope of enhancing children's mental health and perhaps reducing future violence (Enright, Gassin, & Knutson, 2003). Children who learned and practiced forgiveness showed reduced levels of anger and depression, which in turn predicted improved peer relationships and academic achievements (Holler, Martin, & Engright, 2006).

The work of Enright and his colleagues provides concrete practical guidance for those working with victimized children who may or may not forgive their perpetrators in a direct encounter. It is important to consider, first, that children of different ages and developmental levels may understand and in fact grant forgiveness in different ways. These differences should affect the expectations of children of different ages. For example, it is possible that young children (aged 12 years or under) will express forgiveness and at the same time show anger toward their offender that will not subside until some form of compensation is given (Park & Enright, 1997). Young adolescents, in contrast, may be at risk of feeling pressured to forgive by other participants at the encounter, and special attention should be given to their tendency to be affected by peer pressure. At the same time, positive encouragement to forgive by trusted people, as opposed to pressure from the entire group, may help adolescents forgive and consequently experience the emotional relief that might follow.

A cautionary comment, however, is due here, relating to the unique power imbalance that is typically inherent in the relationship between a child victim and an offender who is an older child or an adult. When such a power imbalance exists, it might be particularly risky to put the child in a situation where even the most implicit expectation from him or her to forgive is communicated. Moreover, in some circumstances forgiveness is hardly even an option, as in the case of continuous child abuse

(Herman, 2005). Therefore, the benefits of the apology might be counterbalanced if receiving an apology in itself creates an expectation to forgive. But assuming that apologies can be expressed without any expectation for forgiveness, they are especially valuable in child–adult situations because they represent an articulation of respect for the young victim—an attitude that is particularly cherished by the less powerful. It will therefore be important to further explore the dynamics of apology and forgiveness in unequal situations, such as when the victim is a child and the perpetrator is an adult.

A direct, safe interaction with the offender offers, then, at least in the ideal, several benefits for child victims of crime. The opportunity to openly discuss the crime, express the feelings related to it, and receive answers to pressing questions firsthand from the perpetrator can potentially reduce post-traumatic symptoms. Receiving an apology and, to no lesser extent, granting forgiveness have empirically validated emotional benefits such as enhanced self-esteem and reduced anger and depression.

Group Discussion

Beyond a personal interaction between victims and offenders, some writers have outlined the positive impact that a group discussion in which the crime and its consequences are discussed in the presence of supportive participants might have for the victim.

Shame Management

Studies on bullying behavior and bullying victimization have pointed to the connection between shame management ("acknowledging shame and making it work for you"; Ahmed et al., 2001, p. 4) and victimization. Poor shame-management skills are related to feelings of self-blame, shame, and rejection, and generally internalizing shame instead of discharging it (Ahmed et al., 2001, Chapter 17). It is possible that these patterns can be changed in a group discussion where shame is acknowledged and discharged, self-blame is resolved, and the victim's behavior is validated. The experience can help victims improve their shame-management skills, thus moving away from "victimization careers" (Finkelhor et al., 2005). The Responsible Citizenship Program that was tried in the Australian Capital Territory with year 5 students showed that healthy shame-management skills could be developed within the classroom (Morrison, 2002, 2006). Further research is needed to examine the effectiveness of group discussions in helping child victims discharge and manage shame, and whether improved shame-management skills can actually reduce the risk of future victimization (Ahmed, 2006).

Sense of Belonging

Judith Herman identifies a second element that makes the participation in a group discussion potentially important for trauma victims. This is the sense of belonging it provides, which is an antidote for the feeling of isolation the crime generates:

> Traumatic events destroy the sustaining bonds between individual and community. Those who have survived learn that their sense of self, of worth, of humanity,

> depends upon a feeling of connection to others. The solidarity of a group provides the strongest protection against terror and despair, and the strongest antidote to traumatic experience. Trauma isolates; the group re-creates a sense of belonging. Trauma shames and stigmatizes; the group bears witness and affirms. Trauma degrades the victim; the group exalts her. Trauma dehumanizes the victim; the group restores her humanity (Herman, 1992, p. 214).

This connects with Randall Collins' Interaction Ritual theory and his term "emotional energy," which he argues is created when such rituals are successful (Collins, 2004, p. 108). Giving restorative justice processes as an example, Collins explains how rituals begin with differing emotions and moods (such as shame and anger in the case of victimization), and through the group ritual they are transformed into a unified long-term emotion. Since the group focuses on certain emotions relevant to the gathering, Collins argues, they intensify during the interaction as other emotions or moods are gradually driven out. The outcome is a transformed shared emotion that he calls "emotional energy." In successful processes, such shared emotion is of group solidarity. The restorative justice ritual, he illustrates, provides an opportunity for people to transform their feelings of anger and fear during an intense interaction, and to leave the conference feeling a sense of belonging (Collins, 2004, p. 111).

What happens, though, in unsuccessful rituals? Cook and associates (2006) warn against the "McDonaldization" of the process—the development of a one-size-fits-all mechanism in which apology and remorse are expected from the offender, in exchange for forgiveness and closure on the victim's part, and a sense of concern and empathy by the supporters. When these are the authentic feelings of the participants the process can indeed be a healing experience. But when the process becomes a "rationally elicited product wheeled out to suit stage-managed circumstances" (Cook et al. 2006, p. 93), it may be ineffective in reducing the offender's recidivism, promoting the victim's healing, and empowering the community.

Notwithstanding this concern, however, Sherman, Strang, and their coworkers provide empirical validations of Collins' argument, through findings regarding reduced levels of fear and anger, reduced willingness to seek revenge, and the acceptance of genuine apologies among victims who participated in face-to-face restorative justice conferences (Sherman, Strang, Angel, Woods, Barnes, Bennett, Inkpen, & Rossner, 2005; Strang, Sherman, Angel, Woods, Bennett, Newbury-Birch, & Inkpen, 2006).

Social Acknowledgment and Validation

Social acknowledgment is a victim's experience of positive reactions from his or her community that reflect appreciation of the victim's condition and difficulties (Maercker & Muller, 2004). It is different from social support, which usually refers to emotional and practical support provided by specific family or friends; in contrast, social acknowledgment refers to the reactions of the wider community. Social acknowledgment, or lack of it, might affect victims' emotional healing. For example, in a study of former political prisoners of the former communist East Germany and crime victims, Maercker and Muller (2004) found that lack of social acknowledgment was positively correlated with PTSD symptoms, while the existence of social acknowledgment was negatively correlated with such symptoms. The researchers concluded that social acknowledgment by intimate relatives, friends, and extended community can be therapeutic to traumatized victims.

Social validation (Ahmed et al., 2001) is one of the most important objects victims want to gain from their family and community (Herman, 2005). Validation means not only accepting the victim's story as reliable but supporting the victim's behavior and moral stance as well. Social validation can be helpful for victims when their own victimization is perceived by them as against social norms. For example, a rape victim might feel that being raped is normatively wrong, and social validation of her behavior can help her regain her sense of identity and belonging (Ahmed et al., 2001, p. 191, fn. 3). This explanation fits well with Zehr's (1990, p. 27) argument that one of the important needs of victims is to have an opportunity for their emotions to be expressed and validated. Zehr (2002) further argues that to create new meaning and re-establish order in their lives, victims need to retell their life stories so that their victimization events fit into them. Compassionate listeners are central to this process of retelling as they validate the truthfulness of this new story. With regard to child victims, age differences might affect the importance of social validation. For example, peer and community reactions may be more influential on adolescents than on young children (Finkelhor & Kendall-Tackett, 1997).

In the context of healing from trauma, Herman (1992) raises the importance of supportive listeners in helping the victim to resolve his or her own blame. Feelings of self-blame challenge victims in their healing process and are difficult to resolve without the help of others:

> Beyond the issues of shame and doubt, traumatized people struggle to arrive at a fair and reasonable assessment of their conduct, finding a balance between unrealistic guilt and denial of all moral responsibility. In coming to terms with issues of guilt, the survivor needs the help of others who are willing to recognize that a traumatic event has occurred to suspend their preconceived judgments, and simply to bear witness to her tale. When others can listen without ascribing blame, the survivor can accept her own failure to live up to ideal standards at the moment of extremity. Ultimately, she can come to a realistic judgment of her conduct and a fair attribution of responsibility (1992, p. 68).

Social acknowledgment and validation also provide victims the opportunity to mourn, which is another important element of the healing process (Herman, 1992). While telling the story in detail with the accompanying feelings, and with supportive listeners, the post-trauma symptoms are reduced. Therefore, a social ritual of mourning with support people can be very helpful (1992, p. 70). The sense of loss is particularly central in childhood victimization, and therefore mourning is crucial in children's healing processes (Murray, 1999).

Participating in a safe, supportive group discussion regarding their victimization is important, therefore, for crime victims' healing. It provides an opportunity for a therapeutic mourning ritual, helps victims regain a sense of belonging and identity, and supports victims in managing their shame. A group discussion is a forum in which victims can experience social acknowledgment and validation of their feelings and behavior. Once again, however, it is important to explore the way in which children of various ages experience such group discussions and the extent to which, if at all, they are able to "retell" their story and ask questions similar to adult victims. Furthermore, if the group discussion turns out to be unsafe or involves unsupportive participants (for instance, if there are expressions of victim blaming), then the benefits described here are likely to be lost and further emotional harm can be expected (Herman, 2005).[30]

Support Network

Another significant need of victims in their healing process is being supported by their families, friends, and others who are part of their communities (Caffo et al., 2005; Norris et al., 1997). The support by family members and in particular a strong relationship with the mother are protective factors for children exposed to domestic violence (Holt, Buckley, & Whelan, 2008). In nonfamilial victimization, adolescents regard the support of their older siblings as particularly supportive (Jenkins Tucker, McHalem, & Crouter, 2001). Other family members, such as fathers and grandparents, also provide significant support for children and youths (Furman & Buhrmester, 1985). Why is social support important for crime victims? Different scholars provide varying explanations and empirical support.

Relating to daily stressors among adolescents, Call and Mortimer (2001) suggest an analysis through the concept *arenas of comfort*. According to the authors, people have different settings of relationships with others within their life space, such as family, work, and school. They suggest that when an individual has at least one context in which he or she feels comfortable, accepted, and relaxed, that individual can retreat to that "arena of comfort" in times of stress in the other arenas, and reinvigorate. Therefore, stress and injury in one space can be soothed and buffered through the comfort one experiences in another. In their studies of 1,000 adolescents the authors found that most youths have few arenas of support, which are typically their families, their peers, and their school or workplace. Most adolescents reported feeling comfortable in at least one context, and the majority found comfort in two or more arenas. Based on their findings the authors theorize that this *ecology of comfort*—the different arenas and the distribution of stress and comfort in them—can be manipulated through social intervention as well as the adolescent's own agency. Therefore, they argue that it is possible to strengthen those arenas that provide comfort when other arenas induce stress. Accordingly, they suggest that interventions may focus not only on the problem itself, but on strengthening the other arenas of support, while at the same time raising the adolescent's own awareness of his or her ability to manipulate the ecology of comfort and to alternate support and challenge in their environments.

How well can young victims "manipulate their arenas of comfort," in Call and Mortimer's terms, in order to gain support and deal with stress? To what extent do children and adolescents know how to choose the right people to turn to when they need help? Studying coping mechanisms of youths with daily stressors, Inge Seiffge-Krenke (1995) found through interviewing over 1,000 adolescents that the most popular coping strategy was getting help from friends, followed by talking with parents and other adults, and thinking about the problem. Girls sought help, talked about the problem, expressed emotions, and thought about possible solutions more often than boys, but they also tended to withdraw more frequently. For both girls and boys, the use of internal forms of coping (thinking about the problem and possible solutions) and active coping (seeking social support) increased with age. Age 15 was found to be the turning point after which more mature coping strategies were sought. For example, after that age adolescents were better able to choose the specific people to whom they turn for support. Seiffge-Krenke also found, in accordance with Call and Mortimer (2001), that a positive family environment and to a lesser degree peer relationships may act as stress buffers. She consequently suggests that intervention programs should strengthen and mobilize peer support networks, as this has the potential of helping youths in coping with their difficulties.

On a practical level, Norris and coworkers (1997) found that social support and in particular protective neighbors were effective in reducing fear among victims, thus contributing to a general decrease in the distress they were experiencing. Social support has been found to be a protective factor for children exposed to domestic violence as well (Levendosky & Graham-Bermann, 2001).

It seems, then, that both for adults and young people who deal with difficult situations, having support networks from within and outside the family is important for various reasons. They create a sense of belonging, help resolve feelings of self-blame, provide buffers when other areas in the individual's life are unstable, and can be a source of practical assistance, such as an increased sense of safety. Accordingly, it is expected that processes that activate weak or inactive relationships, and that strengthen existing ones, will generate positive results for victimized children through the provision of emotional and practical support.

Reparation

Although symbolic reparation, in the form of an apology or full acknowledgment of responsibility, by the offender is far more important for crime victims, material reparation is yet another element in the victim's rehabilitation following crime (Strang, 2002; Strang & Sherman, 2003; Zehr, 1990). Of particular importance for victims is receiving restitution directly from the offender, because this reflects social and personal recognition of the offender's concrete responsibility for the act (Harris, Walgrave, & Braithwaite, 2004; Shapland, 1984). While the literature on apology described earlier is illuminating in identifying children's expectation to be compensated in some form before being willing to forgive their wrongdoers, it has yet to be examined what type of compensation children of different ages consider important. Children might have different preferences, and needs, from adult victims. First, although monetary payment can help fund the victimized child's needs, such as counseling, this might not have a significant meaning for the child. Therefore, the specific means of reparation should be considered together with the child. Creativity might be needed here. It is possible that children will favor other forms of restitution, such as help in schoolwork or in commuting safely after school hours, getting a new bicycle in return for the one stolen, or financing a holiday trip for the child. Second, it is questionable who is to become the legal owner of the restitution money—the child or the child's guardian—and whether there might be a conflict of interests in the latter case. For older children it might be appropriate to ensure that the money (or part of it) is given directly to them and not their parents. These child-specific matters call for further examination so that the material needs of victimized children are better addressed. Whatever form the material reparation takes, however, it is important to consider that the need for material restoration is most acute in the first few weeks and months after the incident (Shapland, 1984, p. 278). This finding is important because it means that restitution orders issued as part of the verdict, at the end of lengthy legal processes, do not adequately address the victim's acute need for financial support following the victimization. Fast-track compensation schemes, and ideally mechanisms that produce restitution agreements with offenders, provide a better remedy for victims.

BRIDGING BETWEEN THE NORMATIVE AND DESCRIPTIVE FRAMEWORKS: AN INTEGRATED NEEDS-RIGHTS MODEL FOR CHILD VICTIMS

The previous sections of this chapter reviewed theories and data drawn from the psychosocial literature regarding the aftermath of crime, relevant coping strategies, and the resulting needs of crime victims in general and child victims in particular. But the examination of evidence and theories on the subjective realities of child victims and their needs should be seen in the broader context of this book, which integrates the needs and rights frameworks into a combined template. The search for a combined model follows Gary Melton's *psychological jurisprudence* (Melton 1991, 1992; Melton & Wilcox, 2001), which argues that the integration of legal and psychological knowledge helps define the boundaries of individuals' fundamental rights (Melton, 1991). According to Melton (1992), law promotes human condition by announcing common norms and creating structures for acceptable social behavior that is consistent with these norms (1992, p. 384). To do that, the law must take people seriously. Therefore, knowledge of what is important for people is crucial. In other words:

> if the law is to be successful in its purpose of promotion of human welfare, it must undertake systematic examinations of social reality. Putting this principle into practical terms, if legal authorities are to take people seriously, they must adopt an empirical attitude (Melton, 1992, p. 385).

Social evidence is particularly important to the law relating to children and families:

> Combining an empirical attitude and, perhaps more important, psychological mindedness, psychological jurisprudence invites a bottom-up perspective. By its concern for the dignity even of those whose personhood often has not been fully recognized, psychological jurisprudence opens the door to establishment of a *children's law*. In such a framework, not only would there be due attention to development and developmentally meaningful means of vindicating the rights of children, but there would also be concern for children's experience of law in diverse contexts (Melton & Wilcox, 2001, p. 9).

This exploration of evidence-based findings, Melton claims, often requires social science research. Indeed, he argues that international human rights law sets the stage for the use of social studies, as it relies heavily on the subjective experiences of people as respected human beings. The Convention is particularly compatible with this approach as it leaves much room for assessments drawn from social sciences, especially through the concepts of children's dignity, development, and individual views (Melton, 1992, p. 390; Melton & Wilcox, 2001, p. 10).

The integration of empirical findings regarding children's needs with normative arguments regarding their rights also fits Waldron's (2000) call for using "needs" as a diagnosis, and "rights" to give the diagnosed claims the required status to create obligations (see p. 18). Following this approach, this chapter presented studies that have been conducted to explain subjective experiences of legal processes (for example, studies regarding perceptions of procedural fairness and children's understandings of their rights), as well as studies conducted purely from a psychological or sociological perspective, without considering their legal consequences, such as the studies on control. The latter studies are perhaps more challenging in integrating into a multidisciplinary framework, since they require some speculation regarding their application to the victimization context. Clearly, many of these studies provide not much more than initial hypotheses and ideas for further research. The central argument, however, is that findings such as those presented in this chapter are helpful in identifying needs-based rights for child victims and related principles for action.

This part of the chapter considers what the psychosocial literature presented earlier might add to a human rights framework, and maps the relationships among these contributions to those made by the rights discourse discussed in the previous chapter. The relationships between the various elements of both needs and rights discourses are illustrated in Figure 3.1. This somewhat cluttered model is in fact a double-layered figure combining the human rights elements that were identified and mapped in Chapter 2 (presented in circles) and the psychosocial needs identified in this chapter (presented in boxes). The dashed arrows visualize the interconnections between the different human rights principles, and the dark arrows represent the links between the needs and the varying human rights. Each box—or needs cluster—is positioned between the human rights principles with which it is most closely related.

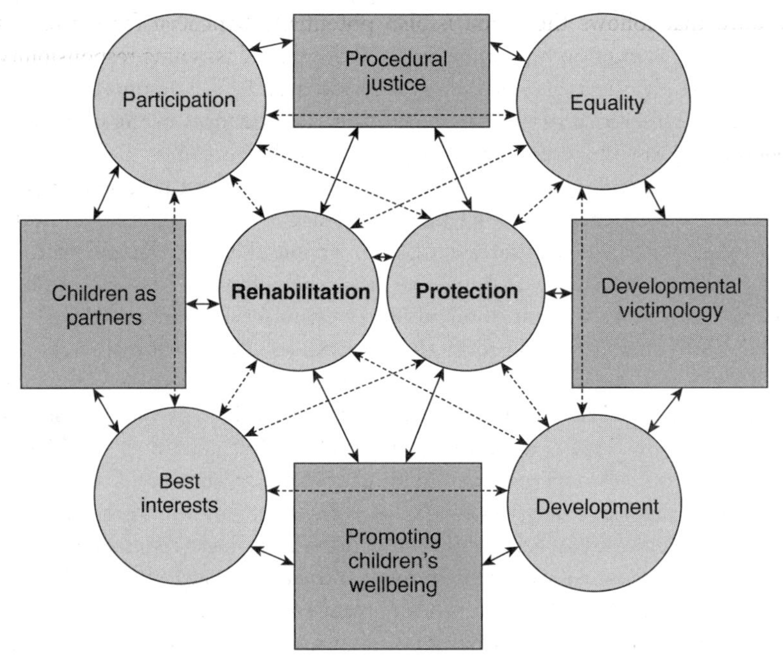

Figure 3.1 Integrating psychosocial and legal discourses: a needs-rights model for child victims.

Best Interests Cluster

Starting from the bottom end of Figure 3.1, the first set of needs can be grouped as "promoting children's wellbeing" because it is associated with the promotion of children's best interests, rehabilitation, and development. It includes findings regarding the needs for support networks, social acknowledgment, validation, and reparation.

Call and Mortimer (2001) emphasize the benefit of strengthening some arenas of comfort when crisis occurs in others. Seiffge-Krenke (1995) talks about the changing significance of various support networks for children as they grow. Maercker and Muller (2004) show a correlation between social acknowledgment and reduced post-trauma symptoms. Ahmed and coworkers (2001) suggest that victims can benefit from having their behavior and feelings validated by others. Finally, victimologists find that material reparation is important for most crime victims (Strang, 2002; Zehr, 1990). All these accounts are clearly related to the rehabilitation of child-victims, and provide detail and concrete meanings to this human rights principle. Similarly, they are informative about what the best interests of child victims might be, and should be considered whenever an individual child's interests are deliberated. Many of the findings in this group also include developmental knowledge and can promote an approach that respects the evolving capacities and specific developmental needs of child victims.

Control Cluster

Moving to the left-side box titled "children as partners," the needs clustered in this box correspond with all three human rights principles of participation, best interests, and rehabilitation. The data regarding the potential benefits of having a sense of control and empowerment during the healing process (Brickman et al., 1982; Frazier, 2003; Lazarus & Folkman, 1984), for instance, suggest that a sense of control in the justice procedure that follows the crime is also potentially beneficial for crime victims, although this assumption has not been tested directly. If assuming responsibility and making active decisions makes victims feel better and heals trauma, then perhaps making active decisions that are related to the consequences of the crime for both the victim and the offender might have similar positive outcomes. To have a sense of control in the justice process, victims need to be able to participate and influence its outcomes. Control, therefore, might be regarded as the psychological equivalent of the participation principle. Additionally, having a sense of control might promote the best interests of child victims and enhance their rehabilitation—an assumption that is, again, based on indirect findings and requires empirical validation.

While studies related to control in children (outside the criminal process) demonstrate the power of control as a coping mechanism, they also act as reminders that exerting control might be harmful in some circumstances, particularly when the situation is not contingent on the child's actions (Langer et al., 2005; Thurber & Weisz, 1997; Weisz, 1986). Therefore, it is possible to speculate that if children's participation in decision-making processes is only token—that is, if adults are not willing to allow children to have a meaningful input—then involving children in such processes might only cause them further pain as well as disappointment (Graham & Fitzgerald, 2005). In other words, children's participation that is meaningless, either due to lack of adequate preparation of the child or because of adults' unwillingness to take the child's views seriously, might be seen as making the situation "uncontrollable" from the child's perspective. In these situations engaging in primary control behavior (trying to influence the process) is futile and can cause further harm to the child. In contrast, where the child is considered a partner in the decision-making process, using a primary control coping strategy through active involvement in the process might enhance the child's wellbeing and promote his or her healing. Indeed, further research is needed regarding the potential benefits, and risks, of involving children as partners in decision-making processes following their victimization, and the ability of children of various ages to have meaningful participation in such procedures.

Other psychosocial concepts that are closely linked to the human rights principles of participation, best interests, and rehabilitation are direct interaction with the perpetrator, the exchange of apology and forgiveness, and group discussion. All three concepts provide additional explanations for the importance of being included in the process that follows victimization instead of being left out: only through participation can victims personally confront their victimizers, ask questions and receive answers, and perhaps gain a better understanding of what has happened to them (Herman, 1992; Lazarus, 1999; Murray, 1999). Similarly, active participation is a precondition for a face-to-face, genuine, voluntary exchange of an apology by the offender and forgiveness by the victim, which have been found to have positive effects on victims' wellbeing (Enright & Kittle, 2000; Petrucci, 2002; Taft, 2000). Moreover, only when victims are regarded as partners in the process can they benefit from meeting others in a group discussion where their self-blame is resolved (Herman, 1992), their shame is discharged (Ahmed et al., 2001, Chapter 17), and their behavior is validated (Maercker & Muller, 2004). Additionally, as Collins (2004) explains, participating in a positive group discussion can create a sense of belonging and transform negative feelings into more positive ones. Since these concepts have been found to have positive effects on victims' short-term wellbeing and recovery from harm, they serve as pointers for the implementation of the child's best interests and rehabilitation human rights principles, in addition to their clear link with the participation right. Clearly, the potential benefits described in the control cluster depend on one crucial condition: that the encounter with the perpetrator and the group discussion are indeed safe, physically and emotionally, for the child. Further examinations are needed to test the different assumptions of the control cluster with regard to child victims as well as the practicality of such imagined encounters in real life.

Procedural Justice Cluster

The discussion on participation and control is closely related to that on procedural fairness, since having a sense of control over the process is considered an important component of procedural justice (Tyler, 1988). But beyond participation, the data on children's perceptions of procedural justice also relate to two other human rights principles, rehabilitation and equality, and were therefore placed in proximity to them in the upper part of Figure 3.1.

Studies on children's perceptions of fairness present important findings regarding the unique challenges of children's participation in delicate matters. Lawrence (2003) found that children do not always regard their own participation (control over the process) as the central element of procedural fairness. Other studies, in contrast, identify children's views of participation as the main component of any fair process (Melton & Limber, 1992). Graham and Fitzgerald (2005) exposed the ambivalence children feel about their participation in divorce proceedings: fears regarding exposure to painful subjects were combined with wishes to somehow be included in decision-making processes. Despite these varying findings, researchers agree that participation is key for any process to be fair, and that it is not a skill children are born with or develop independently. It needs to be learned and practiced continuously; otherwise, it might be useless—even harmful. Indeed, children repeatedly say that if their participation is only token, then they would rather not take part in such processes (Stafford, Laybourn, & Hill, 2003). Procedural justice is related to rehabilitation for its potential in helping victims "put things behind them" after experiencing justice (see Zehr, 1990, p. 28), and equality, through the concepts of neutrality, consistency, and respect, which are central components of procedural fairness, especially for children (Lawrence, 2003; Tyler, 1988).

In practice, the positioning of the "procedural justice" box in between the participation, rehabilitation, and equality human rights circles means that those wishing to take these rights seriously need to adhere to the procedural justice elements that, according to current psychosocial research, are considered important for child victims.

Protection Cluster

Moving to the last box on the right-hand side of the model, the developmental victimology approach (Finkelhor, 2008) and the studies that are derived from it (Finkelhor & Dzuiba-Leatherman, 1994; Finkelhor & Kendall-Tackett, 1997) are instrumental in the understanding and implementation of the equality, protection, and development human rights principles, as suggested in Figure 3.1. For example, Finkelhor and Kendall-Tackett (1997) discuss the effect of age-related developmental tasks on children's reactions to crime; the effect of age on the significance of family, peer, and community support for child victims; and developmental differences in coping capacities. At the same time, developmental victimology emphasizes the importance of conducting longitudinal studies to expand our knowledge on the ways different crimes occurring at different developmental stages affect children in the long run and into adulthood (Finkelhor, 2008, p. 91).

Further, the aggregated data reviewed by Briere and Elliott (1994) illuminate the behavioral, cognitive, and emotional impact of crime on children of different ages. These facts can all be helpful in better addressing the unique needs of children of various developmental levels who are at risk of being victimized or who have already been victimized. For example, children might be better protected against further abuse if distress signs are identified at an early stage. Secondary victimization during the legal process might also be more effectively prevented based on knowledge regarding children's age-related fears, capacities, and difficulties.

Similar examinations should be conducted to expand the developmental approach so that it includes children with special needs. Special groups of children should be studied regarding the impact of crime on them, their available coping mechanisms, perceptions of justice, and specific needs in the legal process that follows crime. Such populations are, for example, children with disabilities, institutionalized children, children who live in rural and peripheral areas, children of immigrants and refugees, and children who are exposed to domestic violence in their homes. In these areas the human rights principles of equality and protection clearly identify a gap in the psychosocial literature. Most of the research concerning victimization of children with disabilities, for example, has focused on their increased risk of being victimized and their difficulties in the criminal justice process (see, for example, Petersilia, 2001, and Vig & Kaminer, 2002). It seems that insufficient attention has been given to exploring ways of enhancing the ability of children with different types of disabilities to gain access to justice mechanisms and to have meaningful roles in them.

It is similarly important to explore differences between boys and girls in the context of crime risk, reactions to crime, and ways of ensuring equal access to meaningful remedies for their victimization. For example, the findings of Finkelhor and Dziuba-Leatherman (2001) regarding the higher risk of boys of suffering homicide, assault, and robbery and of girls of suffering rape, together with their claim that gender differences grow as children get older, are relevant in constructing policies to identify and reduce specific types of crimes against children. The protection cluster further suggests that specific populations of children might be more vulnerable to crime and have less opportunities to disclose their victimization—an inequality that should be addressed. Jody Miller's (2008) book on poor African American girls, for example, reveals how race, gender, and socioeconomic status increase their vulnerability to crime.

Finally, the findings regarding the pervasiveness and severity of emotional impacts of domestic violence on children who witness it in their homes (Hodgkin & Newell, 2002, pp. 260–261; Pinheiro, 2006, p. 70), suggest that taking the equality principle seriously means that these children should be treated as other victimized children and should be provided with the protection and rehabilitation services that best address their needs. This is true both for children who are "merely" witnesses of domestic violence and should be treated as direct victims (Peled, 1996), and for the many children who consequently become victims themselves (Zolotor et al., 2007).

CONCLUSIONS

Various studies on trauma, stress, and coping emphasize the importance of control, fairness, social acknowledgment and validation, direct and positive interaction with the offender, receiving an apology from the offender, and support by family and friends in healing from stressful events. Indeed, these elements fit into the children's human rights framework described in Chapter 2 by giving the human rights principles concrete meanings in the context of childhood victimization. The two frameworks complete each other through a mutual deliberation in which the human rights principles identify areas of concern for the psychosocial literature to explore, and existing evidence-based findings on the needs of child victims shape the interpretation and implementation of the human rights principles. The human rights framework presented in the previous chapter, then, cannot stand alone to address child victims' concerns. It needs to be integrated with relevant knowledge about children's psychosocial needs in order to provide comprehensive guidance as to the adequate responses for childhood victimization from a child's perspective.

While the psychosocial literature provides guidance on the understanding and implementation of children's rights, a needs-alone perspective can similarly prove weak and insufficient. Beyond the political power that the rights component contributes to the model, the human rights principles are useful in identifying where psychosocial studies have neglected certain issues regarding childhood victimization. Indeed, it should come as no surprise that some elements have been studied thoroughly by the psychosocial literature while others have been neglected. Only when applying a human rights approach can elements of inclusion, participation, and equality become visible to victimization studies on children. For example, a large body of research explores the outcomes of traumatic events, post-trauma symptoms, and different treatment techniques regarding child victims. In contrast, very little has been written on the evolving capacities of children in making decisions regarding their victimization, the importance of having a sense of control and empowerment in the legal process that follows crime, and the perceptions of justice from the perspective of child victims. Furthermore, there is insufficient knowledge about the ability of children with special needs to participate in decision-making processes and their coping capacities following traumatic events. Studies on adult victims and adolescents, however, as well as studies on children in other contexts provide some preliminary indications regarding these neglected aspects of childhood victimization. The studies conducted by Seiffge-Krenke (1995) reveal the strengths and coping strategies of children of various ages. Young children's appreciation of apologies is supported by Darby and Schlenker (1982). Studies by Weisz (1986), Thurber and Weisz (1997), and Langer and coworkers (2005) demonstrate the importance of exerting control in controllable yet stressful situations for children. These preliminary findings, together with directions from the human rights framework, can be used as a starting point for further empirical examinations of the various needs of child victims.

Clearly, the matching between specific psychosocial needs and various human rights principles might be criticized as arbitrary, if not forced. For instance, one could ask whether social acknowledgment of harm, validation of victims' behavior, and receiving an apology from the offender are indeed reflected in any of the Convention's articles. Obviously, there are no specific rights granting child victims such elements. However, as Melton (1992) argues, the Convention is sensitive to social science research and empirical findings. Many of its articles, including those entailed in the current child victims' rights model, leave considerable space for interpretation and implementation according to the lived realities of children. Put differently, the broad wording of the Convention and its use of indeterminate concepts actually invites a search for specific meanings in different situations. The psychosocial framework then is called in to fill the human rights principles with substance, while turning the attention to specific challenges or difficulties in their implementation. Accordingly, to return to the example, once social acknowledgment and validation have been found to be beneficial, at least in some circumstances, for child-victims, they may be regarded as concrete reflections of the best interests, rehabilitation, and protection human rights principles and grouped together as paths to promoting children's wellbeing. Similarly, the literature on the benefits of apology might be used as guidance in the understanding of the best interests, rehabilitation, and participation principles.

Still, the parallels drawn here might be criticized for ignoring other possible correlations. The link to developmental victimology analysis of victimization outcomes could be positioned, instead of within the protection cluster, in the best interests cluster. No doubt, findings regarding the various effects of victimization on children of different ages are relevant in uncovering the short- and long-term interests of child victims. Nevertheless, for the interest of clarity and coherence, I linked the developmental victimology literature with other victimology-related findings and left the more sociological literature linked together within the best interest cluster.

Beyond this example, clearly the connections made here between the human rights principles and the psychosocial needs are not axiomatic, may be changed with the emergence of additional findings, and might prove wrong in some specific circumstances. The more important message of the needs-rights model is the value of combining the two frameworks, using them to complete each other through an ongoing dialog.

It is further important to remember that this chapter has provided only short glimpses into the psychosocial literature, reviewing only central findings and offering somewhat simplistic explanations for complex situations and reactions to crime. More comprehensive writing would require more than a single chapter, which would exceed the framework (and the overall goal) of this book.

Finally, and most importantly, every child is different. No textbook, certainly not this one, can provide a prescription for treating victimized children. The theories and data reviewed here and in the psychosocial literature can therefore be used only as a starting point for an individual assessment of the wishes, interests, and needs of the child following his or her victimization.

4

Child Victims in the Criminal Justice System

INTRODUCTION

The previous chapter reviewed empirical findings regarding the psychosocial needs of child victims. This evidence-based examination has been integrated with the normative human rights framework presented in Chapter 2. Together they create a multidisciplinary model that can be used to evaluate public responses to crimes against children. This chapter uses the needs-rights model to examine common legal responses to childhood victimization in adversarial criminal justice systems and their ability to meet the human rights and needs of child victims.

At first glance, the characteristics of the adversarial criminal justice process in Western societies seem to overlook many of the needs-rights of child victims. Their rehabilitation and best interests, while possibly in the background, are not assigned high priority in the process. Child victims' participation is limited and problematic. Important aspects of children's development and the right to equality are further neglected. As to protection, while this is clearly a goal of the criminal justice system (unlike the other human rights principles), the low reporting rates of crimes against children and the evidentiary difficulties associated with such crimes make it difficult for the criminal justice system to reach this goal in a satisfactory manner. Further, an investigation into the psychosocial needs of child victims such as an apology, direct (positive) interaction with the perpetrator, validation, and a sense of control reveals that they are typically not addressed in the criminal process. These matters are discussed in this chapter, as well as some suggestions for making the criminal justice process more oriented toward the needs-rights of child victims.

The chapter begins by uncovering the strains related to the involvement in the criminal justice process for all victims. Because the first and central goal of the criminal justice process is to find out whether the defendant is innocent or guilty, procedural and evidentiary rules are all aimed at ensuring that an innocent person would not be convicted. Consequently, victims are required to discuss their victimization in detail, leaving out (at least until the sentencing stage) any "irrelevant" information such as their feelings, background, or special circumstances. Additionally, the outcomes of the process are typically dichotomous—either acquittal or a finding of guilt—with the offender's incarceration often linked with the latter. These outcomes can cause a significant emotional burden on victims: if the offender is acquitted, then the message is one of disbelief in the victim's story. If the offender is found guilty (and consequently has to endure punishment), then the victim might suffer self-blame. When there is an ongoing relationship between the victim and the offender, economic and emotional losses can also be experienced.

Next, the chapter considers the difficulties that are unique to child victims due to their dependency on adults, lack of experience, and increased vulnerability. Studies focusing on children's involvement in criminal proceedings as witnesses suggest that such involvement may have short- as well as long-term effects on their emotional well-being and behavior.

The chapter then moves on to discuss some of the reforms introduced in many jurisdictions to reduce the negative effects of the process on child victims. These reforms, however, have shown only partial success, and their limitations are discussed as well.

Finally, this chapter evaluates the criminal justice system through the needs-rights model. Analyzed in this way, it becomes clear that even in a utopian criminal justice world where all victim-friendly reforms were to be applied to all cases of child victims, still victims' needs-based rights would not be met in a satisfactory way. The concluding part of this chapter includes some suggestions for making current criminal justice processes more attuned to the needs-rights of child victims.

VICTIMS IN THE CRIMINAL JUSTICE PROCESS: DISTRESSING ELEMENTS

In Western adversarial criminal justice systems the major participants are the state—represented by the prosecutorial authority—and the offender.[31] Victims are typically only witnesses. In many cases, the process ends with a plea bargain, leaving no role for the victim. In other cases, victims are called to give testimony, and while doing so, to put themselves at the hands of defense attorneys who are trained to conduct stringent cross-examinations. Seen as a "piece of evidence" (albeit a central one), victims often are denied opportunities to tell their stories in their own terms, to ask questions that bother them, or to talk about the aftermath of their victimization. Indeed, "If one set out by design to devise a system for provoking intrusive post-traumatic symptoms, one could not do better than a court of law" (Herman, 1992, p. 72).

Kim Scheppele (1989) proposes a social critique of the criminal justice process through the concept of narratives. She criticizes the legal system as differentiating between "insiders" and "outsiders": narratives told by "insiders"—typically white, middle-class men—are accepted and believed. In contrast, narratives told by outsiders (whether they are defendants, victims, or witnesses) such as women, the poor, and people of color are rejected or disbelieved or are not heard at all. Scheppele argues that having one's story disbelieved and transformed into something completely different is one of the most disempowering experiences one can have. The rejection of stories told by the "outsiders" is not necessarily done explicitly; rather, rules of evidence and relevancy restrict their ability to tell their stories in their own way, and exclude much of their narratives. Stories need to fit the legal template: details that do not fit are simply excluded and do not become legal facts. For example, subjective feelings and impressions do not count as relevant in the legal template and therefore are rejected. Similarly, the history of a person that might explain his or her behavior (for example, not resisting sexual abuse) is often excluded from the legal process, which is interested only in the "facts" at the time of the offense.

Caroline Taylor (2004) builds on Scheppele's thesis and provides a feminist critical analysis of the experience of young sexual abuse victims in the court process, based on an in-depth examination of all court hearings of several case studies in Australia. Taylor's argument is that criminal proceedings generate "stock stories" (2004, p. 18) that represent the domination of adult males and reject and undermine the narratives of victims—typically young women and girls. These stock stories are created in the following way. Defense attorneys use the complainant's initial interview (either with the police or in the preliminary hearing) as raw material. They exclude those parts that are undesirable through evidentiary rules and fill the gaps with alternative information, creating a story favorable to the accused. They are able to do so since the adversarial system has developed through its history many rules that are not about truth finding but about providing ammunition to the competing parties. Consequently, instead of telling their story in their own words, victims are required to ignore some parts of their story and even change their testimony to comply with evidentiary rules. These gaps, silences, and inconsistencies in victims' stories are held against them and make their narratives appear less compelling than those of the defense (Taylor, 2004, pp. 24–30).

For example, in one of Taylor's case studies victims were required not to use the word "rape" in their testimony because the offense was legally termed "incest." Victims were even threatened with contempt of court if they continued to use this word in reference to their ongoing sexual abuse by their father (Taylor, 2004, p. 32). Another example is when ongoing abuse is narrowed in the preliminary hearing, due to evidentiary difficulties, to one or two occasions that can be specifically dated. The victim then is prohibited from mentioning other occasions, although in her memory these all may be linked together. These create forced gaps, silences, and sometimes inconsistencies. Juries are aware of only one or two incidents and do not understand that the inconsistencies may result from the victim's difficulty in identifying the specific sequence of events in a particular event.

Moreover, Taylor describes how previous testimonies and interviews provide numerous opportunities to find contradictions and gaps, which are used in an attempt to prove the victim is a liar. Facts about family tensions and the victim's past behavior (often told by the accused) are used to portray the victim as "bad" and suggest revenge and greed as motives. The accused, on the other hand, is forbidden by legal rules from being questioned about past criminal behavior.[32] Furthermore, the accused can choose to remain silent throughout the trial and leave it to the defense attorney to provide legal representation (Taylor, 2004, p. 38). As a result, victims tell their story in an extremely hostile environment. The explicit goal of this storytelling is to provide the defense with opportunities to find inconsistencies and portray them negatively (Taylor, 2004).

Taylor's research is based on a small number of cases in one Australian jurisdiction. It would therefore be wrong to conclude that *all* cases, or at least sexual abuse ones, are dealt with in the same manner everywhere. However, the evidentiary and procedural rules that allow these dynamics, as well as the "competition" between the prosecution and the defense, do exist in most adversarial jurisdictions and are derived from the nature of the adversarial legal process. Moreover, what Taylor demonstrates are not explicitly aggressive tactics against the victim (which might be prohibited or at least limited in some courts, especially where legal reforms have been introduced), but a more subtle degradation of the victim's credibility through a carefully planned use of these legal rules. Such tactics may be resistant to prosecutors' objections, since they often comply with the written word of procedural and evidence law. It is possible therefore to speculate that Taylor's description can well apply to many courts across different jurisdictions, in various levels of accuracy.

PARTICULAR HARDSHIPS ON CHILD VICTIMS IN CRIMINAL COURTS

If the criminal justice process is stressful for adult victims, then it is far more stressful for child victims. First, due to their limited knowledge and lack of experience in such proceedings, children's (particularly young ones) understanding of the process, its importance, and the rationales behind various procedural rules is very limited. Therefore they might experience greater anxieties, resent the need to testify, or believe that they are the ones "in trouble" (Quas & McAuliff, 2009). Second, taken away from their natural environments of school and home, children need to communicate with a large number of unfamiliar adults, many of whom are often not trained or used to speaking with young people. In this adult-oriented environment, children often feel alienated and scared.

Closely related is the problem of language. Professional jargon, while often threatening and unclear to many adults, is particularly threatening for children, whose vocabulary has not fully developed. Even words that professionals think are not "jargon" might be unfamiliar and might enhance the anxiety of young victims. In addition, childhood victimization carries with it some specific characteristics that make the process harder for children. Often, a large number of professionals are involved (such as child protection and education officials) who are not typically involved in crimes against adults. As a result, children sometimes are interviewed multiple times. Combined with their limited understanding of the process, children often think that their reports are somehow "wrong" or that they themselves are under investigation (Morgan & Zedner, 1992, p. 116; Quas & McAuliff, 2009). Further, particularly in intrafamilial crimes, children may incur direct financial and emotional consequences as a result of the defendant's incarceration and the family breakdown. Finally, since children are often considered less reliable witnesses, they are regularly faced with either the acceptance of a plea bargain, or a particularly harsh investigative process in court (Morgan & Zedner, 1992, pp. 121–122). Consequently, the criminal process has become notorious for "revictimizing," or causing a "secondary victimization," for many child victims (Fortin, 2003; Herman, 2003; Morgan & Zedner, 1992; Zedner, 2004).

Unfortunately, in the absence of an overarching childhood victimology theory (with the work of Morgan & Zedner [1992] and Finkelhor et al. [2005] as unique exceptions), all the research work in this area has focused on the experiences of child victims of sexual and intrafamilial crimes and has neglected to study the involvement in the process of young victims of other crimes (Whitcomb, 2003). Accordingly, this section reviews the research regarding mostly victims of sexual and family violence.

Testifying in Court

Testifying in court has consistently been found as a stressful task for children (Eastwood & Patton, 2002; Ghetti et al., 2002; Malloy et al., 2006; Whitcomb, 2003). Increased anxiety during testimony has been linked with being under cross-examination, having to face the accused, discussing personal events in public, the formality and unfamiliarity of the process, and the need to testify multiple times (Cashmore, 1995; Ghetti et al., 2002; Malloy et al., 2006). Repeated testimonies and harsh cross-examinations are correlated with greater distress during testimony as well as with a higher risk of trauma in the longer term, including in adulthood (Ghetti et al., 2002; Malloy et al., 2006; Whitcomb, 2003). In Australia, children who were interviewed following their testimony said that the cross-examination, which could take hours and days, was particularly stressful. They described it as horrible, confusing, and upsetting, and many felt they were being accused of lying (Eastwood & Patton, 2002, p. 123). This is typical of most adversarial systems in which the competing parties are trained to portray the witnesses for the other side as unreliable.[33] Unfortunately, many judges and magistrates have limited or no knowledge of the dynamics of sexual abuse and they tend not to limit cross-examination, even when there is limiting legislation (Eastwood & Patton, 2002, p. 126).

Waiting for the Testimony

Delays in the trial and particularly in the child's testimony can also be stressful for children and at the same time may add evidentiary difficulties, as children's memory can fade (Fortin, 2003). In Australia, in-depth interviews of child victims and their parents revealed that long periods of waiting (lasting an average of 18 months) prevented children from being able to move on with their lives. They were expected to maintain their memory about what happened and were not allowed to discuss it with their families and supporters, and their psychological treatment was put on hold. Typically they spent their time worrying about the upcoming trial. Children reported having nightmares, feeling depressed, feeling great fears, not being able to concentrate at school, as well as self-hatred and suicidal behavior (Eastwood & Patton, 2002, p. 115).

In the Courthouse

In some jurisdictions child witnesses still have to wait (often for long hours, even days) in waiting rooms or corridors that are not geared for children. Often they are worried about meeting the offender and the offender's supporters. Sometimes they are not allowed to leave the room, either for their protection (to prevent an unwanted encounter with the defendant) or for fear of contaminating their testimony. These waiting periods are stressful for children, especially when there are no child-friendly facilities (Malloy et al., 2006; Whitcomb, 2003).

Specific Issues in Intrafamilial Crimes

When allegations of child and spousal abuse occur within families, there are additional difficulties for children. First, reporting the abuse carries the potential of separation from the family, which (even in cases where such separation is in the best interests of the child) is a great source of stress and uncertainty for abused children (Ghetti et al., 2002; Malloy et al., 2006). Second, children might find themselves testifying and being interviewed in multiple proceedings, each of them stressful: in the criminal court (for questions of guilt and penalty), in the juvenile court (for protection measures), and in the family court (as part of family law proceedings) (Myers, 1994). Finally, the need to testify against their caretaker is particularly difficult, since this is often someone whom they still love and hope to be loved by, despite the victimization (Fortin, 2003, p. 461). When child abuse is connected with domestic violence the situation is particularly complex. Reporting paternal child abuse is a challenge for an abused mother who fears her own safety and therefore declines to report her own victimization. Further, many women report the abuse to the police, but once violence has stopped they disengage from the system (Wemmers, 2005). Therefore, abused children who are exposed to domestic violence are not only less likely to become known to the authorities, but those whose cases have been reported might be left to handle the criminal justice process without parental support by either their violent father or their victimized mother, who fears for her own safety.

Summary

Empirical findings indicate that the court process is stressful for child victims of abuse, especially with regard to the child's own testimony. While most or all children who testify endure anxiety during their testimony, many others suffer emotional difficulties that continue in the weeks and months after the trial, especially after being interviewed numerous times and being required to go through unpleasant cross-examination. In extreme situations, testifying in court has been correlated with long-term mental health problems that continue into adulthood—particularly if the child victim did not have maternal support, when the abuse was severe, when children were required to testify repeatedly, and when the trial ended with acquittal (Malloy et al., 2006; Quas & McAuliff, 2009; Whitcomb, 2003).

It is unclear whether child victims of crimes other than sexual and family abuse endure similar difficulties from the criminal justice process, as there is hardly any empirical research investigating the effects of the court process on child victims of other crimes. Referring to child victims generally, Finkelhor and Kendall-Tackett (1997) argue that the effect of testifying in court changes with age, and more specifically that preschool children are actually less distressed by testifying than older children. The authors claim, however, that although children were negatively affected in the more extreme forms of court involvement (such as being interviewed multiple times), criminal prosecution in itself did not put children in a worse position overall (1997, p. 21). There are reasons to believe, however, that involvement in the criminal justice process may be challenging for any victimized child. Many similarities exist, such as the formal, unfamiliar environment; the cross-examination, which is aimed at reducing the witness's reliability; the unpleasant anticipation before giving testimony; and the multiple interviews (Quas & McAuliff, 2009). At the same time, it will be equally reasonable to assume that the less sensitive the matter, the easier it will be for the victim to discuss it, even in open court.

Whether it is the assumption that other types of crimes are easier to discuss or easier to resolve through a guilty plea or whether it is lack of public interest, it is notable that most legal reforms aimed at reducing the stress for child victims have focused solely on victims of family and sexual abuse. Child victims of other crimes such as theft and physical assaults by strangers are usually not provided with special measures of protection, and those who are called to testify are required to do it in the same manner as adults. Even in jurisdictions such as the United Kingdom where all child victims are treated, by law, as vulnerable and deserving special protections, in reality child victims of crimes other than sexual and family abuse, especially older children, are not treated as vulnerable (Burton et al., 2006). Given the negative implications crime has on children that were discussed in the previous chapter, it is reasonable to assume that their involvement in the criminal process is not an easy experience, especially for those already coping with stress, fears, and anger resulting from their victimization.

The next section discusses some modern reforms and their application, especially in cases of sexual and intrafamilial abuse.

RECENT REFORMS AND THEIR LIMITATIONS

Increased awareness regarding the plight of crime victims led many jurisdictions to legislate victims' reforms (Maguire, 1991). Most reforms include steps promoting the rights of victims to be treated with respect and to be protected from further harm, to receive information about the progress of the case dealing with their victimization, and to receive restitution from the offender or, alternatively, state compensation (Groenhuijsen, 2004). In many countries victims' services and victims' compensation programs have been established to address their needs within the criminal process and later in their recovery process (Maguire, 1991). The implementation of these reforms, however, has been limited (Groenhuijsen, 2004; Shapland, 2009). In addition, there is no empirical evidence that the emotional healing of victims has improved in jurisdictions where reforms have been introduced (Herman 2003; Maguire, 1991). Another kind of criticism refers to victims' compensation. According to Zehr (1990), compensation is often limited to violent crimes; it is typically regarded as welfare or charity-based and not as a symbol of the state's legal responsibility for the criminal loss suffered by the victim; many victims, such as those with criminal records, are excluded; and often compensation does not take into account the specific needs of victims.

Many jurisdictions, including the United States, Australia, and Canada, have enacted victim impact statements (VIS, also known as victim personal statements in the United Kingdom), to include victims' views in the sentencing process (Kelly & Erez, 1997; Strang & Sherman, 2003; Wemmers, 2009). It is now questionable, however, whether the use of VIS enhances victims' involvement and satisfaction with the criminal justice process (Erez et al., 1994; Kelly & Erez, 1997; Strang & Sherman, 2003; Wemmers, 1996). Many victims are not informed of their right to provide victim impact statements or do not exercise this right (Kelly & Erez, 1997). Information about VIS often depends on the good will of law enforcement personnel, who may have no incentive to promote victims' participation in the process. As a result, victims' right to participate in the criminal justice process through the submission of VIS is often considered only "lip service" (Kelly & Erez, 1997, p. 242). When victims do provide a VIS, it is often rejected or disregarded by judges (Erez et al., 1994; Shapland, 2009; Taylor, 2004). Furthermore, victims' statements regarding the impact of the crime may relate to only those crimes that have been allowed in the courtroom and not those that have been excluded through evidentiary rulings (Taylor, 2004). Opponents of VISs argue that the punitive nature of the system may expose victims to harsh adversarial investigations regarding their statements (Goldsmith et al. 2003, p. 356), and, when the process outcomes are severe, make them feel guilty and fear retaliation from the offender (Zehr, 1990). From the opposite ideological direction, other opponents fear that including victims' statements will result in harsher sentences, although there is no empirical evidence supporting this concern (Kelly & Erez, 1997).

In addition to these reforms, some child-specific reforms have also been enacted to meet the needs of child victims of special crimes. Examples for these reforms are the following (Burton et al., 2006; Eastwood & Patton, 2002; Fortin, 2003; Malloy et al., 2006; Morgan & Zedner, 1992; Shapland, 2009; Whitcomb, 2003):

- Expedited proceedings
- Special waiting areas
- Reduced formality (i.e., taking off wigs and robes and changing seating arrangements)
- Exemptions from corroborating evidence requirements in cases of child testimony
- The use of video cameras for early interviews
- The use of closed-circuit television (CCTV) to enable children to testify from another room during the trial
- The use of screens to prevent eye contact when CCTV is not available or is undesirable
- Prohibitions on defendants from conducting cross-examinations
- The use of support persons to sit next to children testifying in court
- Special children's courts for sexual abuse cases.

Most of these reforms have arguably eased the stress on child victims, in particular the use of CCTV for children who have to testify in court (Burton et al., 2006; Cashmore, 1995, 2002; Goodman et al., 1998; Malloy et al., 2006; Myers, 1994; Shapland, 2009). For example, in-depth interviews with 130 participants across three Australian jurisdictions (Eastwood & Patton, 2002) revealed that where extensive reforms have taken place, many more children stated that they would report again should they be victimized. In particular, knowing in advance that they would not have to confront the accused, either in the waiting area or during their testimony, was a great relief for victimized children, as were the shortened waiting periods and the child-friendly waiting rooms. Although testifying from a different room via CCTV was still stressful, children nevertheless thought it was somewhat better:

> Having someone yell at you through a television screen is not as upsetting as someone yelling at you from five feet away (Eastwood & Patton, 2002, p. 123).

However, it would be wrong to conclude that with the introduction of these innovative procedures the legal process is benign for child victims. Often the implementation of these reforms is limited and their effectiveness questionable.

First, despite their availability, some of these reforms are only rarely used, either because of questions regarding the defendant's due process rights (especially in the United States, where the right to due process has a constitutional status), or because of the prosecution's concerns that the use of an alternative to the child's live testimony in court will reduce the credibility of the child's testimony, and as a result impair the prospects of proving the case (Eastwood & Patton, 2002; Ghetti et al., 2002; Goodman et al., 1998; Malloy et al., 2006; Whitcomb, 2003). In particular, the U.S. Supreme Court stated that the use of CCTV has to be balanced with the defendant's constitutional right to confront the accuser. Accordingly, CCTV can be used in the United States only if there is proof that the child will be so affected by confronting the accused in court that he or she will not be able to reasonably communicate while testifying (Ghetti et al., 2002; Malloy et al., 2006). This narrow ruling makes it difficult to use CCTV in most cases; indeed, only a small minority of victimized children in the United States are allowed to give their testimony through CCTV (Myers, 1994; Whitcomb, 2003). In the United Kingdom, where comprehensive reform has granted all child victims a "status" of vulnerable witnesses deserving special measures of protection, CCTV is also used only in a minority of cases, either because of due process considerations or because of assumptions regarding the capabilities of older children to testify in court (Burton et al., 2006, pp. 52).

Videotaped forensic interviews are yet another example: in the United States, they are used in only 17% of child sexual abuse trials (Malloy et al., 2006). In the United Kingdom, they are employed in only about a quarter of cases involving child witnesses, despite the statutory presumption for the use of video-recorded interviews (Burton et al., 2006, p. 46). Furthermore, even when such interviews are videotaped, they are usually an addition to the child's live testimony and not an alternative to it, which defeats the purpose of reducing the number of interviews (Malloy et al., 2006). Indeed, there is no evidence that the use of tape-recorded interviews reduces the number of interviews child victims have to endure (Cashmore, 2002).

Other measures are used even less often. The removal of wigs, for instance, is used with only 15% of identified vulnerable witnesses in the United Kingdom (Burton et al., 2006, p. 582). In New South Wales, where a specialized children's court was piloted for sexually abused children, a recent evaluation (Cashmore & Trimboli, 2005) found that despite specific training and child-friendly regulations, not much has changed for child victims of sexual crimes. In particular, cross-examination was still experienced as a stressful, unfair process and judges varied in their motivation and effectiveness in controlling defense attorneys. Delays often still occurred and technical problems with the equipment emerged. Even support persons, although welcomed in theory, did not always escort the child witness to court, for various reasons, such as being required to testify at a later stage (Cashmore, 1995). Having trained volunteers or staff accompany the child as supporters did not resolve this difficulty. From a child's perspective, a victim services volunteer whom the child has met only shortly before the trial does not address his or her need to be escorted by someone he or she is familiar with and trusts (Plotnikoff & Woolfson, 2004).

Furthermore, the use of VISs, while questionable with regard to adult victims, is particularly problematic with young ones. In a study of child witnesses conducted by Judy Cashmore (1995), all court hearings in New South Wales, Australia, dealing with child sexual assaults during a 12-month period in 1991–92 were surveyed, totaling 517 cases. VISs were completed in only 23.4% of convictions, but only 13.8% were submitted to the court for consideration. Younger children (aged 5 to 11) were more likely to complete a statement than older children, and the researcher speculated that this was due to the higher refusal rate by children aged 12 and older.

Another limitation of these reforms is that even when practiced, they do not offer a full remedy. For example, even tape-recorded interviews may be experienced as stressful by children (Fortin, 2003). Moreover, often technical difficulties emerge when certain techniques are being used. For instance, when screens were used in Australia as an alternative to CCTV in order to prevent eye contact between the testifying victim and the defendant, problems arose because children could still hear the accused and see his or her body parts (Cashmore, 1995; Eastwood & Patton, 2002). Even CCTV, which seems to be clearly a positive aid for young victims who need to testify, is not always used to children's satisfaction. There is evidence that some child victims would prefer to be present in the courtroom to tell their story in the defendant's presence and see him or her being punished. At a minimum, children would prefer to be consulted regarding the use of CCTV beforehand (Wade, 2002). This is not the current practice, at least in the United Kingdom, despite existing legislation (Burton et al., 2006; Plotnikoff & Woolfson, 2004). Also, children who testify via CCTV are not allowed to have a family member as a supporter, and if they were informed of this, they might have preferred to give testimony in court, perhaps behind a screen, where they could have a familiar support person sitting next to them (Plotnikoff & Woolfson, 2004). Finally, it is important to remember that typically these innovations are aimed at child victims of sexual and severe violent and family crimes. Other child victims are required, if their case is not resolved through a guilty plea, to participate at the trial as any other witness, without any support (Whitcomb, 2003). Even when reforms are comprehensive and include all child victims, as is the case in the United Kingdom, in reality children who are not sexually assaulted, as well as older children, are often not provided with special protection measures (Burton et al., 2006).

One innovation that has gained wide support in the United States is children advocacy centers, which provide multidisciplinary services to child victims (Finkelhor, 2008, p. 172). Highly trained interviewers conduct videotaped forensic interviews with the involvement of police, prosecution, and child protection officials to minimize the number of needed interviews. However, despite some evidence concerning improved services and reduced charging time, it is still unknown to what extent these child advocacy centers substantially reduce the number of interviews and decrease children's stress (Malloy et al., 2006; Quas & McAuliff, 2009; Whitcomb, 2003).

Another widely accepted reform is the preparation of children for court through age-appropriate explanations of the court process, visits to the courtroom, and child-friendly brochures describing the court experience. Enhancing children's understanding of the process has been found to be effective in decreasing their anxiety and improving their testimony. At the same time, these preparations are considered less controversial in terms of defendants' rights and the prosecution's interests, as long as they do not involve rehearsing or coaching the child (Ghetti et al., 2002; Malloy et al., 2006; Morgan & Zedner, 1992; Whitcomb, 2003). Even this seemingly simple innovation, however, is not implemented uniformly across jurisdictions, and some preparation programs are unsatisfactory. For example, children testifying in one Crown Court in England said that the preparation program did not provide them with sufficient information about their role in the trial, and some complained that it in fact heightened their anxiety (Wade, 2002). Burton and coworkers (2006, p. 42) found that British children could not make informed decisions about their preferred method of testifying since they had not had a court preparation visit at the stage of making those decisions, and therefore did not have a real understanding of how the various measures work.

It seems, then, that while there are some data reporting enhanced satisfaction of child victims when some of these reforms are used, the experience of most child victims in the criminal justice process is still negative (Burton et al., 2006; Cashmore & Trimboli, 2005; Plotnikoff & Woolfson, 2004). First, important reforms such as CCTV, videotaped interviews, and expedited proceedings are typically implemented in cases of family and sexual abuse of children. However, many other young victims, while still vulnerable due to their young age, are often required to testify in court as adults. Second, even in cases of sexual and family abuse, very often prosecutorial considerations and legal constraints lead to the decision not to use stress-reducing techniques, exposing traumatized victims to live testimony in court in front of the defendant. Thirdly, the effectiveness of these reforms has not yet been proved, and seems to vary among jurisdictions.

POTENTIAL BENEFITS OF THE CRIMINAL PROCESS FOR CHILD VICTIMS

Despite evidence regarding the stress associated with children's involvement in the criminal process following their victimization, it is important to remember that not everything is negative in that process, and not all children experience it as stressful or traumatic.

Perhaps the most obvious positive outcome arising from the criminal process from the victim's point of view is when the defendant is found guilty. A finding of guilt delivers a message of trust in the child's testimony, an acknowledgment of the wrong done to him or her, and a public message of denunciation. Indeed, there is evidence concerning the higher prevalence of mental health problems in adulthood for child victims whose cases ended without a finding of guilt (Malloy et al., 2006; Whitcomb, 2003).[34]

In a study of Australian child victims involved in criminal proceedings (Cashmore, 1995), about half of the children thought there were some positive things about going to court.[35] The highest correlate of positive replies was a finding of guilt, and the main positive things in going to court, according to the half who replied positively, were feelings of vindication and that justice was done. This was particularly true for children under 12.

Another positive element in the criminal justice process may be a feeling of empowerment as a result of being able to testify against the perpetrator. It is important to remember that there are individual differences among children. In contrast with the negative experiences many children report, as presented earlier, some children find the opportunity to stand in court (or in a separate room) and tell their story to be an empowering experience (Cashmore, 1995; Ghetti et al., 2002; Peters et al. 1989).

Thirdly, some children find the court experience cathartic—an opportunity to confront their past "once and for all" and put it behind them afterwards (Cashmore, 1995; Peters et al., 1989).

How common are these positive experiences for children? There have been only a few studies comparing the long-term emotional and behavioral problems of testifying and non-testifying child victims (Edelstein et al., 2002; Herman, 2003). There are, however, data that suggest that maternal support and a finding of guilt are the most important determinants of children's short- and long-term reactions to the legal system (Edelstein et al., 2002). Victim inclusion, choice, and empowerment may also enhance victims' satisfaction and improve their mental health compared with victims who are dealt with disrespectfully and are excluded from the process (Herman, 2003). Runyan and colleagues' (1988) study of 100 allegedly abused children indicated that the involvement in juvenile court as witnesses in care and protection proceedings had a positive effect on them. These children showed reduction in anxiety faster than those involved in other proceedings or those whose cases were not brought to court. It is important to note, however, that the results relate to juvenile court proceedings, where a safety plan for the child victims was negotiated, rather than involvement in the criminal process.

Finally, although this text reflects a child-centered perspective, one cannot ignore the societal benefits typically associated with the criminal justice system. These benefits are, in a nutshell:

- Holding the offender wholly responsible for the crime and absolving the victim of blame
- Validating the norm that no one has a right to abuse children
- General deterrence of others against committing similar crimes, through public punishment
- An opportunity for the court to refer offenders to treatment, for prevention of recidivism
- An opportunity to maintain follow-up on offenders through their criminal record (Peters et al., 1989).

These societal benefits, however, while apparently important, represent aspirations rather than empirically demonstrated realities. As the next section will demonstrate, there are serious obstacles to achieving these goals. First, reporting rates of child victimization are very low. Second, the majority of reported cases are resolved through guilty pleas, which, notwithstanding victims' early notification or even consultation, withhold the opportunity for a comprehensive judicial consideration. Finally, there is a shortage of effective treatment programs for offenders. Even when these social benefits were achieved, a human rights approach toward children raises the unavoidable question of whether the price children pay personally in pursuit of these social goals is justified.

To summarize, some children may gain emotional benefits from being involved in the criminal process following their victimization. Nevertheless, the large body of literature describing the hardships this process puts on many children presents quite a negative picture. While some reforms have been introduced to reduce the stress associated with testifying in court, they are limited in their application and often raise legal and practical problems. Furthermore, there are other matters, arising from a child's rights perspective, that are typically neglected when assessing the involvement of child victims in the court process and the success of various reforms. Accordingly, the next section will consider the criminal justice process and its shortcomings through a broader needs-rights perspective.

A NEEDS-RIGHTS EVALUATION

As mentioned earlier, with the use of certain techniques, much of the stress experienced by child victims during the court process can be eliminated or at least reduced, and the satisfaction of child victims with the process may be increased

(Eastwood & Patton, 2002). Accordingly, it is possible to imagine a perfect system where the reforms discussed earlier are all fully implemented, and consequently children are protected against any stress associated with having to confront the offender, speaking about personal matters in public, having to go through aggressive cross-examinations, and having to endure long delays. Two international examples of such "ideal" systems are the International Criminal Court and its treatment of child victims and witnesses, and the 2009 UNDOC/UNICEF Model Law for treating child victims and witnesses of crime. These two examples will be discussed toward the end of this chapter. In practice, however, not only are these reforms limited in application within specific states because of financial, bureaucratic, legal, and professional training obstacles (Burton et al., 2006; Cashmore & Trimboli, 2005). Even in their broadest implementation they are aimed at addressing only some of the human rights and psychosocial needs of child victims.

Chapters 2 and 3 presented an integrated account of the human rights and evidence-based needs of child victims. This model expands the discussion beyond the common themes of court-related anxieties and special protective measures for child victims. While not impeccable in its structure, it illuminates other elements important for child victims as respected individuals, such as participation, equality, and rehabilitation. Accordingly, the following discussion will evaluate the criminal justice process through the needs-rights model. As the model suggests (see p. 84), the human rights principles used as measurements for such evaluation (and presented in circles) are the child's best interests, equality, development, and participation, as well as the two specific rights associated with victimization, namely protection and rehabilitation. These principles are intertwined with each other, and their practical meanings in the context of childhood victimization can best be understood through the evidence-based findings regarding children's needs. These psychosocial needs are grouped into four boxes, each of them corresponding to some of the human rights principles.

Since it is difficult (and in fact futile) to isolate each one of the model's indivisible components, the following discussion follows the division conducted in Chapter 3 into four quarters ("clusters"), each representing one box of psychosocial needs combined with their corresponding human rights principles. The four clusters are *best interests, control, procedural justice*, and *protection*. To apply the model as an evaluation tool for Western criminal justice systems, the following sections discuss each cluster separately. In each cluster, a "Pac-Man" shape represents the criminal justice process's difficulties (often failures) to meet the relevant needs-rights of victimized children.

The Best Interests Cluster

As Figure 4.1 demonstrates, this cluster relates to three interrelated human rights principles: best interests, rehabilitation, and development. This interrelationship can be explained in the following way: while the best interests principle creates an obligation to assess the individual child's wellbeing and give it primacy, the rehabilitation principle emphasizes the long-term interests of child victims and the duty to address them. In assessing the short- and long-term interests of child victims, it is crucial to consider their developmental stage and conditions for their future healthy development.

As the box representing the psychosocial layer of the model shows, the best interests cluster identifies some central needs related with the promotion of the wellbeing

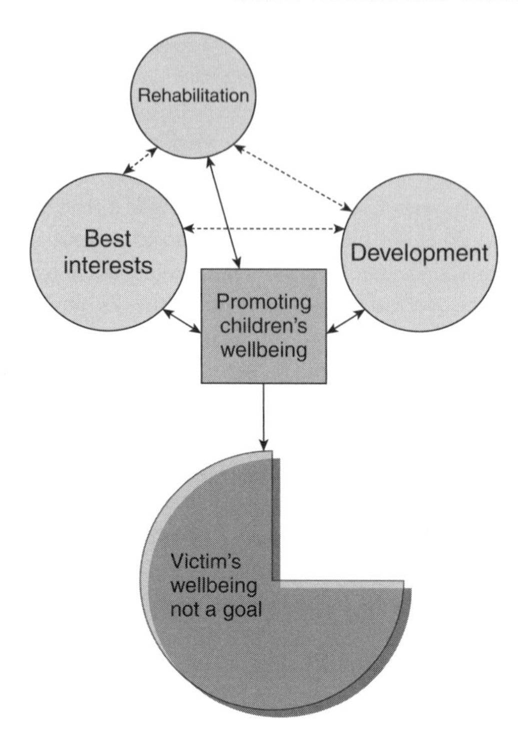

Figure 4.1 The best interests cluster: shortcomings of the criminal justice process.

of child victims. These are the importance of having strong support networks, experiencing acknowledgment of harm and validation of behaviors and feelings, and receiving appropriate reparation. A detailed description of these findings appears in the previous chapter (see p. 85).

As shown by the Pac-Man shape, most of the identified needs-rights included in the best interests cluster are either neglected or in conflict with the goals and *modus operandi* of Western criminal justice processes. The criminal justice system by its nature does not give centrality to the interests of victims, young or adult (Shapland, 2009). The goal of the Western criminal justice system is not to heal, promote wellbeing, or rehabilitate victims. Rather, it focuses on defendants—deciding whether they are legally responsible for a specific crime and on the appropriate punishment, when guilt is proved. While there are social goals, such as public denunciation of the crime, retribution, and incapacitation, that may promote the wellbeing of victims (or children in particular), these goals match the interests of the specific child victims only rarely.

The involvement in the criminal process, and particularly being under cross-examination, is often in direct conflict with the child's needs for protective support networks, social acknowledgment, opportunities to mourn, and even reparation. As this chapter has shown, there is voluminous evidence of the stress related to the child's own testimony, as well as medium- and long-term consequences of testifying in court.

For example, referring to the identified need of victims for social validation, it is possible to argue that by punishing the offender society demonstrates solidarity with the victim and affirms the severity of the crime committed against him or her, thus providing the social acknowledgment and public support victims want (Hudson, 1998, p. 249). However, demonstrating concern over the severity of the offender's behavior is different from showing concern over the severity of the harm done to the victim. The criminal justice system does not demonstrate the latter by punishing the offender (Zehr, 1990).

Moreover, it is argued that even a trial that ends with the imprisonment of the offender may in fact be in conflict with the victim's interests, as it may make the offender unable to compensate him or her. In particular in the case of crimes against children, incarceration does not necessarily promote the child's best interests, rehabilitation, or development. In family abuse cases, for instance, while some children want to be separated from their abusers, most would like the abuse to stop rather than see the abuser (typically a parent) incarcerated (Fortin, 2003, p. 521). Imprisonment, while arguably serving social goals such as retribution and vindication (and admittedly it is sometimes necessary to secure the child's immediate safety), may often be in direct contradiction with the child's best interests, development, and rehabilitation because of its economic and emotional consequences on the child. Furthermore, the criminal sanctions for child abusers rarely ensure that they do not reoffend once they are released. Indeed, in the case of pedophiles, a prison sentence, while promoting public safety (and, again, the child's own safety) in the short term, may reinforce their addiction following release (Fortin, 2003, p. 537).

Further, in direct contrast to their need for a supportive, sympathetic audience, in the criminal justice process victims tell their story in the least supportive manner possible (Taylor, 2004). Instead of bringing together the child's supporters to validate the child's feelings, assertions, and behavior, the adversarial system calls for those who can most effectively rebut the child's reliability as a witness or at least minimize the severity of the harm committed against him or her. In particular, the lengthy cross-examination in a hostile and intimidating courtroom environment in the presence of the abuser reinforces feelings of powerlessness and blame (Eastwood & Patton, 2002).

It is also likely that the timing of the court process does not meet the child's timing of recovery (Herman, 1992). For example, children often do not receive psychological treatment for fear that the therapy will contaminate their testimony (Fortin, 2003, p. 525). The criminal justice process may also interfere in the important process of establishing safety, because of a threat of retaliation by the offender (Herman, 1992, 2003).

Moving beyond the negative aspects of testifying in court, the criminal justice process does not include many rehabilitative and reintegrative elements for crime victims, nor is rehabilitation of victims a goal of the process. Often, in fact, it may enhance feelings of disempowerment, distrust, humiliation, anger, and fear, as demonstrated earlier. These are obstacles in the psychological and social healing process of the child victim. Although in family abuse cases, and to some extent in extrafamilial sexual abuse cases, there are mechanisms outside the criminal justice system that are aimed at providing social and psychological services for victimized children, this is typically not the case for child victims of many other types of crime. Children who have been violently assaulted, robbed, or bullied may fall between the cracks and not receive any psychological treatment or other professional support (Finkelhor, 2008, p. 111). Victim support schemes that provide information, support, and guidance for victims involved in the criminal process may reduce the stress and sense of disempowerment that victims feel during the criminal trial, but they differ from mental health services and have not been proved as contributing to the long-term healing of victims (Maguire, 1991).

While reparation is indeed an identified need of many victims, court-ordered compensation reaches only a small portion of victims (Maguire, 1991; Strang, 2009) and often does not address the specific needs or wishes of those who eventually receive it. Even when compensation is available for victims, this is typically established not according to the specific victim's needs and wishes but rather depending on either set rules (as is generally the case in the United Kingdom and Australia) or the decision of the judge or jury based on their impression of the severity of the crime (as is the case in the United States).

It seems, then, that not only are the child's short-term, long-term, and developmental interests peripheral in the criminal process, but also the process and its outcomes are often in direct opposition to these interests. Moreover, from a child's needs-rights perspective, only very rarely do children experience throughout the criminal process support, social acknowledgment, and validation, and only seldom do they receive individually matched material reparation.

The Control Cluster

As discussed in Chapter 2, the Convention stipulates that any child who is able to form his or her own opinion should be able to express this opinion freely. Furthermore, decision-makers are expected to give such opinion due weight, in accordance with the child's age and maturity. This means that children are to be seen as partners in decision-making processes regarding their lives, they should be well informed, and their opinions should have a gradually greater impact on the outcome of such processes as they age and develop their capacities. Participation is associated with greater self-esteem, trust in others, and self-respect (see Chapter 2) and therefore is intertwined, especially in the context of childhood victimization, with the rehabilitation and best interests human rights principles. As the previous chapter demonstrated, the treatment of children as partners is related to feelings of empowerment and control, it provides opportunities for having a direct interaction with the perpetrator, and it opens the door for an exchange of apology and forgiveness (see p. 75). When all these occur in a safe, respectful manner they might contribute to the short- and long-term interests of child victims, thus addressing the rehabilitation and best interests principles as well. At the same time, when children's involvement in the process occurs against the child's will or in an unsafe manner, children's rehabilitation and wellbeing may be jeopardized. The relationship between the human rights principles of participation, rehabilitation, and best interests (represented in circles) and the needs of child victims emerging in this context (collated into a box) is demonstrated in Figure 4.2.

Does the criminal justice process adhere to these needs-rights? The following discussion suggests that even when children are provided with opportunities to describe how they have been affected by the crime through victim impact statements, there is no real dialog between child victims and those who make decisions, since they are not regarded as partners in the process. Children's overall experience of the process is one of disempowerment, lack of control, and often alienation. The criminal justice process does not foster mutual interactions between victims and offenders, it discourages apologetic expressions, and it does not provide space for any open, constructive discussion about the crime and its effects. The failure of the criminal justice process to treat children as partners based on their control-related needs-rights is shown in Figure 4.2.

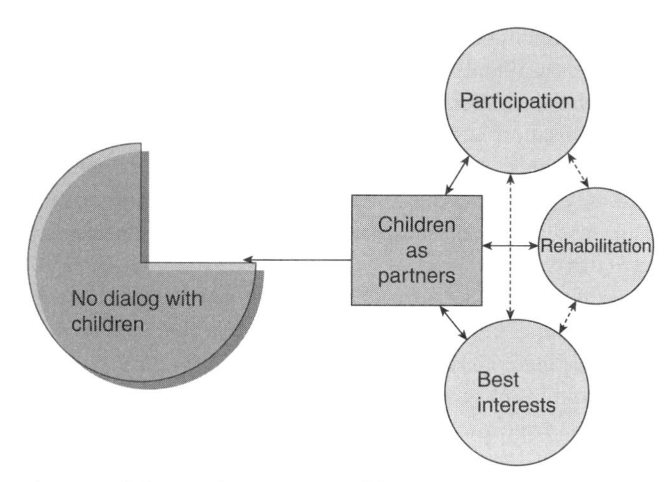

Figure 4.2 The control cluster: shortcomings of the criminal justice process.

Although the introduction of VISs in many jurisdictions reflects an acknowledgment of the victims' right to be heard, given the criminal justice process's basic goals of fact finding (and the necessary protections granted to offenders as a result), it is now questionable whether they are indeed effective in enhancing victims' involvement and satisfaction with the criminal justice process (Strang & Sherman, 2003). First, even when victim impact statements are used regularly, victims can only make representations and requests to judges and prosecutors, who are the decision-makers (Roach, 1999) and who often reject or disregard them (Taylor, 2004). Children give VIS information and have this information considered by judges in a particularly low number of cases (Cashmore, 1995).

Furthermore, victims' input is strictly limited: they may relate to only those crimes that have passed evidentiary obstacles (Taylor, 2004). They can relate to only the past (what happened to them and how the crime affected them) and cannot have a future-oriented deliberation regarding the way the trial should be handled, the guilt of the offender, and the preferred sentence. Finally, the timing of presenting VIS to decision-makers and the identity of those who review it are not contingent upon the victim's preference. While there are good explanations for these limitations, the fact is that victims have very little opportunity to engage in dialog with the criminal justice system (Shapland, 2009). Although it is arguable that victims do not want to be the ones who make the actual decision on the verdict of their victimizer, but rather wish to be heard and consulted (Wemmers, 1996), there is convincing evidence that the use of VISs in practice fails to provide victims with the sense of control and empowerment so important for their healing.

In the context of child victims, there are further questions regarding the use of VISs in practice, the suitability of this instrument for children of different ages, and whether staff are trained in assisting children filling out their statements. Under Roger Hart's (1992) "ladder of participation" (see p. 48), in many cases children's submission of VIS might meet the definition of Hart's third (and criticized) level of the ladder—tokenism. In token participation, children are ostensibly consulted and have a say in the process but are not prepared for it in any meaningful way and are required to communicate in adult terms (1992, p. 9).

Beyond the submission of victim impact statements, the experiences of victims, and child victims in particular, of the process as a whole are of lack of control. There are several reasons for this. First, the victims' role in the process is as witnesses and evidence holders, not partners. Their opinions and wishes are secondary at best when deciding the outcomes of the trial and other decisions along the way. Second, the criminal justice process does not provide means for victims to ask questions or receive answers regarding the reasons for the crime and for their own victimization. In the criminal justice process the victims (and to a great extent the offenders as well) are passive actors (Zehr, 1990, p. 55).

Third, children are being overlooked in particular, not only because adults are used to disregarding their opinions, but also out of motivation to protect them. As described earlier, in many jurisdictions special provisions have been enacted to minimize the exposure of child victims to the criminal justice system. In many instances children under a certain age are exempted from giving testimony altogether. Although these measures are intended to protect children, they also leave those children completely out of the communication loop, unheard and disenfranchised. For example, British children are usually not consulted about their method of testifying, and even when they are, they do not receive full information about the way various measures of testifying work in practice. Many measures are not offered at all. Informed decisions about these measures, therefore, cannot be made (Burton et al., 2006, pp. 42–46).

The passiveness of victims and offenders and the adversarial nature of the process have other consequences. Apologies are rare, and in fact defense attorneys typically advise their clients not to apologize since this may be regarded as an admission of guilt (Brook & Warshwski-Brook, 2009; Rogehr & Gutheil, 2002). Instead of providing space for direct, honest, and respectful dialog between defendants and complainants, the criminal justice process encourages offenders to remain silent and deny responsibility, and minimizes any direct contact between the parties. In the rare occasions when apology is provided, its effectiveness is questionable because of the formal context in which it is expressed: offenders might request that the apology is not used as evidence of their liability; conversely, offenders might be perceived as using the apology as a tactic to achieve a more favorable decision in court. The sincerity of the apology is particularly questionable when the defense attorney apologizes on behalf of the perpetrator (Brook & Warshwski-Brook, 2009). The rarity of apologies in court proceedings and their low credibility in victims' eyes is supported in empirical research (Strang, 2009; Strang & Braithwaite, 2002).

The lack of any opportunity for direct interaction between the parties is particularly common for child victims, where protective measures are taken to limit the child's exposure to the process. Although the encounter with the perpetrator in the formal and alienating setting of the courtroom may indeed be traumatic for children, the prevention of any dialog whatsoever with the perpetrator eliminates any opportunity for closure.

Analyzed with the elements of the control cluster in mind, it becomes clear that even in a utopian criminal justice world where all victim-friendly reforms, including victim impact statements, were applied to all cases of child victims, still victims would have only a limited, indirect influence on the process, and their overall experience is one of exclusion rather than partnership. In fact, it is more likely that once children disclose their victimization they lose control over "their" case and its outcomes, shifting the decision-making power to the professionals in charge. In addition, there is no direct, positive interaction with perpetrators where an apology can be expressed, questions asked, and answers provided in a personal and frank way. There is also no group discussion where children's stories and feelings are validated in the presence of their perpetrator. As a result, the human rights principles of participation, rehabilitation, and best interests are cast aside. Even worse, the disempowerment experienced by children in the courtroom might mirror the victimization experience itself (Eastwood & Patton, 2002, pp. 12–78).

The Procedural Justice Cluster

As Figure 4.3 demonstrates, this third cluster refers to the three human rights principles (presented in circles) of participation, rehabilitation, and equality, all tied together through the psychosocial need for procedural justice, appearing in the box at the center. Indeed, participation (or process control) is central in people's perceptions of procedural justice (Tyler, 1988). In fact, positioning the "procedural justice" need as an explanation (and indeed justification) for the participation right emphasizes the fact that participation does not mean controlling the outcome (which is, apparently, not what victims want—see, for instance, Wemmers, 2004), but rather, perhaps, opportunities to deliberate on it. With victimized children, there is a need to further explore what exactly is the kind of procedural justice they wish for, as the data regarding their views are mixed (Hicks & Lawrence, 1993; Lawrence, 2003; Melton & Limber, 1992). Procedural justice is further related to equality, since neutrality and consistency are also part of people's perceptions of fairness, especially for children (Lawrence, 2003). Procedural justice also corresponds with rehabilitation, since victims who have "experienced justice" might feel closure and are able to move on from

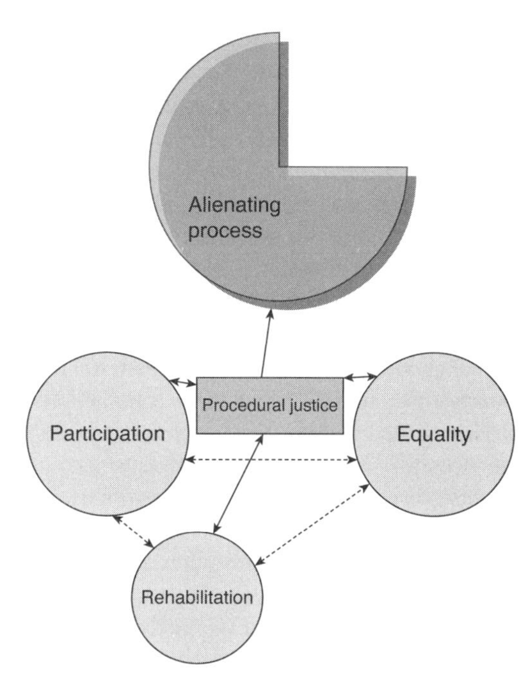

Figure 4.3 The procedural justice cluster: shortcomings of the criminal justice process.

their victimization (Strang, 2002; Zehr, 1990). Do victims in general, and child victims in particular, "experience justice" in the criminal justice process?

Victims who have been involved in the legal process frequently experience it as alienating rather than fair or inclusive. They feel that they were not adequately informed about the progress of their case (Shapland, 2009), were not treated fairly, and did not have an opportunity to express their views, and that as a result the outcome is unfair (Strang, 2002, p. 13). This might be especially the case in the "production line for guilty pleas" (Braithwaite & Strang, 2001, p. 164). When victims are not encouraged to be part of the process, when they are not treated with respect and fairness, and when they do not feel that a fair and just process was applied in their case (Strang, 2002), they might find it difficult to heal. Indeed, in the context of childhood victimization, not only can victimization itself affect the development of children in different ways, but the encounter with the legal process may also interfere with the natural course of children's development. Alienating experiences in the legal process may disrupt the psychological rehabilitation of the child. Conversely, a positive experience of the justice process may leave children with an optimistic lesson about the world and enhance their emotional growth (Murray, 1999).

Beyond the limited opportunities for victims to participate discussed earlier, child victims might also encounter unequal treatment and special difficulties in accessing justice if they belong to marginalized populations. Equality between victims is not a priority of Western criminal justice systems. Victims typically cannot expect equal results in terms of process outcomes, their level of influence on the process, and the protection measures they are granted. Western criminal justice systems focus on offenders, not on victims, and the common conception of equality in justice aims at criminals and their punishment, rather than victims and the remedies they receive. Consequently, legal systems in general do not even attempt to secure equality between child victims. Child victims enduring similar harms see their respective offenders facing different punishments and have varied encounters with criminal justice professionals, because the factors that are considered relevant for the criminal justice system are mostly those relating to the offense and the offender, not the victim.

Perhaps more disturbing, however, is the criminal justice system's blindness to differences between children. As discussed in Chapter 2, the Convention refers to "substantial equality," in the sense that disenfranchised children should, as a matter of right, be provided *more* than "normal" children to remedy their disadvantage (Van Bueren, 1999a). In reality, however, justice systems are often insensitive to the special circumstances faced by some child victims. The result of this lack of sensitivity and flexibility is that the criminal justice process is not equally accessible to all children. Young victims who differ in their socioeconomic status, race, gender, and location receive (if at all) different kinds of services, protection measures, and compensation. One of the outcomes of these differences is children's difficulty in disclosing and reporting victimization in secluded or marginalized communities, where particular difficulties exist. Jody Miller's (2008) description of gendered victimization of girls from African American disadvantaged neighborhoods in St. Louis, Missouri, is a striking example. Lack of sufficient flexibility in the testimony and investigation of children with special needs is another example of the failure to reach substantial equality. Subsequently, children who are marginalized for various reasons (and as a result are often more vulnerable in the first place) are frequently even less protected, and their interests are even more severely neglected, in comparison with middle-class, white, "normal" children.

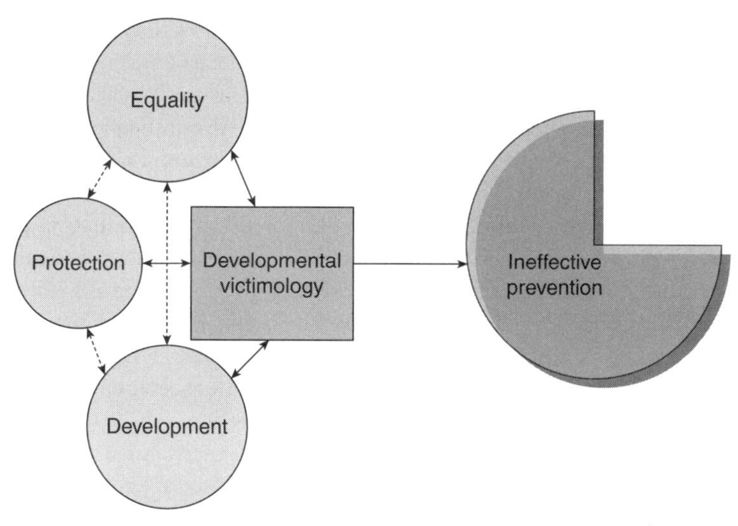

Figure 4.4 The protection cluster: shortcomings of the criminal justice process.

The Protection Cluster

The final needs-rights cluster, shown in Figure 4.4, includes the development, protection, and equality human rights principles (presented in circles), which affect each other and are closely related to topics related to developmental victimology. These topics include the effects of victimization on different children, different coping strategies among children of various ages and groups, and special vulnerabilities of specific populations of children. Indeed, to meet the right of children to be protected from violence within and outside their homes, states need to know more about children at special risk of certain types of victimization and ways of empowering children who are particularly disempowered.

More generally, to meet the human rights framework, legal systems need to examine whether their responses to crimes against children are effective enough in protecting children of various ages and circumstances, or whether it is possible to do more. As the following paragraphs demonstrate, data on crime reports, prosecution, and recidivism rates show quite a pessimistic account of the efficacy of existing criminal justice systems in combating crimes against children. It is reasonable to speculate that children belonging to marginalized populations and children with special needs are the least protected, since they present various challenges in identification, reporting, and prosecuting crimes against them. Indeed, some disabled children have such limited communication abilities that the criminal justice system is unable to protect them (Temkin, 1994). Clearly, to allow these vulnerable children effective access to justice in order to meet their right to protection and equality, special mechanisms are needed to make it possible for them to overcome their communicative and emotional barriers.

Reporting

Given the difficulties relating to the involvement in the criminal process discussed earlier, it is no wonder that only a minority of victims choose to report the crime against them, and a minority of even those choose to follow through the criminal process and give testimony (Shapland, 2009; Zedner, 2004, p. 156). While all crimes are underreported, crimes against children are particularly so: only 28% of violent crimes against youths (ages 12 to 17) are reported to the police (Finkelhor, 2008, p. 103). The emotional barriers to reporting affect both victims and their caretakers. Approximately a third of all victimized children do not tell anyone about their situation, due to fear, shame, and guilt (Finkelhor, 2008, pp. 107–108). Even when victimized children talk about their victimization, their parents often decline to report to the police for reasons such as fear of retraumatizing their children, lack of trust in the police, fear of retaliation, and reluctance to confront an acquainted perpetrator (Finkelhor, 2008, p. 107). In an Australian study of the experiences of child victims in court, many children who had been through the court process stated that they would not report again should a crime be committed against them, even when their cases had been finalized with a conviction (Eastwood & Patton, 2002).

Victims of sexual assaults and maltreated children are the least likely to report (Finkelhor, 2008, p. 152; Russell, 1984). Non-reporting stems from a lack of belief in the system's ability to solve the crime, or from fear of revictimization by it (Roach, 1999, p. 695). In child abuse cases the reporting rates are even lower than adult rape cases—on one estimate 6% for extrafamilial cases and only 2% when the abuse happened in the family (Herman, 2003, p. 161). Put more simply, the vast majority of sexual abuse cases against children are not known at all to the authorities.

Prosecuting

Only a small fraction of the cases that are reported to the authorities proceed to trial (Myers, 1994). Many reports are screened at the investigation stage, and are hardly investigated, if at all. When the police investigation does get through to the prosecution stage, the police have broad discretion in deciding whether to prosecute (Zedner, 2004, p. 147). A central consideration is the case's prospects of being proved in court. Young children (for fears of suggestibility) and older teenagers (for concerns regarding motivation and ability to fabricate accusations) are regarded as posing special difficulties of proof, and therefore crimes against them are less likely to be prosecuted than those relating to children aged 7 to 12 years (Cashmore, 1995; Myers, 1994).

Proving

While only a very small fraction of all offenses result in a conviction—2.2% in Britain (Zedner, 2004, p. 156)—child abuse cases present unique evidentiary difficulties that may reduce prosecution and conviction rates even further. Typically, the child's testimony is the only direct evidence against the defendant, as these kinds of offenses are usually committed only when no one else is present. In addition, often there is no physical evidence; even if there is, children's tendency to delay the reporting of their abuse makes it more difficult to identify physical evidence. Moreover, physical evidence of abuse may not link the abuse with a specific perpetrator. These evidentiary difficulties make the child's testimony central (Malloy et al., 2006). Because the child's testimony is so central, the use of CCTV or prerecorded interviews is problematic from a prosecutorial perspective, as prosecutors often fear that it may reduce the credibility of the child's testimony and create a requirement to present corroborating evidence—and as a result can jeopardize the success of the case (Whitcomb, 2003). At the same time, putting the child on the witness stand not only exposes him or her to the stressors discussed earlier, but it also reduces his or her ability to provide coherent, reliable testimony. This happens either because the child is unable to retrieve memories well under pressure or because of lower motivation to talk (Goodman et al., 1998; Saywitz & Nathanson, 1993). This choice between two evils is particularly common with young children, who are more vulnerable and at the same time less credible witnesses. The result is that younger children, who most need protection, are the least likely to be protected, as their cases are the most difficult to prove (Myers, 1994). Children with disabilities pose similar (and sometimes greater) difficulties, and as a result are insufficiently protected by the system (Temkin, 1994).

With these evidentiary difficulties in mind, it is not surprising that according to one American estimate, approximately two-thirds of the cases that proceed to court end up in a plea bargain, where the defendant pleads guilty to a lesser offense or the prosecution agrees to limit the recommended punishment. When the offender is a juvenile, the case is typically dealt with in the juvenile court, where plea bargains are even more common, at least in the United States (Myers, 1994). Only a small minority of cases end up with a conviction (Myers, 1994). In a study of South Australian court cases against youthful sexual offenders conducted in 1995–2001, Daly and coworkers (2003) found that only 51% of the cases referred to court were finalized (by either admission or proof). Furthermore, the more serious the offense, the less likely it was to be proved in court. Many of the charges were reduced as part of plea bargains or due to evidentiary difficulties. The authors concluded, "From the legal point of view, nothing happened" (Daly et al., 2003, p. 20).

Low Effectiveness of Incarceration

It has been argued that the "crime control" ideology has led to a growth in the jail population but has failed to reduce crime (Fattah, 1998; Roach, 1999; Zedner, 2004, p. 238). More specifically, the incarceration of sexual and domestic violence offenders is considered particularly problematic (Fortin, 2003, p. 521) as it further promotes the offenders' distorted perceptions of violence and sexuality (Hudson, 1998).

The result of these difficulties in reporting, prosecuting, convicting, and effectively punishing is that criminal justice systems are far from being successful in preventing crimes against children, especially child sexual abuse (Fortin, 2003; Roach, 1999). In other words, if governments are committed to the right of children to be protected against violence and abuse, then they must search for ways to increase substantially the reporting rates of crimes against children and to deal with these crimes more effectively. It is questionable whether the criminal justice system alone is able to do that. Furthermore, with these limitations in mind, it is arguable that putting children on the witness stand is simply not worth the cost (Fortin, 2003).

Another concern emerging from the protection cluster is whether responses to crimes against children are sufficiently flexible and can be adjusted according to the specific needs and capabilities typical for each developmental stage and specific needs of individual child victims. For example, one clear difference between children and adults and between children of different ages is the perception of time (Sturgis, 2009). While a month for an adult is a comprehensible time limit, for young children a month may feel like a lifetime. Accordingly, a developmentally sensitive system should schedule court hearings and process cases involving young children promptly, unless there are indications that the opposite would better serve the child's interests.

Developmental data should also be considered in constructing policies regarding the identification of children at risk and prioritizing prevention strategies. For example,

Finkelhor's research group found that teenagers are more at risk of sexual offenses and serious physical assaults, while elementary school children experience higher levels of bullying (Finkelhor et al., 2005). Young children, in contrast, suffer mostly from sibling assaults and property crimes. Finkelhor's data on developmental victimology and the changing patterns of victimization risks and coping strategies throughout childhood (Finkelhor, 2008; Finkelhor & Dzuiba-Leatherman, 1994; Finkelhor & Kendall-Tackett, 1997; Finkelhor et al., 2005) might shed light on where current practices are failing most. There is similarly a need to learn further about how children of different ages, abilities, and specific needs are affected by the criminal justice process and the effectiveness of various techniques in meeting their needs-rights.

CONCLUSIONS

Reviewing the adversarial criminal justice system through a human rights lens in the case of child victims is very telling. It broadens the scope of exploration beyond current research regarding possible emotional difficulties arising from testifying in court and meeting the defendant during the trial. It reveals other weaknesses of the system that are equally disturbing, especially if these legal systems are committed to following the international obligations under the Convention on the Rights of the Child. As Figure 4.5 demonstrates, the full range of children's needs-rights could not be met for child victims, even with the introduction of most progressive reforms. As the "Pac-Mans" demonstrate, the various needs-rights are addressed in the criminal process at varying (yet always unsatisfying) levels.

Perhaps the area where adversarial criminal justice systems score the highest mark is protection. This is not surprising, as preventing crime and protecting the general population is probably the ultimate goal of the criminal mechanism. Despite significant difficulties at all stages of the process (in particular reporting and proving some types of crime, and even more so with regard to children with disabilities), there is no other mechanism at present that provides a systemic response to childhood victimization, and the criminal justice system is still the most widely used mechanism for reporting, responding to, and preventing crimes against children. Therefore, even if the criminal justice system is only partially effective and clearly needs to improve in this regard, it is still the leading alternative at present.

The criminal justice process has also improved remarkably in the past two decades in protecting children who have already been victimized against the emotional harms associated with the process itself. In many jurisdictions far-reaching reforms have been introduced that include the use of videotaped testimony and the use of CCTV or screens during children's live testimony, court preparation, support persons, expedited proceedings, interagency cooperation, and adjustments of the courtroom environment. Jurisdictions differ in the comprehensiveness of their reforms as well as in their implementation, but there is certainly a trend toward reform globally.

Another aspect of children's rights to be protected, however, remains neglected in the current system: some types of violence still harm children on a daily basis, such as sibling assaults, parental corporal punishment, and school bullying, without being effectively addressed (Finkelhor et al., 2005). It might be argued that these types of violence and domination are not suitable for the criminal process. Nevertheless, in evaluating the extent to which the criminal justice process protects children against violence, these data should be considered, particularly in light of findings regarding the severe and pervasive outcomes of these "non-criminal" forms of violence against children (Finkelhor, 2008, p. 97).

If children's right to protection is somewhat addressed through the criminal process, then other needs-rights of child victims are often neglected, if not abandoned altogether. As the analysis in this chapter shows, adversarial criminal justice systems typically do not consider the child's wellbeing as central. This is true for all victims, who are peripheral to the system's *modus operandi*. This is perhaps why the victims' rights movement was so successful in communicating the system's failures. Still, however, since states are bound by the Convention on the Rights of the Child to give primacy to the individual interests of every child in matters concerning him or her, the failure of the criminal process to give considerable weight to children's wellbeing (and, of course, when acting directly against these interests) is even more disturbing.

Further, this chapter shows that there is no true dialog with children, nor are they regarded as partners in the process. Children's participation in the process is nonexistent in many cases, limited in others, and often only token. It is reasonable to maintain that, in psychological terms, the criminal process is an "uncontrollable" situation (see p. 71). While being in an uncontrollable situation is difficult, even more emotionally taxing is engaging in "primary control" coping (trying to influence the situation), expecting high controllability, when in fact the situation is not contingent upon the child's actions. For instance, the use of VISs with children might cause more harm than good when their perspectives are not seriously considered by decision-makers.

Similarly, adversarial criminal justice processes typically do not meet specific developmental needs of child victims of various ages, do not take any measures to promote their psychological recovery and social reintegration, and fail to give special attention to children who have specific needs or who belong to marginalized populations.

Analyzed through a needs-rights perspective, it becomes clear that some elements of the criminal process cannot be changed. In Roach's words, "no one has yet managed to develop a victim centered model which is also consistent with due process or crime control" (1999, p. 707). The criminal justice process in adversarial legal systems is adult- and offender-oriented. It is aimed at establishing guilt or innocence and deciding on the appropriate punishment when guilt is proved. With the threat of being incarcerated or having to endure other financial or social penalties, defendants and defense attorneys are free to use almost any tactic to deny responsibility and reduce the victim's credibility. There is limited room for open, genuine communication between the victim and the offender, who are placed on opposite sides of the competition. There is very little room for apology and remorse, compassion and reintegration. At the same time, fears about the expected results of either punishment or acquittal, combined with fears regarding the process itself, inhibit many children and their parents from reporting the crime and cooperating with the police.

At its best, the crime control model provides indirect recognition of victims without empowering them (Roach, 1999). Indeed, the criminal process cannot, by definition, meet all the needs of victims, and some argue that it should not (Daems, 2009; Groenhuijsen, 1994, p. 174).

At the same time, the needs-rights framework also uncovers elements in the criminal justice process that can be improved. For instance, the protection cluster, directed at a developmental victimology perspective, identifies the need for greater flexibility

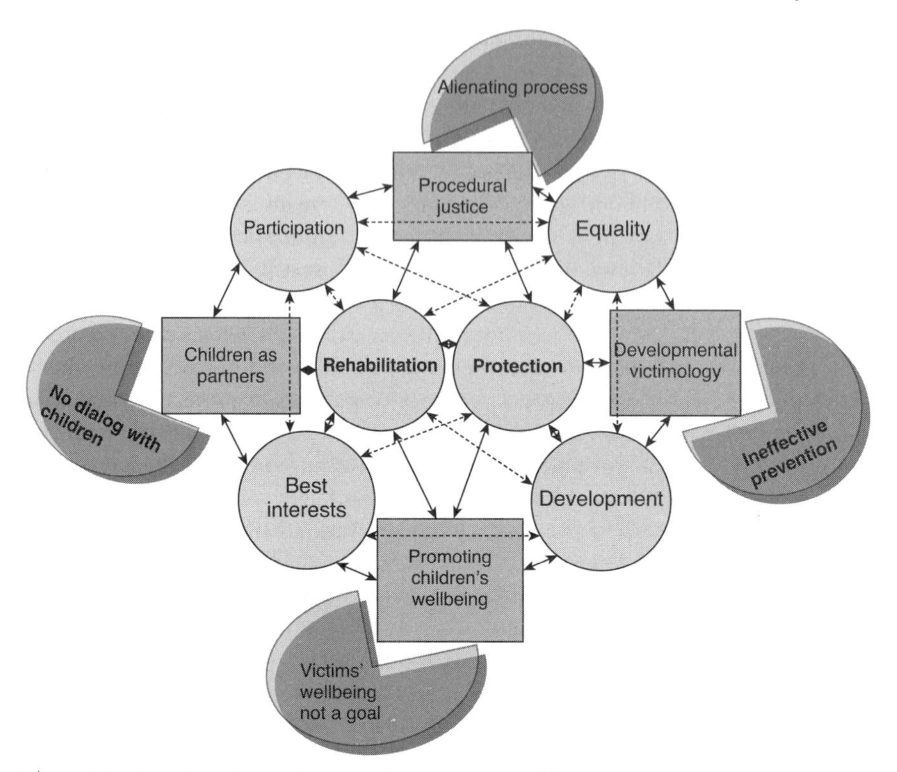

Figure 4.5 A needs-rights evaluation: shortcomings of the criminal justice process.

and adjustments of special measures for children with disabilities. The control cluster demonstrates the need for greater emphasis on consultation with young victims regarding the way they will testify and other protective measures. Treating children as partners also illuminates the importance of listening to children regarding the form of compensation they wish to receive. Using a needs-rights approach can arguably make criminal justice systems more child-friendly, even if they could never meet the full scope of children's needs-rights. The following are two examples of the implementation of a human rights-based approach toward child victims within the criminal process.

UNICEF's guide on children in international criminal justice mechanisms reflects the Convention's provisions and focuses on the best interests of the child, participation, and rehabilitation principles (*International Criminal Justice and Children*, 2002, p. 16). According to the guide, the individual circumstances of each child, including his or her age, gender, and wishes, should be considered at every stage, including the appointment of representatives (2002, p. 16). To promote participation of children, justice mechanisms make accessible aids to make the child's testimony easier and less stressful, such as support people sitting by the child witness, CCTV, and the use of screens. Every child, however, should be consulted prior to the testimony to ensure that the measures meet his or her specific needs and wishes (2002, p. 39). The guide further stresses that to allow children to make an informed decision regarding their participation, they should be fully informed about the process, its goals, and their rights in it, and their views should be heard and carefully considered (2002, pp. 52–53). Justice regimes are urged to protect children against harm and to promote their rehabilitation (2002, p. 49).

Since rehabilitation needs to take place in an environment that "fosters the health, self respect and dignity of the child," as the Convention stipulates, procedural rules should protect children from harm and humiliation. In particular, rules should protect children during cross-examination (2002, p. 50).

Accordingly, the Rules of Procedures and Evidence for the International Criminal Court (ICC) state that in performing their functions, organs of the court "shall take into account the needs of all victims and witnesses . . . in particular children, elderly persons, persons with disabilities and victims of sexual or gender violence" (*International Criminal Justice and Children*, 2002, p. 84, Rule 86). Examples of special measures are hearings behind closed doors, the use of live-link television or recorded testimonies, the duty of the court to prevent harassment or intimidation of a witness, anonymity of the child, and alteration of voice or pictures to protect victims from being identified (2002, p. 85). The court may also order reparation for the victim for damage, loss, or injury. Importantly, there are special arrangements for the representation of child victims (2002, p. 86). The ICC organs include a victims and witnesses unit that provides protective measures, counseling, and other assistance for victims (2002, p. 86). The ICC is designed to be child-friendly. A staff requirement is for some judges to have legal expertise on children. Similar expertise requirements apply to advisers to the prosecutors and the victim assistance unit. All staff members need to go through training on child-related issues (2002, pp. 92–93).

A second example of a human rights-based approach toward child victims is the International Bureau for Children's Rights standards for treatment of child victims and witnesses (*Guidelines on Justice in Matters Involving Child Victims and Witnesses of Crime*, 2005), and the Model Law translating these standards into legislation (UNODC and UNICEF, 2009). The general principles on which the standards and the model law build are those of dignity for all children, non-discrimination, best interests of the child as a primary consideration, protection, harmonious development, and the right to participation.

The model law, designed to assist states to enact child-sensitive legislation regarding the treatment of child victims and witnesses, includes detailed provisions that ensure that the full range of rights mentioned in the Convention on the Rights of the Child and other, nonbinding documents are addressed, provided that the rights of the accused are considered as well. Among the most notable provisions is the right of child victims to be represented, when appropriate, by a legal representative throughout the process (Article 10)—a provision that recognizes these child victims as a third party in the process (Wemmers, 2009). Another important provision is the right of all child victims and witnesses to be assigned a support person (Article 15). Support persons play a key role in escorting the child throughout the process—providing full information, communicating with authorities regarding the case, and providing emotional support and referral to professional services when needed. Article 27 is also notable, authorizing judges to limit cross-examination of child victims and witnesses (after giving due regard to the rights of the accused). Article 28 includes a comprehensive list of special measures that judges are authorized to allow in order to protect the privacy of child victims or witnesses and to prevent secondary victimization. Article 29 provides for the right of victims to restitution from the offender.

It seems, then, that there is much room for improvement in the criminal process, in the directions that many reforms have already taken. The optimal situation for child victims within the criminal justice system would most likely be in a state that adopts the model law in full. It is unclear, however, whether the model law can indeed be enacted in domestic legislation within the existing criminal justice framework. The far-reaching protection measures for child victims, their representation by a legal representative, and the resource-intensive requirements that would arise from such a law would make it more aspirational than realistic. Beyond the budgetary difficulties, the model law is expected to raise objections especially from defense attorneys and others advocating for defendants' rights. Indeed, the model law seems to tilt the balance more toward victims and away from offenders, at least in the case of child victims. The removal of the requirement for corroborating evidence in cases where the child victim is the sole witness, and limitation of cross-examination of victims are two examples of amendments aimed at easing the process for victimized children—but at the same time they remove basic safeguards designed to secure defendants (and society) against false accusations (Fattah, 1997). At the same time, even in a complete child-sensitive framework such as that of the International Criminal Court or the one portrayed in the model law, some aspects of the criminal justice process will not change, since it is based on fact finding and punishment. These are in conflict with the needs of all victims, but perhaps child victims in particular, to tell their stories in their own terms, have their harms acknowledged, receive an apology from the offender, and experience a sense of control and empowerment during the process.

Is there another option, one that is able to meet the needs and rights of both victims and offenders, without jeopardizing any of them, an alternative that can protect child victims and at the same time respect their human rights? The next chapter explores the restorative alternative, in which, at least theoretically, admitting offenders are held accountable while at the same time victims' needs and basic human rights are promoted. If restorative justice offers a valid alternative, then the impossible dilemma between retribution (at the cost of exposing children to stressful, traumatic, and degrading proceedings and the possibility of family breakdown) and protection (at the cost of giving up any denunciation of the crime) might become unnecessary.

5

Restorative Justice Experiences Involving Child Victims

INTRODUCTION

The previous chapter argued that the rights and needs of children who have been victimized are not fully met when their cases are handled by the criminal justice system. Child victims need and deserve to take an active part in the process that follows their victimization, or at least to have the choice to decide not to take part in it. Child victims need and deserve a fair process in which they are treated with respect; their specific needs, interests, and wishes are considered; and their rehabilitation is a central concern. Possible specific needs of child victims might be having a group discussion whereby their harm is acknowledged, their behavior is validated, the perpetrator apologizes, and reparation is negotiated. The criminal justice process, as shown in Chapter 4, completely neglects many of these needs-rights, fails to address some of them even when considered, and often traumatizes children through their exposure to an unfriendly process as witnesses.

In contrast, restorative justice fits well, at least in the ideal, the needs-rights model for child victims. As this chapter will show, restorative justice offers an environment where victims are provided an opportunity to have significant control over the process that follows their victimization and its outcomes by being active partners in it. The victim's family, friends, and significant others are invited and encouraged to provide support, both during and after the process. The participants ideally listen to the victim's story, acknowledge the harm, and validate the victim's behavior. Issues of self-blame have the potential of being resolved as the victim is given an opportunity to discuss his or her behavior with sympathetic listeners. At the same time, offenders are expected to take full responsibility for the harm they have caused the victim, and ideally to apologize. Moreover, the flexible, creative nature of restorative justice allows a range of different processes and accommodations to meet the needs and varying coping preferences of different children, according to their age and specific needs. Of course, restorative processes occur only upon the offender's admission of the offense—which arguably would eliminate any of the victim's hardships in the criminal process described in the previous chapter. But restorative justice proponents claim that restorative justice expands the numbers of admissions, and the victims of those offenders who would plea guilty anyway benefit from a direct encounter, which the criminal justice process would deny.

Moreover, restorative justice might hold particular potential for young victims. The studies discussed in Chapter 3 by Call and Mortimer (2001) and Seiffge-Krenke

(1995), for example, suggest that to the extent that restorative justice processes provide an opportunity for different arenas of comfort to be strengthened and for new ones to be created, supporting young victims and acting as stress buffers, such processes are indeed valuable for victimized children. Indeed, there is evidence that in a restorative justice conference family ties can grow stronger (Burford & Pennell, 1998). Other people may become more sensitive to the child victim's difficulties following the crime and offer their friendship and support in more active ways. This by itself (notwithstanding the process outcomes with regard to the offender's behavior) might help children cope with stress.

At the same time, restorative justice may put children in vulnerable, or undesirable, situations. For example, without adequate preparation, support, and debriefing, children's sadness and pain might grow following their participation in a restorative process (Graham & Fitzgerald, 2005). Further, children do not always want to take part in decision-making processes and might prefer knowing that the decision has been made by a neutral, fair adult who provides them with full information about it later (Lawrence, 2003). Finally, concerns about pressuring victims to forgive their apologizing perpetrators should be addressed, especially when there are clear power imbalances between a young victim and an older offender or other participants. These concerns, as well as the potential benefits of restorative justice for child victims, should be explored in real-life situations. This chapter delves into the questions regarding whether, when, and in what conditions restorative justice is beneficial for child victims by looking at existing findings and analyzing them through a needs-rights perspective. It is clear, however, that much more child-centered research is needed before these questions can be fully addressed. Still, the theoretical framework combined with the findings presented here offer sufficient basis for the construction of small-scale child-inclusive restorative justice programs that, following appropriate testing, can be applied more broadly.

The chapter begins with a short description of the three most prevalent restorative processes: victim–offender mediation, conferencing, and circles. Next, it reviews five exemplary restorative justice programs involving child victims and discusses their levels of success, as well as the emerging challenges, in addressing the needs-rights of child victims. These documented experiences dealt restoratively with different crimes against children, including serious crimes such as child abuse, spousal abuse, and sexual assault. They were chosen because each one of them provides unique knowledge about aspects of childhood victimization, and together they offer a broad spectrum of examples regarding possible difficulties, as well as achievements, in the area.

New Zealand was chosen as the only jurisdiction whereby under national legislation all juvenile justice cases (except for murder and manslaughter) and child protection cases are dealt with through family group conferences (FGCs) as the default option. The wealth of knowledge that has been accumulated in this country, where since 1989 an attempt has been made to deal with most cases of juvenile offending restoratively, is invaluable. Beyond the "quantitative" advantage of having thousands of youth-offending cases (many of them involving child victims) to learn from, the fact that restorative justice is the baseline mechanism used in New Zealand at a national level can also tell us how a restorative approach affects a whole community. It can tell us, for example, whether reporting levels of crimes against children have changed as a result of the move toward a restorative system. It can also tell us whether the levels of youth crime in general have gone down (Sherman & Strang, 2007, p. 24). From a child victim perspective, a national restorative system may also reveal the risks (and advantages) of having restorative justice as the routine reaction to crimes committed by youths, rather than a specialized, small, or experimental program.

Australia followed New Zealand, and starting from the early 1990s all of its jurisdictions have been practicing restorative justice programs, either through legislation or local initiatives. The two Australian restorative justice schemes described in this chapter are examples of the two most common (and highly debated) restorative conferencing schemes. The Australian Capital Territory (ACT)'s Reintegrative Shaming Experiments (RISE) are unique for using randomized control groups for comparing court and conference experiences for victims and offenders. Beyond a review of the RISE project, this chapter uses unpublished information from it revealing the experiences of child victims participating in the study. South Australia was chosen mainly because of its routine use of family conferences to respond to juvenile offenses, including sexual assaults of children and adults, and the detailed qualitative and quantitative evaluation data available through the South Australian Juvenile Justice report.

Canada has been known for its innovative approach in restorative justice and its responsiveness to local initiatives, especially in Aboriginal communities (Goel, 2010). Two local Canadian projects, both addressing family violence and child abuse, are discussed in this chapter. The Community Holistic Circle Healing Program (CHCH) at the Hollow Water community in Manitoba was chosen because of its reputation as a successful community-based program designed to uncover and respond to intergenerational family abuse and violence. While not being tested in a purely scientific way, multiple reports of this program, some written by indigenous writers who themselves were child victims, indicate success in discovering and reducing family violence. At the same time, some concerns regarding the voices of women and children emerge and perhaps can be used as a warning sign for other programs with similar goals. The Newfoundland and Labrador Family Group Decision Making (FGDM) pilot project was chosen, despite the fact that it was active for only one year (1993–94), because of the "feminist praxis" it used to address violence against children and women, and the detailed evaluation accompanying this program. While not presented as an alternative to criminal proceedings, this program and its evaluation provide many insights about the unique concerns that emerge in sensitive and complex situations such as sexual and physical abuse of children by family members. Since the Newfoundland and Labrador FGDM project was practiced in a child protection context, a discussion on child protection restorative processes will precede its review.

The chapter further discusses the major concerns that emerge in relation to the involvement of child victims in restorative processes, and considers some of the possible solutions deployed in the case studies. The final section uses the needs-rights template to evaluate the picture emerging from these programs.

THREE MAJOR FORMS OF RESTORATIVE JUSTICE PROCESSES

As mentioned in Chapter 1, restorative justice is a process whereby parties with a stake in a specific offense (typically victims, offenders, and the affected community) collectively resolve how to deal with the aftermath of the offense and its implications for the future (Braithwaite, 1999; Marshall, 1999). The three processes most considered as restorative are victim–offender mediation, conferencing (or, in many cases, FGCs), and circles (Schiff, 2003; Strang, 2002). They are designed to put victims at the center, to encourage them to tell their stories, and to provide them with the opportunity to gain some control over the outcomes of the process. In most of these processes victims are also able to hear their family members and the offender's family condemning the crime and acknowledging their harm.

In *victim–offender mediation*, or victim–offender conferences (Zehr, 2002, p. 49), the offender and the victim meet, with the support of a mediator, and discuss the crime and its aftermath.[36] A restitution agreement is then reached. The mediator plays an active role in negotiating this agreement with the victim and the offender. The completion of the agreement is monitored in the follow-up phase (Umbreit, 1999).

Family group conferencing or family group decision making involves more participants. Typically, an FGC involves the offender, the victim, and their respective communities of support, including usually family members and friends, teachers, spiritual leaders, or others who have meaningful relationships with them. A facilitator provides the setting and leads the discussion, but otherwise leaves as much as possible of the discussion to the participants to work out for themselves. Other professionals, such as police and social workers, may also be present to provide information. The objective, however, is for the decisions to be made by the stakeholders, not the professionals. In some programs, an important part of the process is family private time, where professionals and other stakeholders leave the room, and the offender and his or her family remain to decide on a plan. After an agreement is reached, the other participants are invited in and the plan then needs to be approved by the facilitator.

Circles are yet a broader forum of decision making, in the sense that they create opportunities for the involvement of a whole indigenous community and its traditions. *Sentencing circles* are post-conviction mechanisms designed as an alternative to court sentencing hearings. They are practiced largely in indigenous communities in North America and in some jurisdictions in Australia as a means to rehabilitate offenders, reduce recidivism rates, and empower the community. The participants in sentencing circles are the victim and the offender, their families, community elders, and other community members, as well as state officials—the sentencing judge, defense attorney, public prosecutor, and often the social worker or probation officer. The participants sit together in a circle and talk about the offense and the desired outcome until a consensus is reached regarding the disposition. While the sentencing judge can decide to return the case to court, in practice judges rarely reject sentences proposed by a circle (Goel, 2010, p. 65). Sentencing circles hold political significance, as they are perceived as an opportunity for indigenous communities to regain their independence in controlling crime by themselves, highlight past injustices committed by the majority community, and reduce the numbers of incarcerated indigenous offenders (Goel, 2000, 2010). *Healing circles* are even more traditional variants of the circle paradigm, where non-indigenous judges do not sit in the circle with a veto power. The Hollow Water circles, for example, are often referred to as healing circles.

These three types of practices are "restorative" in both values and process, and involve a dialog between victims and offenders (Shapland, 2003, p. 197). Other procedures, such as community boards or panels, are often regarded as restorative, although they typically do not involve direct communication between the victim and the offender (Schiff, 2003). Since these partially restorative processes pose different questions and perhaps are less problematic (and less promising) from a child victim perspective, they will not be discussed in this chapter.

POTENTIAL BENEFITS OF RESTORATIVE JUSTICE FOR VICTIMS

As discussed in Chapter 3, the common needs and wishes of crime victims are having opportunities for meaningful participation, emotional and material reparation, and fair, respectful treatment (Shapland, 1984; Strang, 2002; Strang & Sherman, 2003). From a victim perspective, it seems that restorative justice processes, when conducted appropriately, may address these needs and rights better than a court process.

First, a central value of restorative justice is respect for people (Wemmers, 2009). This is not an obvious value; as we saw in the previous chapter, the criminal justice system treats victims as objects with at best evidentiary value. Vulnerable witnesses such as children are treated (again, at best) as objects of protection. To be treated as an individual subject of rights, with legitimate interests in the particular case and with valid expectations from the process and its outcomes, can be no less than a healing experience for victims.

A second core element of restorative justice is reparation (Wemmers, 2009). While material reparation is an expressed goal that most processes reach in a satisfactory way (Sherman & Strang, 2007), symbolic reparation, one of the most important needs of victims, is more difficult to achieve. Retzinger and Scheff (1996) argue that the "core sequence" of successful restorative justice processes, the basis for victims' satisfaction and healing and for offenders' rehabilitation, is the expression of shame and remorse by the offender and some (even partial) expression of forgiveness by the victim. This exchange of emotions is the basis for symbolic reparation. Indeed, restorative justice provides a natural setting for apology because of the informal, sometimes even intimate, nature of the gathering, which allows all parties to communicate face to face and exchange verbal as well as nonverbal messages (Brook & Warshwski-Brook, 2009).

Another benefit for crime victims of restorative justice is the opportunity to discharge their shame in constructive ways that can help them heal from their victimization (Ahmed et al., 2001). When facilitators are successful in channeling expressions of indignation and anger toward the offender into expressions of deeper emotions such as shame, fear, and grief, then victims can begin to overcome their shame and move on in their healing process (Retzinger & Scheff, 1996).

Finally, and perhaps most importantly, is the concept of participation, which in restorative justice means meaningful participation—partnership—of victims, offenders, and their supporters. From the victims' perspective, restorative justice processes provide an opportunity to engage in a safe, respectful, and nondominating deliberation regarding the crime and its outcomes. Opinions, feelings, and information are exchanged between the participants affecting each other until a consensual restoration plan is reached. This dialog and the active role victims take in it enables them to feel a sense of control over the process itself and its outcomes, which, as we saw in Chapter 3, is an important way to cope with stress and trauma.

How often does restorative justice fulfill its promise for crime victims? Despite great variations in restorative justice models and practices (Stubbs, 2010), studies are overwhelmingly consistent in showing that restorative justice provides significant benefits for victims in terms of measurements such as fairness, accountability, satisfaction, repentance and forgiveness, emotional wellbeing, and feelings of safety (Latimer et al., 2005; Poulson, 2003; Sherman & Strang, 2007; Strang, 2002; Strang et al., 2006).

Russ Immarigeon (1999) provides a literature review of victims' perspectives on restorative justice practices, particularly victim–offender mediation and FGCs. Summarizing numerous studies from Canada, the United States, Australia, and New Zealand on victims' satisfaction, perception of fairness, participation, and completion of restoration agreements, Immarigeon concludes that findings are significantly encouraging for victims. In Canada, for example, victims who met with their offenders in mediation programs were more likely to receive answers to their questions, more likely to value the offenders' apologies, more likely to negotiate restitution, and less likely to fear revictimization and remain upset about the crime and the offender. In the United Kingdom, victims who participated in direct mediation showed greater levels of satisfaction with the system; they found the apology, as well as the negotiation of restitution, important. Finally, in the United States a number of studies showed high satisfaction levels among victims who participated in mediation (Immarigeon, 1999, pp. 310–311).

Immarigeon further cites research conducted by Maxwell and Morris (1993) on FGCs for cases of youth crime, which showed that approximately 60% of participating victims found the conferences helpful. In general, victims felt better because they were included rather than excluded from the process. Some negative impacts were also identified among a quarter of the victims, but Maxwell and Morris argue that these findings challenge the implementation, rather than the concept, of FGCs.[37]

More recent reviews continue to present similarly—perhaps even more—positive results regarding the effects of restorative justice on victims and their satisfaction with it. In an assessment of all available, "reasonably unbiased" evidence of restorative justice,[38] Sherman and Strang (2007) conclude that "evaluation results almost always indicate a high level of satisfaction with the process, despite a wide range of rigour in those tests" (2007, p. 62). While a "small minority within well-conducted studies" felt that the restorative justice experience was counterproductive and made them feel worse, the authors state that "such strong and consistent positive findings about victim benefits in the great majority of cases lead us to conclude that victims will generally benefit from participation whenever they have the opportunity to do so" (Sherman & Strang, 2007, p. 62).

Crime reduction is another parameter for measuring the potential of restorative justice from victims' perspective, because public safety is clearly in victims' interest. Several meta-analytic reviews (Andrews & Bonta, 2003; Bonta et al., 2006; Smith et al., 2002) concluded that restorative justice interventions are associated with reductions in recidivism, although it is also known today that in some circumstances restorative justice might increase recidivism (Sherman, 2000; Sherman & Strang, 2007). Notwithstanding this cautionary finding, restorative justice can be positively considered as an appealing alternative for crime victims.

Particular Potential Benefits in Family Violence and Other Serious Crimes

Most empirical tests, however, have been conducted with restorative justice programs addressing minor to medium-level property and violent crimes. Very little is known regarding the effectiveness of restorative justice in cases of domestic violence, child abuse, and serious sexual crimes, based on either randomized assignment or a control group comparison (Cossins, 2008; Stubbs, 2010). The question, therefore arises: is restorative justice as beneficial for victims of such crimes as it is for victims of "trivial" (albeit sometimes serious) crimes? On the one hand, it seems that it is the disempowered victims who have the most to gain from it. On the other, perhaps the virtues of restorative justice are not that virtuous for victims of gendered crimes. A discussion on the concerns raised with regards to restorative justice in cases of family violence and sexual abuse will appear later in this chapter. First, however, it is worth considering the potential benefits of restorative justice, particularly in cases of domestic violence, child abuse, and sexual assault.

Perhaps the central benefit for victims in restorative justice is the sense of empowerment they achieve through telling their stories and being listened to. The empowerment experience might become an antidote for disempowerment, humiliation, and loss of control and is therefore particularly beneficial for victims of sexual assaults, who typically feel disempowered by the criminal justice system. As Barbara Hudson writes:

> All versions of restorative justice have at their center the opportunity provided for the victim to recount what the offence meant to her. Instead of giving evidence in answer to questions, having to follow rules and maintain relevance to the questions at issue, she is able to say whatever is important to her (Hudson, 2003, p. 179).

Lawrence Sherman (2000) suggests that restorative justice is likely to be effective in domestic violence cases if it is practiced in a manner compatible with the following theories of crime and crime prevention:

- John Braithwaite's reintegrative shaming theory (1989) is drawn from family life; family members who had "offended" are forgiven after their act has been condemned. Since in domestic violence it is likely that the relationships will continue after the victimization, Sherman (2000) argues, the "family" basis for analysis is most appropriate. The involvement of extended family members increases the opportunity and the effectiveness of shaming, while at the same time allowing the offender to be reintegrated as well.
- Tom Tyler's (1990) procedural justice theory suggests that offenders who perceive the legal process as unfair become angry and thus are more prone to reoffend. Conversely, offenders' feeling of being treated fairly may reduce reoffending, including in domestic violence cases. Restorative justice, Sherman (2000) claims, with its egalitarian nature is perceived as fairer (Strang & Braithwaite, 2002, p. 127) and therefore is likely to reduce reoffending.
- Routine activities theory (Cohen & Felson, 1979) suggests that offending is related to opportunities to offend, such as the presence of a suitable target with no capable guardians who could prevent a motivated offender from committing the crime. Restorative justice uses family and community members to monitor and support the offender and create positive opportunities for offenders to be involved in other activities. The use of the extended family to monitor family violence is likely to be very effective, Sherman (2000) argues, as relatives are able to have unplanned visits and have access to intimate information.

Accordingly, Sherman calls for careful experimentation of restorative justice in domestic violence cases, particularly when considering the unsatisfying results of the formal court system (Sherman, 2000, pp. 287–288).

Regarding non-family-related severe crimes, Alison Morris (2002b) argues that there are significant benefits in using restorative justice practices: restorative justice achieves denunciation of serious crimes through the presence of the abuser's family and friends, and it takes crime very seriously by focusing on its specific consequences and searches for meaningful ways of holding offenders accountable. Maxwell and Morris (2001) present data on two pilot projects in New Zealand, where community panel meetings with some restorative justice characteristics took place as diversion for adult offenders who had committed medium-serious offenses, mostly property and some violent crimes. The projects are unique in the seriousness of the offenses and the participation of repeat adult offenders. At 6 months and after a year, project offenders were less likely to be reconvicted and were involved in crimes that were less serious than those committed by control group offenders who were randomly referred to court.

At least in theory, then, restorative justice fits well with a needs-rights approach toward victims, and is even perhaps particularly beneficial (despite natural concerns) for victims of serious crimes. Those victims are most likely to yearn for respectful treatment, material and symbolic reparation, and opportunities to take an active role in the process and discharge their shame. More specifically with regard to participation and the related need of empowerment and a sense of control, restorative justice is predicated on these concepts and thus provides opportunities for victims to play an active role and have these rights-needs met, provided that power imbalance issues are addressed (Nixon et al., 2005, p. 34). Nevertheless, the controversy over the appropriateness (and risks) of restorative justice in the context of domestic violence, child abuse, and gender crimes continues, and questions regarding victims' safety, the prospects for conflict resolution, and risks of manipulations and pressure persist (Cossins, 2008; Stubbs, 2010). Although the debate focuses largely on women, much of it relates to abused children, who are either indirect victims of spousal abuse or direct victims of abuse by their caretakers (Schechter & Edleson, 1999). Does restorative justice pose similar benefits—or similar risks—for these child victims? Can it meet their needs-rights without exposing them to further harm? Aiming to contribute to the debate from a child-centered perspective, the next section explores empirical findings regarding the involvement of child victims in restorative justice programs.

RELEVANT RESTORATIVE JUSTICE EXPERIENCES

The previous section provided a brief overview of the various models of restorative justice and its central potential benefits for victims. Indeed, there are now sufficient data indicating that victims do much better through restorative processes than in the court. The next question is, then, is restorative justice as beneficial for child victims as it is for adults? In what circumstances is it mostly beneficial, and are there cases in which restorative justice may actually harm children? As already noted, there is a dearth of scientific knowledge regarding the involvement of children in restorative justice processes. Using the limited findings that are available, this section explores the experience accumulated in five different restorative justice initiatives in New Zealand, Australia, and Canada. All these programs have included child victims, some more than others; they have all been evaluated and therefore provide valuable lessons from their levels of success, and most of them (except the RISE experience) included sexual assaults against children, possibly the most controversial crime with regard to restorative justice (Cossins, 2008). Moreover, these programs provide a broad spectrum of approaches as they vary in their underlying theories as well as practice.

New Zealand

New Zealand was the first jurisdiction in the world to integrate the use of restorative justice into the mainstream of its juvenile justice system through the Children, Young Persons and Their Families Act of 1989. With this nationwide legislation, drawn from traditional Maori justice mechanisms, the broad use of FGCs in youth offending is unprecedented in the English-speaking world (Maxwell & Morris, 1993, p. 1). According to the Act, all juvenile offenders across New Zealand, with very limited exceptions, are referred to FGCs either by the police or the youth court. In 1998, for example, 6,309 youth justice referrals were made to FGCs (Maxwell et al., 2004, p. 26). The centrality of FGCs in the New Zealand youth justice system is reflected in the development of practical experience as well as a wealth of research, and has made New Zealand a world leader in the field.

At the heart of FGCs in New Zealand is the emphasis on the extended family, the *whanau*, as the central force in promoting the young offender's rehabilitation. But also central is the emphasis on the interests of the victim (Maxwell & Morris, 2006). Morris and Maxwell (1998) describe a typical FGC. It includes the young offender and his or her family members and supporters, the victim or victim's representative, a support person for the victim, the police, and a mediator—an employee of the Department of Social Welfare. At the start of the conference the facts are introduced and acknowledged by the offender; then all participants discuss the offense and its effects, the reasons for the offending, and the offender's background. There is family private time in which the offender and the offender's family make a proposed plan. This is later introduced to the rest of the participants, and if all is agreed, the plan is signed. A typical plan can include an apology, community work, reparation for the victim, or involvement in a rehabilitation program by the offender.

Earlier evaluations have raised some concerns. In 1990–91, approximately one-third of the victims said they felt worse as a result of attending the FGC, and less than a half were satisfied with the outcomes (Maxwell & Morris, 1993, pp. 119–120). Less than half of the conferences were attended by the victims. A third of the victims who did not attend said they had not been invited at all; others could not attend because of the timing of the conference or because they had not been informed early enough to make arrangements (Maxwell & Morris, 1993, p. 79). Other concerns related to the participation of young offenders: nearly half felt that they had not been involved in the process, and only about one third said that they felt involved (Maxwell & Morris, 1993, p. 109). This result is of concern in the context of child victims as it may be related to any child–adult dynamics, including those between an adult offender and a child victim. Indeed, the researchers commented that the young people who were asked about their involvement in the process replied in a way that indicated that:

> they were either excluded by the adults present (literally by the adults ignoring them almost entirely or by the way in which adults asked questions) or that they did not feel able to participate through feelings of shame, embarrassment or simply not knowing what to say (Maxwell & Morris, 1993, p. 110).

Furthermore, Maxwell and Morris noted that parents felt more involved in the process than the young offenders, and suggested that these differences in views reflect parents' belief that it was inappropriate for their child to participate in the decision-making process (Maxwell & Morris, 1993, p. 111).

These results raised some concerns against expanding and applying the FGC practice in other jurisdictions and in other crimes. In particular, the suitability of FGC for sensitive matters such as family violence was questioned. Low victim participation and satisfaction have been seen as reflecting an offender-oriented initiative. Power imbalances, victims' safety and a higher risk of victimization when the conference is unsuccessful, and facilitators who themselves are too threatened to address offenders' behavior have been some of the main concerns (Busch, 2002).

Reflecting back, however, Morris (2002a, p. 92) argues that these results came from poor practice and failure to implement restorative justice values, rather than from a failure of conferencing itself. Indeed, the early evaluations emphasized the importance of preparing families and victims before the conference so that they know what to expect, and commented that this had not been done in many cases (Maxwell & Morris, 1993, pp. 85–86). For example, victims who were asked to be the first to speak at the conference felt intimidated and were caught unprepared (Maxwell & Morris, 1993, p. 88). Alternatively, positive feelings of victims were linked with careful briefings prior to the conference, involvement in the process, having an opportunity to release bad feelings, being able to affect the outcomes, and having the opportunity to confront the offender and the offender's family (Maxwell & Morris, 1993, p. 118).

Another concern that Morris (2002a) regards as practice-related is power imbalances between youth offenders and others at the conference. Technically, argues Morris, all members are present at the FGC, but in fact, on occasions, the young offender's views are overlooked by the families. This, however, can be resolved if young people are actively encouraged and supported to speak and are listened to by the adults. This specific concern is again of general relevance for child victims, as it is a typical problem in many child–adult communications.

The Final Report on the New Zealand Youth Justice System Project (Maxwell et al., 2004) delivered somewhat better results. About half of the young offenders felt involved in the decision-making process. While two thirds felt that they were able to say what they wanted, over a third felt too intimidated to say what they wanted to say (Maxwell et al., 2004, pp. 123–126). In a program that puts the stakeholders' participation at the center, these may not be considered highly satisfactory results. Some examples of young offenders' expressions were "He spoke to Dad the whole time, not me" and "I wish my Mum had not talked so much" (Maxwell et al., 2004, p. 126). In one out of five cases, some of the participants were overlooked—mainly family members, with the young person himself or herself being ignored in some of these conferences. The police or coordinators dominated these discussions (Maxwell et al., 2004, p. 172). With victims, the situation was relatively better: over a half felt involved in making decisions, and 86% felt they had the opportunity to say what they wanted (Maxwell et al., 2004, p. 155). Still, however, these data present quite disappointing outcomes with regard to both victims' and offenders' participation, particularly when compared with other programs (Kurki, 2003; Poulson, 2003; Sieppert et al., 2000). They might be related to the fact that in over half of the conferences, the observers noted that the youth justice coordinator was one of the most dominant figures in determining the final decision, in contrast with his or her originally prescribed role

(Maxwell et al., 2004, p. 169). Youth advocates, in contrast, were seen as less dominating and as playing positive roles in informing young offenders and speaking on their behalf (Maxwell et al., 2004, p. 171).

Concluding that the successes, and failures, of FGCs in New Zealand are predominately practice-related, the New Zealand evaluation group pointed to the following effective practices that were correlated with positive outcomes for families and victims (Maxwell et al., 2004, p. 302):

- Participants are well prepared for the conference.
- Participants are greeted and introduced, and encouraged to be actively involved.
- Participants understand what is happening at the conference.
- Participants are treated fairly and with respect.
- Participants are able to have an input on the outcomes.
- Participants experience genuine remorse from the offender and believe the offender will try to make up for the crime and refrain from reoffending.

On a systemic level, a more optimistic picture emerges. Soon after the introduction of the Children, Young Persons and Their Families Act of 1989, the number of court cases involving young offenders dropped markedly, and so did the figures describing custodial sentences against them (Maxwell & Morris, 2006). Despite some increase in both measures in the beginning of the 21st century, still the data clearly indicate that young offenders are now diverted away from the criminal justice system and from prisons in New Zealand. Perhaps more indicative is the decline in police apprehension of both children and youths between 1995 and 2007, with 2007 having the lowest apprehension rates since 1995 (Duncan, 2009).

South Australia

South Australia in 1993 was the first Australian state to enact a restorative justice law, incorporating conferences as one of the responses to youth crime (Daly, 2001). The South Australia Young Offenders Act of 1993 adopted, with some modifications, the New Zealand model, and conferences are run by facilitators under the youth court umbrella. The South Australian family conferences scheme is unique for its inclusion of a wide array of juvenile crimes, and data on its outcomes (Daly, 2001, 2002; Daly et al., 1998, 2003; Daly & Stubbs, 2006) are illuminating regarding the experiences of child victims of sexual assaults committed by siblings, peers, or stranger juvenile offenders.

The Young Offenders Act of 1993 provides discretionary authority to the police in referring "minor" criminal offenses committed by a "juvenile" (aged 10 to 17) to an FGC. Since the definition of "minor offense' has been left open for police interpretation, the police refer quite serious cases to conferences, including sexual offenses (Daly et al., 1998). This enabled Kathleen Daly's research group to conduct systematic archival research describing court and conference cases of sexual offenses. The research included documents concerning all South Australian finalized cases between January 1995 and June 2001 that involved juvenile offenders charged with at least one sexual offense, categorized as cautioned, court-handled, or conference-handled.

The total number of sex-offense cases was 387. In general, the more serious crimes were court-handled and the least serious ones were cautioned, leaving conferencing at the "middle" level. However, an analysis of the seriousness of the crimes "proved"[39] shows that the legal seriousness (maximum sentence expected for the offense) of proved crimes in court cases was reduced to the same legal seriousness of conference cases. Plea bargains (the defendant's agreement to plea guilty for a lesser crime) or incomplete evidence led to this erosion between the original charge and the proved offense, an erosion that did not happen in conference cases (Daly et al., 2003, p. 7). Additionally, of the cases referred to court, only 51% were finalized (by either admission or proof). Almost all conferences, in contrast, resulted in admissions made by the offender. Furthermore, the more serious the offense, the less likely it was to be proved in court (Daly et al., 2003, p. 8). This finding is somewhat different from data published by the South Australian Attorney General's Department cited by Daly in an earlier publication, according to which only one-third of sexual offenses referred to the youth court were finalized during 1998 (Daly, 2002). This difference may result from the smaller number of cases analyzed in the 2001–03 study, as well as the longer period studied there (years 1995–2001). Whether the disposition rate is closer to a third or to a half of the cases, Daly and coworkers (2003, p. 4) emphasize that among the conference cases, no fewer than 94% were finalized, and therefore conference victims (and in particular victims of severe crimes) had more chances of hearing the crime being acknowledged during that process.

It is important to remember, however, that cases in this study were not randomly assigned to either court or conference, and therefore any conclusion should be qualified by the selection bias concern. In particular, since admission is a precondition for referring a case to a conference, it is only natural that admissions (and apologies) were expressed almost exclusively in conferences and not in court proceedings. It would be imprudent, then, to conclude that conference cases have more chances of being finalized because of the nature of the process.

Daly and coworkers' findings are nonetheless important in describing what happens in each process and the characteristics of each. One important finding is victims' ages. The median age in all cases was between 8.6 and 13 years. Conference cases had the youngest victims, with 16% being under 5. Moreover, the age gap between victims and offenders was higher in conference cases (median of 6.1 years vs. 4.2 in court cases). Interestingly, conference cases had a higher rate of intrafamilial cases, with babysitter and caretaker cases included in this category (Daly et al., 2003, p. 11). Most conference victims received an apology from the offender, whether verbally or in writing; this was rarely the case in the court process. Further, a higher rate of conference offenders were ordered to stay away from victims compared with court offenders (Daly et al., 2003, p. 17). Ninety-four percent of conference offenders complied with their undertakings. It took twice as long for court cases to be finalized compared with conferences (Daly et al., 2003, p. 19). Daly and her colleagues emphasize that on average, sexual offense victims would have to attend court 6 times, and nearly 20% would have to attend 10 times or more (Daly et al., 2003, p. 20). They conclude that:

> Conferences have the potential to offer victims a greater degree of justice than court. The YP's [Young Person] admission to the offence serves as an important public validation of the harm suffered by the victim, and the conference offers a forum for apology and reparation. For victims whose cases go to court, half will

> be disappointed (and perhaps angry and disillusioned) when charges are withdrawn or dismissed after lengthy proceedings. On all measures of what YPs have to do for victims (apology), for the community (community service), and for themselves (Mary Street counselling),[40] it appears that conferences outperform court . . . our data suggest that the court, not conference, is the site of cheap justice (Daly et al., 2003, pp. 20–21).

Once again, however, it should be noted that since cases were referred to either court, caution, or conference according to police discretion and not randomly, many of these differences may be attributed to characteristics of the offender (such as admission of guilt) or the offense, rather than to the process itself.

Earlier research work by Daly's group included two waves of conference observations and interviews, one in 1998 and one in 1999 (Daly, 2001). Focusing on property and violence (including sexual) offenses, the research goal was not to compare outcomes with those of court cases, but to study the procedure itself, the relationship between participants' social status and their perception of the process, the relationship between the victim and the offender, and the connection between the perception of the conference as "fair" with its level of success (Daly, 2001).

In general, results from this research were positive for victims in terms of victim satisfaction and victims' reduced anger and fear. However, not all victims benefited from conferencing. Conference observers commented that 11% of the conferences "revictimized" victims.[41] Observers also noted that in eight cases (9% of the observed conferences), participants intimidated others, with the offender intimidating the victim in three of them (Daly, 2001).[42] In the interviews conducted later, 18% of the victims said they felt upset after the conference by what the offender or the offender's supporters had said. Additionally, 13% of the victims noted in their interviews that they felt they had been "pushed into things."

These findings show that while most victims benefit from conferences and are satisfied with them, for some, conferences might be a negative, even harmful experience (Cossins, 2008). Children might be particularly vulnerable to intimidation, pressure, and silencing.

The South Australian Family Conference Team practitioners provide some "inside information" about the dynamics in sexual offense conferences (Doig & Wallace, 1999). They indicate that conferences were particularly useful in dealing with sexual offenses when there were existing relationships between offender and victim and when there were prospects of future contact, as with offenses by siblings or other family members.[43] When the victim was a child, preparations included discussions with the parents about possible ways to have the child's viewpoint heard and considered at the conference, sometimes with an appointed counselor to represent the child. Victims as young as 9 participated in conferences, and team members found that with adequate counseling and parental support, their participation often had a powerful role:

> For example, a 9-year-old girl whose brother had been forcing her to have sexual intercourse for several months, and who, when she had disclosed the abuse, had been accused by her father of "leading her brother on," decided that she wanted to be at the family conference. She found it very satisfying to hear her brother admit to his abusive behavior and was able to confront her father about how he

had made her feel; and both her brother and her father apologized to her during the conference (Doig & Wallace, 1999).

Doig and Wallace (1999) add that when an offense had been committed by one family member against another, often parents (particularly mothers) were required to take sides during the criminal justice process. In conferences, they argue, as the offense was condemned independently from the offender, this was not needed. Parents could support both offender and victim, while condemning the act at the same time.

The Australian Capital Territory

Conferences in the Australian Capital Territory (ACT) more or less followed the "Wagga" model, named after the first restorative justice program in Australia, which was conducted in Wagga Wagga, New South Wales (Daly, 2001). Accordingly, conferences in the ACT were facilitated, until 2004, by the police and were not statute-based.[44] Conceptually, they were heavily influenced by John Braithwaite's reintegrative shaming theory (Braithwaite, 1989). RISE used a randomized experimental design to compare outcomes of court and conference cases in property, violence, and drunk-driving offenses (Strang, 2002). The RISE researchers were able to make definite conclusions regarding the effects of restorative justice on both victims and offenders because the randomized referral to either court or restorative justice processes ensured that no other preexisting variables—expected (such as admission, remorse, and accountability) or unexpected—influenced the outcomes.

Restorative justice was found usually to be beneficial for victims (Strang & Sherman, 2003, p. 42). Victims were found to benefit from conferences in the areas most important for them: meaningful involvement in the process, an opportunity to meet with the offender and receive an apology, emotional and material reparation, an increased sense of safety, closure and healing, and finally being treated with fairness and respect (Strang & Sherman, 2003). The most significant benefits for victims were found in the emotional aspects of healing and restoration. Offenders too were satisfied with the process and felt it was fair and respectful. Restorative justice, accordingly, was described as a "win–win situation" for both victims and offenders (Strang, 2002, p. 200).

As to the effectiveness of restorative justice in crime prevention, conferences that followed violent offenses were shown to reduce reoffending rates dramatically, in comparison to the randomly assigned court cases (Sherman et al., 2000). The results were negative, however, in property and to a lesser extent in drunk-driving crimes (Sherman et al., 2000).

Child Victims in RISE

RISE provides important data in the current context for two major reasons. First, its rigorous design ensures reliable comparisons between court and conference cases, without being vulnerable to selection bias concerns. Second, most files include a combination of police reports, conference observations, and questionnaires answered by both victims and offenders, thus revealing much of what "actually happened." It did not, however, differentiate between adult and minor victims in the application of court or conference treatment. Nor did the RISE researchers make any concrete reference to the distinct experiences of victims who were under the age of 18 while participating in the experiment. To fill this gap, and while residing in Canberra where the experiment took place, I later examined all the RISE files dealing with property and violence offenses against child victims.[45]

The RISE data are drawn from 175 cases of property offenses and 100 cases of violence offenses.[46] There were two "waves" of interviews. A first wave was conducted shortly after the disposition through court or conference, a second wave 2 years later (Strang, 2002, pp. 66, 74). Five property cases and 28 violence cases involved children and youth as victims, either as primary victims or jointly with adults. Given the limited number of cases, I did not attempt to draw statistical conclusions. Still, the general impression was that, like the general population of the study (adults and children), conference child victims were more satisfied, stated more often that their rights had been respected, and reported greater emotional healing than court child victims. Exploring the files, however, it was possible to identify a few cases that went wrong. The following discussion addresses the issues and concerns that arose in those less-successful cases in which child victims were involved, as well as in some court cases in which young victims were involved. Because the examples describing restorative processes involving young victims are so sparse in the literature, each case is brought in a relatively detailed manner, providing a glimpse into the "banal" victimization of children and its outcomes.

Parent–Child Differences

One issue of concern emerging from the RISE materials is the role of parents in representing the child victim, and the different ways children and their parents experience conferences. In some of the RISE cases parents were very interested in holding the conference. They spoke on behalf of the child throughout the conference and reported a high level of satisfaction—while the child was not satisfied and felt that there was no restoration. Conversely, when parents prohibited their child from participating in a conference against the child's will, again the conference received low scores in the victim's interview. Dependence on the guardian's consent is unique to child victims, and the presumption that the parents' decision would always promote the child's best interests, and even more so the child's wishes, is naïve. Although it is impossible to make decisive conclusions based on the following examples, they are clearly in line with the discussions in earlier chapters on the right and need of children to participate in decision-making processes affecting their lives, in a way that is attuned to their needs and wishes, and to have a sense of control in the process. Perhaps these examples highlight the need to grant some autonomy for victims who are under the age of 18 but are beyond a certain age, say 16, and let them participate (or not) in conferences even when their parents think they should not (or should). Perhaps they are reminders of the importance to speak directly with young victims participating in conferences, even when their parents seem to represent their views effectively: we have seen that meaningful participation is not only a way to achieve the desired outcomes, but, even more importantly, a coping mechanism, an opportunity to experience procedural justice, and a way of managing shame and resolving questions of blame and fear.

Examples:

- In case #JVC081,[47] an 18-year-old victim had been punched in the jaw by a neighbor in what seemed to be an ongoing dispute. As a result, the victim was hospitalized, underwent surgery, and consequently missed a job interview.

The observer's notes portray a positive conference but commented that the victim's mother did most of the talking. When asked about the incident, the victim described the facts briefly. Then his mother gave a very graphic and emotional account of what had happened to him afterwards, with the hospitalization, not being able to eat, going through physiotherapy, and needing orthodontic work as well. It seemed that the mother's account was what changed the atmosphere and made the offender feel genuine remorse and to apologize. Toward the end of the conference the offender's supporters suggested that the two shake hands. The offender did this willingly and apologized again. The victim cooperated and simply said, "That's OK." At the interview, however, the victim reported that he felt dissatisfied and angry and was suffering various physical damage, such as sleeplessness and headaches, which the conference did little to repair. He felt the conference had been "somewhat fair" and that he could influence its outcomes, but at the same time said he felt awkward during the conference, regretted not being repaid, and was dissatisfied with the outcome. He was very unforgiving toward the offender, whose apology was "somewhat" sincere, did not feel that he could put the incident behind him, and felt that the offender had not learned a lesson. His mother, in contrast, thought the apology was sincere.

- In case #JPP155, a 13-year-old victim joined his parents in the conference following a theft at their home. The child reported that the reason he had come to the conference was "because Dad said I had to go." The RISE observer commented on this file that the offender was going to court two days later on another matter, and therefore there was very little cooperation on his side. Furthermore, the observer commented that there was some pressure from the conference facilitator to reach an agreement: "He just said—is that all right with you? And we didn't like to say it wasn't." Perhaps not surprisingly, the child was not very satisfied, felt he could not influence the conference outcomes, felt too intimidated to speak freely, did not have enough control, and felt pushed around by other people. The young victim felt that the conference respected his rights a little, that it had been unhelpful, and that his emotional condition remained the same afterward.
- A contrary example is case #JVC007, in which a 17-year-old boy had been assaulted in a fight. As a result of the assault he suffered an eye injury and was treated in a hospital. The victim's parents did not want their son to take part in the conference, and consequently the case was referred instead to caution. The "first wave" interview revealed a very negative experience for this young victim. He reported that he had not been given any information about what would happen and what was expected of him. He "strongly disagreed" that he could trust the police during the case. The offender had not apologized to him (which is not surprising since a direct encounter never happened). The victim reported feeling very dissatisfied, angry, and bitter. As a result of the way his case was handled, his respect for the police went down a little. He scored very low on all the questions regarding trust in others and said he anticipated that the offender would reoffend against someone else. He "strongly agreed" that as a result of the offense he suffered a loss of dignity, self-respect, and self-confidence. Other negative effects the victim reported

of were fear of being alone, sleeplessness, headaches and other physical symptoms, general increase of suspicion or distrust, loss of confidence, and loss of self-esteem. Although it is possible that this specific victim had preexisting difficulties that affected his reaction to the non-delivered conference, it is equally possible that participating in a conference as he had hoped to would have given him some redress. Notwithstanding the uncertainty regarding this victim, his case is a reminder of the concern of overprotecting young victims and declining their wishes to participate in face-to-face conferences with their perpetrators.

Victim Exclusion

Parents' overprotectiveness is not the only reason why young victims might miss an opportunity to participate at a restorative justice process. Other reasons can be more trivial, such as a system's failure to deliver a timely invitation. This was probably the case in the following example, which tells us what might happen to victims who were promised a conference but never had the chance to participate in it.[48]

In case #JVC076, a conference followed a violent threat with a knife pulled on a 17-year-old victim after he had not returned shoes to the offender's friend. The observer's comments describe a very positive, fruitful conference for the offender and his family. The victim, however, was not well informed prior to the conference and did not attend the conference. Consequently, the victim reported being very dissatisfied, angry, and bitter; he also reported suffering loss of trust, confidence, and self-esteem, which were not healed by the conference. Naturally, the offender did not apologize to him, and the victim expected the offender to reoffend against someone else. As a result of the way his case was handled, his respect for the law and the justice system went down.

Gaps between Satisfaction and Emotional Healing of Victims

An interesting gap repeatedly appeared in several court and conference cases involving child victims. Some victims reported high levels of satisfaction but low levels of emotional healing. Why did this happen? Let's begin with looking at the *court* cases:

- In case #JVC004 a 13-year-old victim had been assaulted by two brothers. The case was dealt with in court, and the victim did not attend the hearing. He reported being very satisfied with the process and the outcome. However, he also reported feeling frightened and sleepless, suffering headaches or other physical symptoms, coupled with a loss of confidence.
- In case #JVC019 a 15-year-old girl had been assaulted by another girl, resulting in a broken nose. The case was dealt with in court. The victim did not attend the court hearing; she said she would have gone had she been informed about. The victim reported feeling satisfied in the "first wave" and very satisfied in the "second wave" interviews. However, many of the emotional problems reported in the first interview were still bothering her 2 years later.
- In case #JVC025 a 17-year-old girl had been attacked by two males near a bus stop. The case was referred to court, and the offenders were given a 12-month good behavior bond. The observer's comments reveal that the

victim went to court to attend the hearing with her mother but was not allowed to enter the courtroom. Nevertheless, the victim was satisfied with the outcome, was glad the case had been referred to court and not to a conference, and thought the offenders had learned their lesson. At the same time, she reported being very upset and bitter about the process and the fact she could not participate in it, and feeling afraid that one of her offenders would attack her again. She also reported suffering from sleeplessness, headaches, and feelings of distrust.

In all of these three cases, the victims did not attend the court hearing, most likely because the offenders were juveniles and therefore their cases were adjudicated *in camera*. In all of these cases, the victims reported having emotional and some physical problems, although they were satisfied with the process. It is interesting to see that a similar gap appeared among the *conference* victims:

- In case #JVC051, a 17-year-old boy had been assaulted and attended the resultant conference with his mother. The mother reported being very dissatisfied, explaining that the offender's parents were not at the conference and that his only supporters were his peers. In the atmosphere that was created, she explained, there was no denouncing of the offense and it was impossible for them to communicate effectively and reflect on the criminal nature of the offender's behavior. The victim himself reported being quite satisfied. At the same time, he stated that he felt too intimidated to speak freely at the conference. He further reported fears of being left alone, headaches, and loss of self-esteem and self-confidence, and felt less trusting. The victim also stated that his sense of security had not been restored and that the conference was not helpful in solving these problems.
- In case #JPP129, a 17-year-old had been one of several victims of Internet fraud. The victim did not attend the consequent conference, but nevertheless received compensation and an apology from the offenders. It was interesting to discover that despite the victim's satisfaction and perception of the process as very fair, he reported in the "second wave" interview ("first wave" was not conducted) a loss of trust along with feelings of insecurity and suspicion, from which he did not recover at all.

In these conference examples, again, either the victim did not attend (as in the case of the Internet fraud) or there was a problem in communicating with the offender, and there was strong dissatisfaction by the victim's mother (as in the first case). Similar to the above-mentioned court victims, these conference victims experienced only minimal healing from their harm, even when they reported high levels of satisfaction. This raises the question whether, despite low expectations of young victims to take active part in the decision-making process, their participation is crucial for their emotional healing. In other words, perhaps children are not used to (and are not trained or encouraged to) being active partners in decision-making processes regarding their own matters. Nevertheless, facilitators should perhaps encourage them not only to attend but also to express their views in conferences, as their meaningful participation may prove important for their healing. Naturally, these are merely anecdotal cases, but they are in line with what the literature showed us in Chapter 3: that a sense of control and a positive, supportive group discussion may act as antidotes for trauma, although children and youths are not always clear about wanting to participate in decision-making processes.

Victims with Special Needs

Unsuccessful conferences in which special measures were not taken to address the specific needs of victims may be very harmful for them. The following case provides an example of the need to ensure that facilitators are well trained and that conferences are sufficiently equipped to meet the needs of physically, mentally, or emotionally challenged victims. This is a key requirement not only for ensuring the conference success in these situations, but also for protecting the right to equality of all children, including those with special needs, and specifically the accessibility of such conferences to all children.

- In case #JVC016, a 17-year-old mentally disabled boy had been punched in his head outside the nightclub he was attending. The case was referred to a conference. The observer commented that the conference was very poorly conducted, and that the facilitator did not manage to support the boy's participation, although it seems that in a better setting he could have managed well. As part of the restoration plan, the offender was expected to invite the victim for a meal at McDonald's, despite the victim's fear of him. When looking at the responses given by the victim in the questionnaire, it was striking that in all indicators the conference was a failure from the victim's perspective. Most importantly, the victim reported that he had not understood the process, that his views were not respected, and that he was pushed into the decision that was made. He further stated that the conference was very unfair and that he was not treated with respect. He also reported feeling afraid and angry at the offender after the conference. His trust in others was very low, and he stated that following the conference he was a little less trusting than before. The conference was also not helpful for the victim in overcoming his emotional harms and provided no sense of "closure" for the victim. The "second wave" interview revealed considerable emotional harm and anger. According to the victim, meeting the offender at the conference was "a major upset; I would never do it again." Following the conference, the RISE observer reported that the McDonald's meeting never took place; apparently there was never any intention on the part of the victim, or his mother, that this would happen, but they chose not to argue about it in the conference. They evidently felt so disempowered by the time of the outcome agreement that they just wanted the conference to end.[49]

The Significance of Expressing Emotions

Some "emotional" conferences, in which participants spoke freely about their feelings and could express their emotions without embarrassment (such as weeping), were very successful for the victim, even when the outcomes did not include significant material restoration. This is not surprising, considering the literature reviewed in Chapter 3 regarding the benefits of a direct interaction with the perpetrator in which shame is discharged, harm is acknowledged, and apology and forgiveness are exchanged. This fact is important as often adults want to protect children from emotional experiences, worrying that they might cause them further trauma. The following examples are reminders of the potential benefits of such emotional experiences for young victims:

- In case #JPP106 a unique coat had been stolen from a 15-year-old victim by another girl. After a very emotional conference (according to the observer's comments), the victim stated that the process had "helped a lot" toward healing from her emotional harm. She reported that the conference had been very fair and helpful. In the "second wave" interview she reported feeling very satisfied, stated that she was fully rehabilitated from her emotional injuries, and said that meeting the offender had been "a major upset but felt better afterward."
- In case #JVC075, a 17-year-old girl had been struck by another schoolmate, an assault that was the culmination of an ongoing social conflict between the two girls. During a long and emotional conference the offender apologized and the two discussed the sources of their dispute. Following the conference the victim reported feeling very satisfied with it. She stated that it had helped her a lot in healing from her emotional harm, that she felt safer, and that her sense of dignity was increased.

Technical Issues

Finally, the following case demonstrates how ostensibly minor technical failures may add up to complete disaster. The physical environment, room temperature, seating arrangements, preventing any unnecessary delays, and other operational matters should be thoroughly thought through prior to the process, because, for conference participants coming from different backgrounds with varying sensitivities and heavy loads of stress, fear, and anger, small problems may be experienced as detrimental. Indeed, if we take the needs of the participants seriously and treat them with respect, then both minor issues of comfort (such as separate waiting areas) and major ones (such as translation services) should receive due attention.

- In case #JVC032, a conference was held after a 16-year-old boy had been punched twice in the face by a young adult. The offender was an uncle of an 11-year-old boy whom the victim had previously pushed. The assault resulted in some serious injury in the victim's nose and he was later hospitalized for surgery. The conference was apparently so badly organized that it was one of the original study's examples of failed conferences, described in detail (see Strang, 2002, pp. 146–148). All parties had to wait outside the conference room in the same waiting area in the police station for a considerable amount of time before its commencement, a situation that made the victim feel very uncomfortable. During the conference, the offender's family did not speak much English and spoke Cambodian to each other, leaving the victim and his family feeling alienated and not understanding much of the discussion. Perhaps most importantly, the offender did not show any remorse and kept arguing that the victim was as responsible as he was for what had happened. Not surprisingly, the interview

> showed very bad results from the victim's viewpoint. As a result of the offense, the victim suffered loss of dignity, headaches and other physical symptoms, and a general increase in suspicion to others. The conference was not at all helpful in overcoming these difficulties or in repairing the harm done to him. According to the questionnaire, the victim felt awkward during the conference. He felt that the conference did not make the offender understand the harm he had caused him and did not take into account the harm he had suffered. Although the offender apologized, the victim thought this was not at all sincere (the victim's mother later said that she assumed that the letter of apology, prepared as part of the conference outcome, was written by someone else [see Strang, 2002, p. 147]). He felt that the conference was only somewhat fair and respected his rights "a little." He was very unsatisfied with the way it was handled, was very angry and bitter, regretted that his case was assigned to a conference, and would not choose to attend a conference again. The victim was also very unforgiving, very angry, and very unsympathetic with the offender after the conference. As a result of his experience with the case, his respect for the justice system and for the law went down a lot, and his own sense of dignity was reduced a little after the conference.

The concerns that surfaced from the RISE files highlight some of the challenges involving the participation of young victims in restorative justice practices. While they should not be regarded as exhaustive due to the small number of cases analyzed, these issues deserve consideration.

At a minimum, these cases demonstrate that at least for some young victims being involved in the process that follows their victimization is desirable and appropriate. These cases tell us what we have already known from the literature reviewed in earlier chapters: that participation in restorative conferences should not be prohibited for young victims simply because of their age. Furthermore, and again in accordance with the literature, some of these cases are reminders that participation can be an important and effective step in the healing process. In other words, active participation is not only something that some young victims *want,* it is something that they often *need* for their emotional recovery. This is not surprising, considering the empirical findings and theories regarding the importance of control, procedural justice, and direct interaction with the perpetrator, discussed in Chapter 3.

One of the differences between adults and children is that children do not always know the extent to which they are allowed, and able, to have an input in the conference outcomes, nor are they critical when denied such an opportunity. It is important to remember that children are not active participants in decision-making processes in their daily lives. Adults make decisions for them regularly, regarding their education, health, lifestyle, and so forth. It should come as no surprise then that some children have low expectations for active participation in restorative conferences, and that they may not articulate disappointment when not provided adequate opportunities to have a say in the process. Nevertheless, the limited recovery of these children supports the arguments regarding children's psychological needs to have some control over the process, to meet the offender, and to exchange information. To use the psychosocial terminology presented in Chapter 3, children might perceive these processes as uncontrollable and use secondary control coping mechanisms only (controlling their own behavior and feelings) instead of believing that they can influence the process and participating in it more meaningfully. These "passive" attributions and behaviors are typically less effective in dealing with emotional difficulties (see p. 71), which perhaps might explain the persistent negative symptoms of children who did not have meaningful participation. These of course are not conclusive findings, but rather speculations that warrant further testing. It is possible to suggest, however, that at least for some children, merely having the option of being present at a conference is not enough. Child victims should be well prepared and informed, and facilitators should be creative and flexible in order for these young victims to have meaningful participation in restorative conferences. If the child's healing is a central goal of the process, then his or her participation must be actively pursued.

A further point of interest is the appropriateness of regarding parents as their children's representatives speaking on their behalf in restorative conferences. While it is only natural to seek the parents' opinions regarding their child's participation at a restorative conference, the parents' opinions do not always correspond with those of the young victims. Often children and their parents disagree, and at a minimum there should be room for considering the child's opinion, if not accepting it. Some of the cases discussed here demonstrate that parents do not always represent their child's wishes, nor are they aware of their child's psychological need to be actively involved in the process. Moreover, at the conference itself it may be easier to turn to the parents on different matters; parents may also volunteer their opinions more easily than their children, and facilitators naturally assume that their opinions are compatible with those of the child. But if the child's active participation at the conference is important for his or her healing, then turning to the parent defeats the purpose. Children should therefore be encouraged to express their views at every stage of the conference, even when it seems that the parent represents the child's opinion.

Hollow Water

The Hollow Water Community Holistic Circle Healing (CHCH) program in Manitoba, Canada, is notable for its success in promoting the wellbeing of an entire community afflicted by intergenerational violence and abuse. It has not been evaluated in any systematic methodology, although there are detailed descriptions of its evolution, as well as some indications regarding its successes and potential risks (Couture, 2001; Lajeunesse, 1993; Roberts & Roach, 2003; Ross, 1996). It is worthwhile exploring, however, since unlike the other case studies this is a community circle sentencing program initiated and conducted in and by an Aboriginal community, which has demonstrated significant achievements in uncovering and combating family abuse.

The program was initiated in 1984, when a group of professionals from within and outside the community hoped to address behavioral problems of community youths. Gradually it became clear that the children had been facing problems in their homes, including alcohol and drug abuse and violence. A more thorough inquiry into the problematic behaviors of the parents revealed a broader picture of intragenerational sexual abuse. To address this reality, the team members began to work together to unravel the secrets and heal the victimizers and the victims. Abusers were encouraged to admit their crimes and to go through a healing process before being sentenced by the court, and most abusers chose this option instead of pleading not guilty and facing a trial. One of the greatest achievements of the team was the large numbers of admissions, which would never have been reached through the criminal justice system (Braithwaite, 1999, p. 16). Furthermore, out of 48 cases of admission, only 5 did not successfully complete the program (Ross, 1996, p. 36).

The 13 stages of the healing process, which typically takes 2 to 5 years, include:

> the initial disclosure of abuse, protecting the child, confronting the victimizer, assisting the (non-offending) spouse, assisting the families of all concerned, coordinating the team approach, assisting the victimizer to admit and accept responsibility, preparing the victim, victimizer and families for the Special Gathering, guiding the Special Gathering through the creation of a Healing Contract, implementation of the Healing Contract and, finally, holding a Cleansing Ceremony designed, in their words, to mark 'the completion of the Healing Contract, the restoration of balance to the victimizer, and a new beginning for all involved' (Ross, 1996, pp. 32–33).

The Canadian Solicitor General's report on the Hollow Water experience provides some indications as to its success. Of the 91 offenders who have been charged and processed through the project, only 2 reoffended since the first disclosure at 1987 (Couture, 2001, p. 25). Another positive indication for the success of the project is the rising levels of "wellness," a local measure that refers to various indicators such as children's general health, number of people completing their studies, parenting skills, empowerment of individuals in the community, increased community responsibility and resources, increased sense of safety, reduced prevalence of violence, and return to traditional ceremonies (Couture, 2001, p. 5). From a rating of 0–3 in the years 1984 to 1986, the wellness levels in 1999 rose to 5–6 (Couture, 2001, p. 51). Additionally, the data showed that children stayed in school longer, and people were returning to live in Hollow Water—both indicators of positive growth.

Unfortunately, the experience of the Hollow Water CHCH process was not systematically evaluated in criminological terms in comparison with court proceedings. It is also unclear whether other compounding factors affected the community's wellness, such as governmental attempts to confront racial and cultural inequalities or general improvements in Canadian communities' standard of living. Furthermore, Dickson-Gilmore and La Prairie (2005) illuminate some problems in the program. First, they argue that it focused more on offenders than on victims, especially in the crucial stage of deciding whether to engage in the CHCH program or prosecute. Offenders were involved in that stage, while victims were not (Dickson-Gilmore & La Prairie, 2005, p. 172). Another concern is the questionable reliability of the recidivism data. These were based only on cases that were identified, prosecuted, and successfully completed, instead of using a broader definition. Therefore, they claim (albeit without offering alternative indicators) that the exceptionally low recidivism rate of 2% is somewhat suspicious (Dickson-Gilmore & La Prairie, 2005, p. 176). Another concern raised by Dickson-Gilmore and La Prairie (2005, p. 178) is that the reduction in reported violence and abuse may have been a result of victims' reluctance to report in the atmosphere of success that had been created within a context of a colonized community striving to achieve some levels of autonomy. At the same time, these reduced reporting rates might lead to budget cuts from the government, therefore further endangering the most vulnerable members of that community (Dickson-Gilmore & La Prairie, 2005, p. 178).

It is unclear to what extent these concerns are warranted, since there are no data supporting them either. There is merit, however, in adopting a skeptic account in considering future projects and evaluations, and greater attention to victims' unique accounts should be given both in constructing programs and in evaluating them. Similar to Annie Cossins' (2008) pessimistic reading of the South Australia experience, Dickson-Gilmore and La Prairie (2005, p. 178) remind us of the importance of intensive follow-up and monitoring because of the high risk of revictimization in child abuse cases. Notwithstanding this cautionary reminder, the Hollow Water experience provides a remarkable example of a community-based restorative justice process that has had success, at least at the community and family restoration level, in disclosing and addressing violence and sexual abuse against women and children (Braithwaite, 2002b).

Newfoundland and Labrador

The Family Group Decision-Making Project (FGDM) in Newfoundland and Labrador Province in Canada is particularly valuable because of its special construction as a demonstration project, with a rigorous and detailed evaluation conducted during and after its implementation, as well as a follow-up study. It provides a good example of how the two interrelated problems of domestic violence and child abuse have been treated jointly, in a restorative manner (Pennell & Burford, 2000b). This well-documented experiment included three different types of community (Aboriginal, rural, and urban) as well as a range of types of abuse (sexual, physical, emotional, and social) against both children and adults (Pennell & Burford, 1995, par. 9.1). While not using a randomized control group sampling, the project did compare the outcome results with those of a control group who were treated with more traditional methods.

The Newfoundland case study is different from the others presented here as it might be identified as closer to the child protection context than to criminal justice. Although women, and not only children, were the subjects of many FGDM gatherings following abuse by their husbands or teenage children, the project was designed as an alternative to child protection practices. Indeed, the mission and philosophy statements of the project made it clear that the justice system maintains its role separately (Burford et al., 1995, p. 70). That means that while gatherings searched for means of ensuring the safety and wellbeing of family members, their occurrence and results did not replace the criminal process and its outcomes against perpetrators. This different context warrants some explanation and a review of child protection conferences in general before returning to the Newfoundland experience.

Child Protection Conferencing

Family group conferencing (or FGDM) in child protection cases is closely related to conferencing in the criminal justice context, as it shares the goal of securing victims' safety and enhancing the stakeholders' participation. It also shares the goal of reaching a more "family-centered" practice in which family and "like-family" members are central in the decision making and implementation (Pennell, 2006). Other child welfare goals that social workers seek to achieve through the use of FGCs are strengths-based perspective, community-based service delivery, family preservation, and enhanced use of kinship-care (Merkel-Holguin, 2000). Cultural safety and sensitivity are also central in child welfare FGCs (Pennell & Anderson, 2005).

Originating from the same 1989 legislative reform in New Zealand that established youth justice conferencing as the mainstream reaction to youth crime, child protection conferencing is being used today in many jurisdictions in North America, Europe (especially the United Kingdom), Australia, and New Zealand (Brown, 2003; Sieppert et al., 2000). Unlike in the criminal justice context, however, the child in these proceedings is central to the process. Here the focus is not the offense and ways to repair the harm, but the child at risk and ways to secure the child's safety and wellbeing. The conference is not an alternative to a criminal justice process against the offender; rather, it is an alternative to other decision-making processes regarding a placement and safety plan for the child. The typical stakeholders in such proceedings are the child and the child's family only; there is no "offender's family"—although often an offending family member or members may be present.

Morris (2002a) captures the differences and similarities between the two practices:

> Care and protection and youth justice family group conferences do have very different objectives: youth justice family group conferences are concerned primarily with holding offenders accountable and making amends to victims; and care and protection family group conferences are concerned primarily with the victims' safety. Critical for both, however, is giving victims a voice and meeting victims' needs. Both also focus on taking steps to prevent the recurrence of the offending or victimization. Thus they share a common restorative core (Morris, 2002a, p. 90).

Child protection and youth justice conferences have some additional common features: involving the stakeholders in determining the appropriate response to the act, reaching a consensual plan, informality and flexibility in the process, and the use of a facilitator (Morris, 2002a, p. 91).

The similarities between child protection and youth justice conferences justify a review of the success of the former. In general, child protection conferences have been found to be successful: children are present in the vast majority of conferences (Robertson, 1996), including children as young as 5; children aged 11 or 12 and over are regularly present at conferences, and their presence was generally described as "painful but appropriate" (Marsh & Crow, 1998, pp. 93, 103). More children attend and participate in conferences compared with other child protection decision-making processes, although some raise concerns about the difficulties that their participation causes them (Nixon et al., 2005, p. 34). Most conferences ended with an agreement to a plan (Fraser & Norton, 1996; Robertson, 1996), sometimes with surprisingly creative solutions (Marsh & Crow, 1998, p. 145). Participants show high levels of satisfaction and children benefit from the process (Marsh & Crow, 1998, p. 120). Child protection FGCs have shown positive outcomes in a wide range of situations, including child physical and sexual abuse, neglect, parents' drug use, and domestic violence. FGCs were also successful in "multiproblem" families such as sexual abuse and domestic violence cases (Jones & Finnegan, 2004). Although there are some indications that implementation is not always satisfactory (Marsh & Crow, 2000; Merkel-Holguin, 2000, p. 146; Robertson, 1996), it has been suggested that other child protection procedures do not generate higher implementation rates (Marsh & Crow, 2000, p. 148). In light of the growing body of positive findings, family group conferencing is supported as a best practice by the U.S. Office of Juvenile Justice and Delinquency Prevention (Nixon et al., 2005, p. 3).

Despite the large body of literature discussing family group decision-making in child protection cases,[50] there is very little research about the actual participation of children in them (Campell, 1997; Dalrymple, 2002). The limited research on child participation in such proceedings indicates that even when they are present at conferences, children are rarely active participants in them, and they do not feel as if they are being heard (Dalrymple, 2002).

To learn about how family group conferencing is actually practiced in different places, Nixon and coworkers (2005) conducted an online international survey of child protection FGCs. Two hundred twenty-five program representatives from 17 countries completed the survey in part or in whole, the majority of them being from the United States (143), Canada (32), the United Kingdom (18), Australia (9), and New Zealand (9). As the authors state, while the data collected in this survey is not representative of practices around the globe, it nevertheless provides a snapshot of what was happening in a particular point in time in various programs internationally (Nixon et al., 2005, p. 5). One of the practice-related issues addressed in that study was child participation. While most programs had children attending conferences most of the time, children's participation varied. The authors found, however, that with good preparation, adequate planning, and sometimes a support person or an advocate, children "can experience good levels of participation in conferences" (Nixon et al., 2005, p. 35). Most programs had restrictions on children's participation, typically due to the nature of the discussion or the child's age and understanding. Children's safety was a major concern (Nixon et al., 2005, p. 36). However, only in very few programs were children themselves asked whether they wanted to participate. It was also clear that procedures regarding the participation of children were not regulated but were more in the hands of practitioners (Nixon et al., 2005, p. 37).

Back to Newfoundland and Labrador

The goal of this 1-year experimental project was to reduce violence against women and children within families and to promote their wellbeing. Thirty-two families were treated and a total of 384 family members participated in 37 conferences (for 4 families, conferences were reconvened). Conferences included an average of 10 or 11 family members and 2 or 3 professionals. After the referral, conference coordinators started with preparation, which took 3 to 4 weeks. Preparations included identifying the right people to invite, preparing the participants, taking the required steps to protect family members during the conference, and taking care of practical matters, such as transportation. In comparison to the length of the preparation phase, the conferences themselves took just 5.5 hours on average. Conferences typically included five steps (Pennell & Burford, 2000b, pp. 140–141):

1. Opening (sometimes with a culturally appropriate ceremony), setting the ground rules and giving information about the offenses and existing services
2. Family private time
3. The coordinator and other professionals are invited in and review the plan reached by the family.

4. Approving the plan, either immediately or (in cases of budgetary difficulties) some time later. Plans often included counseling, addiction treatment, in-home support, child care, transportation, material assistance, and recreation.
5. Implementation of the plan

The implementation of the project's goals was evaluated by a number of measures, including the researchers' observations of family private time (Pennell & Burford, 1995). These valuable reflections provide an unusual perspective on such proceedings. Conference outcomes were also evaluated by a range of measures, such as direct reports of abuse and indirect indicators of abuse, which were triangulated to overcome the underreporting of these offenses (Pennell & Burford, 1995, 2000a). In addition, two comparable samples—one of families whose cases were dealt with by the Child Protective Services (CPS), the other of families from the community—served as control groups.[51]

Two of the evaluation measures—follow-up interviews with family members (progress reports) and the CPS notes (child protection events)—revealed that conferences reduced violence in families and strengthened family ties (Pennell & Burford, 2000b). The majority of interviewees thought that the conference had been beneficial and described how the conference strengthened positive ties among family members. The child protection events demonstrated not only greater family unity (less separation) but also greater safety for children within families. Among the project cases the number of violent events was reduced after the conference, while in the CPS control group there was an increase in child protection events.

The Implementation Report published in 1995 indicated that the vast majority of participants were satisfied with the way the conference was run (Pennell & Burford, 1995, par. 7.1.2), including biological parents who were considered as the abusers (Pennell & Burford, 1995, par. 7.5.3). Furthermore, all but one of the conferences ended with an adequate plan (Pennell & Burford, 1995, par. 7.5.1). The conference that did not wind up with a plan was the only one that failed. In that conference, the abused mother had as her support person her abusing husband, and none of the children attended or had their views heard otherwise. The abusing husband managed to manipulate the family group and scare them, and as a result the group was denying the abuse altogether by the end of the conference. The researchers attributed this failure to the lack of a genuine support person for the woman and the fact that the children's views were not heard (Pennell & Burford, 1995, par. 7.5.2).[52]

Despite the goal of family wellbeing, the plans put the highest priority on children's safety and considered the children's interests as central. In one conference, for example, instead of removing the abused child from the home, it was suggested that the abusing father live elsewhere until he treated his substance abuse problem.[53] The father agreed to that suggestion (Pennell & Burford, 1995, par. 7.5.4.9).

Children's Participation in the Newfoundland and Labrador Experiment

Of special importance here is the data concerning young victims' participation in these conferences and methods that coordinators used to enhance the input children had in them.

Stakeholders' participation seemed central in the project, as reflected in the steps taken by the coordinators to enhance such participation, and the detailed discussion regarding methods that were found helpful in achieving this goal. Indeed, comparing the project and the control groups, the outcomes report concluded that through conferencing, the voices of young people were more likely to be heard and acknowledged (Burford & Pennell, 1998, p. 271). This was possible, however, only with adequate preparation (Burford & Pennell, 1998, p. 264). In most cases, family members were identified as the main decision-makers in conferences, although abused people themselves were identified only in a minority of cases as the decision-makers (Pennell & Burfordm 1995, par. 6.5.1). This does not mean that the abused people did not have a say in the process; instead, it might indicate that while they were able to articulate their difficulties and state their wishes, others were more active in searching for solutions. This, in fact, matches claims that victims in general want a say, but not a decisive role (Wemmers, 2004). It is also an appropriate finding, considering professionals' concerns of putting "too much weight" on the shoulders of young victims.

Support persons were found to be particularly important for young people to escort them and help them articulate their views (Burford & Pennell, 1998, p. 264). Additionally, the researchers emphasized the importance of coordinators being creative in finding specific ways to enhance children's participation that were appropriate for each family, without trying to impose a "one-size-fits-all" strategy for all children (Burford & Pennell, 1998, p. 264).

One of the most effective tactics in advancing children's participation was the early preparation of a personal statement. It was found particularly useful with young participants because, as one researcher wrote:

> even the most vocal young people clam up at the FGC . . . [The young people would] at first talk like . . . they would/could go in there and say what they want. And then when they would get in there they wouldn't say a word—be totally intimidated. What became clear is that they had to write down their views ahead of time, come prepared with a statement of what they wanted to say, because that was the only way that they were heard. Sometimes they read it themselves, but more times they had their support person say it for them. But it was prepared ahead of time between them and their support person (Pennell & Burford 1995, par. 4.17).

A coordinator reflected:

> Always have it down in writing. And usually have their support person read it . . . Toward the end [of the project], I always required it of any young people, any teenagers. The ones that I didn't do it with and the ones afterwards where I did do it, there was [sic] dramatic differences in the way that the teenagers were able to participate in the FGC (Pennell & Burford 1995, par. 5.3.4.1).

In addition, providing clear information about the conference at the preparation phase was crucial to the success of conferences, as well as taking care of technical arrangements to allow all relevant stakeholders to participate in the conference conveniently (Pennell & Burford, 1995, par. 4.22).

Flexibility was also found to be important. For example, in one case a teenage girl did not want to sit with the rest of the family. To allow her participation and to remind the family group of her centrality in the discussion, the coordinator left the door panel open to the next room, and left an empty seat at the conference room (Pennell & Burford, 1995, par. 5.1.8).

A striking example of a young victim ensuring her control over the process was that of an abused girl who volunteered to be the note-taker at the family private time. The coordinator wrote that she did "a fabulous job," and that it allowed her to be in control. When asked in the follow-up interview whether she was satisfied with the plan, she replied: "I wrote it, didn't I" (Pennell & Burford, 1995, par. 5.5.3).

It was further noted that when a conference was reconvened for the second time, participants were more active in their participation, particularly young people who had often been reluctant to talk at the first conference (Pennell & Burford, 1995, par. 6.6.2).

Children below the age of 12 normally did not attend conferences, due to their length or the subject matter. Efforts were made, however, to use the preparation phase to make their views known at the conference. Accordingly, preparations included (1) private discussions between the coordinator and the child (with the coordinator later expressing the child's wishes at the conference); (2) letters written by the child to be read at the conference; and (3) the appointment of a representative to speak on behalf of the child during the conference. In some cases, very young children's photos were placed in the middle of the conference room to remind the participants of the centrality of the child in the discussion. Children who did attend conferences chose a support person to accompany them through the process (Pennell & Burford, 1995, p. 76).

As to the information-provision stage, evaluations were usually positive, although a remark was made about the special care that needs to be taken when a presentation is given with a child in the room. It was further suggested by one observer that children perhaps should leave the room at that stage (Pennell & Burford, 1995, par. 5.3.2.5).

Concerns Regarding Revictimization of Children

With the family private time as a central aspect of the process, some fears were raised, mainly regarding the family turning against the victim and revictimizing him or her, and of the family being so dysfunctional that it would not be able to reach a plan. These fears, however, generally proved to be unfounded (Pennell & Burford, 1995, par. 6.1). Moreover, there were no cases of violence during conferences, nor was there conference-related violence later on (Pennell & Burford, 1995, par. 6.1.1). Fears were particularly expressed with regard to sexual abuse. A central concern was that abusers would use manipulation and control similar to those in the abusive relationship to turn the family group against the victim and to deny the accusation, while revictimizing the victim. The researchers found, however, that cases involving sexual abuse were particularly helpful for victims as they got the facts "out in the open" and provided more support and empathy to the victims, who were until that time isolated in their victimization (Pennell & Burford, 1995, par. 6.1.2). Moreover, one of the most powerful elements of conferences was the disclosure of abuse in detail, in front of all the decision-makers. This was found to have a sustained and significant effect on the participants (Burford & Pennell, 1998, p. 267).

Not all cases, though, were free of manipulation of young people. In one case, for example, the father invited his daughters for dinner the night before the conference, something he had never done before, and stated at the beginning of the conference that he might not live for the next 5 years. It was perceived as "buying their silence" (Pennell & Burford, 1995, par. 6.5.3).

Project Outcomes

The outcome report published in 1998 indicates that over 85% of the participants thought that the plan had been completely or somewhat carried out (Burford & Pennell, 1998, p. 55). Many family members expressed the wish for a reconvened conference to talk about the problems that had emerged since the first conference (Burford & Pennell, 1998, p. 63). Overall, most of the participants (67%) thought that their family situation had been improved as a result of the conference (Burford & Pennell, 1998, p. 64). However, positive responses were even more common among family members who were directly involved in the abuse, either as victims or abusers: 85% of them thought that their families were "better off" following the conference (Burford & Pennell, 1998, p. 66). In cases where participants felt that their families were "worse off" after the conference, the main themes that emerged were of family separation (such as the removal of the child from home) and lack of follow-through on the plan.

The most outstanding impact of the conferences, however, was that of strengthened family ties and feelings of unity (Burford & Pennell, 1998, p. 68). Furthermore, a recurring theme was that of enhanced caring for children within their families (Burford & Pennell, 1998, p. 71). Children's increased safety was evident in the number of substantiated abuse or neglect cases, which dropped from 16 before the conference to 8 after the conference (Burford & Pennell, 1998, p. 81). A more general indicator was that of the Total Child Protection Events measurement: child protection events dropped from 233 before the conference to 117 after the conference (Burford & Pennell, 1998, p. 91). Of these events, the most dramatic difference was identified in the "CPS Child Activity" category, events that were directly linked with child abuse activities. In the project group, the number of such events declined from 120 before the conference to 69 after the conference, while in the comparison group the numbers rose from 71 to 94 (Burford & Pennell, 1998, p. 100).

An important measurement that focused on children's wellbeing was the Looking After Children (LAC) questionnaire, which comprised a list of age-appropriate indicators of the child's development and wellbeing regarding many aspects of life such as health, education, relationships, and identity. The LAC questionnaire is a key instrument because unlike CPS-related measurements it can identify unreported revictimization of children, which is a high risk in family abuse cases. This measurement revealed that out of the 26 project children who had LAC data from before and after the conference, 16 improved in their wellbeing, 9 regressed, and 1 remained the same (Burford & Pennell, 1998, p. 146). In the comparison groups, greater proportions of children regressed in their wellbeing (Burford & Pennell, 1998, p. 148). Moreover, the mean percentage of positive change was the largest in the project group (Burford & Pennell, 1998, p. 149). The greatest progress in comparison with the control group was in the area of family and social relationships (Burford & Pennell, 1998, p. 151). With these positive indicators it would be unlikely to assume that children in the treatment group were reabused but did not report their victimization; the LAC instrument would probably have identified increased victimization symptoms if that was the case. It is important to remember, however, that the project children's starting point was lower than the control group, and that they had a lot of "catching up" to do (Burford & Pennell, 1998, p. 258). The LAC measurement also indicated that project children had many other problems, which stopping the abuse did not solve. Therefore, the authors emphasized the importance of continued support for children in such families and the provision of long-term services (Burford & Pennell, 1998, p. 164). The researchers concluded that no kind of abuse should be excluded from the practice of FGCs, including sexual offending and domestic violence. These issues, they argue, surface at conferences and it would be counterproductive to suggest that they are irrelevant to the discussion or that they ought to be prohibited on principle (Burford & Pennell, 1998, p. 161). At the same time, the authors noted that some families have so many problems to resolve that they must have intensive follow-up and long-term services in order to meet their needs, including reconvened conferences (Burford & Pennell, 1998, pp. 161–162). Therefore, they suggest that similar projects should include long-term services and policies and protocols to ensure follow-up for families (Burford & Pennell, 1998, p. 253).

Relying on a well-designed comparison and evaluation, then, Pennell and Burford (2002) have been able to conclude that conferencing can be effective in stopping child maltreatment and domestic violence.

DISCUSSION: CONCERNS AND CHALLENGES

The cases presented in this chapter have all included child victims as participants in restorative justice conferences or circles, and by and large have done so successfully. However, some difficulties have also been noted. Not all victims, young and adult, were satisfied, nor were they all healed from their victimization. Significantly, it seems that the participation of young people, whether as offenders or victims, was often quite minimal, despite the centrality of this aspect in restorative justice values. Are these problems practice-related, as the New Zealand researchers claim (Maxwell & Morris, 1993; Morris 2002a), or are they inherent to the *modus operandi* of restorative justice in the case of child victims?

Even when considering the less successful experiences, it is still worth noting that studies (including those based on a randomized assignment of only *admitting* offenders to either court or conference) have consistently shown higher levels of satisfaction and better recovery signs for the majority of "conferenced" victims, including children, in comparison to court victims (McCold & Wachtel, 1998; McGarrell et al., 2000; Poulson, 2003; Strang, 2002). Furthermore, the Newfoundland and Labrador experiment demonstrated that when significant efforts are made to allow young victims to actively participate, their participation can be considerable and the outcome results are better than those achieved by other practices. Moreover, victims' voices and victims' empowerment are at the heart of the restorative justice approach. It is therefore possible, at this stage of restorative justice, when the participation of young victims is still in its infancy, to speculate that with improved practices (such as the ones demonstrated in Newfoundland and Labrador), better results can be expected. At the same time, this is an appropriate stage for learning from past experiences to improve future ones.

With this cautious optimism in mind, the goal of the section below is to consider the central difficulties that emerge from the less successful cases in these experiences and explore ways of overcoming them.

Revictimization of Child Victims

Perhaps the most serious concern regarding the involvement of young victims in restorative processes is the fear of exposing them to a revictimizing and intimidating encounter with the offender and the offender's support group. Such cases of revictimization and intimidation were recorded, though at very low rates, in the RISE program in the ACT (Strang, 2002, pp. 139–150), as well as in New Zealand (Maxwell & Morris, 1993, p. 88) and in South Australia (Daly, 2001). However, it was possible to identify at least some of the reasons for these failures: (1) inadequate preparation of victims; (2) inadequate search for support persons; (3) operational issues (such as an encounter with the offender's family in the waiting area); and critically (4) facilitators who were either too dominating or too passive in the protection of victims' interests. Conversely, victims responded positively to conferences when they (1) were adequately prepared for what would happen; (2) were greeted and introduced in the beginning of the conference; (3) understood what was happening; (4) were treated with respect; (5) were involved in the decision making; and (6) received what they saw as a genuine apology from the offender (Maxwell et al., 2004, p. 302).

Considering the greater vulnerability of young victims to revictimization in conferences, the training and personal skills of the facilitator are critical to the success of restorative justice involving child victims (Fraser & Norton, 1996; Marsh & Crow, 1996; Maxwell & Morris, 1996). An insensitive facilitator can cause harm, or fail to prevent the revictimization of a young victim, even when all formal requirements are met. On the other hand, one of the safeguards of a large circle (as opposed to one-on-one casework) is that insensitivity on the part of the caseworker can be made up for by other, more sensitive adults in the circle. Additionally, a thorough, face-to-face preparation of the victim (and, equally important, the offender) prior to the conference has been recognized as crucial from the victim's perspective (Maxwell et al., 2004; Pennell & Burford, 1995, p. 82; Umbreit, 1998). The preparation phase allows the facilitator to evaluate the willingness of the offender to take responsibility for the crime without blaming the victim (and thus screening out offenders who might do just this). It provides the victim an opportunity to become familiar and develop trust with the facilitator, so that there is a free exchange of information between them. Moreover, when during the preparation phase victims are given adequate information, they know what to expect from the process and what will be expected of them.

Naturally, when the victim is a child the individual preparation is even more important. It might be understood as an opportunity to identify the specific needs-rights of the child and provide him or her with the appropriate tools to overcome his or her weaker position due to age, lack of experience, and past victimization. Therefore, it should be conducted in an age-appropriate manner. The preparation phase further provides an opportunity for the facilitator to exclude the child from the conference and decide on alternative participation methods, be it according to the child's own wishes or the facilitator's concerns about the child's wellbeing. For example, in some child protection FGCs in New Zealand, facilitators decided to exclude either the child or the alleged abuser from conferences, in light of fears of additional trauma for the child (Robertson, 1996). In South Australian juvenile justice conferences, when victims were reluctant to participate, other options were suggested during the preparation phase, such as nominating a friend or a victim's advocate to represent them at the conference. Other methods were the use of a tape recorder, letters, or photos, in which victims could provide their perspectives without the need to be present at the conference (Wundersitz & Hetzel, 1996).

In Newfoundland and Labrador, children who did participate in conferences were, as a requirement, escorted by an adult support person of their choice.[54] The role of the support person was to provide emotional support, to speak on behalf of the child as needed, and to leave the room with the child for a break when this was required (Pennell & Burford, 1995, p. 76). Another lesson learned is the importance of practical details, such as having an extra room available for children who get bored or need a rest from an emotionally charged conference (Marsh & Crow, 1998, pp. 54–55).

It seems, then, that the flexibility of the process allows for a wide array of arrangements that can significantly minimize the risk of revictimization of child victims. A thorough preparation provides opportunities to screen out unsuitable cases (for example, when there is a risk of victim blaming) and to choose the specific arrangements that best suit the wishes and needs of the child victim. Manipulation, domination, and intimidation are expected to be prohibited from the outset. If they occur during the process, the group dynamics are designed to ensure an immediate reaction by either the stakeholders or, as a last resort, by the professionals. Naturally, however, there is no guarantee against revictimization, only ideas of how to minimize the risk.

Revictimization of children can occur not only during the conference, in the form of intimidation, domination, or blame, but children might also be revictimized by their offender after the process, through the same or a similar crime. The risk of such revictimization is particularly high when the offender and the child are acquaintances. To address this risk, monitoring should always be part of the conference plan; children should always be invited and encouraged to report their revictimization to someone trusted, perhaps even given a direct-line telephone number to make it easier for them to report.

Children Being Silenced by Adults

In the context of juvenile justice conferences, one of the concerns that has been raised is of young people being silenced by a "room full of adults" (Haines, 1998), or simply being less involved than the adults participating in the conference (Umbreit, 1998). The concerns that were raised with regard to young offenders and their ability to participate in an adult-dominated discourse are relevant to young victims as well. The same issues emerge: child–adult imbalance; adults paying lip service to giving the young person the opportunity to speak, without giving due consideration to his or her views; and young participants being "pushed into things" in the decision-making phase. John Braithwaite (2002a, p. 159) suggests addressing this child–adult imbalance by adding support circles for both sides that include youngsters and adults, men and women. Here, again, individual preparation is very important for the young participant, as lack of preparation may result in insufficient understanding of the process and lack of meaningful participation (Umbreit, 1998). At the same time, care should be taken not to dominate young participants in the course of informing them of the process and the possible outcomes (Morris et al., 1996).

Procedural fairness may also be helpful in preventing (or minimizing the risk of) young participants from being overlooked, by a protocol requirement to ask for the young participant's opinion at every stage of the process. However, to ensure the *effective* participation of young people, it is suggested that balance can be regained by supporting the less powerful participants and by restraining the more powerful ones (Morris, 2002b). Such empowerment of the disempowered participants can be achieved through victims' advocates, community activists, and others who are able to promote the victims' views and perspectives (Hudson, 1998). The role of victims' advocates is particularly important in complex cases such as in domestic violence, where women's advocates can contribute to the understanding of the woman's difficulties and to bridge the ostensibly conflicting interests of women and children (Pennell & Anderson, 2005, pp. 176–177). The role of professionals and community members in supporting victims during restorative conferences should, however, be well defined, and caution should be taken not to mute the victim and other participants by introducing yet another professional in the room. Different models of child "representation" need to be considered.[55] At this stage the point should be made that child victims may benefit from having someone present on their behalf at the process, not only to secure their wellbeing but also to enhance their participation.

Young Victims Being Pressured to be Forgiving

Some programs, especially in the earlier stages of restorative justice, have been perceived as offender-oriented. This led to criticism regarding insensitivity toward the victim and facilitators putting explicit or implicit pressure on victims to help rehabilitate offenders, and to grant forgiveness, thus enhancing victims' feelings of revictimization (Umbreit, 1998). Victims' feelings of being coerced to agree with others may occur even in a more victim-centered practice, if the conference is unbalanced and facilitation is inadequate. Indeed, Braithwaite (2002a, p. 15) warns against asking or expecting victims to forgive. Forgiveness, Braithwaite says, is a gift victims can give, and making it a duty would destroy its power. Asked specifically about this point, however, victims in the RISE project did not generally feel pressured to forgive or prevented from expressing their anger (Strang, 2002, p. 125), and this was true for young victims as well.

Rushmi Goel (2000, 2010) raises a similar concern regarding the current practice of sentencing circles in Canada as a means of resolving domestic violence cases. In such cases, Goel argues, the power imbalance is too great to overcome in a procedure aimed at healing the offender and the community. This is more so in the Aboriginal context, whereby women can feel obliged to promote their community's interest to show successful outcomes. The political goals behind sentencing circles, Goel continues, hinder the restorative goals, discouraging women from disclosing the full range of violence and reporting further abuse. Such disclosures, women fear, might lead to the failure of the circle, which in turn may lead to the offender's incarceration and to lower success rates of the community in controlling crime. The pressure to reconcile in order to follow communal values of forgiveness and to reach a consensual disposition is simply too great, especially for a victim who has already been weakened by the dynamics of abuse itself.

Goel's concerns about Aboriginal women in domestic violence situations might also be relevant to child victims, perhaps even more so because of children's natural tendency to be influenced by adults' implicit or explicit messages. Great caution should be taken not to give children an impression that they are under any pressure to agree to what others are suggesting, or to "make things easier" for the participants to resolve. It is difficult to conclude, for example, whether children in the highly publicized Hollow Water CHCH program were under such pressure, especially in light of the vast differences between Couture's optimistic evaluation (2001) and Dickson-Gilmore and La Prairie's critical review of it (2005). It seems, however, that the positive external indications (the increase in "wellness," the growing population, and the longer years children attend school) suggest that at least some positive results there were genuine and not a result of any political pressure. Notwithstanding the questions regarding the level of success of the Hollow Water CHCH program, it is important to remember that in this program extensive work has been invested to ensure the wellbeing of the victims, as well as other members of the community.

Child Abuse: A Special Case Warranting Special Consideration

Even if there are ways to overcome the special vulnerabilities and weaker position of children and to include them in restorative justice processes, still there are additional challenges in child abuse cases that warrant further discussion. These include extreme power imbalance, the ongoing nature of the relationship, and the safety of the child. These concerns emerge not only in cases of child sexual abuse (Cossins, 2008) but in domestic violence cases as well (Stubbs, 2010) and will be discussed here concurrently under the title "family violence."[56]

Because of the unique characteristics of family violence, some argue that victims of family violence (both children and women) have needs that differ from those that restorative justice can meet. As Julie Stubbs claims:

> while restorative justice literature emphasizes participation, apology and reparation, victims of domestic violence have emphasized safety and external validation of their attempts to stop abuse, together with deterrence and rehabilitation, over other possible outcomes (Stubbs, 2002, p. 51).

Annie Cossins raises similar claims regarding the inappropriateness of restorative justice for cases of child sexual abuse (Cossins, 2008). She argues that because of the ongoing, escalating nature of sexual abuse of children, the major achievements of restorative justice for victims, such as a greater sense of sympathy toward the offender, forgiveness, reparation, and safety, are irrelevant for child victims of such crimes.

Is it a question, then, of *how* restorative justice is practiced in cases of child abuse (and domestic violence), or is it simply that restorative justice cannot, even in its ideal form, address the unique needs of abused women and children? The following paragraphs unravel the various claims against restorative justice in these unique circumstances.

Power imbalance is perhaps the principal concern in cases of family violence. In cases of prolonged child abuse, not only are there often age differences between victim and offender, but there is also usually a relationship of control and coercion, where the child is "trained" to obey the victimizer (Morris, 2002a). Similarly, in domestic violence, the cycle of violence creates a relationship of subordination and control where the victims are passive and obedient. The power of the batterer is so great in this relationship that the victims often feel that nothing they can do will change the situation. Instead, victims often choose to remain silent. This power imbalance, it is argued, presents a serious challenge to restorative justice (Busch, 2002; Stubbs, 2002). It affects the bargaining power of the parties during the process, minimizing the chances for a fair agreement (Kreiger, 2002). Fearing retaliation, a battered woman is unlikely to speak openly about her view of the preferred outcomes of the process in front of her abuser (Frederick & Lizdas, 2010, p. 51). Here is, for example, a quote from a woman participating in a focus group facilitated by women's organizations in Nova Scotia regarding the suitability of restorative justice in cases of domestic violence:

> How could you think straight when the person who had instilled so much fear in you . . . for years and years and years, I can't do it. All of that would come back. Even if just little bits and pieces come out, it would be so unnerving, that you couldn't think straight. They know us, they know the triggers . . . it would be that look, the look, the dead cold look. I would just have to see that and think, "I am in trouble." I would want to run out of the room . . . they have their looks or their hand motions, you know? (Rubin, 2010, p. 85).

This criticism, it can be argued, relates mostly to victim–offender mediation, where the victim faces the offender without any supporters to help her in the deliberation. Indeed, in contrast with conferences and community circles, mediation does not seem to provide an adequate framework for resolving these problematic situations, because the victim's family members and supporters are not present and therefore cannot protest when manipulation, domination, or victim blaming occurs (Braithwaite, 2002a, pp. 251–253). Still, however, victims of family abuse are likely to find it difficult to speak freely even when surrounded with supporters who denounce the behavior of the abuser. Furthermore, unlike other victims, battered women may be more reluctant to provide their opinions about the preferred outcomes of the restorative process, even in the presence of their supporters, and would perhaps rather allow professionals to take a more dominant role, especially when a custodial outcome is suitable:

> I would rather have the court send a message to my partner that his behavior was unsociable, unacceptable, than to sit in a small room and try . . . because then it's me . . . and I don't want to be there. I don't even want to be in court. But to be there in a small room and being responsible for helping to determine the outcome, to me, is about the worst place I could possibly imagine (Rubin, 2010, p. 86).

Lorreta Frederick and Kristine Lizdas argue that because of these concerns, battered women should never be asked to sit in a group with their abuser and supporters to discuss alternative ways to resolve the problem;[57] only if they *desire* to do so should such a group discussion be held with them. Furthermore, if their input is asked for, they should be fully informed as to who will have access to that information and should be assisted in considering the risks and benefits of each alternative (Frederick & Lizdas, 2010, p. 51). Victims of family violence might alternatively prefer having restorative processes held without them, as long as their needs are attended in the process and they are represented by a family member or another designated person of their choice (Jülich, 2010).

It is possible to argue that, for the same reasons, abused children should not be asked to participate in a group discussion regarding their victimization in the presence of their abuser, unless they themselves express a wish to do so. Even when they opt to participate, caution should be taken not to ask them directly about the preferred outcomes of the process, unless the victim has specifically requested to address this question. The baseline assumption in any process involving a young victim of family violence should be that, after being dominated and abused for a prolonged period of time by a close family member, the victim is unlikely to be willing and able to speak up in front of the abuser, unless he or she expresses a will to do so.

It is important to remember, however, that despite the resemblances between domestic violence and child abuse, there are also distinct characteristics to each form of victimization. One difference is that child victims of intrafamilial abuse, by nature of their definition, grow up. Their physiological, social, and biological maturation changes the nature of their relationship with their abuser and makes it possible (and desirable) for many of them to confront the abuser. Accordingly, while young children are perhaps still likely to be trapped in a relationship of subordination and terror, teenagers and youths, sometimes by now as tall and physically strong as their abuser, might be more prepared to speak up in a face-to-face, direct encounter. For battered women, in contrast, time in itself does not provide such possibilities and much more is needed to transform the distribution of power between the victim and the perpetrator. In any event, clearly a thorough case-by-case evaluation should be conducted when abused children are involved, and the options should be clearly explained to them in advance so that an appropriate form of participation is designed that suits their needs, wishes, and abilities at the time of the conference. The advantage of restorative justice is that it allows such a tailor-made approach.

A second concern typical of family violence and child sexual abuse is the continual nature of the violence, the prospects for the future relationship between the offender and the victim, and concerns for the victim's safety—these are typically peripheral in most other crimes (Cossins, 2008; Stubbs, 2002, p. 51). Accordingly, process outcomes of cases involving family violence may combine voluntary as well as coercive measures such as custody or no-contact orders (Herman, 2005). Extensive monitoring mechanisms are also needed, including emergency buttons, community services for victims and offenders, and ongoing surveillance. A related concern, therefore, is that communities lack the resources needed to address the safety needs of victims before, during, and particularly after the restorative process (Cossins, 2008). This concern is particularly salient in indigenous communities in which local services are often under-resourced or lacking altogether (Stubbs, 2010, p. 113). The safety concerns of abused children remind us that the "restorativeness" of the process is essential, but not sufficient: safety measures and support services after the process are crucial to prevent further victimization.

A third concern raised by feminists against the use of restorative justice in domestic violence cases is that of privatization and trivialization of the crime: arguably, domestic violence has been ignored and pushed into the private sphere for too long, with courts acknowledging the severity of the problem only in recent years. Restorative justice practices, it is argued, might reverse this positive change (Braithwaite, 2002a, p. 152; Kreiger, 2002). This is definitely the case with children witnessing domestic violence, who only now are beginning to be viewed as victims by state authorities. Furthermore, feminists worry that communities might be tolerant toward domestic violence (Herman, 2005), and that instead of asking the batterer "Why did you do it?" community and family members would ask the victim "Why didn't you leave?" (Frederick & Lizdas, 2010). A failure to generate a clear message against the violence (or worse, victim blaming) may result not only in further victimization and isolation of the victim, but also in increased risk for her safety, because the perpetrator's behavior is not unanimously rejected (Frederick & Lizdas, 2010). This concern may be relevant in some forms of child abuse as well, where family members may believe that this is a "family matter" or that the child's behavior justified some form of violence. A related claim regarding the (in)appropriateness of community-based justice is that shifting power to the local community is a way to absolve the state from its responsibility toward victims and reduce public expenses, relying on the good will of citizens to safeguard victims and rehabilitate offenders (Jülich, 2010). Accordingly, any restorative justice program addressing family violence would need to clearly establish the responsibility of both the community and the state to protect victims and denounce the abuse.

An additional argument against restorative justice in the case of domestic violence is the centrality of apology in it, which is often used as a tactic by batterers and is highly suspect in these crimes (Daly & Stubbs, 2006). It is unclear, however, to what extent this concern emerges in "direct" child abuse cases. Certainly in sexual abuse, even a seemingly sincere apology would not suffice, and a primary goal of the professionals involved is to make sure that the abuse does not recur.

In contrast with these arguments, restorative justice proponents claim that particularly in serious crimes, victims can benefit more from a restorative process, as the emotional restoration is much greater through such a response (Marshall, 1999, p. 18; Strang, 2002, p. 198). Indeed, restorative justice has a lot to offer victims of violent crimes, including putting the victim's story at the center, as well as the more rehabilitative, restorative alternatives to punishment. Furthermore, restorative justice can deliver compensation and restore the relationships between the parties involved, when these outcomes are desirable (Hudson, 2002, p. 622; Pranis, 2002).

Child victims in particular, it is argued, have an interest in the restorative option instead of the criminal justice alternative, especially in cases of intrafamilial abuse:

> children tend to love their parents come what may, and want the behavior to stop rather than their father imprisoned; children may be afraid of the consequences of breaking up the family (Hudson, 2002, p. 622).

Although many children do want their abusers to be sent away, even if that means imprisonment, surely for at least some children the opportunity to tell their story in a nonthreatening way, to be listened to, and to find a consensus-based solution that secures their safety is desirable. Additionally, restorative justice provides victimized children an opportunity to talk (or have others talk on their behalf) about their present and future cost-related needs, and consequently reach a restitution agreement that the court is less likely to order.

Despite these advantages, the concerns regarding the involvement of abused children in restorative justice processes are helpful in sensitizing restorative justice theory and practice to the special case of family violence. They are crucial for making restorative processes more nuanced in ways that address specific issues of race, gender, sexual orientation, culture. and socioeconomic status. The following are some examples of different ways to address these concerns.

To address the power imbalance, in both domestic violence and child abuse cases, restorative justice proponents suggest that victims must be especially empowered, and coordinators have to ensure that the victim's voice and interests are heard, not only with regard to the outcome, but also when discussing the harms. To achieve this in child abuse cases, adequate child representation is crucial (Bazemore & Earle, 2002).

When concerns regarding domestic violence exist, women's advocates or other domestic violence experts should be present to educate the participants about the effects of domestic violence, to address victim blaming, and to secure the woman's safety needs (Pennell & Anderson, 2005, pp. 176–177). The participation of the victim, whether an abused child or a battered woman, should be considered with them, assessing the risks and benefits of each alternative (Frederick & Lizdas, 2010). When considering these options, however, it is important to remember that the victim's input may be expressed through a written statement or by a representative, whether the victim is present or not. Using the experience accumulated in New Zealand, for instance, Allison Morris suggests that power imbalance can be addressed by supporting the abused child and by challenging or excluding the abuser. Morris provides an example where a sexually abused girl wrote a letter to her abusive stepfather and gave it to her grandmother to read at the conference, in front of the family members (2002a, p. 102). Furthermore, the flexible nature of restorative justice permits the involvement of multiple supporters for the victim, including family members and friends; other participants, such as the family doctor or a schoolteacher, may also act as protectors against any controlling, manipulative, or aggressive behavior (Braithwaite & Daly, 1994). Professionals can also prevent the abuse of power imbalances by rejecting unfair outcomes that are at odds with the child's wishes or best interests.

Another important way of addressing extreme power imbalances is the use of indirect contact between victims and offenders (Zehr, 1990, p. 206). With indirect contact, victims can still benefit from the advantages of restorative justice while enjoying the safety of not meeting their offender.[58] They are able to ask questions and receive answers (through the involvement of professionals or others who represent them), to express their own feelings and wishes, and to have an impact on the final resolution, and they are more likely to receive an apology and/or significant material restoration than through a court process.

Further, the safety of the child must always be a precondition for, and a central goal of, the process. In fact, addressing the concern for children's safety, it is argued that conferences are more effective in this regard than professional-led proceedings, because they use the strengths of the extended family. Family members, it is argued, are more available than state services in conducting unplanned visits, providing temporary placement, and monitoring the behavior of the offender (Morris, 2002a, p. 103). The Newfoundland and Labrador experience showed that the safety of abused children can be maintained during and after the conferences, and that these processes can prove effective in reducing future family violence (Burford & Pennell, 1998). The success of the process, however, depends largely on what happens outside the "justice room": during the preparation and screening stage, in the monitoring and service-provision stage, and at the evaluation level (Ptacek, 2010).

Addressing concerns about the offender trivializing the abuse or shifting his responsibility onto others (thus revictimizing the child), facilitators can encourage the offender to take responsibility and family members to condemn the abuse (Morris, 2002a, p. 104).

Another relevant field is child protection, where sexual, physical, and emotional abuse is often the subject of discussion. The findings presented earlier regarding the relative success of FGCs in producing safety plans for abused children and the high satisfaction levels suggest that even in these sensitive and complex matters, families can sit together and reach an agreement.

One important finding involves the benefits of child representation in child protection FGCs. In Wiltshire, England, a pilot project for child representation in child protection FGCs was conducted by an independent advocacy service. The underlying premise in the project was that:

> if the conference is another adult decision-making forum, then advocacy support is crucial, but... ideally such support should be someone that the young person knows (Dalrymple, 2002, pp. 292–293).

Accordingly, whenever the child chose someone he or she knew, that person was prepared by the coordinator before the conference. When there was no such "natural advocate," an independent, trained youth advocate was provided. In follow-up interviews, out of 44 children, all but 1 reported feeling involved or very involved at the conference. Having an independent advocate made the children feel powerful at the *personal level* (they had someone "under their command," saying exactly what they wanted him or her to say). They also felt empowered within the *family context* (the advocate spoke on behalf of them with their families in ways that they did not have the courage or ability to speak); and *with the professionals*, as the advocate made it possible for them to have an impact on the outcomes. With various techniques, the perspectives of the children were revealed to both the adult family members and professionals, and made the decisions more informed and child-focused. Furthermore, children generally reported feeling that they had some control over the process and their input in it. They were able to decide for themselves whether to stay in the room or leave, whether to speak for themselves or have the advocate speak on their behalf, and what to tell the adults (Dalrymple, 2002).

The positive results in the Wiltshire experience, together with the positive effect of support persons found in the Newfoundland and Labrador program, show that either support persons or advocates may enable children to have meaningful participation in such proceedings even after repeated abuse had occurred. Moreover, it is suggested that the empowerment of children should start as early as the preparation stage. Children should be asked whom they would like to invite to the conference and whom they wish to exclude. The child's view on this matter should be central, though it is possible to propose extra support for the child instead of totally excluding someone (Marsh & Crow, 1998, p. 52).

Even those who are skeptical of the use of restorative justice in cases of family violence agree that, if programs are carefully designed to address the concerns associated with these crimes, restorative justice can indeed be successful (Cossins, 2008; Herman, 2005; Stubbs, 2010). For example, the influential "Greenbook" suggests that courts should refer parties to mediation in cases of child abuse combined with domestic violence only in the following conditions:

1. Mediators are trained thoroughly in the dynamics of domestic and family violence, including child maltreatment, as well as in the dynamics of substance abuse, basic psychology and family systems theory, the developmental needs of children, the workings of the local child protection and juvenile court systems, local domestic violence services, and other local community resources.

2. The mediation program provides specialized procedures designed to protect victims of domestic violence from intimidation by alleged perpetrators and to correct power imbalances created by the violence with interventions, including the performance of differential assessments of the domestic violence issue, the offering of individual—as opposed to conjoint—sessions for the victim and alleged perpetrator so that they never have direct contact with each other, and permitting the victim to have an advocate in attendance throughout the process.
3. The mediation process also provides for the participation of victim and child advocates, the child protection agency, other interested family members and individuals, as well as all involved attorneys and GALs [Guardians ad Litem] or CASAs [Court Appointed Special Advocates], to reinforce further the balance of power and ensure that the rights of the participants are protected in the search for a resolution that focuses upon the safety and best interest of the child and the safety of all family members.
4. Mediators are vigilant when involved in discussions concerning the factual basis of the abuse of the child or victim-parent in order to prevent victim blaming and/or collusion with the batterer's denial, minimization, or discounting of the significance of the violence or abuse (Schechter & Edleson, 1999, pp. 90–91).

When following these conditions, the Greenbook summarizes, mediation can "effectively empower victims of violence and enhance their safety as well as the safety of their children and other family members" (Schechter & Edleson, 1999, p. 102).

Annie Cossins, providing an elaborate discussion on the failure of restorative justice to address the needs of sexually abused children, in fact reiterates the known challenges that child abuse cases create for restorative justice (Cossins, 2008). Basing her argument on a re-reading of the findings in the South Australian youth justice conferences, Cossins emphasizes the need to conduct victim-centered processes, combined with extended monitoring and rehabilitative services. But restorative justice programs that withstood the challenge of family violence and child abuse such as Newfoundland and Labrador adopted most of these recommendations. They demonstrated that when appropriate steps were taken to prevent further victimization, these types of crimes were dealt with effectively through restorative justice conferences (Daly, 2002; Daly & Stubbs, 2006; Doig & Wallace, 1999; Pennell & Burford, 2002). Moreover, Cossins' criticism of restorative justice was not supported with any empirical findings suggesting that restorative justice resulted in worse outcomes for child victims of sexual abuse.

It seems, then, that the disagreement between the proponents and opponents of the use of restorative justice in cases of family violence is rooted not in whether or not this is appropriate altogether, but rather *when* restorative justice would be appropriate, and in what ways it should be managed. Whether or not one is optimistic about the ability of restorative processes to overcome these challenges, it is clear that if restorative justice is to be practiced in child abuse cases, it must be constructed differently than for other crimes against children, and perhaps in conjunction with domestic violence cases, considering the strong connection between the two phenomena. This was the case in the Newfoundland and Labrador experience, where a "feminist praxis" was used and intensive work was invested in securing the safety and empowerment of abused family members, both women and children (Pennell & Burford, 2000a, 2002).

A Lenient Response?

Even if, from the child victim's perspective, restorative justice may be an appealing alternative, including in child abuse cases, there might be other arguments against it, external to the child's interests but nevertheless important. One of these concerns is the appropriateness of restorative justice as a response to serious crimes. Perhaps serious crimes such as physical and sexual violence against children should be left for the court to resolve because of the grave violation of communal norms. Perhaps restorative justice does not provide a sufficient moral reaction in such cases. The criminal process addresses the public call for condemnation in cases of severe crimes, an aspect that is missing in restorative justice practices (Hudson, 2002). Further, perhaps it is simply against basic perceptions of fairness to "let offenders go" without being punished in such severe cases. In addition, concerns exist with regard to perpetrators who are clearly dangerous to society or who are unwilling to repair the harm and refrain from future crime (Hudson, 1998).

Clearly, whether one chooses to adhere to a punitive approach or a restorative one depends largely on personal and political preferences. There are, however, some evidence-based considerations. First, while only offenders who admit having offended can be referred to restorative justice, among those not referred to restorative processes only a small minority of court cases are finalized with a finding of guilt and the consequent public condemnation and punishment (Daly et al., 2003; Roach, 1999; Zedner, 2004). The majority of cases are either not prosecuted at all, or a plea bargain is reached. The reality, then, is that while restorative justice suits only some offenders, the criminal process does not punish or condemn most of them, or, as Daly's research group put it, in most cases "nothing happens" (Daly et al., 2003).

Second, the public call for punishment and condemnation is not supported by findings about victims' wishes, which are typically about the fairness of the process rather than its outcomes, and more about material and emotional reparation rather than punishment alone (Strang, 2002; Wemmers, 2009).

Third, the expression of disapproval of the act may be generated through the open, equal, and nondominated nature of the restorative justice process, where "weak" victims can speak freely, and the process encourages progressive views (Hudson, 1998). A clear message, therefore, can emerge from a restorative justice conference against abusive behavior, especially when combined with community rehabilitative services and state enforcement mechanisms in cases of noncompliance. Furthermore, the bigger the conference the stronger the message of appropriate behavior would be. When not only family members of the offender but also others who are significant in their lives participate, it becomes clear that the norms set through the conference are community norms, not just family norms (Pranis, 2000).

Clearly, however, the process and the outcomes have to fit the severity of the crime, and one possible response of restorative justice to serious crimes is to include retribution in the process (Daly, 2002). While there is much controversy around this matter (see Daly, 2002, and Duff, 1996), punishment is not completely irreconcilable with restorative justice values (Strang, 2002, p. 204), as long as it is not perceived as a goal in and of itself (Zehr, 1990, p. 210).

In addition, a flexible restorative justice scheme might allow for severe crimes to be dealt with restoratively after a court process has started, either before or after sentencing, such as the case in the ACT under its 2004 Crimes (Restorative Justice) Act.

This "modular" approach allows for both punishment and restoration to occur, integrating the formal court process with restorative elements. With regard to "clearly dangerous criminals," Braithwaite suggests climbing up the enforcement pyramid, which has restorative justice at its base and incarceration at its top, with gradually more restrictive alternatives in between (Braithwaite, 2002a, pp. 32–41). This should be complemented with public education as to the wrongfulness of violence so that crimes that are dealt through the lowest level of the enforcement pyramid (restorative practices) are not perceived as minor (Hudson, 1998).

CONCLUSIONS

We have seen that there are benefits of restorative justice for victims, compared with the court process. This is true especially in violent offenses and in other emotionally charged crimes. Unlike criminal justice processes, the victim's perspective is central in restorative justice, thus making it possible to meet the specific needs of victims, including disempowered ones such as children. Moreover, there are some indications that restorative justice can reduce violence, at least in some contexts, thus promoting the broader interests of the community beyond the interests of the specific victim.

The five case studies discussed in this chapter provide examples of restorative justice processes that have been used, with varying levels of success, in cases of crimes against children, including very young ones. The generally positive results from these experiences support the claim that child victims can benefit from restorative justice, while at the same time providing valuable lessons as to the difficulties that emerge. The flexibility that characterizes restorative justice makes it possible for children to participate in these processes in ways that fit their specific ages and capabilities. In some cases, children may be able to express themselves independently (possibly with some creative methods such as drawings, letters, stories, and so forth); in others, children may need assistance from other people, such as a victim advocate (be it a family member or a professional acting on their behalf). In extreme situations and with young children, an indirect conference may be appropriate. In all cases, however, thorough preparation, including an age-appropriate explanation of the process, is central to the successful participation of the child victim.

Indeed, the values and principles underlying restorative justice described in Chapter 1 are consistent with the needs-rights of child victims reviewed in Chapters 2 and 3. Restorative justice aims to provide victims an opportunity to have significant control over the process that follows their victimization by being active partners in the process and affecting its outcomes. This helps victims regain their sense of control in their lives and can be an important element in their healing process (Frazier, 2003; Lazarus & Folkman, 1984; Zehr, 2002). Furthermore, restorative justice invites and encourages the victim's family, friends, and significant others to provide support for the victim, both during and after the conference. The victim's "arenas of comfort" (Call & Mortimer, 2001) are strengthened and activated. In successful conferences, participants listen to the victim's story, acknowledge the harm, and validate the victim's behavior, thus empowering the victim (Pranis, 2002), resolving their sense of shame (Ahmed et al., 2001), and helping them make sense of what happened (Zehr, 2002). Issues of self-blame have the potential to be resolved, as the victim is given an opportunity to discuss his or her behavior with sympathetic listeners (Herman, 1992).

In addition, offenders are expected to take full responsibility for the harm they have caused to the victim, and ideally to apologize. This provides an opportunity for victims to grant forgiveness, thus overcoming negative feelings of anger and low self-esteem and enhancing their sense of hope and self-worth (Enright & Fitzgibbons, 2000). Moreover, a positive interaction between the offender and the victim may engender in the latter more positive feelings toward the perpetrator, or at least permits a better understanding of the crime and its circumstances. This in turn provides an opportunity for positive reappraisal to occur, which helps the victim cope with the aftermath of the crime (Lazarus, 1999). Additionally, the opportunity to hear the offender's story and to feel some level of sympathy toward him or her may create a sense of growth in the victim, even at a young age (Murray, 1999). Finally, experiencing fair treatment and procedural justice may help the victim heal from the event (Herman, 2003).

These of course are outcomes of an ideal restorative justice process, at least for the victim. Although there is today consistent and strong evidence of the emotional benefits of restorative justice for crime victims in general (Sherman & Strang, 2007; Strang et al., 2006), it is yet to be examined how often such processes are conducted in a way closest to this ideal when child victims are involved. Clearly, a face-to-face encounter with their perpetrator might, if gone wrong, have just the opposite outcomes to those described above: adults' domination may create a sense of powerlessness and betrayal; victim blaming or even supporters' silence may amplify feelings of self-blame, shame, and confusion; and insincere apologies might induce anger, distrust, and bitterness. Consequently, failed conferences may result in further emotional harms to child victims and leave them feeling unsatisfied, angry, and suspicious. Cases of family abuse pose particularly complex challenges, and each case needs to be carefully considered to evaluate the prospects of a community- and family-based discussion, with or without a direct encounter between the perpetrator and the victim. Because of the high correlation between domestic violence and child abuse, restorative programs involving abused children should always screen for domestic violence so that they can address it properly (Schechter & Edleson, 1999, p. 61), considering not only the complex needs of the child but also the mother's own difficulties as a source of information and support (Ptacek, 2010). The risk of recidivism is also particularly high in family violence cases, challenging programs to find ways to monitor, report, and prevent further harms to children.

The programs reviewed in this chapter, however, show that there is room for optimism. Some of the experiences discussed earlier, such as those in Newfoundland and Labrador and in Hollow Water, are examples of promising practices addressing childhood victimization that can be carefully adapted in other places. Nevertheless, special caution should be taken in adapting existing models from other cultures. Any program should fit the community where it is being implemented, with the specific adjustments needed (Umbreit, 1998). General principles, and not specific programs or rules, are more useful in constructing a restorative justice approach with regard to child victims. An attuned, enculturated imagination is needed to bring these principles to life in any specific place and time. The next chapter, therefore, will propose general principles for a child-inclusive approach in restorative justice processes in cases of child victimization.

6

Victims to Partners

Child-Inclusive Restorative Justice

INTRODUCTION

As discussed in the previous chapter, restorative justice has gained popularity in the past two decades as either an alternative or a complementing practice to the criminal justice process. Child victims have been involved in such processes in many parts of the world, such as New Zealand (Morris, 2002a), Australia (Ban, 2000; Daly et al., 2003; Strang, 2002), the United States (Merkel-Holguin, 2000; Pennell & Weil, 2000), Canada (Pennell & Burford, 1996, 2000b), and the United Kingdom (Dalrymple, 2002; Marsh & Crow, 1996). While child victims have not been the focus of evaluation studies on these programs, still the existing data reveal that young children can take part in such processes, their satisfaction can be high, and their safety and wellbeing can be enhanced through the process.

The generally positive results of restorative practices from a child victim's perspective reviewed in Chapter 5 make it an attractive alternative to the criminal justice process. Chapter 5 also showed, however, that restorative justice can harm children. Therefore, it would be wrong to include child victims in the "routine" practice of restorative justice. Rather, it might be appropriate to create specific programs for child victims, and perhaps special programs for specific crimes against children (i.e., family and sexual abuse), to enable adequate training, facilitation, and investment that will produce safe and successful processes for children of various ages. In crafting such programs, a needs-rights approach can maximize their success and minimize the risks to children. A systematic implementation of the needs-rights model offers some subsidiary principles for action for child-inclusive restorative justice programs. This is the subject of this chapter.

Accordingly, this chapter translates the ideas and theories that were presented in previous chapters into practical methods within a restorative justice framework. Rights (Chapter 2) and needs (Chapter 3) are connected to principles for action. Earlier in this book, the Convention's four guiding principles of best interests, equality, participation, and the right to life, survival, and development, adjoined the right to be protected from abuse and neglect, and the right to rehabilitation and reintegration, and formed a human rights framework for child victims. To convert these human rights into practical principles and produce a holistic model, however, findings from the psychosocial literature regarding the needs of child victims were integrated. Following the model presented in the end of Chapter 3 (see p. 83), these two disciplines were connected to create a combined needs-rights model. Related needs were linked with correlated rights to create clusters that indicate the interrelationships between them. In this integrated model the human rights principles provide the normative aspirations and identify areas that should be explored empirically. The psychosocial findings support (or potentially negate) the linked normative arguments, and help translate the general norms into principles for action.

These principles for action are more specific than the human rights principles presented in Chapter 2, but they are sufficiently broad and flexible to be interpreted in different ways in various cultures, programs, and contexts. Hence, they should be regarded as subsidiary, instructional principles rather than a list of specific requirements.

For example, the literature on control is indicative of the importance of active participation and perceiving the situation as controllable for the wellbeing of victims (Frazier, 2003; Herman, 2003; Thurber & Weisz, 1997), while warning against forced participation of children (Murray, 1999) and token inclusion of children when in fact they have no input on the outcomes (Langer et al., 2005). Together with the normative principles of participation, rehabilitation, and best interests, it emphasizes the importance of treating child victims as partners. Other examples are studies discussing the importance of support of family and friends (Call & Mortimer, 2001; Morgan & Zedner 1992, p. 169), acknowledgment of harm (Herman, 1992), and validation of the victim's behavior (Ahmed et al., 2001, p. 191) in promoting the wellbeing of the victim (or his or her best interests, development, and rehabilitation, to use the Convention's terminology). Similarly, studies identify the rehabilitative and adaptive potential of receiving an apology and forgiving and the ability of children, even young ones, to appreciate both (Darby & Schlenker, 1982; Enright & Kittle, 2000; Petrucci, 2002). Finally, some studies discuss children's coping mechanisms and reactions to crime from a developmental perspective (Finkelhor & Kendall-Tackett, 1997; Seiffge-Krenke, 1995), thereby illuminating the varying needs across childhood.

While relying on international norms on the one hand and on psychosocial literature on the other, many of the practical methods of realizing the rights of child victims are drawn from positive experiences of restorative justice initiatives involving child victims, such as those discussed in Chapter 5. Others are adapted from the criminal justice context, including UNICEF's guidelines for the International Criminal Court (see p. 116) and the United Nations Model Law for involving child victims and witnesses in criminal proceedings (UNODC and UNICEF, 2009) (see p. 117).

The first four sections in this chapter discuss the subsidiary principles for action that might be derived from the needs-rights framework. Each section relates to one of the four "clusters" of the model, presented in Chapter 3: best interests, control, procedural justice, and protection. Grouping the model's elements into clusters seems to be more appropriate than an individual matching of each human rights principle with suggested principles for action, because of the indivisibility of the human rights principles and the arbitrariness of such an individual matching. In the figures drawn to illustrate each cluster, each oval in which the subsidiary principles are articulated should be seen as "floating" and "connecting" in the vicinity of the human rights principles and psychosocial needs included in the corresponding cluster, while still having some ties with the other parts of the complete needs-rights model.

The final section of this chapter proposes a set of eight heuristic principles that, if followed by professionals, are likely to produce reasonably satisfying child-inclusive restorative practices. A child-inclusive process is, arguably, one that regards children as active, equally respected partners in it. It does not mean that children participate in the same manner that adults do, nor does it suggest that children are simply included in it. Rather, instead of being treated as passive objects of the discussion, children involved in such a process are treated with respect, and can exercise their human rights in it in a way that suits their best interests and wishes. At the same time, a child-inclusive approach is not identical to a child-centered approach, a phrase often used in child protection discourse. The latter, while being a vague concept, suggests that children's interests are the only criteria for decision making, or at least the central and trumping ones. In the context of justice mechanisms, however, other interests exist, such as those of the perpetrator to a fair trial, and should not be understated. Although the best interests of the child should have primacy (as required by the Convention), it is acknowledged that other interests, such as those of defendants (and victimized women when domestic violence is an issue), are also vital and must be guaranteed as well. This could be especially true when the perpetrator is also a child, and therefore deserves equal protection of the human rights provided in the Convention. Accordingly, a child-inclusive approach realizes the existence and importance of other stakeholders and at the same time reflects a respectful, rights-based attitude toward child victims.

The following section, then, discusses the bottom part of the needs-rights model: the best interests cluster.

THE BEST INTERESTS CLUSTER OF SUBSIDIARY PRINCIPLES

As explained in Chapter 3, the best interests cluster includes the best interests, rehabilitation, and development human rights principles, as well as psychosocial findings regarding paths to promote the wellbeing of child victims such as support networks, acknowledgment of harm, validation of behavior, and material reparation. While the best interests principle is a broad, perhaps vague term, rehabilitation relates to the long-term wellbeing of children and development relates to the changing interests of children as they age. All elements of this cluster, then, associate with different aspects of children's wellbeing. Figure 6.1 demonstrates the subsidiary principles for action that derive from the best interests cluster.

Starting from the best interests principle itself, perhaps its most important contribution as a human rights principle is the obligation it creates for decision-makers to consider the individual needs of each and every child under their authority (rather than relying on general assumptions about "what's best for children") and to give primacy to these specific considerations.

In the restorative justice context, to ensure that the best interests of the individual child are given primacy, a thorough assessment should be conducted prior to any such process, to verify its appropriateness in the particular circumstances. Most importantly, it is vital to explore (1) whether there is a risk of victim blaming and manipulation during the process; (2) whether the victim is prepared to have a direct encounter with the perpetrator, and if so, what measures can be taken to secure the child's wellbeing during the encounter; (3) whether there is adequate support for the victim; (4) whether there is a high probability of a convincing safety plan; and (5) whether there is a high risk of revictimization by the process. Additionally, the timing of the conference, its location, and the list of invitees should be designed with the

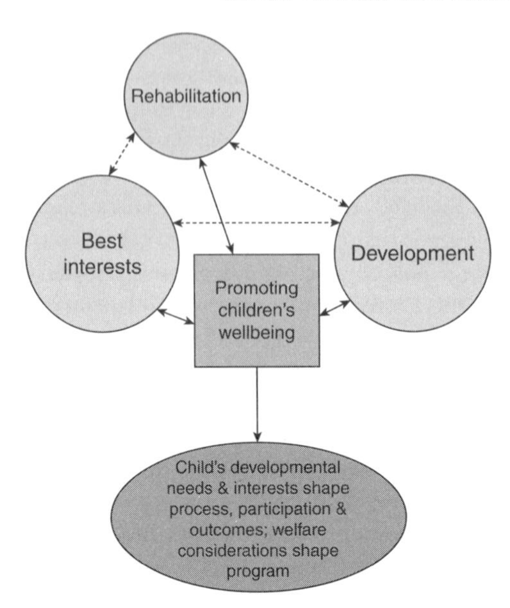

Figure 6.1 The best interests cluster: subsidiary principles for action in restorative justice settings.

interests of the child in mind. Finally, the outcomes of the process should promote the best interests of the child. Accordingly, it should at a minimum ensure the safety of the child, include reparation (material, symbolic, or both) that meets the specific needs and wishes of the child, and strengthen the child's support system.

Clearly, some of these subsidiary principles also derive from rehabilitative (such as reparation) and developmental (such as readiness to confront the perpetrator) considerations. The best interests principle, however, includes a "formula" for balancing the child's interests with the interests of others, namely the "primary consideration" formula specified in Article 3(1) of the Convention. Therefore, it is useful, at least in the context of this cluster, to use it as a general provision, while filling it with more specific rehabilitative and developmental content through the other principles.

Although the best interests principle is ostensibly simple to accept, it would be naïve to assume that its practical application is without problems. In particular, other important interests may compete with the child's interests, such as the perpetrator's. For example, the child's interest to have only the offender present at the process without his or her support group contrasts with the offender's interest (although the child's true interest might actually be having the offender's support group present, because only then can the offender feel shame, take full responsibility, and suggest a comprehensive restoration plan). Deciding on a large amount of restitution might help the child get therapy but might delay the offender's rehabilitation due to financial stress (although, again, the offender's extended family, if included in the process, can make arrangements to secure the interests of both sides in this regard). Does the best interests principle suggest that other interests should be ignored? Clearly, the answer is no. The competing interests need to be discussed and negotiated, with special attention given to those of the child. No magic solution exists, but arguably restorative justice provides space for an open, respectful negotiation where creativity, initiative, and involvement of supporters might lead to resolutions that jointly promote the interests of victims, offenders, and the other stakeholders. A final example arises in the context of children witnessing domestic violence. What should be decided regarding contact arrangements between the abusive father and the child, assuming the child wants such contact? A strict children's rights approach might lead to a decision that contact should be secured for the interests of the child, as long as his or her safety is secured, even if that prevents the mother from relocating or taking other measures to secure her own safety. But as the analysis of the Convention's provisions in Chapter 1 suggested, the best interests principle should be understood broadly, highlighting the shared interests of children and their abused mothers. An outcome plan addressing the mother's safety (for instance, residing temporarily at a relative's home) may promote the child's interests in the wider sense even if that means not seeing the abusive father for a while, because it will improve the mother's wellbeing and strengthen the child–mother relationship (Schechter & Edleson, 1999, p. 19).

Beyond individual considerations regarding specific children and their circumstances, the best interests cluster is also helpful in providing guidance about which process is most suitable for the short- and long-term wellbeing of children. It suggests that authorities are obliged to give primacy to children's wellbeing when crafting new child-inclusive restorative justice programs and when choosing the most suitable type of process for discussing crimes against children. Restorative conferences and circles are designed to bring together the support systems of victims and offenders, thus helping empower vulnerable stakeholders (Bazemore & Earle, 2002; Pennell & Burford, 2000a). More specifically, Chapter 5 demonstrated that family group conferences have had considerable success in discussing all family-related crimes, including domestic violence and sexual abuse of children. Conferencing was the process chosen and conducted in Newfoundland and Labrador (Pennell & Burford, 1995, 2000b), New Zealand (Morris, 2002a), the Australian Capital Territory (Strang, 2002), and South Australia (Daly et al., 2003). Traditional dyadic mediation, in contrast, does not include the support circles of either victims or offenders, and might expose the victim to unsafe and unbalanced situations (Busch, 2002). It seems, therefore, that the best interests cluster indicates a preference for programs that bring together victims, offenders, and their supportive communities, such as conferencing or community circles. Further evaluations, however, are needed of the latter, to address the concerns raised in regard to them, especially in cases of family violence (Dickson-Gilmore & La Prairie, 2005; Frederick & Lizdas, 2010; Goel, 2000; Stubbs, 2010).

In addition to the choice of process, the wellbeing of child victims should be a central consideration in the training, program protocol, location, and physical design of the program. For instance, programs should consider the age of their target population in choosing and designing the physical environment of the restorative process. Children should feel comfortable and have age-appropriate activities to engage with when necessary while the process takes place.

The best interests cluster also implies that accepting material restoration from the offender is important for victims' rehabilitation (Strang, 2002; Strang & Sherman, 2003; Zehr, 1990). Considering the developmental and rehabilitative normative principles, it is important that reparation agreements represent, when feasible, the lifetime consequences of childhood victimization. As discussed in Chapter 3, however, special attention should also be given to the child's specific wishes and material needs.

Another subsidiary principle deriving from the best interests cluster is that state authorities should foster the healthy development of children. Therefore, not only are restorative processes obliged to promote the emotional and physical healing of the child through the process outcome, but the process itself should be seen as providing an educational and developmental experience for the child. In particular, the value of active participation should be understood in a developmental context as well as an independent right. Indeed, Chapter 2 showed that providing children with opportunities to participate in decision-making processes enhances their development by promoting their negotiation skills, ability to express their views, self-esteem, and sense of belonging (see p. 44).

In sum, the short- and long-term interests of children should be the cornerstone of every child-inclusive restorative justice program, not only in its preliminary design, but in the application of the process with each and every child as well. When involving child victims, it is important to consider their age-specific needs and vulnerabilities. Therefore, the process should be designed according to the child's level of development and wishes, to maximize its rehabilitative potential for the child, and the reparation agreement should be tailored to the child's specific circumstances. Fortunately, one of the features of restorative justice is the ability to apply flexibility and creativity in its implementation, as long as it is based on the wishes and interests of the specific participants and does not violate their human rights.

THE CONTROL CLUSTER OF SUBSIDIARY PRINCIPLES

The control cluster presented in Figure 6.2 demonstrates the interconnections between children's participation and their short- and long-term interests. Development, however,

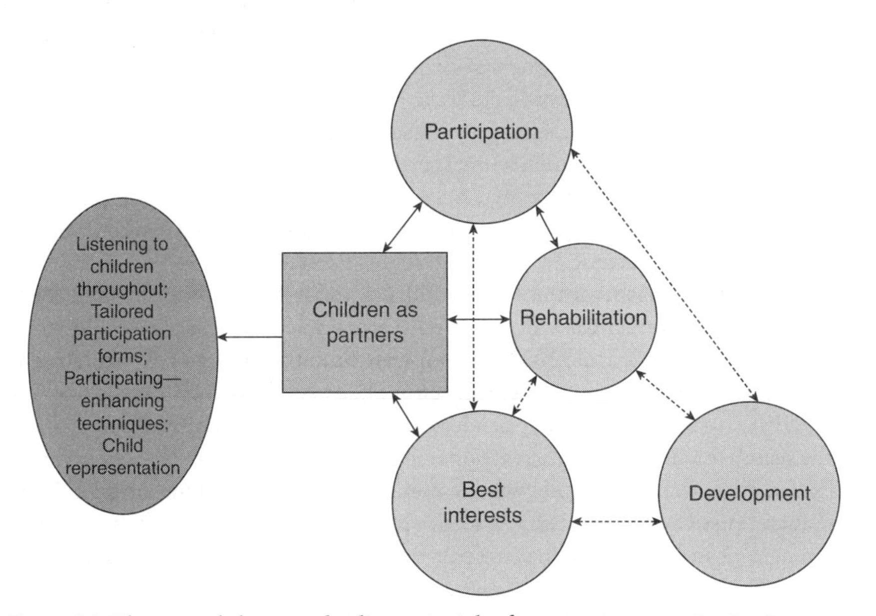

Figure 6.2 The control cluster: subsidiary principles for action in restorative justice settings.

is also salient in constructing forms of participation since there are significant differences in the emotional, cognitive, and social capabilities of children of various ages in engaging in shared decision-making processes. Findings regarding these developmental changes are relevant and important. Accordingly, despite the temptation to use a symmetrical model of four relatively even clusters, development was integrated into this cluster, in addition to its position in the protection cluster (see p. 179) and the best interests cluster (see p. 166).

Participating in restorative conferences is not only a right of children; often it might contribute to their short- and long-term wellbeing or, in other words, promote their best interests and rehabilitation. The psychosocial literature presented in Chapter 3 reveals the rehabilitative effects of a safe, open encounter with the perpetrator whereby the victim can ask questions and receive answers about the crime (Zehr, 1990), hear the perpetrator's perspective (Lazarus, 1999; Murray, 1999), receive a sincere apology and grant forgiveness (Bibas & Bierschbach, 2004, p. 113; Enright & Fitzgibbons, 2000; Enright & Kittle, 2000; Taft 2000), discharge shame (Ahmed et al., 2001, Chapter 17), and resolve self-blame (Herman, 1992, pp. 68, 199; Zehr, 2002). These typically cannot occur (or cannot be effective from the victim's perspective) without the victim's own participation. Restorative justice provides such opportunities where the victim, the offender, their supporters, and a facilitator meet together in a process that fosters partnership, respect, and nondomination.

Angel's 2006 findings regarding the positive mental health impacts of restorative justice provide evidence of the rehabilitative power of such processes. Based on her findings regarding reduced post-trauma symptoms among conference victims compared with court victims from randomized controlled trials in Australia, the United Kingdom, and the United States, Angel claims that although restorative justice conferences are typically a single event, they may be sufficiently powerful to have a similar effect to that of multiple cognitive behavioral therapy sessions.

While these findings have not included child victims, they provide a first therapeutic jurisprudence account of the relationship between the mental health of victims and their participation in restorative justice processes that follow their victimization. Clearly, it is important to conduct similar studies on child victims to explore whether such direct encounters hold the same potential for children. The existing psychosocial literature, however, makes a sufficiently strong argument for careful experiments with safe, supportive, and open encounters between child victims and their perpetrators in order to test whether these encounters promote emotional healing and rehabilitation as they do for adult victims.

In any case, findings regarding child victims' need for a sense of control and need to be empowered, listened to, and respected (Graham & Fitzgerald, 2005; Melton & Limber, 1992; Stafford et al., 2003) demonstrate both the potential of restorative justice and the great challenge it presents when applied to child victims. On the one hand, restorative justice treats victims, offenders, and their affected communities as partners in the search for an appropriate reaction to crime. At the same time, considering children's limited experiences and evolving communication skills, involving children in restorative justice settings requires some special arrangements. Although children as young as 3 and 4 are potentially capable of expressing their views, intentions, and difficulties (Smith, 2002), a child-inclusive restorative justice process needs to find ways of involving children as partners in the process, in accordance with their specific age, needs, abilities, and wishes. Adults also need to develop their ability to listen to children and understand their messages. Furthermore, it is important to be attentive to children and respect their views not only during the process but also before it, while making the decision regarding the form of participation.

One example of seeking young children's viewpoints is the "Storycrafting" method, developed by the Finnish organization STAKES. Storycrafting is suitable for 1- to 6-year-old children and was found to be effective in bringing out children's thoughts and viewpoints (Riihelä, 2001, 2002). According to the method, the child is asked to tell a story. The adult promises to write the story using the child's exact words while the story is told. The adult further reassures the child that there is no right or wrong story, that he or she is simply interested in hearing the child's thoughts and feelings. When the child is done, the adult reads the story to the child, and any corrections or changes the child makes are integrated into it (Riihelä, 2002, p. 7). The success of the method in improving communication between young children and adults, including regarding painful matters such as divorce, was explained by Riihelä (2001, p. 2) as follows:

> Oftentimes the situation loses its meaningfulness from the child's perspective because the adults ask the children about things they already know about. This is why the children in some way have to be told, that "Everyone has their own way of thinking. I am interested in how you think. Since I am the other person I cannot know your way of thinking." Once a child said to me with a surprised expression: "You mean you are interested in what I'm thinking?"

Since 1995, Storycrafting has been used in numerous Finnish municipalities and adopted in other Nordic countries. It was accepted in 1999 as a preferable therapeutic method in the European Network on Promoting Mental Health for children aged 0 to 6 years (Riihelä, 2001, p. 4).

There is no evidence that Storycrafting is as effective in the context of child victimization and restorative decision-making processes. Nonetheless, it demonstrates how, with creativity and awareness of children's own perspectives, it is possible to understand their worlds better than when using adult-oriented methods. This method can perhaps be tested with very young child victims as a way to achieve their meaningful participation without having them present at the conference itself.

While participation might have a powerful rehabilitative role, it is important to remember that forcing children to take control may be sometimes experienced as dominating them yet again and could interfere with their healing journey (Murray, 1999). Therefore, participation should always be considered together with the wellbeing of the child. Whichever the chosen form of participation, being treated as a partner in the process means also receiving ongoing information about its progress, in a way suitable for the child's level of development and understanding.

As mentioned earlier in this section, developmental findings are central in the discussion of children's participation. A related concept is that of "evolving capacities." Children develop their capacities constantly and gradually, and their families and surrounding communities need to foster their development by providing guidance while allowing growing freedoms and autonomy.

Accordingly, restorative processes need to be adjusted according to such developmental issues at every stage of the process, and these adjustments should be based on general scientific data as well as individual assessments. Consequently, the preparation of the child and the information given to him or her, the form of participation, the list of invitees, the location of the process, and its goals should all be shaped in a way appropriate to the developmental level of the specific child.

The Convention, however, makes it clear that every child who is able to form an opinion (even toddlers can) has the right to have these views heard and considered. In other words, every child has a right to participate in a decision-making process, and the key question is *how*. A needs-rights approach requires evidence-based findings, as well as specific assessments, before children are excluded from processes regarding their victimization. Indeed, developmental studies have found that 3-year-old children are able to recognize that other people have different viewpoints (Hart, 1992, p. 32; Selman, 1980, p. 132; Smith, 2002, pp. 82–83). Yet other studies have shown the limited intellectual and emotional capacities of children and adolescents, which make them unable to make rational, future-focused decisions (for a review, see Lansdown, 2005, pp. 23–24). One explanation for the different findings might be that developmental studies used experimental designs that take children away from their natural environment, thus inhibiting their true capacities to make rational decisions (Lansdown, 2005, p. 25). Another explanation is that children and young adolescents are perhaps still not ready to make rational decisions on their own, but they are able from a very young age to engage with others in discussions regarding their daily lives. In fact, the differentiation between making decisions alone and engaging in shared decision-making matches the Newfoundland finding that while young victims participated in the process, they were typically not the main decision-makers (Pennell & Burford, 1995, par. 6.5.1).

Whatever the reason might be, the differences between the studies suggest that an individual assessment regarding the capabilities and wishes of the child is necessary in every case, as well as a gradual understanding of the concept of participation. Taking part in the process does not necessarily mean being present at the conference, speaking up, and having an equal voice to the other participants, although this might be the preference for adolescents and some younger children. It can mean, for instance, sending a message through someone else. It might mean being present at the conference without taking an active role in it, or participating in part of it and then leaving the conference room. These are all specific forms of participation that can be tailored according to the specific needs, abilities, and wishes of the individual child. This gradual understanding of children's partnership fits with Flekkøy and Kaufman's (1997, pp. 65–67) suggestion to evaluate the appropriate level of participation with regard to each child, balancing his or her best interests and evolving capacities. Indeed, this balancing between developmental and best interests considerations to determine the level and form of participation mirrors the control cluster, which combines these concepts.

Nevertheless, considering the rehabilitative effects of participation and the right to participate, it is essential not to be overprotective of children through allowing "best interests" considerations to trump children's wishes. Indeed, children often feel overprotected and want to participate in proceedings that adults regard as potentially harmful (Lansdown, 2005, p. 35). More specifically, children expressed a desire to have a voice in family and school matters, including in domestic violence situations (Prout, 2001, p. 198). Marshall (1997) compared the views of child protection professionals with those of children who had had direct experience with the child protection system. She found that children wanted to take part in decision-making processes following child protection events much more than professionals were willing to let them. For example, in a situation where negative attitudes toward the child could be expressed during the process, children thought that they would probably hear them anyway, so there was no point in protecting them against such expressions. Children also said that it was not possible to "wrap people up in cotton wool" (Marshall, 1997, p. 74). This finding suggests that professionals are perhaps too often willing to give up children's "participation" for the sake of their "best interests," even though the latter might not necessarily be in conflict with the former. Moreover, professionals' unwillingness to take any risk of an unpleasant process for children could arguably be seen, in some cases, as a defensive organizational strategy to protect themselves from possible accusations, rather than the result of a genuine consideration of potential benefits and risks in each case.

Indeed, experience shows that even very young children are able to be present in restorative justice processes or actively participate in them. In South Australia, 9-year-old victims participated in conferences and generally did well, with adequate preparation and support (see p. 131). In child protection family group conferences in the United Kingdom, children were present in the vast majority of conferences, and some were as young as 5 (see p. 143). Restorative justice processes involved very young children in the school context. For example, 10- and 11-year-old children participated in "Whole School" programs in the Australian Capital Territory (Morrison, 2002), and 5-year-old children participated in restorative practices in schools in Nottingham, United Kingdom (Hopkins, 2002). Children aged 6 and older were involved, with high rates of participation and satisfaction, in school-related family group conferences in Hampshire, United Kingdom (Crow et al., 2004).

Seiffge-Krenke's (1995) work is an example of a developmental study that can be helpful in designing a developmentally sensitive restorative program. She identified developmental differences between boys and girls of various ages in terms of their ability to actively choose and approach support people in coping with stress. Her findings suggest that children over the age of 15 should be quite free to choose whom to invite to the conference, while younger children should be given more intense help in this regard (see p. 81). This, however, is a general assumption that can be rebutted when a young child exhibits resourcefulness in specifying a large, varying list of supporters, or when an older teenager displays passiveness at that stage.

One of the possible outcomes of a direct and genuine encounter between the victim and the offender is the exchange of an apology and forgiveness. The rehabilitative benefits of receiving an apology and granting forgiveness were discussed in Chapter 3 (see p. 75). It is important to give special consideration, however, to children's greater tendency to behave according to others' expectations, especially at certain ages. Thus, there is a need to ensure that children are not pressured to accept the apology or to offer forgiveness. The developmental studies regarding children's evolving capacities to forgive and accept apologies (Darby & Schlenker, 1982; Enright & Fitzgibbons, 2000; Park & Enright, 1997), as well as their changing propensity to submit to peer or family pressure (Holland et al., 2000; Park & Enright, 1997), can give useful guidance in this matter.

Participation-Enhancing Techniques

Once a decision is made that a child victim will be present and actively participate at a restorative process, it is important to consider participation-enhancing techniques.

Meaningful participation cannot be achieved simply by allowing children to state their views (Marshall, 1997, p. 75). Certain techniques are required to help children overcome their disadvantage due to age, dependence on others, and lack of experience. The ability to participate in decision making does not depend on cognitive capacities alone. For example, Roger Hart argues that the child's stage of social and emotional development, cultural and individual differences, as well as motivational barriers, may affect the child's apparent capacity to participate. Low self-esteem can be a critical barrier to participation, as children can develop coping mechanisms such as being silent and obedient. Accordingly, he claims that enhancing their self-esteem (through, for example, situations where their capabilities come to the fore) may encourage them to speak up (Hart, 1992, pp. 31–33). Indeed, focusing on children's strengths rather than their vulnerabilities and weaknesses may increase their trust in themselves and enhance their motivation to take an active role in the process. The "note-taker" from Newfoundland (see p. 147) is a good example of a victim who found a way to participate in a manner that made her feel confident and in control.

Additionally, children are often not used to being listened to and taken seriously, and there is no reason to believe they will spontaneously make a meaningful contribution without first enhancing their understanding of the process, their trust in the other participants, and their belief that their views really matter. To gain the child's trust in himself or herself and in the facilitator, empowerment should start before the conference itself. Thorough, lengthy preparations should include rapport building, assessing the child's best interests and wishes, constructing the invitees list with the child, deciding on the child's form of participation, and making the necessary steps to promote it. These not only help the facilitator prepare the conference, but they also set the stage for partnership-based decision making. For example, the most effective methods of ensuring the meaningful participation of child victims in the Newfoundland and Labrador experiment were assigning support persons; providing clear, detailed information about the process; and preparing written statements to help children articulate their views at the conference (Pennell & Burford, 1995, pp. 76, 94, 108–109).

The following points, made by Kathleen Marshall (1997, p. 106), summarize the suggested principles for enhancing children's participation:

- The child is prepared and given access to appropriate information.
- The child is helped in thinking in advance about his or her views.
- The child should know who will be present, and if there is anyone whose attendance might threaten the child, it should be reconsidered.
- Measures should be taken to ensure that the procedure meets the needs of the child and that no distressing "surprises" will emerge.
- Adults should avoid "adult language" and should be aware of the impact their communication will have on the child.
- During the process someone should be in charge of securing the interests of the child.
- Toward the end, it is important to make sure that the child understands the agreement fully, and that if he or she has different opinions they are clearly expressed, if the child wishes so.
- A follow-up is done with the child to make sure he or she understands what happened and to ensure his or her wellbeing.

The Sierra Leone Truth and Reconciliation Commission: A Test Case

One example of an effort to promote children's participation in a restorative process is that of the Truth and Reconciliation Commission (TRC) for Sierra Leone. While not a criminal but a public process of community healing, this experience is significant for giving children's testimonies centrality in an unprecedented way. Special policies, guidelines, and directions were constructed by a group of national and international experts together with children and under the auspices of UNICEF to promote the safe and effective participation of children as both victims and perpetrators of atrocities in Sierra Leone's armed conflict during the 1990s (Mann & Theuermann, 2001). According to the guidelines, statements by children should be taken by well-trained personnel, and each child should be accompanied by a social worker, preferably from his or her existing social network. In accordance with the Convention's evolving capacities principle, the statement-taker and the social worker are required to assess, together, the child's willingness to testify, the child's ability to give testimony, the child's level of understanding of giving a statement to the TRC, and the ability to deal with emotional outcomes of his or her testimony. Instead of setting strict age limits, the guidelines propose grouping children into three categories, which the statement-takers and social workers are expected to consider while assessing these issues: (1) children under 6, who should generally be excluded from the discussion; (2) children aged 7 to 12, about whom a specific decision should be made; and (3) children aged 13 to 18, who are assumed to be able to express their opinions on political and social issues (Mann & Theuermann, 2001, pp. 26–28).

The guidelines for taking statements from children testifying for the TRC provide an exemplary framework for enhancing children's understanding, participation, and wellbeing in relation to the process (Mann & Theuermann, 2001, pp. 28–32):

- Preparation: Children testifying for the TRC should receive age-appropriate information about the process, their role, and other people's roles in it.
- The environment should be child-friendly. The interview should be held in an informal setting, preferably one familiar to the child. Before starting, children should have the opportunity to familiarize themselves with the place, and some friendly discussion between the participants should take place prior to the formal interview.
- Methods of expression: Staff should be equipped with alternative measures of communication to assist children, such as drawing and figurative materials, role-play sessions, and so forth. Training should ensure that these techniques are used and then analyzed in an appropriate manner.
- Listening to children: Children should not be interrupted while talking, and questions should be open-ended. Generally, interviews should not last more than an hour, including a 10-minute break. For children under the age of 12, the interview should be no longer than 45 minutes.
- Children's wellbeing: The child's emotional state should be monitored throughout the session, and if a child seems to need a break it should be provided. The interview should be concluded with an emotional debriefing so that the participants can express and confront their feelings at the end of the session. Follow-up support by the social worker should also be available.

These guidelines include some helpful ideas that can be adapted in other restorative justice settings. Naturally, some of the assumptions in the report may be culture-specific, such as the time limitation according to age, and additional guidelines might be required. It is also important to remember the sociopolitical context from which these guidelines resulted: the forced involvement of children in war crimes and extreme crimes against humanity, making them both deeply traumatized victims and violent offenders. Nevertheless, they can arguably be used as a starting point in the development of program protocols.

Another unique contribution of these guidelines is the inclusion of the views of youths while they were being formulated. Importantly, the children thought that the process of telling their stories could be a form of healing, and stressed the importance of providing opportunities for children to practice their right to talk about their experiences. They also emphasized that children should be allowed to express themselves in various forms, including songs, facial expressions, written statements, drawings, and actions. Importantly, they stressed the difficulties children face in expressing themselves when there are adults around, as they are brought up to be silent near adults and not to participate. This provides a challenge to any promotion of the participation of children (Mann & Theuermann, 2001, pp. 43–44).

Certainly, children in other countries and in different contexts may have other ideas regarding their participation in restorative processes. To increase the likelihood that children of various ages feel comfortable in the process, it may be appropriate to include young people in the planning teams of new programs and to ensure their meaningful involvement in program design, similar to Pennell's (1999) suggestion regarding the inclusion of different community representatives in the construction of new programs.

Child Representation

The Convention's participation principle explicitly states the right of children to be adequately represented in administrative and judicial processes (Article 12(2) of the Convention). Indeed, an emerging theme in restorative justice experiences involving child victims is the importance of someone representing and supporting the child during the process. This reflects an understanding that the involvement of advocates for victims who are disadvantaged in the process can reduce power imbalances and child silencing during conferences (Bazemore & Earle, 2002).

However, there are different approaches as to who should represent the child and what exactly is to be represented: the interests of the victim, or his or her wishes.

Bazemore and Earle (2002, p. 170) propose, for instance, that in family violence matters victims' advocates should sometimes represent not only the views of the victim but also the victim's interests and harms in order to discuss reparation, even when the victim is reluctant to do so. This proposition mirrors beliefs about battered women's "learned helplessness" (Dobash & Dobash, 1992, p. 220)—the notion that women who routinely experience abuse by their spouses will gradually become passive, will not seek help, and will not cooperate with help providers because they do not believe that anyone can help them escape their all-powerful abusive partners. But the idea that advocates will take over, Bazemore and Earle admit (2002, p. 170), could be seen as manipulative. Furthermore, it can arguably create the very disempowering effect that victims' advocates want to defeat. Child victims witnessing domestic violence or suffering from direct abuse by family members are likely to be in a similar trap, because any intervention by authorities might be perceived by them as either pointless or, worse, dangerous. An active advocate may take the stance the child would not dare to take, but at the same time this "taking over" might create the same sense of domination and control the child has been dealing with at home.

In other words, the representation of children in restorative processes might, instead of enhancing their participation, do just the opposite. It is therefore important to identify ways of helping children participating while not "taking over." For example, if the victim and the victim's advocate (or supporter) reach a prior agreement that the advocate will raise issues that the victim feels unable or unwilling to raise, then this strategy might be helpful for the victim.

There are various forms of child representation in restorative justice processes, from support persons who monitor children's wellbeing and safety, as was the case in the Newfoundland and Labrador experiment (Pennell & Burford, 1995), through appointed counselors, as in South Australian juvenile justice conferences (Doig & Wallace, 1999), adult survivors in family violence cases (Bazemore & Earle, 2002), to barristers/solicitors or lay advocates, as legislated in New Zealand (Children, Young Persons and Their Families Act of 1989). It seems that there is no one preferred model for child representation in restorative justice processes. Involving lawyers in the process could lead to legalistic, adversarial, and disempowering results similar to those that characterize the legal process, and stands against the ethos of restorative justice (Braithwaite, 2002a, pp. 249–250). In particular, the involvement of lawyers in family private time might create a sense of professional dominance over the family and reduce the family members' sense of safety expressing their views. At the same time, it is possible to argue that children present a special case that justifies the participation of lawyers to ensure that their viewpoints are being adequately considered.

Katherine Hunt Federle (1996) proposes an empowering lawyering model for child representation, under which lawyers who represent children must encourage active involvement of their clients, refrain from subordinating lawyering practices, and be generally aware of and try to minimize the disempowering effect of the lawyer–client relationship. This might be a lawyering style appropriate for restorative justice, and can perhaps be used as a condition for involving lawyers as child representatives in the process (see Braithwaite, 2002a, pp. 250–251, for a similar proposition regarding collaborative lawyering in divorce proceedings).

Conversely, supporters from the victim's natural environment know the child best and could conceivably offer a less dominating, more democratic form of representation. Family members and friends, however, have their own views and feelings, which might influence their ability to provide an objective representation of the child's wishes, and can potentially also dominate the discussion instead of empowering the child. Accordingly, perhaps only trained advocates can overcome the power imbalance between young victims and the adult participants and represent the child's wishes and interests effectively, without prejudice. Further research is warranted to explore the benefits and limitations of each model. Whichever the choice is, the support person or representative should be thoroughly prepared for the role and be sensitized to its challenges.

The Wiltshire family group conferencing project (see p. 158) provides an illustration of the efficacy of child representation in child protection proceedings in the

United Kingdom. As discussed in Chapter 5, the evaluation study showed that children felt involved and empowered, and their perspectives were made known to both family members and professionals, with the provision of either "natural" or trained advocates (Dalrymple, 2002).

In sum, involving children of various ages and from different familial and cultural contexts in the decision-making process is challenging and requires careful design, thorough training, and intensive individual work with each child. However, a true, developmentally appropriate inclusive process is not only a fulfillment of an important human right of children, but it also increases the likelihood that the process and its outcomes will enhance the child's wellbeing, rehabilitation, and satisfaction with the process.

THE PROCEDURAL JUSTICE CLUSTER OF SUBSIDIARY PRINCIPLES

As explained in Chapter 3, the procedural justice cluster displays the interrelationship between the human rights principles of equality, rehabilitation, and participation and the concept of procedural justice. While equality in opportunities and treatment and participation in the process are both *elements* of procedural fairness, rehabilitation is a possible positive *outcome* of a fair process.

As Figure 6.3 shows, to meet the equality principle (and thus provide fair treatment and equal rehabilitative opportunities), all child victims should have access to restorative justice mechanisms and should be able to expect equal responsiveness to their rights and needs. This means that, as much as resources are available, restorative justice

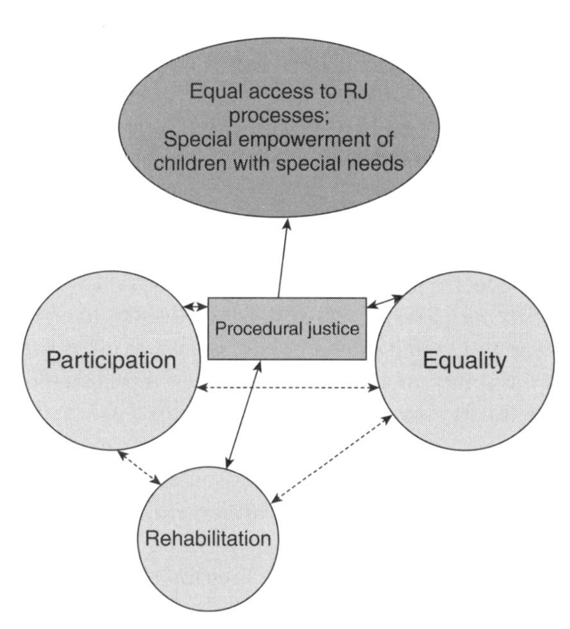

Figure 6.3 The procedural justice cluster: subsidiary principles for action in restorative justice settings (RJ = restorative justice).

programs should be located in different areas and should be accessible for all children.

A second aspect of the equality principle is that children with particular barriers or disadvantages should be provided special assistance to equalize their opportunities to participate meaningfully in such processes. The relationship between equality (or lack of it) and participation becomes salient here. It has been suggested, for instance, that children from low-income families would find it harder to actively participate, both because their parents value obedience rather than participation and because they are used to seeing their parents being passive while others make decisions. Therefore, the challenge of "liberating their voices" could arguably be greater (Hart, 1992, p. 33). Similarly, some cultures encourage children to be obedient and subordinate to adults, and this should be considered with participants before and during restorative processes.

It is difficult to believe that a single process can change patterns of behavior and transform silent children into charismatic leaders of discussion. It is important, however, to be aware of these social and cultural barriers and create a relationship based on respect, empathy, and sensitivity with the child. Technical aids might also enhance the participation of disadvantaged children. For example, translators might make children from minority groups feel more comfortable at a restorative justice conference. Special aids might help children with disabilities to overcome their physical, mental, or emotional limitations. Free transportation can potentially make processes more accessible for children and extended families living in isolated communities where programs are not available. Finally, children who are institutionalized should have full access to restorative mechanisms that take into account their difficulties in reporting crimes against them, their particular dependency on staff, special concerns regarding their supporters, and other specific circumstances that make it more difficult for them to participate.

A somewhat different concern emerging from the equality–fairness–participation trio relates to victims whose perpetrators are unwilling to take responsibility and participate in restorative processes, and those whose perpetrators are not found. Are the needs-rights of these victims to equality, procedural justice, participation, and, as a result, rehabilitation, violated? It might be argued that governments can only make restorative justice processes available to child victims and cannot guarantee the willingness of either victims or perpetrators to participate in them. Hence, when the perpetrator is not found or is unwilling to participate in such a process, the child victim is not necessarily discriminated against—but rather, perhaps, simply unlucky.[59] Naturally, it is vital to find other ways of promoting the wellbeing, rehabilitation, and participation of children without a known "willful perpetrator." For example, providing these victims with equal opportunities for restoration and justice might mean having some alternative processes available with their supporters, other victims, or other offenders. Clearly, restorative mechanisms that are not "deliberative" are substantially different and have other effects (Sherman & Strang, 2004), but these can be the best alternative when a fully restorative encounter is not feasible.

Restorative justice, then, needs to be both universal in its accessibility, and diverse in its application, to fulfill the needs-rights of children included in the procedural justice cluster. Clearly, financial limitations pose a serious problem in achieving this goal. Regarding translators, special aids, and free transport for disadvantaged children as part of their human rights, however, may generate a change in priorities and increase the accessibility of these mechanisms to all populations.

THE PROTECTION CLUSTER OF SUBSIDIARY PRINCIPLES

As Figure 6.4 shows, to understand children's various vulnerabilities, coping mechanisms, and different reactions to crimes, it might be useful to consider collectively the human rights principles of equality, development, and protection. Indeed, the developmental victimology perspective instructs us that developmental differences as well as special needs and belonging to different population groups affect both vulnerabilities and strengths of children. Gaining knowledge about these issues might help states target the protection of children and reduce the risk of both victimization itself and revictimization during the process.

As discussed in Chapter 2, the right to protection has been interpreted as not only creating an obligation on governments and public organs to prevent childhood victimization to the maximum extent possible, but it also implies the prevention of harms associated with children's involvement in the process following their victimization. An additional meaning of the protection principle emerges from Finkelhor's research group (Finkelhor & Kendall-Tackett, 1997; Finklehor et al., 2005). They argue that the consequences of corporal punishment and peer and sibling violence can be as devastating as criminal forms of violence against children, and therefore should be regarded as crimes. Consequently, to fully meet the right of children to be protected from all forms of injury and abuse, states should seek ways to prevent these (often noncriminal) forms of violence and domination as well. Restorative justice can be a suitable platform to address bullying, sibling violence, and noncriminal corporal punishment without criminalizing these acts.

An important question in this context is whether restorative justice is more effective than the criminal justice process in reducing crimes (as well as noncriminal forms

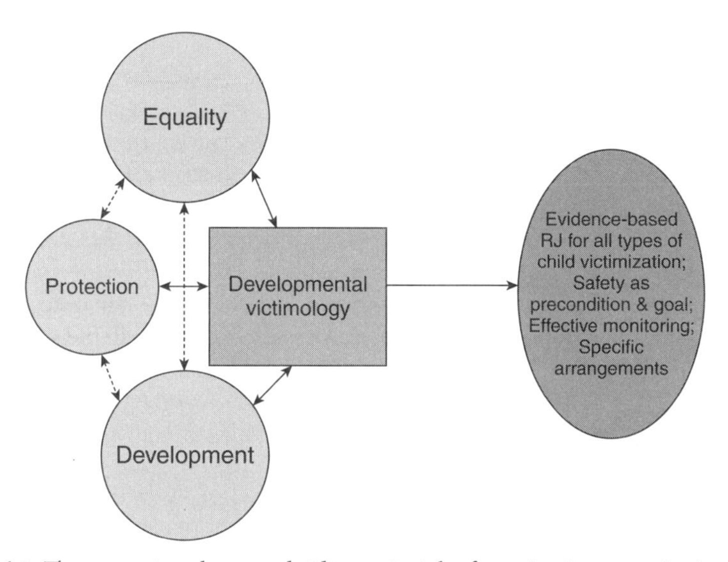

Figure 6.4 The protection cluster: subsidiary principles for action in restorative justice settings (RJ = restorative justice).

of violence) against children. Current recidivism studies on restorative processes (with mainly adult victims) showed mostly (yet not solely) positive results (Bonta et al., 2002; Braithwaite, 2002b; Latimer et al., 2005; Sherman & Strang, 2004, 2007). However, none of the randomized controlled tests conducted until now has focused on recidivism rates in crimes against children, nor on the most problematic types of such crimes. Of particular concern is the question whether restorative justice can ensure the safety of sexually abused children and those who are exposed to family violence. This lack of data can be addressed only with a foundation of carefully designed studies with randomized control groups involving offenders and victims of such crimes.

It is important to note, however, that restorative justice emerged, among other reasons, because of the unsatisfactory results of the criminal justice system in identifying, prosecuting, and reducing crime. With this in mind (and considering the other positive effects of restorative justice on victims) it is arguable that to prove successful, restorative processes should be merely as effective as the criminal justice process in identifying and reducing crimes against children. The Hollow Water and the Newfoundland and Labrador programs in Canada have shown that restorative justice mechanisms might be at least as (and perhaps more) effective than the criminal process in identifying and reducing family violence (Braithwaite, 2000; Pennell & Burford, 2002).

In the noncriminal context, child protection family group conferences have increased children's safety (Marsh & Crow, 2000, p. 208; Nixon, 2000, p. 99), and school-based restorative justice programs have improved children's sense of safety (Morrison, 2002) and reduced behavioral problems (Crow et al., 2004, p. 42). Restorative justice has not specifically targeted noncriminal family violence such as the use of corporal punishment by parents and sibling assaults, although these matters could have been raised during conferences. Small-scale experiments should perhaps be designed to address these types of violence as well.

A first step, then, in fulfilling the protection cluster is to design small-scale experimental projects that include child victims of different crimes and other forms of violence, and test their effectiveness in reducing violence, both against the particular children whose cases are dealt with through these mechanisms, and against other children. To test whether restorative justice can reduce crimes against children on the community level, there would be a need for a systemic use of restorative justice in a specific locality—say, a court jurisdiction in which all crimes against children are referred, as the default option, to restorative justice mechanisms (Sherman & Strang, 2007, p. 90). Beyond the potential financial damage, operating large-scale programs nationally without testing them first can presumably increase the risk of childhood victimization, and would constitute a violation of children's human rights. Nevertheless, the reduction of young people's involvement in the criminal justice system, as well as incarceration and apprehension rates, in New Zealand may be indicative of the positive systemic outcomes of restorative justice when implemented nationally (Duncan, 2009; Maxwell & Morris, 2006).

A second requirement drawn from the protection cluster is securing the safety of the specific child during and following his or her involvement in the process. Careful screening of cases should be conducted to exclude children who are at an increased risk of being revictimized by the process, due to the crime (for example, when the child is not only a direct victim of abuse but also witnesses the abusive behavior of one parent against the other), their young age, or special needs. In such cases it is possible either to consider alternative measures of participation for children, or to decide not to hold a conference at all. Addressing the specific needs of the child might also increase the likelihood of the process being a positive instead of a distressing experience. The example of an outcome plan requiring the offender to take his terrified victim for a meal at McDonald's discussed in Chapter 5 (see p. 137) demonstrated how young victims can be revictimized in restorative conferences when their needs and feelings are not adequately addressed.

The safety of the child must not be just a precondition for facilitating the conference, but the central goal of the process as well. Accordingly, a safety plan for the child should be a key element of the outcome agreement. To ensure that this goal is achieved, it is important to go beyond the agreement itself and monitor its compliance by everyone. While ideally family members and other stakeholders are in the best position to conduct such monitoring, professionals should stay involved and "monitor the monitoring" (Burford & Pennell, 1998, p. 253). Additionally, considering children's difficulties in reporting their victimization, especially in cases of family violence, it is important to ensure that children know who they can (and are invited to) contact if they are victimized again or if the conference plan is violated.

Included in the protection cluster are developmental considerations (the right to development) and concerns regarding children with special needs (the right to equality). Surely, all people under the age of 18 should not be treated similarly simply because of their legal status as minors. There are considerable physical, emotional, mental, and cognitive differences between younger and older children and between children with various capabilities. Therefore, policies need to consider scientific knowledge about developmental stages (and the limitations of such general assumptions), and use this knowledge as a starting point for individual assessments, in order to meet the rights and needs of children of all ages and with various types of needs.

In sum, the protection cluster creates an obligation that no restorative process should be conducted without taking adequate measures to ensure the safety of the child before, during, and following the process, as illustrated by the prudence of Pennell and Burford's method (1995, 2002). In doing so, the individual capacities of the child and any special needs should be considered. Additionally, restorative practices might be used for noncriminal violent acts against children, such as bullying, sibling violence, and parental corporal punishment, thus broadening the scope of protection provided.

CHILD-INCLUSIVE RESTORATIVE JUSTICE: HEURISTICS FOR PRACTITIONERS

This chapter used the needs-rights framework for proposing subsidiary principles for child-inclusive restorative justice. Seen as a whole, the needs-rights approach for restorative justice presented in Figure 6.5 suggests that child victims are not merely objects of protection at the mercy of the authorities, but rather full partners whose emotional wellbeing, empowerment, and participation are central goals in the process. This fits neatly into the underlying restorative justice values of empowerment, rehabilitation, and repair of harm for all stakeholders. The needs-rights model also reminds us of the importance of paying special attention to children as a vulnerable

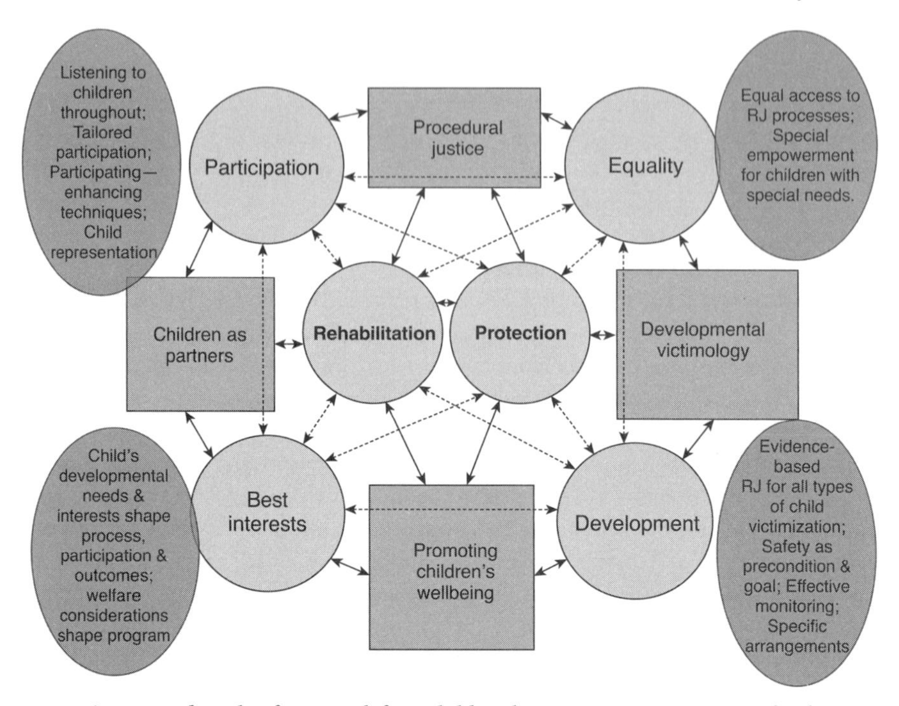

Figure 6.5 A needs-rights framework for a child-inclusive restorative justice: subsidiary principles for action (RJ = restorative justice).

population who are, despite their vulnerability, entitled to be included in public discourse. Moreover, the model can help professionals both in the child protection and the criminal justice arenas to identify issues of concern beyond the protective elements that are usually the focus of child-related policies.

Accordingly, this chapter divided the model, similarly to the method employed in Chapter 4 regarding the criminal justice process, into four clusters: best interests, control, procedural justice, and protection. Based on theories and existing empirical findings, subsidiary principles that might promote the ideas represented in each cluster were suggested. These subsidiary principles are a little less abstract than the human rights principles, and move us closer to the world of practice. The importance of such subsidiary principles is that they may have a "gatekeeper" role by grounding practice in certain values, hence assisting in creating new programs, retaining their quality, and helping stakeholders guard against abuses (Bazemore & Earle, 2002). They are also designed to be flexible enough to accommodate adaptation of various restorative justice practices to multiple settings and cultures, as opposed to more specific manuals for action that may fit only specific contexts.

An underlying idea behind these subsidiary principles is that of restorative justice as a social movement aimed at promoting equality among human beings. Therefore, child-inclusive restorative justice seeks to find ways that structurally empower children, help them overcome their inherently weaker status, and enable them to participate in adult discourse as equal partners. Children are less experienced in group discussion, they are less articulate than adults, they are usually not used to speaking up and making their views known, and when they do those views are often misinterpreted or downplayed by adults. Children also often regard adults, and professionals in particular, as authority figures and may find it difficult to engage in an open conversation with them; this may be especially true in more traditional communities. The younger the child, the greater these barriers are. Hence, the Convention's equality principle should be understood in its broader meaning under which children are equally valued people in society who need assistance to learn how to exercise their rights.

To move these principles even closer to practitioners, it is possible to articulate them in eight *heuristics*, which, if followed by practitioners, might move them closer to meeting the needs-rights of child victims without needing to go through the laborious task of addressing each one of the model's components separately. One limitation of the model is the large number of elements it includes and the complex interrelationships between them. While it is hoped that the needs-rights model would be valuable for the development of theory, policies, and further studies on child victims, a simpler framework is more useful for practitioners.

It is important to note, however, that the suggested heuristics are aimed at filling the specific niche of child victims involved in restorative justice settings. Many other values, principles, and rules are relevant when practicing the various models of restorative justice. In victim–offender mediation, for example, concepts drawn from the alternative dispute resolution movement, such as the privacy of the parties and neutrality of the mediator, apply. Family group conferences, to give another example, are embedded within or with close proximity to social work practices and theory. Values regarding group empowerment, mutual interdependence, and shared responsibility are salient. Even more closely related, Joan Pennell and Gary Anderson, two prominent writers in the field of family group conferences, offered in their 2005 comprehensive guide *Widening the Circle* nine principles for conference implementation in cases of family violence. These principles are, to name a few: have the conference belong to the family group; foster understanding of the family and creativity in planning; help the stakeholders take part safely and effectively; tap into the strengths of the family group in making a plan; and promote carrying out the plan (Pennell & Anderson, 2005, p. 8). The proposed heuristics build on Pennell and Anderson's principles; unlike them, however, they are by definition child-focused and are designed to be applicable to not only family group conferences but other child-inclusive restorative practices as well. Similarly relevant (and yet equivalently different) are the recommendations stated in the National Council of Juvenile and Family Court Judges' "Greenbook" (Schechter & Edleson, 1999). The principles and recommendations in the Greenbook offer a holistic, comprehensive approach for addressing cases of domestic violence and child maltreatment, and many of them are echoed in the following heuristics as well as in the principles suggested in this chapter. It is important to remember, however, that the victimization of children takes many different forms and often does not occur in the context of family violence. Furthermore, even in cases of family violence, the suggested heuristics and principles are derived from the perspective of children's needs-rights, thus providing a different way to approach such cases.

The eight heuristics are:

1. Holism
2. Tailor-made process
3. Children as partners
4. Participation as a continuum

5. Liberating children's voices
6. Let go
7. Restorative process as a goal
8. Empowering advocacy

The first heuristic principle emerging from the needs-rights approach is that of *holism*: child victims need to be treated in a manner that considers them as whole human beings and addresses the full scope of their rights and needs. Accordingly, providing protection and meeting immediate needs alone are insufficient. Children's rights to participation, rehabilitation, maximal development, and equality need to be met as well, and adults need to consider their strengths, social circumstances, and developmental needs too. Furthermore, these aspects of being a child victim are intertwined and affect each other. One right cannot be considered apart from the others, and ignoring one means making incomplete, sometimes wrong decisions. Holism means continuity as well. As found in the Newfoundland and Labrador experience, when social services stopped being provided once the crisis was over, families felt disappointed and children's wellbeing was compromised (Burford & Pennell, 1998, p. 164). Accordingly, holism should imply that restorative processes are only part of the full picture; children who have suffered victimization (particularly, but not only, those who suffered family abuse) need continual support and various services that should be provided until they are psychologically and socially rehabilitated. The idea of holism also suggests that children's different worlds should be considered together and should not be dealt with separately. Put differently, professionals need to make the child's life their starting point rather than the perspective of any individual state authority such as school, child protection services, or the police. If a child is being bullied at school and is also experiencing or witnessing family violence, these problems should all be included in a restorative process. Without addressing the full scope of violence experienced by children it is difficult to believe that their safety and rehabilitation can be secured.

This point should perhaps be reiterated because a holistic approach to child victims in restorative justice has particular benefits for some of the most problematic forms of childhood victimization. Because of the secretive nature of domestic violence (Peled, 1996), for instance, children witnessing it may conceal the circumstances they live in. But in a holistic approach, indications of domestic violence emerging during a restorative process following, say, bullying, are examined and addressed as well, in a process that can evolve into a combination of justice-, education-, and child protection-related processes. Moreover, a holistic approach also means addressing the interests of the abused caretaker (as well as the other family members' interests) to meet the full scope of children's rights and needs. Therefore, a holistic approach to restorative justice can bring together child protection and women's advocates—who often disagree regarding the appropriate reaction to the violence—to support the stakeholders in finding consensual solutions that address the interests of the child, the parent, and the family as a whole. Such collaborative work is recognized as "best practice" in the field of child protection and domestic violence (Schechter & Edleson, 1999; Wolfe & Jaffe, 2001).

A second heuristic is that each restorative process should be designed as a *tailor-made process* rather than a standard procedure. To meet the complete scope of the child's needs and rights, and to enable children to overcome their lack of experience and developmental limitations and become true partners, each process should be designed, to the maximum extent possible, according to the child's wishes, interests, and developmental and social circumstances.

Following Minow's argument discussed in Chapter 2 for "taking the perspective of the other" (1990), it is arguable that only in an environment that accommodates the child's specific wishes and needs can children feel that they are listened to and fully respected, and can begin to believe they are able to overcome their inherent weakness due to age. In other words, crafting the form of participation and other elements of the process around the wishes and interests of child victims can structurally empower them and provide the "push" they need for having an equal voice in the process. Creativity and flexibility are needed to allow for different settings and special adjustments. Processes may differ and may be adjusted according to the child's interests and wishes, in terms of locations, timing, invitation list, form of participation of the child, choice of advocate, the number of meetings, the length of each meeting and the breaks taken, special activities organized before or during the gathering, the language used, the outcome plan, the form of reparation, and the form of apology expected. Children obviously should not be the architects of the whole process, but their wishes should carry special weight so that they feel right from the preparation phase that they can actually influence the process.

The diversity in facilities and professional expertise and training required in different circumstances suggests that one program in each geographical area might be insufficient: a restorative process with a 6-year-old will look very different from one with a 15-year-old. Sexual abuse against children requires different training and settings than those for victims of burglary or bullying. Family violence and abuse presents yet another set of unique challenges not existing in other offenses against children. The variety is so great that it seems desirable (although, admittedly, unrealistic in many places) to have separate programs with specifically trained staffs for different age groups and different types of crimes against children. At a minimum, programs addressing "special" categories of victimization such as sexual and family abuse should ensure that they provide initial and ongoing training for their staff; involve community members, experts in the relevant fields, and state representatives; and have adequate screening and monitoring mechanisms at hand (Schechter & Edleson, 1999).

In addition, children are sometimes victims of crimes together with other adult victims, such as in house burglaries. In these cases they can join a "standard" adult restorative process. Still, regarding them as human rights holders means their inclusion in the process, in accordance with their wishes and interests, while paying due consideration to their specific needs. It seems, then, that a tailor-made model creates great diversities among processes even when identical crimes are discussed. This diversity could raise concerns regarding discrimination, varying levels of professionalism, and risk for the wellbeing of child victims themselves. In such a diverse network, the human rights of child victims (as well as other stakeholders) become central in guarding against malpractice, domination, and harm to stakeholders.

A third heuristic derived from a needs-rights approach is that of *children as partners*: child victims and professionals handling their cases are partners in designing the process, making it happen, reaching an outcome plan, and monitoring its implementation. Despite their age, children possess unique perspectives important in making the process meet their needs and rights. Partnership with children means more than allowing them to deliver their opinions and then make decisions that dramatically affect their lives without them. To treat children with respect and to address their right and need for meaningful participation, professionals and family members need to engage with them in a mutual, ongoing dialog. Starting from the early preparation stage, children and facilitators need to work in a partnership in which each partner contributes according to his or her own perspective, experience, and capacity until the outcome plan is implemented. To make this partnership work, professionals need to make active efforts to seek children's viewpoints, listen to them, understand their messages, and translate them into action. The Finnish Storycrafting method (Riihelä, 2001) demonstrates how adults can find new ways of listening to very young children and gaining knowledge about their worlds without imposing on them adult methods of communication.

A fourth heuristic is that of *participation as a continuum*. We know that very young children can form opinions and communicate in varying levels. We also know the developmental benefits of having opportunities to participate, as well as the importance of having a sense of control over the process in the healing journey. A utilitarian argument of reaching better outcomes also supports children's participation, as well as the moral argument relying on their human rights. We also know, however, that for some children, in some situations, being encouraged to participate might be experienced as yet another form of domination and control, expose them to information that they do not wish to be exposed to, or put them under undesirable pressure. Therefore, special caution should be taken when discussing the form of participation with the child. An understanding of participation as a continuum (following Flekkøy & Kaufman, 1997) might be appropriate. At one end of the continuum is the child's wish not to take part in the process. This is still a form of participation, as the child is given an opportunity to make his or her choice on this matter. Asking the child for his or her views makes a great difference from the child's perspective, and even having an option is empowering. Even toddlers can deliver messages of not wanting to speak, draw, play, or think about matters regarding their lives, and this should be respected as well. At the other end of the continuum is full, active participation of the child in the process, and children can be creative in the ways they feel comfortable in participating. In between these two extremes exists an endless number of other options, including indirect ("shuttle") conferences, having a one-way mirror that allows the child to watch the conference without being seen so that he or she can decide if and when to join the group, having someone speak on behalf of the child, and so forth. According to the previous principles, the form of participation is created in partnership between the child and the facilitator, and can be changed at any stage if the child wishes so.

Hart's concept of *liberating children's voices* (Hart, 1992) is another heuristic principle. It suggests that it is the facilitator's duty to actively seek the child's viewpoint. It captures the challenge of overcoming social, developmental, physical, and familial barriers and finding the specific way suitable for each child to speak up. Its underlying assumption is that children have valid stories to tell and that with the right tools, adults can understand and learn from them. This is a strengths-based approach that focuses on the capacities of the child instead of his or her weaknesses. Hart's suggestion to engage in activities that demonstrate the child's strengths and talents (1992) is an example of a method that enhances the child's self-esteem and makes it easier for him or her to take part in an open conversation. Liberating children's voices relates also to Pranis's (2002) account on the empowering effect of telling one's story and being listened to respectfully. Children in particular are often overlooked, especially those who have been victimized. Therefore, having their voices liberated and listened to by "a room full of adults" (Haines, 1998) is in itself an empowering, healing experience.

An additional heuristic is what might be called the *let go* approach. Professionals, like parents, have to take calculated risks with children in allowing them to practice their evolving capacities, even when the cost might be great worries and sometimes painful outcomes. As Waldron (2000) explains, being overly paternalistic might violate the child's human rights just as much as neglecting the child's needs for assistance and support (see the discussion on Waldron's theory on p. 18). Therefore, just as parents learn to let their children climb trees, walk on narrow logs, and go out at night when children insist they are ready for it, professionals too need to understand that participating in a restorative process may be a risk the child is ready to take and is appropriate developmentally, despite their own concerns. Marshall's study on children's views regarding their participation in family group conferences demonstrates that children want to take these risks more often than professionals are willing to let them (Marshall, 1997), and suggests that professionals' overprotectiveness might sometimes derive from "risk management" policy rather than from truly child-centered considerations. The other side of this principle is, however, that like parents, professionals too have to provide emotional support, thorough preparation, and close supervision when letting children make their choices. When a child crosses the road alone for the first time, it often occurs only after numerous explanations, warnings, and practice. The parent might be standing (or hiding) within earshot, ready to jump and grab the child away should a speeding car suddenly appear. Similarly, when children express wishes to take part in conferences, facilitators should respect this wish even when they fear the child could get hurt in the process. They should, however, provide full, clear information about the process and its expected outcomes, try to construct a safe setting for discussion with the child, and monitor the child's emotional wellbeing throughout the process. Emotional debriefing after the process, as conducted in Sierra Leone (Mann & Theuermann, 2001, p. 32), is an example of the emotional support needed in such cases.

A related heuristic principle is *restorative process as a goal.* Considering the importance of having opportunities to take part in decision-making processes and having a safe and positive encounter with the perpetrator, a respectful, nondominating restorative justice process can be seen as an important goal in itself, no matter what the outcomes are. The accumulated experience from school-based restorative practices suggests that children who participate in such processes improve their conflict resolution skills, develop empathy for others, and improve their ability to communicate (Crow et al., 2004, p. 42; Morrison, 2002). Moreover, by simply being listened to respectfully and being able to be *partners* in a collaborative decision-making process, children learn that they are respected members of civil society and that their views matter. Put differently, in restorative settings children can be empowered through the respectful listening of others to their stories (Pranis, 2002), in contrast to the adversarial court environment in which children's stories are systematically distorted, questioned, and disqualified (Scheppele, 1989). The process itself can also teach family members to treat children with respect and listen to their messages. While the restorative process is not the equivalent of, nor a replacement for, counseling, Angel's findings (2006) show that restorative justice can reduce trauma symptoms in a way comparable to therapy, at least in the short term. Furthermore, as the evidence described in Chapter 5 indicates, restorative justice can be a positive experience that might enhance the child's feelings of forgiveness and satisfaction and reduce anger and fear, no matter what the outcomes are. At the same time, this principle warns professionals against dominating processes, even when the outcomes seem to address the child's interests.

Finally, Federle's "empowering lawyering" model (1996) might be translated into an *empowering advocacy* principle, under which every child who participates in a restorative justice process should be supported by someone—either from the child's natural environment or a trained professional—whose role is to advocate for the child's rights and interests. Such advocates face the challenge of promoting the child's interests without taking over and silencing the child. The disempowering advocacy dilemma exists in many social movements. Advocacy organizations and human rights lawyers often promote their clients' cause while silencing them yet again and leaving them uninformed and passive out of good will. On the one hand, the higher the advocate is located in the social ladder (for example, a white male lawyer), the more likely it is that the client's interests will be accepted. Powerful advocates, however, are typically more distant from their clients and use more subordinating practices. In contrast, the lower the advocate is located in the social ladder (for instance, an unprofessional female volunteer from the victim's community, or even another teenager), the less effective they presumably will be in promoting the child's interests, but it is easier to assume that they will engage in a more equal conversation with the child victim.[60] The empowering advocacy principle suggests that while the child's interests should be effectively represented in the process, the child should be constantly in a position to decide on the specific role of the advocate and take over whenever he or she is ready to do so. It requires programs to provide advocacy effective enough to be able to overcome manipulations and power imbalances against the child by the perpetrator or other adults. Accordingly, highly trained professionals or skillful, thoroughly prepared "natural" advocates should be employed for this position. At the same time, advocates should be aware of their tendency to use professional jargon and other threatening practices, which they should avoid with child victims. Professional advocates should also be sensitive of the income disparities between them and the children and their families and should respect cultural, socioeconomic, and ethnic differences.

IS A CHILD-INCLUSIVE RESTORATIVE JUSTICE REALISTIC? A COST–BENEFIT ANALYSIS

It seems, then, that child victims deserve and require individual, intensive treatment to be able to participate on an equal basis in restorative processes. Even more intensive work is needed in complex cases such as multiple victimization and child abuse. This means investing considerable amounts of money and work in treating each child. Are all these efforts worthwhile? Naturally, an ethical reply would be that this is part of children's human rights and therefore society is obliged to provide these justice mechanisms, according to the Convention on the Rights of the Child. Since the criminal justice process falls short in meeting the full range of children's human rights, a child-inclusive alternative has to be created.

There is, however, a utilitarian justification as well. As the following cost–benefit analysis demonstrates, a child–inclusive restorative justice for child victims could actually *reduce* the costs of justice.

The Costs

Let's begin by looking at the extra costs expected from a child-inclusive restorative justice system.

The most significant expenditure would most likely result from the involvement of a range of professionals in the design, management, and day-to-day practice of programs. To comprehensively address the full range of child victimization, programs would need to involve experts in diverse fields such as domestic violence, child abuse, education, mental health, and child advocacy. Some of these professionals, such as children's advocates, would probably be involved in most cases, while others (such as experts in domestic violence) need to be available upon request. Above all, facilitators would need to be highly trained and have very low caseloads so that they can conduct thorough and intensive preparation, debriefing, and follow-up beyond the restorative encounter itself.

Another type of expenditure derives from the flexibility needed for programs to be child-inclusive. Programs should be able to offer meeting places with one-way mirrors, separate meeting rooms, separate waiting areas, play areas, perhaps even media facilities to show the child's televised message on the screen. Processes can last two or more meetings; relatives and other significant supporters who live far off should be financially supported, when needed, to make the trip to the conference. Facilitators should be able to conduct personal face-to-face visits to the central stakeholders, in flexible hours, before and after the process. And children and others involved should be able to contact the program at any time to report further victimization, ask questions, and make requests.

We can envision, then, "boutique" programs, with highly paid professionals working with only a few children at a time, surrounded by multitalented teams, in child-friendly, spacious, and well-equipped facilities. And such programs should be accessible for all children state-wide, with special accommodations for children with special needs, to meet the equality principle. Can this realistically be the standard for all victimized children?

The Savings

In their review of the evidence on restorative justice, Lawrence Sherman and Heather Strang suggest that there is no need for budgetary increases to expand the use of restorative justice. Rather, they argue, it is possible to reallocate the existing funds that are likely to be reduced through the expanded use of restorative justice (Sherman & Strang, 2007, p. 86). Sherman and Strang mention three ways in which the increased use of restorative justice can reduce costs: one is reducing the costs related to the multiple court hearings in each process, including fees for clerical and security personnel, private and public attorneys, and law enforcement officials appearing in court. The costs related to one restorative process, even one involving many professionals and intensive pre- and post-conference work, are significantly lower. Secondly, the reduced use of incarceration as a result of an expansion of restorative justice (the review demonstrates that restorative justice is at least as effective as incarceration in preventing crime) is likely to significantly reduce the costs related to custody, estimated as 35,000 Euro per year for each offender. Thirdly, restorative justice has been found to reduce post-trauma symptoms, and therefore is likely to reduce health-related costs for victims (Sherman & Strang, 2007, p. 86). Considering the severe and long-lasting effects of child abuse, child-inclusive restorative justice may be particularly cost-effective both because of its rehabilitative effects (significantly reducing expenses for health-related treatment) and because of children's increased safety (as the Newfoundland and Labrador program demonstrated).

In addition to these savings, the child-inclusive restorative justice process envisioned here can be cost-effective in three additional ways. First, while complex cases require the involvement of various professionals, it is also likely that the child's supporters and surrounding community will use their own resources to contribute to the outcome plan, including the provision of support, monitoring, safety measures (when needed), and practical aid. Communities may also offer a comfortable meeting place familiar to the child. Secondly, a holistic approach means that one large, well-invested process might address numerous problems that, alternatively, would have been treated separately in relation to the child and his or her caretakers. One such process is likely to cost less than multiple discussions and decision-making processes within the education, child protection, juvenile justice, and criminal justice systems. Thirdly, processes in which children's views are actually considered produce more sustainable outcome plans because they meet the expressed needs and wishes of the child; they also reduce the child's anger and vindictiveness. Consequently, child-inclusive processes reduce the likelihood of the need for additional decision-making processes.

It is possible, then, that a systemic change toward child-inclusive restorative justice might, at least after the initial investment, become cost-effective as a result of the significant savings it can lead to, particularly in the long term.

A FINAL (IDEALISTIC) COMMENT

There is, however, a broader social benefit in the development of child-inclusive restorative justice that goes beyond monetary calculations. If adult victims can be positively affected by such processes, as demonstrated in the studies reviewed in this book, then children might be affected by it even more. Because children are still developing, restorative justice in fact has great potential to affect their growth positively, sending children into the adult world with an optimistic message about the power of deliberation, respect, empathy, forgiveness, and trust in others. It could conceivably also develop children's abilities to negotiate with others and enhance their self-esteem and sense of competence. Sending victimized children away empowered, forgiving, and equipped with improved negotiation skills has the potential to reduce violence, promote deliberative democracy, and enhance social justice.

Potential is not reality, however, and we should not be surprised by the empirical experience we have documented of a few restorative justice conferences that were less than perfect, or damaging, from children's viewpoints. It seems, nevertheless, that practitioners who follow the eight heuristics suggested might find that they are able to address the needs-rights of child victims without neglecting the vital interests of the other stakeholders. If they do that, the normative and empirical considerations synthesized in this book suggest that it is likely that damage to children will be rare and their liberation from fear and oppression common.

7

Conclusions

The goal of this book has been to identify better ways of addressing the difficulties faced by victimized children. To achieve this goal, a first task was to provide a multidimensional explanation of the worlds of child victims of various crimes. A second task was to examine the appropriateness (and potential) of two justice paradigms, namely the criminal and the restorative, as responses to children's victimization. Throughout the book, two complementary epistemologies were used—children's human rights and their psychosocial needs. An integrated needs-rights framework was developed, based on relevant human rights principles set out in the Convention on the Rights of the Child on the one hand, and on empirical research drawn from psychosocial literature about child victims' needs on the other. This needs-rights model was then deployed to evaluate existing criminal justice processes in adversarial legal systems, and to propose practical principles for action in restorative justice settings. Using the needs-rights model it became clear that the adversarial criminal justice process can, at best, meet some of the needs of child victims, but is limited in its ability to address the full scope of their needs-rights. Restorative justice, in contrast, was found to be potentially appropriate. Since, however, what is known about child victims and restorative justice today is limited because so much is as yet untested, the needs-rights model was used again to suggest subsidiary principles that might reduce the risk of harm and maximize the potential of restorative justice to meet the needs and rights of child victims. To translate the, by then, cluttered model of Figure 6.5 into simple instructions, a set of heuristics was proposed, which, if followed by practitioners, is likely to bring programs closer to the needs-rights of child victims.

A HUMAN RIGHTS DISCOURSE IN THE CASE OF CHILD VICTIMS

A human rights discourse has been used in this book not only because it reflects respect for children as human beings, as equal members of society. Rights can also be a vehicle to structurally empower children, according to Federle's "empowering rights perspective" (1995). At the same time, the needs-rights framework does not propose an adversarial, individualistic strategy to strengthen children's status. Rather, it follows Minow's (1990) relational approach in which rights may be seen as arising from and defining relationships between people.

The social justice viewpoint on which this book is based, then, necessitates a human rights framework to discuss children's issues. To deploy a human rights epistemology, Chapter 2 adopted a legal theory that includes children in the rights discourse: the interest theory of rights (MacCormick, 1982). The interest theory treats children, as well as people with mental illnesses and those with intellectual disabilities, as human rights holders, similar to other population groups. The alternative will theory (Hart, 1982) has its claims, but it excludes those weakened populations and treats them as objects of protection only. The interest theory, in contrast, represents an inclusive, egalitarian viewpoint that fits well with the underlying values this book defends.

Within the human rights epistemology, the United Nations Convention on the Rights of the Child offers one existing authoritative and compelling Bill of Rights for children, and was thus used here as the normative template of children's rights. Not only has the Convention been ratified by the greatest number of states ever to ratify a treaty, but its substance also represents a holistic approach that combines welfare and self-determination: freedom of expression and autonomy are intertwined with best interests and developmental considerations. The family is presented as the most important social unit for children, while at the same time children's rights as separate entities within their families are acknowledged. Children's special vulnerabilities are considered and addressed as well as their cultural, religious, and economic rights. This holistic approach is compatible with the interest theory of rights because it puts children's dignity as human beings and respect for their needs at the center. It is also compatible with Federle's empowering perspective because it grants children the full range of human rights, including the right to have their opinions heard and considered. Moreover, the Convention's emphasis on the importance of the family, community, and national identity accommodates Minow's social relations approach to rights.

Six provisions from the Convention provided an integrated foundation of "human rights principles": the four "guiding principles" of best interests, participation, development, and equality, as well as two victim-related provisions, namely the right to protection and the right to rehabilitation. The structure of the human rights model, presented in Chapter 2 (Figure 7.1), shows that the four guiding principles have an equal, independent status while influencing each other as well as the two victimization-specific principles. Rehabilitation and protection, on the other hand, have perhaps a lower status in the hierarchy of child victims' human rights. They might be seen as specific

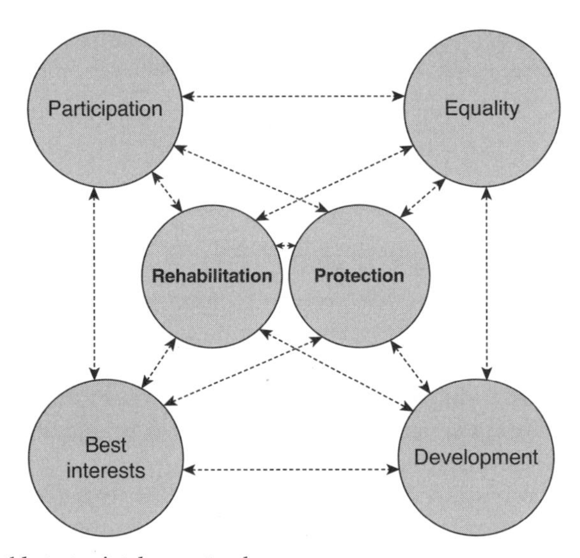

Figure 7.1 Child victims' rights: a visual account.

requirements deriving from the four general guiding principles, in particular the best interests principle.

Other related (yet nonbinding) human rights documents, particularly the *Basic Principles of Justice for Victims of Crime and Abuse of Power* (1985), the model law on child victims and witnesses (UNODC and UNICEF, 2009), and the *Basic Principles on the Use of Restorative Justice Programmes in Criminal Matters* (2002) (RJ Principles), have not been explicitly included in the model, but their provisions, and especially those relevant to child victims, are incorporated, either directly or indirectly, in the human rights principles presented in the model. For example, awareness of power imbalances, the centrality of safety, support persons for children, the provision of full information, and nondomination—are part of the RJ Principles, and are all addressed through the Convention's provisions as interpreted in Chapters 2 and 6. Similarly, the *Guidelines on Justice in Matters Involving Child Victims and Witnesses of Crime* (2005) are based on the Convention's provisions and include similar principles, albeit in the criminal justice context.

AN INTEGRATED NEEDS-RIGHTS MODEL

It needs to be said, however, that a legal document such as the Convention, which is based on a negotiated consensus regarding the rights of children, does not give a detailed account of the practical implementations of these rights. If legal theory and practices are to promote the wellbeing of members of society, then they need to look at the daily realities of people in constructing laws, regulations, and policies. To understand such realities and what is required to improve them it is necessary to rely on social science research. This is the underlying assumption of *psychological jurisprudence* (Melton, 1992; Melton & Wilcox, 2001), which calls for the cooperation of law and psychology to allow evidence-based judicial and policy decisions. This use of empirical evidence about people's lives might not only make law more attuned to promoting people's welfare, but it has the potential also to increase its perceived legitimacy among the public (Melton, 1992). Relying on empirical research is particularly important in regard to children's law, because many decisions regarding their daily lives are made by others (Melton & Wilcox, 2001).

Accordingly, a second set of literature, regarding the psychosocial needs of child victims, was reviewed in Chapter 3 and integrated into a combined needs-rights model. As Figure 7.2 demonstrates, there is a mutual relationship between the human rights principles and the psychosocial needs. The human rights principles set the normative framework of discussion and direct us to the relevant fields of research. The needs layer provides the substance, as well as justifications, for the implementation of the human rights principles. It also provides warnings against possibly damaging use of rights, such as encouraging children to exert control in uncontrollable situations (Langer et al., 2005). Once in the model, these psychosocial needs benefit from the normative strength of internationally recognized human rights principles.

AN INCHOATE MODEL

As the model demonstrates, however, there are no clear-cut matches between individual human right principles and specific findings, and pairing each psychosocial need with

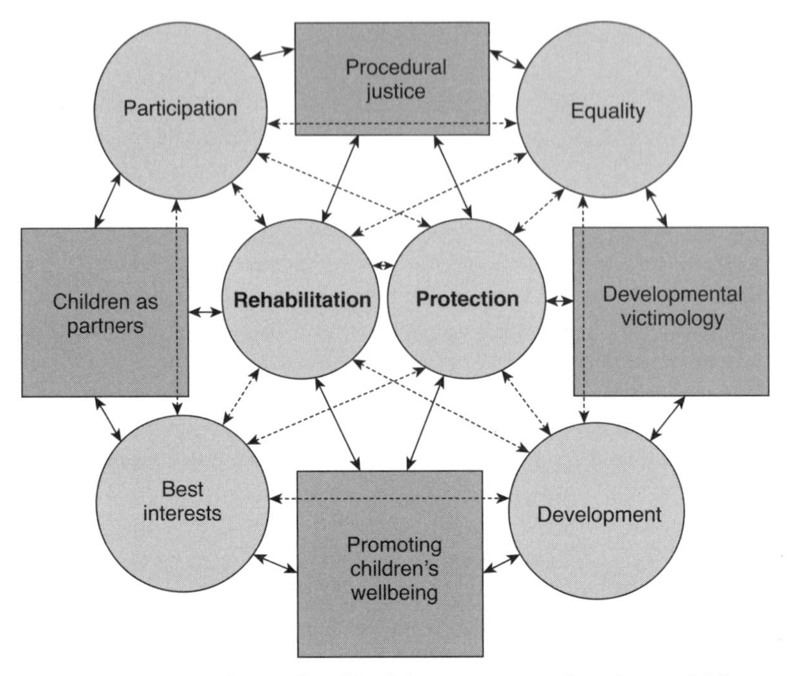

Figure 7.2 Integrating psychosocial and legal discourses: a needs-rights model for child victims.

a human rights principle would occasionally require some arbitrary categorizations. Instead, four key concepts drawn from the psychosocial literature (promoting children's wellbeing, children as partners, procedural justice for children, and developmental victimology) were each linked to different human rights, creating four "clusters," as follows:

- The best interests cluster at the bottom of the model links the best interests, rehabilitation, and development human rights principles with relevant empirical findings relating to children's wellbeing, such as the importance of support networks, acknowledgment of harm, validation of behavior, and reparation.
- The control cluster on the left side of the model places findings justifying the treatment of children as partners (such as the importance of control, direct interaction with the perpetrator, group discussion, apology, and forgiveness) with the three human rights principles of participation, rehabilitation, and best interests.
- The procedural justice cluster at the top of the model enjoins participation, rehabilitation, and equality, and the concept of procedural justice as understood in the psychosocial literature.
- Finally, the protection cluster on the right side of the model connects the human rights principles of equality, development, and protection with developmental victimology findings (and perhaps more so, with a need for further exploration) regarding the effects of age and special needs and circumstances on the impact of victimization, coping strategies, and special vulnerabilities.

Clearly, even with the grouping into clusters, there are links that go beyond this ostensibly neat division. For example, psychosocial data associated with the protection cluster can also be relevant to children's rehabilitation, as they might indicate the existence of special rehabilitative needs of children with disabilities. There is also mutual connection between development and participation in the current context. It became clear to me during the research that participation is directly related to the child's developmental level. Therefore, particularly in restorative justice, where there is room for flexibility in methods of participation, developmental considerations should be integrated into the crafting of participative alternatives available for children of various ages. Accordingly, Chapter 6 used a revised control cluster that included development (see p. 168). The location of the psychosocial boxes, then, should be regarded as the "best available placement" rather than a perfect fit.

Bridging the legal and psychosocial literatures required further adjustments: since each layer of the model uses a different vocabulary, different concepts may actually be closely related. For instance, studies on control in the psychosocial literature are related to (but do not always match perfectly) the participation principle and its normative explanations, and were therefore grouped under the "partnership" concept; children's wellbeing could be regarded as the psychosocial twin of the legal best interests concept, and so on. These connections were made through the model, in the absence of explicit links in the literature acknowledging them.

It is also important to note that psychosocial needs are a dynamic layer in the model. Empirical evidence develops with time and new studies can potentially affect not only our understanding of the meaning of the rights, but also their status in the model. For example, studies on young children's participation in family group conferences could conceivably lead to the conclusion that children under a certain age should not be present at such proceedings because the risk of further harm is higher than the expected benefits (such a conclusion would need to be carefully scrutinized, however, because of the human rights violation it creates). Moreover, studies on long-term outcomes of justice processes might suggest that addressing the short-term needs of children (or their best interests) is in fact an instrument for ensuring their emotional rehabilitation. A conclusion could be drawn from such findings that the right to rehabilitation is secondary to the best interests principle, at least in the context of childhood victimization. In any case, the rights and the needs layers affect each other and are also interrelated within themselves, as the model demonstrates.

A final methodological qualification: the model was not based on the views of children themselves regarding their wishes and needs as victims. Although Chapter 3 included some studies on children's views (for example, regarding procedural justice—see Hicks & Lawrence, 1993; Lawrence, 2003; and Melton & Limber, 1992). I am unaware of any study in which children were asked specifically about their perceptions of their needs and rights as victims, within the criminal justice system or in restorative settings. Perhaps the next step in developing child-inclusive restorative justice is to conduct such studies.

A NEEDS-RIGHTS EVALUATION: THE CRIMINAL JUSTICE PROCESS

Once broken into four needs-rights clusters, the needs-rights model provided a method for identifying the weaknesses, as well as the achievements, of the criminal justice

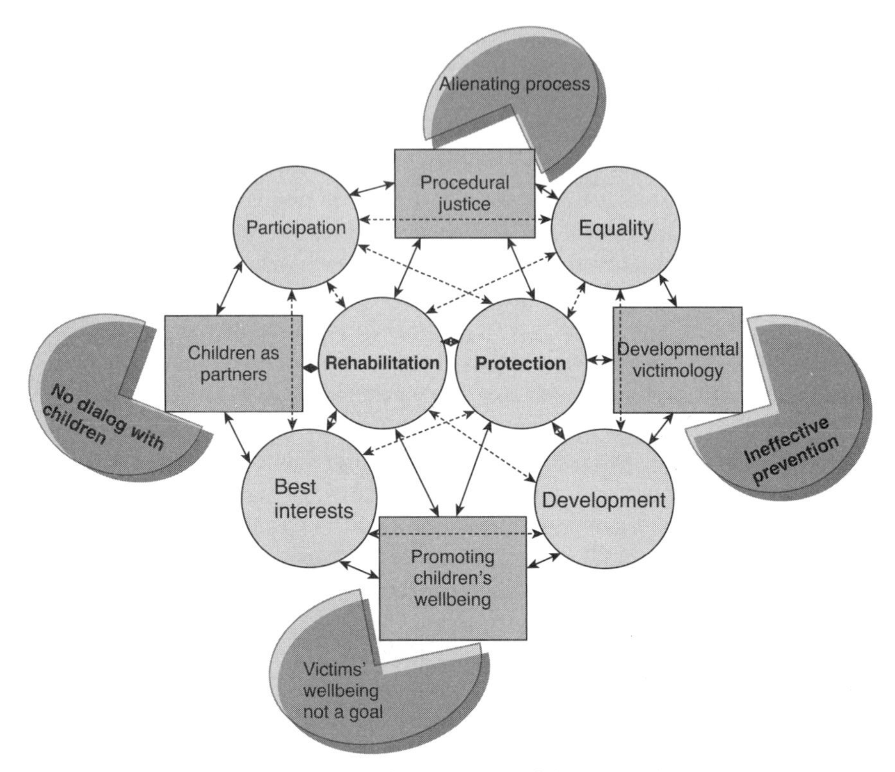

Figure 7.3 A needs-rights evaluation: shortcomings of the criminal justice process.

process in adversarial legal systems. Such an analysis was conducted in Chapter 4. It revealed that the criminal justice process addresses the needs-rights of child victims in only limited ways, as Figure 7.3 demonstrates.

The Protection Cluster

The right to protection[61] is implemented in perhaps the most satisfying way in the criminal process. Despite the significant difficulties in all stages of the process, the criminal justice system is still the only available large-scale mechanism of preventing, reporting, and responding to crimes against children. Protection against revictimization of children by the process itself has also been improved (in some jurisdictions more than in others) through victims' reforms. The current system, however, still largely fails to protect children from noncriminal violence such as sibling assaults, parental corporal punishment, and school bullying (Finkelhor et al., 2005). Furthermore, the criminal justice process struggles with the protection of children of abused mothers—victims of domestic violence—due to, among other reasons, its dichotomous treatment of those it defines as victims and those it defines as offenders. If the criminal justice process is intrinsically unsuitable for treating such forms of violence, then other mechanisms, such as restorative justice, should be considered to address them.

Beyond the right to protection and its subsidiaries, other elements of the protection cluster relating to the right to equality (nondiscrimination) and development receive less satisfactory attention in the criminal process. The criminal justice system fails to take a nuanced, developmental victimology approach, as the needs-rights of child victims postulate. As argued in Chapter 4, children with special needs have particular reporting barriers, and they pose considerable challenges to the system in investigating, prosecuting, and proving their cases. Children belonging to minority groups and residing in disadvantaged communities are also at higher risk for becoming victims, face greater barriers in reporting crimes against them, and are less likely to receive the appropriate treatment addressing their needs as crime victims. One example is the African American girls from urban, disadvantaged neighborhoods in St. Louis studied in Jody Miller's (2008) ethnography. These girls suffer from special vulnerabilities resulting from gender-based stereotypes, poverty, and systemic isolation, which lead to an increased risk of victimization, an increased prevalence of victim blaming, norms that call for bystanders not to intervene, and reluctance to report. From a needs-rights perspective, the criminal justice system fails to provide them with equal protection against victimization. Finally, young children (as well as teenagers, for different reasons) present other distinctive obstacles related to their cognitive and emotional development, and their cases are also less likely to be proved in court.

Despite the relatively high score that the protection right receives, then, the protection cluster as a whole receives an unsatisfactory mark (see p. 179). There is, however, perhaps the prospect of improvement. With better understanding of various disabilities, for instance, the criminal justice process can become more accessible for child victims with special needs, and better able to effectively prosecute crimes against them (Temkin, 1994). Police officers and other criminal justice personnel reacting to domestic violence reports can better address the needs (and rights) of children witnessing the violence if they treat them as victims themselves (Peled, 1996). Children advocacy centers and other child-centered initiatives can make the justice system more accessible for children of minority groups as well as for very young children.

The Best Interests Cluster

In comparison with the protection cluster, the best interests cluster points to even more disturbing shortcomings of the criminal justice process, with limited potential for improvement. The promotion of child victims' wellbeing is by definition not a primary consideration in a process that focuses on defendants. Although efforts are taken to meet some specific needs of child victims through testimony reforms, compensation schemes, and victim support programs, when direct conflict arises between the interests of the victim and those of the offender or the prosecution, the victim's interests lag behind. The court process is not designed to be a vehicle to meet the interests of the child, although there are efforts to make it the least negative experience possible. Proving guilt or innocence is the goal of the process and the victim is an evidentiary instrument (albeit a special one) in achieving this goal. The decision whether or not to call the child to the witness stand depends on the child's ability to promote the prosecution's case, not on the child's interests. Although children sometimes do not testify because of fears for their wellbeing (though often they still testify despite these fears, if the prosecution believes they can strengthen the case), the opposite does not occur: children do not testify "merely" because this might promote their wellbeing. It seems, then, that the criminal system can at best reduce harms to children, and perhaps even provide closure and empowerment coincidentally. It does not, however, seek to promote the best interests of children proactively and separately from the prosecution's interests.

The long-term and developmental interests of children (reflected in the rehabilitation and development human rights principles) are even more rarely considered in typical criminal processes. Material reparation is still not an integral part of the process, although there are now compensation schemes outside the criminal process. Furthermore, the nature of the process is adversarial and often hostile, and it does not provide opportunities to receive support, validation, and acknowledgment. Therefore, the criminal justice process often fails to meet the ingredients of the best interests cluster, and major changes cannot be expected without a shift in the very nature of the adversarial system (see p. 166).

The Control and Procedural Justice Clusters

Similar examinations were conducted with regard to the other two needs-rights clusters, control (see p. 168) and procedural justice (see p. 177). The point is that the model illuminates the limitations of the criminal justice process in meeting each of the needs-rights clusters, as well as the potential for improvement in some areas. This needs-rights analysis provides a more comprehensive assessment framework for the criminal justice process than previous evaluations that focused on specific aspects of children's involvement in court proceedings. The control cluster, for instance, demonstrates how even with victim-oriented mechanisms such as VISs, children can have only very limited influence on the process, if any. Even when they are allowed to report how the crime affected them, very rarely do they get any opportunity to engage in a mutual, respectful dialog with the decision-makers in the process or with the perpetrator, and their overall experience of it is one of lack of control. Similarly, the procedural justice cluster highlighted the inability of the criminal justice system to secure a sense of procedural justice for young victims: a feeling that they were able to affect the process and its outcomes and that they were listened to and respectfully considered. Rather than being partners in the resolution of "their case," children are typically left outside the "justice room." Consequently, children's overall experience of the criminal justice process is as an alienating one rather than inclusive.

RESTORATIVE JUSTICE AND CHILD VICTIMS: THE POTENTIAL

Considering the overall low marks the criminal justice process receives with regard to child victims, the need for an alternative justice mechanism that addresses the needs-rights of child victims more fully becomes clear. At least in the ideal, the needs-rights of child victims can be addressed effectively in restorative justice settings. Restorative justice seeks to achieve healing for the stakeholders, promotion of their wellbeing, and respect for their wishes and narratives while ensuring their safety. At the same time, restorative justice aims to promote rights in their broader meaning, corresponding to Minow's relational approach (1986). This broad meaning of rights includes rights that strengthen the interrelations between the child and the state (protective rights), others that promote relationships within the family (certain freedoms and rights against abuse and neglect in the family), as well as autonomous rights that promote the independence of the child. It also includes duties of others (parents and state) and the child. In an ideal restorative setting, people's relationships can be strengthened and each participant is encouraged to take responsibility while concurrently his or her rights are protected and promoted.

At the same time child victims are undoubtedly a "special case" warranting special attention for restorative justice programs, because of their limited experience, developing capacities, and greater dependency on others. Childhood, furthermore, is a broad and vague term that refers to vastly different developmental stages, abilities, and levels of dependency. When considering the inclusion of child victims in restorative justice programs, it is therefore important to treat each age group or developmental stage within the definition of childhood (age 18 and under) distinctly. Clearly, then, there is a need for a thorough examination of whether, when, how, and in what conditions restorative justice "works" for child victims of various ages.

Unfortunately, there is currently little research on restorative justice that focuses on the inclusion of child victims in these processes. Chapter 5 introduced major evaluation studies from well-known programs across the world and discussed the participation of children and the effectiveness of these experiences in enhancing children's wellbeing, wishes, and interests. Clearly, restorative justice and its evaluation are still in their infancy in terms of childhood victimization. Therefore, a full evaluation, similar to that conducted with regard to the criminal justice process, would be ineffective. Nevertheless, Chapter 5 demonstrated the substantial potential that restorative justice carries for child victims, as well as the concerns it raises. Importantly, it showed how programs such as the Family Group Decision Making Project in Newfoundland and Labrador managed to include child victims in a meaningful way in processes that followed child abuse, neglect, and domestic violence, while securing cultural sensitivity and family empowerment (Pennell & Anderson, 2005).

FULFILLING THE POTENTIAL: USING A NEEDS-RIGHTS MODEL AS A GUIDE

Even in theory, however, a child-inclusive restorative program needs to take into account other participants whose interests and rights are no less valid. Furthermore, in practice it is natural to expect processes that are less than perfect and facilitators who are not completely aware of the special vulnerabilities of children. Further tension exists between the need for flexibility and the expectation from all restorative practices to maintain high standards and address the human rights of all participants.

Therefore, a needs-rights framework might enhance the ability of restorative justice to meet the human rights of child victims in their broad meaning. Such a framework may perhaps also provide safeguards against malpractice, at least with regard to child victims, since programs are expected to meet the full range of the interrelated needs-rights of child victims. Accordingly, Chapter 6 deployed the model presented in Chapter 3. It discussed each of the four needs-rights clusters of the model and suggested subsidiary principles for action in restorative settings (Figure 7.4).

The best interests cluster suggested that individual assessments are needed with regard to every child victim involved in a restorative process, to identify the child's distinct short- and long-term needs and to plan the process accordingly. The wellbeing

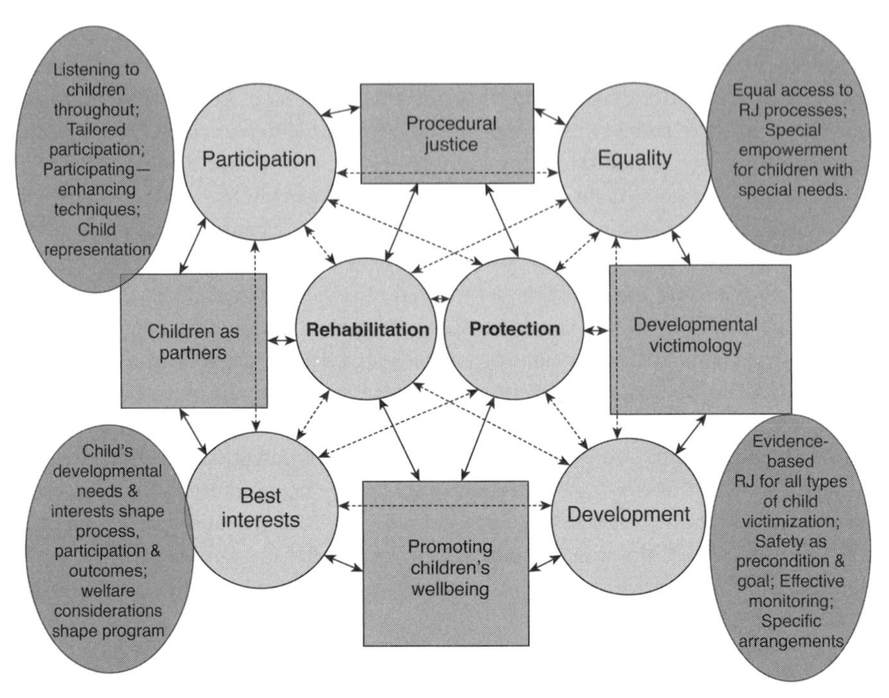

Figure 7.4 A needs-rights framework for child-inclusive restorative justice: subsidiary principles for action (RJ = restorative justice).

of children, we know by now, should be seen in a broad perspective, which considers children's lives within their families, communities, and cultures. The shared interests of children and their caretakers then become salient, even in ostensibly conflicted situations such as when child abuse is committed by an abused mother. More broadly, this cluster guides us to design programs in a way that will best meet the welfare of children according to the types of crime it is designed to approach, the age of the children it is assigned to treat, and the culture and community characteristics within which it operates. Furthermore, restorative justice is seen, in the context of this cluster, as an educational process with possible developmental benefits for children of various ages. At the same time, developmental considerations affect the specific needs and wishes of children. Therefore, each process and its outcomes (including, for instance, the types of reparation) should be tailored to the interests and wishes of the child involved in the process.

The control cluster highlighted the importance of involving children in decisions and listening to their views throughout the entire process, from the initial phase of constructing the invitee lists to the final stage where outcomes are discussed and monitoring mechanisms are considered. At the same time, the control cluster guides us to provide various age-appropriate participation alternatives to meet the specific needs and capabilities of individual children, considering the developmental stage they are in. This section also discussed some techniques to enhance the ability of children to have meaningful input in restorative processes, including child representation.

The procedural justice cluster pointed to the importance of ensuring equal access to restorative justice for children from various geographical areas, cultures, and communities and of different ages. It also suggested that to provide a truly fair and respectful process, programs need to be sensitive to and address children's special needs resulting from disability, ethnicity, and complex situations in their homes.

Finally, practical principles associated with the protection cluster were identified, such as the need to broaden the scope of protection of children to all forms of violence, from sibling and peer assaults to parental noncriminal (and criminal) violence, including the treatment of children who witness domestic violence in their homes as direct victims. The protection cluster also identified the centrality of the child's safety as both a precondition and a goal of the process, the importance of effective follow-up, and ways of providing special protections for children with special needs.

Applying the needs-rights model to restorative justice has helped clarify the relationships between the human rights principles and the hierarchy within them. For example, while the best interests principle is considered a general value that includes rehabilitation, protection, and development, the development principle has other, independent meanings. It emphasizes the importance of increasing children's autonomies and freedoms as they grow. At the same time, development is connected with, and influences, the understanding of the Convention's other guiding principles. It adds a gradual, developmental element to the participation principle, and fine-tunes the equality principle to allow children with disabilities to fulfill their potential to the maximum level.

WORKING HEURISTICALLY: FROM THEORY TO A SIMPLE BLUEPRINT

Since the needs-rights model and the subsidiary principles for action deriving from it create a somewhat cluttered picture, practitioners will need a simple-to-follow method to make this model useful. Accordingly, Chapter 6 concluded with a set of eight heuristics for child-inclusive restorative justice:

1. *Holism* suggests that it is important to consider the child's life as a whole and to address the full scope of the child's needs-rights while balancing them with each other, instead of a fragmented perspective aimed at the immediate issues emerging directly from the victimization.
2. A *tailor-made process* complements the previous heuristic by suggesting that each process should be fitted to the specific needs-rights of the child victim, instead of using a one-size-fits-all approach.
3. *Children as partners* points to the importance of crafting restorative processes *with* the child, instead of *for* the child, and of valuing children's contributions to our understanding of their needs and wishes, even at a young age.
4. *Participation as a continuum* makes children's right to participation possible even when they are very young or vulnerable or have special needs. It opens the door for the full range of participation options, starting from making the choice not to participate at all, up to being an active party in the restorative process.
5. *Liberating children's voices* suggests that each child has a valid story to tell and that it is adults' obligation to find ways to allow these stories to be told and understood even when they are different from adults' forms of expression.

6. *Let go* calls on practitioners to reflect whether they are being overprotective of children for reasons that are not about the rights-needs of the child. It suggests that, like parents, practitioners need to realize that to develop, children need—and often want—to take risks. Practitioners should allow them to act accordingly, while providing maximum preparation, support, and follow-up.
7. *Restorative process as a goal* suggests that notwithstanding their outcomes, restorative processes, when conducted well, might have an important educative and healing role in children's development and therefore should be seen as a goal in itself.
8. *Empowering advocacy* points to the importance of finding ways to strengthen children's position in the restorative process through the use of special advocates, while refraining from silencing or disempowering them through the very provision of such advocates.

None of the eight heuristics can be associated with any specific human rights principle or a psychosocial need. Rather, each principle relates to multiple needs-rights. For example, *restorative process as a goal* is based on the healing effect of taking part in such processes as well as its educative value, and therefore is possibly linked to rehabilitation, best interests, and development. *Liberating children's voices* refers to the challenge of overcoming the various social and developmental barriers to speaking up that children face, and again is justified by the rehabilitative value of being heard. It therefore corresponds with the equality, development, and rehabilitation principles. The *let go* heuristic helps balance participation and protection through a developmental perspective that fosters the evolving capacities of children. Accordingly, it is linked to the participation, protection, and development principles. A final example, *children as partners,* deepens the meaning of participation as starting from the early preparation stage, reminds professionals that they must actively seek children's involvement while treating them with respect as equal partners, and warns against forced participation. Therefore, it can be associated with the participation, best interests, and equality principles.

Holism is somewhat different because it provides methodological guidance for addressing the full range of rights and needs of children and for understanding each right as interrelated with the others while transforming them into action. The idea of *holism* might, then, be taken not as a directive but an overarching methodological tool. Accordingly, not only the rights and needs of child victims should be addressed as a whole in each case; the heuristic principles themselves should be understood as intertwined and indivisible. Moreover, *holism* also indicates that child victims should not be treated as two-dimensional, stereotypical images of victims. Instead, each child should be treated as a whole human being with strengths and weaknesses, wishes and interests, history and aspirations for the future.

A METHODOLOGICAL CONTRIBUTION

The steps taken here to explore the experiences of child victims and to search for ways to address their interests can be seen as a general methodology, one that can be applied to other contexts as well. This methodology includes the following steps.

First, a search for a consensual set of human rights norms was conducted. In the case of children, the CRC was a natural candidate. From this document, six human rights principles were identified as being most relevant to the context of child victims. Each of these principles was explained and justified, and the interrelationships between them were demonstrated graphically.

Second, empirical evidence on the meanings of these rights for child victims was sought from the psychosocial literature. The exploration of various theories and findings regarding elements such as control, apology and forgiveness, social support, and children's development, resulted in a heavily laden Chapter 3.

A third step was to marry the human rights with the psychosocial discourses. Indeed, each of these frameworks suffers from significant weaknesses. Human rights are criticized for being indeterminate, adversarial, and culturally blind. Human needs are considered ineffective in generating change and are difficult to map. The integration of both discourses in the end of Chapter 3 into a unified needs-rights model makes a robust framework that is more resistant to criticism from both directions. The human rights of child victims, when linked with psychosocial findings, are more concrete, are based on empirical evidence, and are clearly family- and community-oriented. Psychosocial elements related to childhood victimization, once linked with human rights, are identified more easily, mapped, armed with normative bite, and used as guides for social action. The division into four needs-rights clusters made the description of this cluttered model somewhat easier, and at the same time captured the indivisibility of many of its components.

Once a needs-rights model was established, a shift was made from theory to practice. Practices regarding child victims in the criminal justice process were evaluated critically in Chapter 4. Perhaps more importantly, subsidiary principles for child-inclusive restorative justice were proposed in Chapter 6. In both exercises, the analysis was conducted through the four need-rights clusters.

Finally, to make the subsidiary principles more accessible for restorative justice practitioners, a set of eight heuristics was proposed. Their importance is in translating a complex model, laden with details drawn from various fields, into very simple rules—almost clichés. These seemingly banal rules, however, are grounded in the findings presented in the full model, and therefore have a stronger status than other commonplace beliefs that are not grounded in the model. Practitioners who follow these rules would be therefore walking on relatively stable ground (as much as this is possible when working with individual human beings coming from different backgrounds and holding distinctive idiosyncrasies) and are likely to meet the full range of needs-rights of child victims. If, however, uncertainty appears, the full model provides the definitive template for testing whether all our obligations to children have been met. The full model is needed because there are a great variety of special circumstances that can shake the normally robust heuristics.

MOVING BEYOND CHILD VICTIMS

Child victims, however, are not the only stakeholders in the process that follows their victimization. As to the other participants, and in particular perpetrators, it has been suggested that human rights should be used as safeguards against disrespect, domination, and other forms of bad practice, in addition to having a role in providing guidance for action (Braithwaite, 2002a, p. 13). Admittedly, a restorative process designed entirely according to the victim's wishes and interests can potentially create conditions that are damaging from the offender's perspective. A balancing measure should be taken then, but a child-prioritizing one. The offender's basic human rights should not be violated and his or her interests should not be ignored. Nevertheless, the weaker position of the child and the need to provide him or her with extra support should never be pushed aside. Therefore, every empowering technique that meets the wishes and interests of the child should receive high priority, and can justifiably be denied only when it creates a significant violation of the offender's interests. In most cases, however, when victims experience the process as fair, offenders are more likely to experience it as fair as well, as Heather Strang's analysis of victims' and offenders' views of conferences demonstrated (Strang, 2002).

A different situation occurs when both victim and offender are minors. The offender then enjoys the same human rights protections provided in the Convention. Furthermore, the assumption of the inherently weakened position of a victim compared to an adult perpetrator does not apply here (assuming there is no significant age difference between the two parties).[62] When both victim and offender are minors, the balancing between the parties' interests can be based on equality. Still, both victim and offender should enjoy special measures to enhance their position in relation to adult participants, either professionals or communities of care.

Put more generally, if restorative justice is to promote social justice (Braithwaite, 2003a) through processes in which weakened populations are empowered, then every disadvantaged participant should enjoy special protections and have high priority. Hence, children (and the younger the child, the more support is needed), women in domestic violence situations, people with disabilities, people belonging to minority groups, elderly people, and poor consumers victimized by powerful corporations should all have their human rights and psychosocial needs actively promoted. Naturally, restorative processes often occur when two of the parties belong to disadvantaged groups. The weakened position of one participant should not negate the other's weakness. Each weakened party deserves to have his or her specific disadvantage addressed through empowerment, protection, and individual treatment. In most cases, the evidence from evaluations of restorative justice suggests, this will not be a win–lose situation (Strang, 2002, p. 250). Victims and offenders can receive whatever it is they need to participate effectively in restorative settings, and empowering one would not necessarily put the other party at a disadvantage. It is possible, in fact, that knowledge about the other's disempowered background will increase empathy and reduce fear between the two parties.

If other weakened populations should enjoy special protections and be empowered to express their views, wishes, and feelings, then the methodology presented here can be used (and is being used in many jurisdictions) to provide a holistic framework for promoting their needs-rights. A consensual set of human rights should be identified for such specific populations as a first step.[63] Then there is a need to seek empirical evidence on the meanings of these rights for that specific population. This exercise has the potential to lead to new understandings of human rights, clarify their importance, and identify gaps in both the normative framework and the social science research. The third step is to examine separate pairs, or clusters, of needs-rights, and draw a set of subsidiary principles for promoting them in restorative settings. Finally, heuristics can be produced that simplify the model and make its practice possible for practitioners. Naturally, this simple methodology requires theoretical research as well as empirical experimentation before applying its outcomes in large-scale projects. The idea, however, of marrying legal templates with the psychosocial literature is simple and has, as shown, much merit.

LOOKING FORWARD: DIRECTIONS FOR THE IMPLEMENTATION OF RESTORATIVE JUSTICE IN CHILDREN'S LIVES

Assuming we have established ways to deliver child-inclusive restorative justice, where do we place it in relation with the mainstream criminal justice process? Realistically, it seems that, at least in the coming years, restorative justice would not *replace* all criminal justice processes following childhood victimization. First, a precondition to hold a restorative justice process is the offender's admission of guilt and willingness to participate in such a process. Even if restorative justice becomes an attractive alternative for many offenders, there would still be those who would prefer to have their day in court and prove their innocence. In these cases, restorative justice would not be applicable. There would also be cases in which young victims would prefer not to be involved but would rather see justice being served publicly, in court. Finally, there would likely be cases in which the public interest would be to turn to the punitive process even when both victim and offender are willing to participate in a restorative process, such as when the offender has an extensive criminal record or when the crime is of special magnitude. In these cases, the criminal justice process is more likely to be used. Nevertheless, restorative justice can be used (and is being used in many jurisdictions) in such cases as an *addition* to the criminal justice process—for example, as part of the sentencing decision, or even later, during incarceration. Furthermore, the needs-rights of child victims and the restorative values sketched in this book can become useful in criminal justice processes as well, and integrated into the justice system. For instance, child victims can be represented in court so that their voices would be heard and their views considered, as happens, for example, in the International Criminal Court (Wemmers, 2009). Furthermore, to address the rehabilitative, developmental, and protective needs (and rights) of child victims, the criminal justice system should be complemented with adequate social services that provide multidimensional, short- and long-term responses to the various types of childhood victimization.

If we look further to the future, however, it is possible to imagine a system in which evidence-based, enculturated, child-inclusive restorative justice processes are so successful that they manage to generate systemic change. Successful processes are expected to provide high satisfaction rates among victims, including those who are disadvantaged by their belonging to a minority group, disability, or other reasons. Offenders' satisfaction rates are also expected to be high, including in cases of family violence, as the evidence has shown us. Consequently, with some marketing efforts and constant fine-tuning as new evidence appears, restorative justice can become the preferred option for both victims and offenders. Reporting rates of crimes against children can be significantly higher, once the threat of a crude adversarial process and cruel outcomes is removed. With higher reporting rates, deterrence is likely to be enhanced and crime can be expected to drop (Braithwaite, 2002a). The Hollow Water community is an example in which restorative justice, when used systemically, increased the number of cases disclosed and reduced recidivism afterwards (Couture, 2001). At the same time, child victims would not only be willing to disclose crime against them more easily, but they (and their parents) would be more open to participating in by now well-established restorative justice practices. More child-inclusive restorative processes would lead, in turn, not only to reduced recidivism, but also to reduced poly-victimization as well, because child victims will be more likely to rehabilitate. An optimistic finale for this book concludes, then, that respect for child victims and for their needs-rights would not only improve the way we react to childhood victimization, but it can also actually make childhood victimization less common.

NOTES

Chapter 1

1. See further discussions on the capacities of very young children to recognize others' viewpoints (p. 169) and regarding Darby and Schlenker's (1982) finding that at age 3 children are able to appreciate apologies (p. 75).
2. Over 20 countries, however, have enacted laws prohibiting corporal punishment of children since Sweden started doing so in 1979. For further details see the Global Initiative to End All Corporal Punishment of Children. Retrieved from http://www.endcorporalpunishment.org/children/countries.html, last accessed on March 27, 2011. Even in jurisdictions in which no general ban on corporal punishment exists, certain levels of corporal punishment are typically considered criminal, such as acts causing grievous bodily harm.
3. Further explanation regarding the differences and similarities between child protection and criminal justice family group conferences is provided in Chapter 5, including some discussion about the theory and practice of child protection family group conferences.
4. A more detailed explanation of these three most common forms of restorative practices will be presented in Chapter 5.

Chapter 2

5. See, for instance, Gilligan (1982) and Olsen (1992).
6. As this book shows, however, a more complex needs-rights model does acknowledge the broader familial context in identifying the optimal solution from the child's perspective and is more likely to identify the woman's wellbeing as promoting the needs and/or rights of the child.
7. The specific meaning of the participation right granted to children in the Convention will be discussed in detail later in this chapter.
8. For a detailed explanation see Rawls (1999, Chapter 3).
9. A somewhat similar way of describing the shift between paternalism and autonomy is Flekkøy and Kaufman's (1997, p. 50) distinction between having rights and exercising rights. This distinction reflects the idea that children, like all other human beings, are born with certain freedoms and basic rights. Vulnerable and inexperienced, young children often cannot exercise these freedoms, but it is adults' obligation to take off the veil of protection, or paternalism, as soon as the children are ready to make their own decisions.
10. Maslow's hierarchy has five levels: (1) physiological—hunger, thirst, shelter, sex, etc.;(2) safety—security, protection from physical and emotional harm; (3) social—affection, belonging, acceptance, friendship; (4) esteem (also called ego)—the internal

ones are self-respect, autonomy, and achievement, and the external ones are status, recognition, and attention; (5) self-actualization (doing things).

11. These principles are discussed in detail as part of the analysis of the Convention's articles.
12. This, however, is not the political reality in the United States today.
13. Under Article 51 of the Convention, states are allowed to make reservations regarding specific articles upon ratification, as long as they are not incompatible with the purpose of the Convention.
14. General Guidelines Regarding the Form and Contents of Initial Reports to be Submitted by State Parties under Article 44, Paragraph 1(a), of the Convention, adopted by the committee at its 22nd meeting, on Oct. 15, 1989.
15. See Committee on the Rights of the Child's (2005) General Guidelines (hereafter known as Guidelines for Periodic Reports).
16. See also the Committee's general discussion day on children with disabilities, in particular paragraphs 330, 331, 334, 335 (CRC/C/69).
17. For a detailed discussion of the wording of the best interest principle and its weight, see Marshall (1997, pp. 8–11).
18. The committee emphasizes the strength of the wording "to ensure" and the fact that it includes both active and proactive obligations (Hodgkin & Newell, 2002, pp. 42–47).
19. Chapter 4 discusses the competing interests in the context of the criminal justice process in further detail.
20. See the discussion on Rawls's work earlier in this chapter.
21. The limitations of the best-interests test were most notably discussed by Mnookin (1975).
22. Guatemala Initial Report Concluding Observations (IRCO), Addendum 58, paragraph 20, cited in Hodgkin and Newell (2002, p. 89).
23. Report on the Fifth Session, January 1994, CRC/C/24, Annex V, p. 63.
24. With the appropriate accommodations to their specific needs—see the discussion on equality earlier in this chapter.
25. Article 12(1) states: "the views of the child being given due weight in accordance with the age and maturity of the child."
26. The various child representation models will be discussed in Chapter 6.

Chapter 3

27. Although women can be violent toward their male partners, the terminology I use here is not gender-neutral because most cases of severe violence are conducted by men against women. This, however, should not be understood as ignoring the opposite scenarios or same-sex intimate violence.
28. As one anonymous reviewer rightly commented, many children and youths who are abused by a family member or witness the abuse of their mother want their relationship with the abuser to end. This, however, does not contradict Herman's description of children's fantasies of gaining their abuser's love and affection.
29. This example was provided by a victim support practitioner at the conference "Innovation: Promising Practices for Victims and Witnesses in the Criminal Justice System," Oct. 23–24, 2003, at the Australian National University, Canberra, Australia.

30. In Chapter 5, some restorative justice programs involving children are reviewed, with initial findings regarding the actual outcomes of such group discussions from child victims' perspectives.

Chapter 4

31. In some inquisitorial legal systems, such as Austria, Germany, Norway, Poland, Sweden, and Yugoslavia, victims have the right to act as subsidiary, or supporting, prosecutors by submitting evidence and participating in the legal debate (see Tobolowsky, 1999, p. 25). However, in Western, adversarial legal systems victims typically have a passive role in the process. The conflict, as Nils Christie (1977) famously noted, was "stolen" by the system away from the hands of the direct parties.
32. This is not the case in some jurisdictions. In the United Kingdom, for instance, a defendant's criminal record can be admitted on a "tit-for-tat" basis where the defendant has attacked the character of a prosecution witness.
33. In inquisitorial systems, in contrast, there is less intimidation and cross-examinations are not inherently confrontational, since they are conducted by the judge (Groenhuijsen, 1994, p. 169).
34. This of course does not suggest that all acquittals are erroneous.
35. While another half reported that there was nothing positive about it.

Chapter 5

36. When direct mediation is undesirable, the parties sometimes communicate indirectly by some form of "shuttle diplomacy" by the mediator (Zehr, 2002, p. 47).
37. These results will be discussed in more detail later in this chapter.
38. Their review focused on tests that were based either on randomized assignment to treatment and control groups, or included comparable control groups.
39. "Proved" means either that the court accepted a guilty plea or found the defendant guilty at trial: see Daly et al., 2003, p. 2.
40. A prevention program for adolescent sex offenders.
41. Twenty-eight percent of the victims were under 18 years old, but it is unknown how many of them were revictimized.
42. All three victims were under 18.
43. Prospects for continuing relationships, however, might be a serious barrier for victims to agree to meet their offenders in the first place: see Crawford & Burden, 2005, p. 39.
44. The Crimes (Restorative Justice) Act of 2004 regulated the operation of restorative justice practices in the ACT through a new restorative justice unit, thereby shifting from the "Wagga" to the New Zealand model.
45. I am very grateful to Heather Strang, who provided me with access to the RISE files involving child victims.
46. These figures relate to two out of the four experiments that were conducted in RISE: property (with a personal victim) and violence. The other two, drunk driving and shoplifting, are of less relevance here and therefore are not included in the following analysis.
47. These were the original file numbers used in the RISE experiment.
48. The negative consequences of undelivered conferences were affirmed statistically. See Sherman & Strang, 2007.
49. Communication with Heather Strang, April 28, 2003.
50. See, for example, Gunderson, 2003; Hudson et al., 1996; Marsh & Crow, 1998; Sieppert et al., 2000.

51. For a detailed description of the evaluation instruments and methodology, see Pennell & Burford, 1995, pp. 21–36.
52. This is in fact an interesting case because it tells us that, at least for that family, the children's views could have been helpful for addressing the spousal abuse. This point exceeds the framework of the current discussion, but it is worth noting that the mutual ties between domestic violence and child abuse go beyond the co-occurrence of abuse and its outcomes on victims. They are also relevant to the discussion regarding ways of addressing the two phenomena and, more specifically, the importance of children's participation in processes resulting from them.
53. This is in fact one of the solutions suggested by the National Council of Juvenile and Family Court Judges' guidelines for effective interventions in cases of domestic violence and child maltreatment, popularly called the "Greenbook." See Schechter & Edleson, 1999, p. 110.
54. This requirement applied to any child participating in conferences, either as a victim, a family member, or an offender. Indeed, many children who were not identified as victims at the start of a conference were found to have also been victimized by the end of the process.
55. This will be discussed in Chapter 6.
56. The following paragraphs do not present a comprehensive discussion of the appropriateness (or inappropriateness) of restorative justice in cases of domestic violence, as such a discussion would exceed the scope of this chapter, which, as the rest of the book, refers to all forms of childhood victimization. Strang & Braithwaite (2002) and Ptacek (2010) are two edited collections introducing a range of perspectives on both the dangers and the potential benefits of restorative justice in cases of domestic violence.
57. This is also the Greenbook's recommendation: see Schechter & Edleson, 1999, p. 90.
58. It is yet to be tested, however, to what extent indirect restorative processes actually help victims.

Chapter 6

59. It is possible, however, that the existence of a restorative alternative would encourage more offenders to admit their crime, as the Hollow Water program demonstrated, and thus would make reparation available to more child victims (see p. 140).
60. I have seen this dilemma time and time again in my own work as a children's advocate and in other social organizations: unprofessional volunteers kept close contact with the clients and managed to build a relationship of trust and partnership, but only high-profile attorneys who hardly ever even spoke with the clients managed to make significant legal achievements in difficult cases. In most cases, however, overworked, underpaid, idealistic, typically female legal practitioners working at nongovernmental organizations (like myself) tried to provide quality advocacy services to their clients *and* develop a relationship based on respect with them.

Chapter 7

61. In contrast with the protection cluster.
62. It is, however, possible that one of the parties is weakened through socioeconomic status, language barriers, or special needs. These, naturally, should be addressed.
63. Such human rights documents may be international treaties or, in domestic policies, constitutional and other human rights laws.

BIBLIOGRAPHY

Ahmed, E. (2006). Understanding bullying from a shame management perspective: findings from a three-year follow-up study. *Educational and Child Psychology, 23*(2), 25–39.

Ahmed, E., Harris, N., Braithwaite, J., & Braithwaite, V. (2001). *Shame management through reintegration*. Cambridge Criminology Series. Cambridge, U.K.: Cambridge University Press.

Alston, P. (1994). The best interests principle: towards a reconciliation of culture and human rights. In P. Alston (Ed.), *The best interests of the child: reconciling culture and human rights* (pp. 1–25). Oxford: Clarendon Press.

Anderson, T. (2005). *PTSD in children and adolescents, Technical Report GCP–05–04*. Chicago: Great Cities Institute.

Andrews, D. A., & Bonta, J. (2003). *The psychology of criminal conduct*. Cincinnati: Anderson.

Angel, C. M. (2006). Restorative justice conceptualized as a cognitive behavioral therapeutic approach: an overview. Unpublished Paper.

Archard, D. W. (2002). Children's rights. In E. N. Zalta (Ed.), *The Stanford encyclopedia of philosophy*. URL: http://plato.stanford.edu/archives/win2002/entries/rights-children/

Ban, P. (2000). Family group conferences in four Australian states. In G. Burford & J. Hudson (Eds.), *Family group conferencing: new directions in community-centered child and family practice* (pp. 232–241). New York: Aldine De Gruyter.

Bandman, B. (1973). Do children have any natural rights? A look at rights and claims in legal, moral and educational discourse. *Proceedings of the 29th Annual Meeting of the Philosophy of Education Society* (pp. 234–246).

Basic Principles of Justice for Victims of Crime and Abuse of Power (1985). General Assembly Resolution 40/34, annex, adopted Nov. 29, 1982.

Basic Principles on the Use of Restorative Justice Programmes in Criminal Matters (2002). Economic and Social Council Resolution 2002/12.

Bazemore, G., & Earle, T. H. (2002). Balance in the response to family violence: challenging restorative principles. In H. Strang & J. Braithwaite (Eds.), *Restorative justice and family violence* (p. 153). Cambridge: Cambridge University Press.

Bennett Woodhouse, B. (1998). From property to parenthood: a child-centered perspective on parents' rights. *Georgetown Journal on Fighting Poverty*, 5, 313–319.

Bianchi, H., & van Swaaningen, R. (1990). *The politics of redress: crime, punishment, and penal abolition*. Michigan: Unwin Hyman.

Bibas, S., & Bierschbach, R. A. (2004). Integrating remorse and apology into criminal procedure. *Yale Law Journal, 114*, 85–148.

Bojer, H. (2000). Children and theories of social justice. *Feminist Economics, 6*(2), 23–39.

Bonta, J., Jesseman, R., Rugge, T., & Cormier, R. (2006). Restorative justice and recidivism: promises made, promises kept? In D. Sullivan & L. Tifft (Eds.), *Handbook of restorative justice: a global perspective* (pp. 108–120). Oxon: Routledge.

Bonta, J., Wallace-Capretta, S., Rooney, J., & Mcanoy, K. (2002). An outcome evaluation of a restorative justice alternative to incarceration. *Contemporary Justice Review, 5*(4), 319–338.

Braithwaite, J. (1989). *Crime, shame and reintegration*. Cambridge: Cambridge University Press.

Braithwaite, J. (1999). Restorative justice: assessing optimistic and pessimistic accounts. *Crime and Justice, 25*, 1–127.

Braithwaite, J. (2000) Restorative justice and social justice. *Saskatchewan Law Review, 63*, 185–194.

Braithwaite, J. (2002a). *Restorative justice and responsive regulation*. New York: Oxford University Press.

Braithwaite, J. (2002b). Setting standards for restorative justice. *British Journal of Criminology, 42*(3), 563–577.

Braithwaite, J. (2003a). Holism, justice and atonement. *Utah Law Review 2003*(1), 389–412.

Braithwaite, J. (2003b). Principles of restorative justice. In A. Von-Hirsch, J. V. Roberts, & A. Bottoms (Eds.), *Restorative justice and criminal justice: competing or reconcilable paradigms?* (pp. 1–20). Portland, OR: Hart Publishing.

Braithwaite, J., & Daly, K. (1994). Masculinities, violence and communitarian control. In N. Tim & B. Stanko (Eds.), *Just boys doing business: men, masculinity and crime* (pp. 221–251). London: Routledge.

Braithwaite, J., & Strang, H. (2001). Introduction: restorative justice and civil society. In H. Strang & J. Braithwaite (Eds.), *Restorative justice and civil society* (pp. 1–13). Cambridge: Cambridge University Press.

Brennan, S., & Noggle, R. (1997). The moral status of children: children's rights, parents' rights, and family justice. *Social Theory and Practice, 23*(1), 1–26.

Brickman, P., Rabinowitz, V. C., Karuza, J. J., Coates, D., Cohn, E., & Kidder, L. (1982). Models of helping and coping. *American Psychologist, 37*(4), 368–384.

Bridgeman, J., & Monk, D. (2000). Introduction: reflections on the relationship between feminism and child law. In J. Bridgeman & D. Monk (Eds.), *Feminist perspectives on child law* (pp. 1–18). London: Cavendish Publishing.

Briere, J., & Elliott, D. (1994). Immediate and long-term impacts of child sexual abuse. *The Future of Children 4*(2), 54–69.

Brook, E., & Warshwski-Brook, S. (2009). The healing nature of apology and its contribution toward emotional reparation and closure in restorative justice encounters. In S. G. Shoham, P. Knepper, & M. Kett (Eds.), *International handbook of victimology* (pp. 511–536). Boca Raton: CRC Press.

Brown, L. (2003). Mainstream or margin? The current use of family group conferences in child welfare practice in the UK. *Child and Family Social Work, 8*, 331–340.

Burford, G., & Pennell, J. (1998). *Family group decision-making project: outcome report, Technical Report 1*. Memorial University of Newfoundland.

Burford, G., Pennell, J., & MacLeod, S. (1995). *Manual for coordinators and communities: the organization and practice of family group decision-making*. Memorial University of Newfoundland, School of Social Work.

Burton, M., Evans, R., & Sanders, A. (2006). *Are special measures for vulnerable and intimidated witnesses working? Evidence from the criminal justice agencies, Technical Report 01/06*. Home Office.

Busch, R. (2002). Domestic violence and restorative justice initiatives: who pays if we get it wrong? In H. Strang & J. Braithwaite (Eds.), *Restorative Justice and Family Violence* (pp. 223–249). Cambridge: Cambridge University Press.

Caffo, E., Forresi, B., & Strik-Lievers, B. (2005). Impact, psychological sequelae and management of trauma affecting children and adolescents. *Current Opinion in Psychiatry, 18*(4), 422–428.

Call, K. T., & Mortimer, J. T. (2001). *Arenas of comfort in adolescence: a study of adjustment in context*. Mahwah, NJ: Lawrence Erlbaum Associates.

Campbell, T. D. (1992). The rights of the minor: as person, as child, as juvenile, as future adult. In P. Alston, S. Parker, & J. Seymour (Eds.), *Children, rights, and the law* (pp. 1–23). Oxford: Clarendon Press.

Campell, L. (1997). Family involvement in decision-making in child protection and care: four types of case conference, *Child and Family Social Work, 2*, 1–11.

Cashmore, J. (1995). *The evidence of children, Technical report*. Judicial Commission of New South Wales.

Cashmore, J. (2002). Innovative procedures for child witnesses. In H. L. Westcott, G. M. Davies, & R. H. Bull (Eds.), *Children's testimony: a handbook of psychological research and forensic practice* (pp. 203–218). West Sussex: John Wiley and Sons.

Cashmore, J., & Trimboli, L. (2005). *An evaluation of the NSW child sexual assault specialist jurisdiction pilot, technical report*. NSW Bureau of Crime Statistics and Research.

Charlesworth, H., & Chinkin, C. (2000). *The boundaries of international law*. Manchester: Manchester University Press.

Christie, N. (1977). Conflicts as property. *British Journal of Criminology, 17*, 1–15.

Coady, C. A. J. (1992). Theory, rights and children: a comment on O'Neill and Campbell. In P. Alston, S. Parker, & J. Seymour (Eds.), *Children, rights, and the law* (pp. 43–51). Oxford: Clarendon Press.

Cohen, L. E., & Felson, M. (1979). Social change and crime rate trends: a routine activity approach, *American Sociological Review, 44*, 588–608.

Collins, R. (2004). *Interaction ritual chains*. Princeton & Oxford: Princeton University Press.

Committee on the Rights of the Child (2005). General Guidelines regarding the Form and Content of Periodic Reports to be Submitted by States Parties Under Article 44, Paragraph 1 (b), of the Convention. CRC/C/58/Rev.1, Accepted 29 November 2005.

Cook, B., David, F., & Grant, A. (1999). *Victims' needs, victims' rights: policies and programs for victims of crime in Australia*. Canberra: Australian Institute of Criminology.

Cook, K. J., Daly, K., & Stubbs, J. (2006). Introduction. *Theoretical Criminology, 10*(1), 5–7.

Cossins, A. (2008). Restorative justice and child sex offences. *British Journal of Criminology, 48*(3), 359–378.

Couture, J. (2001). *A cost-benefit analysis of Hollow Water's Community Holistic Circle Healing Process, Technical Report A PC 20 CA*. Aboriginal Peoples Collection, Canada.

Covell, K., & How, B. R. (2009). *Children, families and violence*. London & Philadelphia: Jessica Kingsley Publishers.

Crawford, A., & Burden, T. (2005). *Integrating victims in restorative youth justice*. Bristol: The Policy Press.

Crow, G., Holton, E., & Marsh, P. (2004). *Supporting pupils, schools and families: an evaluation of the Hampshire Family Group Conferences in Education Project*. Sheffield: University of Sheffield and Hampshire Education Department.

Daems, T. (2009). Death of a metaphor? Healing victims and restorative justice. In S. G. Shoham, P. Knepper, & M. Kett (Eds.), *International handbook of victimology* (pp. 491–510). Boca Raton: CRC Press.

Dalrymple, J. (2002). Family group conferences and youth advocacy: the participation of children and young people in family decision-making, *European Journal of Social Work*, *5*(3), 287–299.

Daly, K. (2001). Conferencing in Australia and New Zealand: variations, research findings, and prospects. In A. Morris & G. Maxwell (Eds.), *Restorative justice for juveniles: conferencing, mediation and circles* (pp. 59–84). Portland, OR: Hart Publishing.

Daly, K. (2002). Sexual assault and restorative justice. In H. Strang & J. Braithwaite (Eds.), *Restorative justice and domestic violence* (pp. 62–88). Cambridge: Cambridge University Press.

Daly, K., Curtis-Fawley, S., & Bouhours, B. (2003). *Sexual offence cases finalized in court, by conference, and by formal caution in South Australia for young offenders, 1995–2001, technical report.* South Australia: School of Criminology and Criminal Justice, Griffith University.

Daly, K., & Stubbs, J. (2006). Feminist engagement with restorative justice. *Theoretical Criminology*, *10*(1), 9–28.

Daly, K., Venables, M., McKenna, M., Mumford, L., & Christie-Johnston, J. (1998). *South Australia juvenile justice research on conferencing: project overview and research instruments, technical report 1.* Queensland: School of Criminology and Criminal Justice, Griffith University.

Darby, B. W., & Schlenker, B. R. (1982). Children's reactions to apologies. *Journal of Personality and Social Psychology*, *43*(4), 742–753.

Davis, R. C., Taylor, B., & Lurigio, A. J. (1996). Adjusting to criminal victimization: the correlates of postcrime distress. *Violence and Victims*, *11*(1), 21–38.

de Haan, W. (1990). *The politics of redress: crime, punishment, and penal abolition.* Washington DC: Unwin Hyman.

Declaration of Geneva (1924). Council of the League of Nations Assembly.

Detrick, S., Doek, J., & Cantwell, N. (Eds.) (1992). *The United Nations Convention on the Rights of the Child: A Guide to the "Travaux Preparatoires."* Boston: M. Nijhoff.

Dickson-Gilmore, J., & La Prairie, C. (2005). *Will the circle be unbroken?* Toronto: University of Toronto Press.

Dobash, R. E., & Dobash, R. P. (1992). *Women, violence and social change.* London: Routledge.

Doig, M., & Wallace, B. (1999). *Family Conference Team, Youth Court of South Australia, Restoration for Victims of Crime Conference.* Australian Institute of Criminology in conjunction with Victims Referral and Assistance Service, Melbourne.

Doyal, L., & Gough, I. (1991). *A theory of human need.* London: Macmillan.

Duff, R. A. (1996). Penal communications: recent work in the philosophy of punishment. *Crime and Justice*, *20*, 1–98.

Duncan, A. (2009). *Child and youth offending statistics in New Zealand: 1992 to 2007.* Wellington: Ministry of Justice.

Durrant, J. A. (2000). *A generation without smacking: the impact of Sweden's ban on physical punishment.* London: Save the Children.

Dworkin, R. M. (1981). *Taking rights seriously*. London: Duckworth.

Dwyer, J. G. (2006). *The relationship rights of children.* New York: Cambridge University Press.

Eastwood, C., & Patton, W. (2002). *The experiences of child complainants of sexual abuse in the criminal justice system, technical report.* Report to the Criminology Research Council. Available at: *http://www.aic.gov.au/crc/reports/eastwood.html*

Edelstein, R. S., Goodman, G. S., Ghetti, S., Alexander, K. W., Quas, J. A., Redlich, A. D., Schaaf, J. M., & Cordon, I. M. (2002). Child witnesses' experiences post-court: effects of legal involvement. In H. L. Westcott, G. M. Davies, & R. H. C. Bull (Eds.), *Children's testimony* (pp. 261–277). West Sussex: John Wiley and Sons.

Edleson, J. L. (1999). Children's witnessing of adult domestic violence. *Journal of Interpersonal Violence, 14*, 839–870.

Eekelaar, J. (1992). The importance of thinking that children have rights. In P. Alston, S. Parker, & J. Seymour (Eds.), *Children, rights, and the law* (pp. 22–235). Oxford: Clarendon Press.

Enright, R. D., & Fitzgibbons, R. P. (2000). *Helping clients forgive: an empirical guide for resolving anger and restoring hope.* Washington DC: American Psychological Association.

Enright, R. D., Gassin, E. A., & Knuston, J. A. (2003). Waging peace through forgiveness education in Belfast, Northern Ireland: a review and proposal for mental health improvement of children. *Journal of Research in Education, 13*(1), 1–11.

Enright, R. D., & Kittle, B. A. (2000). Forgiveness in psychology and law: the meeting of moral development and restorative justice. *Fordham Urban Law Journal, 27*, 1621–1631.

Erez, E., Roeger, L., & O'Connell, M. (1994). Victim impact statements in South Australia. In C. Sumner, M. Israel, M. O'Connell, & R. Sarre (Eds.), *International victimology: selected papers from the 8th International Symposium* (pp. 205–216). Canberra: Australian Institute of Criminology.

Ezer, T. (2004). A positive right to protection for children. *Yale Human Rights and Development Law Journal, 7*, 1–50.

Fantuzzo, J. W., & Mohr, W. K. (1999). Prevalence and effects of child exposure to domestic violence. *The Future of Children, 9*(3), 21–32.

Farson, R. (1974). *Birthrights.* New York: Macmillan.

Fattah, E. A. (1997). Toward a victim policy aimed at healing, not suffering. In R. C. Davis, A. J. Lurigio, & W. G. Skogan (Eds.), *Victims of crime* (2nd ed., pp. 257–272). Thousand Oaks, CA: Sage.

Fattah, E. A. (1998). A critical assessment of two justice paradigms: contrasting the restorative and retributive justice models. In E. Fattah & T. Peters (Eds.), *Support for crime victims in a comparative perspective* (pp. 99–110). Leuven: Leuven University Press.

Federle, K. H. (1994). Rights flow downhill. *International Journal of Children's Rights, 2*, 343–368.

Federle, K. H. (1995). Looking ahead: an empowerment perspective on the rights of children. *Temple Law Review, 68*(4), 1585–1606.

Federle, K. H. (1996). The ethics of empowerment: rethinking the role of lawyers in interviewing and counseling the child client. *Fordham Law Review, 64*(5), 1655–1698.

Feinberg, J. (1980). *Rights, justice, and the bounds of liberty: essays in social philosophy.* Princeton Series of Collected Essays. Princeton: Princeton University Press.

Finkelhor, D. (2008). *Childhood victimization: violence, crime, and abuse in the lives of young people.* New York: Oxford University Press.

Finkelhor, D., & Dziuba-Leatherman, J. (2001). Victimization of children. In R. Bull (Ed.), *Children and the law: the essential readings* (pp. 5–28). Oxford: Blackwell Publishers.

Finkelhor, D., & Dzuiba-Leatherman, J. (1994). Victimization of children. *American Psychologist, 49*(3), 173–183.

Finkelhor, D., & Kendall-Tackett, K. (1997). A developmental perspective on the childhood impact of crime, abuse, and violent victimization. In D. Cicchetti & S. L. Toth (Eds.), *Developmental perspectives on trauma: theory, research, and intervention* (pp. 1–32). New York: University of Rochester Press.

Finkelhor, D., Ormrod, R., Turner, H., & Hamby, S. L. (2005). The victimization of children and youth: a comprehensive, national survey. *Child Maltreatment, 10*(1), 5–25.

Flekkøy, M. G., & Kaufman, N. H. (1997). *The participation rights of the child: rights and responsibilities in family and society*. London, U.K., & Bristol, PA: Jessica Kingsley.

Folger, R. (1977). Distributive and procedural justice: combined impact of "voice" and improvement on experienced inequity. *Journal of Personality and Social Psychology, 35*, 108–119.

Fortin, J. (2003). *Children's rights and the developing law* (2nd ed). London: Butterworths.

Fraser, S., & Norton, J. (1996). Family group conferencing in New Zealand child protection work. In J. Hudson, A. Morris, G. Maxwell, & B. Galaway (Eds.), *Family group conferences: perspectives on policy and practice* (pp. 37–48). Leichhardt, NSW, Australia: The Federation Press; Criminal Justice Press.

Frazier, P. A. (2003). Perceived control and distress following sexual assault: a longitudinal test of a new model. *Journal of Personality and Social Psychology, 84*(6), 1257–1269.

Frederick, L., & Lizdas, K. C. (2010). The role of restorative justice in the battered women's movement. In J. Ptacek (Ed.), *Restorative justice and violence against women* (pp. 39–59). New York: Oxford University Press.

Freeman, M. D. A. (1983). *The rights and wrongs of children*. London: Frances Pinter.

Freeman, M. D. A. (1992). Taking children's rights more seriously. In P. Alston, S. Parker, & J. Seymour (Eds.), *Children, rights, and the law* (pp. 52–71). Oxford: Clarendon Press.

Freeman, M. D. A. (1998). The sociology of childhood and children's rights. *International Journal of Children's Rights, 6*, 433–444.

Freeman, M. D. A. (2002). Human rights, children's rights and judgment—some thoughts on reconciling universality and pluralism. *International Journal of Children's Rights, 10*, 345–354.

Furman, W., & Buhrmester, D. (1985). Children's perceptions of the personal relationships in their social networks. *Developmental Psychology, 21*(6), 1016–1024.

Garner, J., & Nishith, P. (1997). Victims of domestic violence. In R. C. Davis, A. J. Lurigio, & W. G. Skogan (Eds.), *Victims of crime*. Thousand Oaks, CA: Sage Publications.

Ghetti, S., Weede, K. A., & Goodman, G. S. (2002). Legal involvement in child sexual abuse cases: consequences and interventions. *International Journal of Law and Psychiatry, 25*, 235–251.

Gilligan, C. (1982). *In a different voice*. Cambridge: Harvard University Press.

Glennon, T., & Schwartz, R. (1995). Forward: looking back, looking ahead: the evolution of children's rights. *Temple Law Review, 68*(4), 1557–1572.

Goel, R. (2000). No women at the center: the use of the Canadian sentencing circle in domestic violence cases. *Wisconsin Women's Law Journal, 15*, 293–334.

Goel, R. (2010). Aboriginal women and political pursuit in Canadian sentencing circles: at cross roads or cross purposes? In J. Ptacek (Ed.), *Restorative justice and violence against women* (pp. 60–78). New York: Oxford University Press.

Goldsmith, A., Israel, M., & Dally, K. (Eds.) (2003). *Crime and justice: an Australian text book in criminology* (2nd ed). Lawbook Co.

Gonzales, C. M., & Tyler, T. R. (2008). The psychology of enfranchisement: engaging and fostering inclusion of members through voting and decision-making procedures. *Journal of Social Issues, 64*, 447–466.

Goodman, G. S., Tobey, A. E., Batterman-Faunce, J. M., Orcutt, H., Thomas, S., Shapiro, C., & Sachenmaier, T. (1998). Face-to-face confrontation: effects of closed-circuit technology on children's eyewitness testimony and jurors' decisions. *Law and Human Behavior, 22*, 165–203.

Gordon West, W., & Morris, R. (Eds.) (2000). *The case for penal abolition*. Canadian Scholars' Press.

Graham, A., & Fitzgerald, R. (2005). *Taking account of the "to and fro" of children's experiences in family law*. Childhoods 2005 Conference.

Greenberg, J. (1987). Using diaries to promote procedural justice in performance appraisals. *Social Justice Research, 1*, 219–234.

Groenhuijsen, M. (1994). Conflicts of victims' interests and offenders' rights in the criminal justice system: a European perspective. In C. Sumner, M. Israel, M. O'Connell, & R. Sarre (Eds.), *International victimology: selected papers from the 8th International Symposium* (pp. 163–176). Canberra: Australian Institute of Criminology.

Groenhuijsen, M. (2004). Victims' rights and restorative justice: piecemeal reform of the criminal justice system or a change of paradigm? In K. Hendrik & M. Malsch (Eds.), *Crime, victims and justice: essays on principles and practice* (pp. 63–79). Hampshire: Ashgate Publishing Limited.

Guidelines on Justice in Matters Involving Child Victims and Witnesses of Crime (2005). Economic and Social Council, UN. (E/CN. 15/2005/20).

Gunderson, K. (2003). *Addressing child protection and group issues through the use of family group conferencing*. Presented at 4th International Conference on Conferencing and Circles.

Hafen, B. C., & Hafen, J. O. (1996). Abandoning children to their autonomy: the United Nations Convention on the Rights of the Child. *Harvard International Law Journal, 37*(2), 449–491.

Haines, K. (1998). Some principled objections to a restorative justice approach to working with juvenile offenders. In L. Walgrave (Ed.), *Restorative justice for juveniles: potentialities, risks and problems for research* (pp. 93–114). Leuven: Leuven University Press.

Harris, N., Walgrave, L., & Braithwaite, J. (2004). Emotional dynamics in restorative conferences. *Theoretical Criminology, 8*(2), 191–210.

Hart, H. L. A. (1982). *Essays on Bentham: studies in jurisprudence and political theory*. Oxford: Clarendon.

Hart, R. A. (1992). Children's participation: from tokenism to citizenship. *Technical Report Innocenti Essays, 4*, UNICEF.

Herman, J. L. (1992). *Trauma and recovery*. New York: Basic Books.

Herman, J. L. (2003). The mental health of crime victims: impact of legal intervention. *Journal of Traumatic Stress, 16*(2), 159–166.

Herman, J. L. (2005). Justice from the victim' perspective. *Violence Against Women, 11*(5), 571–602.

Hicks, A. J., & Lawrence, J. A. (1993). Children's criteria for procedural justice: developing a young people's procedural justice scale. *Social Justice Research, 6*(2), 163–182.

Higgins, T. E. (1999). Regarding rights: an essay honoring the fiftieth anniversary of the Universal Declaration of Human Rights. *Columbia Human Rights Law Review, 30*, 225–247.

Hodgkin, R., & Newell, P. (2002). *Implementation handbook for the Convention on the Rights of the Child*. New York: UNICEF.

Holland, J., Thomson, R., Henderson, S., McGrellis, S., & Sharpe, S. (2000). Catching on, wising up and learning from your mistakes: young people's accounts of moral development. *International Journal of Children's Rights, 8*, 271–294.

Holler, A. C., Martin, J., & Enrigh, R. D. (2006). Restoring justice through forgiveness: the case of children in Northern Ireland. In D. Sullivan & L. Tifft (Eds.), *The handbook of restorative justice: a global perspective* (pp. 311–320). London: Routledge.

Holt, J. (1974). *Escape from childhood.* New York: E. P. Dutton.

Holt, S., Buckley, H., & Whelan, S. (2008). The impact of exposure to domestic violence on children and young people: a review of the literature. *Child Abuse and Neglect, 32*(8), 797–810.

Hopkins, B. (2002). Restorative justice in schools. *Support for Learning, 17*(3), 144–149.

Hudson, B. (1998). Restorative justice: the challenge of sexual and racial violence. *Journal of Law and Society, 25,* 237–256.

Hudson, B. (2002). Restorative justice and gendered violence. *British Journal of Criminology, 42,* 616–634.

Hudson, B. (2003). *Justice in the risk society: challenging and re-affirming "justice" in late modernity.* Lancashire: Sage Publications.

Hudson, J., Morris, A., Maxwell, G., & Galaway, B. (1996). *Family group conferencing: perspectives on policy and practice.* Leichhardt, NSW: Federation Press.

Immarigeon, R. (1999). Restorative justice, juvenile offenders and crime victims: a review of the literature. In G. Bazemore & L. Walgrave (Eds.), *Restorative juvenile justice: repairing the harm of youth crime* (pp. 305–326). Monsey, NY: Criminal Justice Press.

International Criminal Justice and Children (2002). No Peace Without Justice and UNICEF Innocenti Research Centre.

Jenkins Tucker, C., McHalem, S. M., & Crouter, A. C. (2001). Conditions of sibling support in adolescence. *Journal of Family Psychology, 15*(2), 254–271.

Jones, L. P., & Finnegan, D. (2004). Family unity meetings: decision making and placement outcomes. *Journal of Family Social Work, 7*(4), 23–43.

Jülich, S. (2010). Restorative justice and gendered violence in New Zealand: a glimmer of hope. In J. Ptacek (Ed.), *Restorative justice and violence against women* (pp. 239–254). New York: Oxford University.

Kelly, D. P., & Erez, E. (1997). Victim participation in the criminal justice system. In R. C. Davis, A. J. Lurigio, & W. G. Skogan (Eds.), *Victims of crime.* Thousand Oaks, CA: Sage Publications.

Kennedy, D. (1997). *A critique of adjudication (fin de siecle).* Cambridge: Harvard University Press.

Keppel-Benson, J. M., & Ollendick, T. H. (1993). Posttraumatic stress disorder in children and adolescents. In C. F. Saylor (Ed.), *Children and disasters,* (pp. 29–43). New York: Plenum Press.

King, M. (1994). Children's rights as communications: reflections on autopoietic theory and the United Nations Convention. *Modern Law Review, 57,* 385–401.

Klare, K. (1991). Legal theory and democratic reconstruction: reflections on 1989. *University of British Columbia Law Review, 25,* 69–104.

Koper, G., Knippenberg, D. V., Bouhuijs, F., Vermunt, R., & Wilke, H. (1993). Procedural fairness and self-esteem. *European Journal of Social Psychology, 23,* 313–325.

Kreiger, S. (2002). The dangers of mediation in domestic violence cases. *Cardozo Women's Law Journal, 8,* 235.

Kurki, L. (2003). Evaluating restorative justice practices. In A. Von Hirsh, J. V. Roberts, & A. Bottoms (Eds.), *Restorative justice and criminal justice: competing or reconcilable paradigms?* (pp. 293–314). Portland, OR: Hart Publications.

Lajeunesse, T. (1993). *Community holistic circle healing: Hollow Water First Nation, technical report APC 6 CA.* Aboriginal Peoples Collection, Canada.

LaMontagne, L. L., Hepworth, J. T., Johnson, B. D., & Cohen, F. (1996). Children's perspective coping and its effects on postoperative anxiety and return to normal activity. *Nursing Research, 45*(3), 141–147.

Langer, D. A., Chen, E., & Luhmann, J. D. (2005). Attributions and coping in children's pain experiences. *Journal of Pediatric Psychology, 30*(7), 615–622.

Lansdown, G. (2001). *Promoting children's participation in democratic decision-making, technical report.* UNICEF Innocenti Insight.

Lansdown, G. (2005). *The evolving capacities of the child.* Florence, Italy: UNICEF.

Latimer, J., Dowden, C., & Muise, D. (2005). The effectiveness of restorative justice practices: a meta-analysis. *Prison Journal, 85*(2), 127–144.

Lawrence, J. A. (2003). *Safeguarding fairness for children in interactions with adults in authority: computer-based investigations of the judgments of secondary school students, technical report.* Report to Criminology Research Council.

Lazarus, R. S. (1999). *Stress and emotion: a new synthesis.* New York: Springer.

Lazarus, R. S., & Folkman, S. (1984). *Stress, appraisal and coping.* New York: Springer.

Levendosky, A. A., & Graham-Bermann, S. A. (2001). Parenting in battered women: the effects of domestic violence on women and their children. *Journal of Family Violence, 16*(2), 171–192.

Leventhal, G. (1980). What should be done with equity theory? New approaches to the fairness in social relationships. In K. J. Gergen, M. S. Greenberg, & R. H. Willis (Eds.), *Social exchange: advances in theory and research* (pp. 27–55). New York: Plenum Press.

Lim, H., & Roche, J. (2000). Feminism and children's rights. In J. Bridgeman & D. Monk (Eds.), *Feminist perspectives on child law* (pp. 227–250). London: Cavendish Publishing.

Lind, E. A., & Tyler, T. R. (1988). *The social psychology of procedural justice.* New York: Plenum.

MacCormick, N. (1982). *Legal rights and social democracy: essays in legal and political philosophy.* Oxford: Clarendon Press.

Maercker, A., & Muller, J. (2004). Social acknowledgment as a victim or survivor: a scale to measure a recovery factor of PTSD. *Journal of Traumatic Stress, 17*(4), 345–351.

Maguire, M. (1985). Victims' needs and victim services-indications from research. *Victimology, 10*(1–4), 539–559.

Maguire, M. (1991). The needs and rights of victims of crime. *Crime and Justice, 14,* 363–433.

Malloy, L. C., Mitchell, E. B., Block, S. D., Quas, J. A., & Goodman, G. S. (2006). Children's eyewitness memory: Balancing children's needs and defendants' rights when seeking the truth. In M. P. Toglia, J. D. Read, D. F. Ross, & R. Lindsay, *Handbook of eyewitness psychology: Volume 1: Memory for events* (pp. 545–574). Mahwah, NJ: Lawrence Erlbaum Associates, Inc.

Mann, N., & Theuermann, B. (2001). *Children and the Truth and Reconciliation Commission for Sierra Leone, technical report.* UNICEF, National Forum for Human Rights and UNAMSIL/Human Rights.

Marmor, A. (1997). On the limits of rights. *Law and Philosophy, 16*(1), 1–18.

Marsh, P., & Crow, G. (1996). Family group conferences in child welfare services in England and Wales. In J. Hudson, A. Morris, G. Maxwell, & B. Galaway (Eds.), *Family group conferences: perspectives on policy and practice* (pp. 152–166). Leichhardt, NSW: The Federation Press; Criminal Justice Press.

Marsh, P., & Crow, G. (1998). *Family group conferences in child welfare.* Malden, MA: Blackwell Science.

Marsh, P., & Crow, G. (2000). Conferencing in England and Wales. In G. Burford & J. Hudson (Eds.), *Family group conferencing: new directions in community-centered child and family practice* (pp. 206–217). New York: Aldine De Gruyter.

Marshall, K. (1997). *Children's rights in the balance: the participation–protection debate.* Edinburgh: The Stationery Office.

Marshall, T. F. (1999). *Restorative justice: an overview, technical report.* London: Home Office.

Martineau, S. (1997). Reconstructing childhood: toward a praxis of inclusion. In A. McGillivray (Ed.), *Governing childhood* (pp. 225–249). Vermont: Dartmouth Publishing Company.

Maruna, S. (2001). *Making good: how ex-convicts reform and rebuild their lives.* Washington DC: American Psychological Association.

Maslow, A. (1954). *Motivation and personality.* New York: Harper.

Mawby, R., & Kirchnoff, G. (1996). Coping with crime: a comparison of victim's experiences in England and Germany. In P. Davies, P. Francis, & V. Jupp (Eds.), *Understanding victimization* (pp. 55–70). Northumbria: Social Science Press.

Maxwell, G., Kingi, V., Robertson, J., Morris, A., & Cunningham, C. (2004). *Achieving effective outcomes in youth justice: final report.* Ministry of Social Development, New Zealand.

Maxwell, G. M., & Morris, A. (1993). *Family, victims and culture: youth justice in New Zealand.* Wellington: Social Policy Agency and Institute of Criminology, Victoria University of Wellington.

Maxwell, G., & Morris, A. (1996). Research on family group conferences with young offenders in New Zealand. In J. Hudson, A. Morris, G. Maxwell, & B. Galaway (Eds.), *Family group conferences: perspectives on policy and practice* (pp. 88–110). Leichhardt, NSW: The Federation Press; Criminal Justice Press.

Maxwell, G., & Morris, A. (2001). Putting restorative justice into practice for adult offenders. *Howard Journal of Criminal Justice, 40*(1), 55–69.

Maxwell, G., & Morris, A. (2006). Youth justice in New Zealand: restorative justice in practice? *Journal of Social Issues, 62*(2), 239–258.

McCold, P., & Wachtel, B. (1998). *Restorative policing experiment: the Bethlehem, Pennsylvania, Police Family Group Conferencing Project.* Pipersville, PA: Community Service Foundation.

McGarrell, E. F., Olivares, K., Crawford, K., & Kroovand, N. (2000). *Returning justice to the community: the Indianapolis juvenile restorative justice experiment.* Indianapolis: Hudson Institute.

Melton, G. B. (1991). Socialization in the global community: respect for the dignity of children. *American Psychologist, 46*(1), 66–71.

Melton, G. B. (1992). The law is a good thing (psychology is, too): human rights in psychological jurisprudence. *Law and Human Behavior, 16*(4), 381–398.

Melton, G. B. (1999). Parents and children: legal reform to facilitate children's participation, *American Psychologist, 54*(11), 935–944.

Melton, G. B., & Limber, S. P. (1992). What children's rights mean to children: children's own views. In M. Freeman & P. Veerman (Eds.), *The ideologies of children's rights* (pp. 167–187). Dordrecht, The Netherlands: Kluwer Academic Publishers.

Melton, G. B., & Wilcox, B. L. (2001). Children's law: toward a new realism. *Law and Human Behavior, 25*(1), 3–12.

Merkel-Holguin, L. (2000). Diversions and departures in the implementation of family group conferencing in the United States. In G. Burford & J. Hudson (Eds.), *Family group conferencing: new directions in community-centered child and family practice* (pp. 224–231). New York: Aldine De Gruyter.

Mill, J. S. (1859). *On liberty.*

Miller, J. (2008). *Getting played: African American girls, urban inequality, and gendered violence.* New York: New York University Press.

Minow, M. (1986). Rights for the next generation: a feminist approach to children's rights. *Harvard Women's Law Journal, 9*, 1–24.

Minow, M. (1990). *Making all the difference: inclusion, exclusion and American law*. Ithaca, NY: Cornell University Press.

Minow, M. (1995a). Children's rights: where we've been, and where we're going. *Temple Law Review, 68*, 1573–1584.

Minow, M. (1995b). Whatever happened to children's rights? *Minnesota Law Review, 80*, 267–298.

Mnookin, R. (1975). Child-custody adjudication: judicial functions in the face of indeterminacy. *Law and Contemporary Problems, 39*, 226.

Moore, D., & McDonald, J. (2000). *Transforming conflict*. Sydney: Transformative Justice Australia PTY Ltd.

Morgan, J., & Zedner, L. (1992). *Child victims: crime, impact, and criminal justice*. Oxford: Clarendon Press.

Morris, A. (2002a). Children and family violence: restorative messages from New Zealand. In H. Strang & J. Braithwaite (Eds.), *Restorative justice and family violence* (pp. 89–107). Cambridge: Cambridge University Press.

Morris, A. (2002b). Critiquing the critics. *British Journal of Criminology, 42*, 595–615.

Morris, A., & Maxwell, G. (1998). Restorative justice in New Zealand: family group conferences as a case study. *Western Criminology Review*. Available at: http://wcr.sonoma.edu/v1n1/morris.html.

Morris, A., & Maxwell, G. (2001). Implementing restorative justice: What works? In A. Morris & G. Maxwell (Eds.), *Restorative justice for juveniles: conferencing, mediation and circles* (pp. 268–281). Portland, OR: Hart Publishing.

Morris, A., Maxwell, G., Hudson, J., & Galaway, B. (1996). Concluding thoughts. In J. Hudson, A. Morris, G. Maxwell, & B. Galaway (Eds.), *Family group conferences: perspectives on policy and practice* (pp. 221–234). Leichhardt, NSW: The Federation Press; Criminal Justice Press.

Morrison, B. (2002). Bullying and victimisation in schools: a restorative justice approach. *Trends and Issues in Crime and Criminal Justice, 219*, 1–6.

Morrison, B. (2006). *Restoring safe school communities: a whole school response to bullying, violence and alienation*. Sydney: Federation Press.

Morrow, V. (1999). "We are people too": children's and young people's perspectives on children's rights and decision-making in England. *International Journal of Children's Rights, 7*, 149–170.

Murray, J. (1999). Children and loss. *Children and crime: victims and offenders conference*. Brisbane, Australia: Australian Institute of Criminology.

Myers, J. E. B. (1994). Adjudication of child sexual abuse cases. *The Future of Children, 4*(2), 84–101.

Nixon, P. (2000). Family group conference connections: shared problems and solutions. In G. Burford & J. Hudson (Eds.), *Family group conferencing: new directions in community-centered child and family practice* (pp. 93–104). New York: Aldine De Gruyter.

Nixon, P., Burford, G., Quinn, A., & Edelbaum, J. (2005). *A survey of international practices, policy and research on family group conferencing and related practices*. Available at: http://www.frg.org.uk/pdfs/Family%20Group%20practices%20report.pdf

Norris, F. H., Kaniasty, K., & Thompson, M. p. (1997). The psychological consequences of crime: Findings from a longitudinal population-based study. In R. C. Davis, A. J. Lurigio, & W. G. Skogan (Eds.), *Victims of crime* (pp. 146–166). Thousand Oaks, CA: Sage Publications.

Nussbaum, M. C. (2000). *Women and human development: the capabilities approach*. Cambridge: Cambridge University Press.

Ochaíta, E., & Espinosa, M. A. (1997). Children's participation in family and school life: a psychological and development approach. *International Journal of Children's Rights, 5*, 179–297.

Ochaíta, E., & Espinosa, M. A. (2001). Needs of children and adolescents as a basis for the justification of their rights. *International Journal of Children's Rights, 9*, 313–337.

Ohbuchi, K.-I., Kameda, M., & Agarie, N. (1989). Apology as aggression control: its role in mediating appraisal of and response to harm. *Journal of Personality and Social Psychology, 56*(2), 219–227.

Olsen, F. (1992). Children's rights: some feminist approaches to the United Nations Convention on the Rights of the Child. In P. Alston, S. Parker, & J. Seymour (Eds.), *Children, rights, and the law* (pp. 192–220). Oxford: Clarendon Press.

O'Neill, O. (1992). Children's rights and children's lives. In P. Alston, S. Parker, & J. Seymour (Eds.), *Children, rights, and the law* (pp. 24–42). Oxford: Clarendon Press.

Pais, M. S. (1997). The Convention on the Rights of the Child. *Manual on Human Rights Reporting Under Six Major International Human Rights Instruments*. Geneva.

Park, Y. O., & Enright, R. D. (1997). The development of forgiveness in the context of adolescent friendship conflict in Korea. *Journal of Adolescence, 20*, 393–402.

Peled, E. (1996). Secondary victims no more: refocusing intervention with children. In J. L. Edleson & T. C. Eisikovits (Eds.), *Future interventions with battered women and their families* (pp. 125–154). Thousand Oaks, CA: Sage.

Pennell, J. (1999). Mainstreaming family group conferencing: building and sustaining partnerships. *Building strong partnerships for restorative practices* (pp. 72–82). Burlington, VT: Department of Social Work, University of Vermont; State of Vermont Department of Social and Rehabilitation Services and the Department of Corrections; and Real Justice.

Pennell, J. (2006). Restorative practices and child welfare: toward an inclusive civil society, *Journal of Social Issues, 62*(2), 259–280.

Pennell, J., & Anderson, G. (2005). *Widening the circle: the practice and evaluation of family group conferencing with children, youths, and their families*. Washington DC: NASW Press.

Pennell, J., & Burford, G. (1995). *Family group decision-making: new roles for "old" partners in resolving family violence: implementation report, technical report 1*. St. John's, NF: Memorial University of Newfoundland, School of Social Work.

Pennell, J., & Burford, G. (1996). Attending to context: family group decision-making in Canada. In J. Hudson, A. Morris, G. Maxwell, & B. Galaway (Eds.), *Family group conferences: perspectives on policy and practice* (pp. 206–220). Leichhardt, NSW: The Federation Press; Criminal Justice Press.

Pennell, J., & Burford, G. (2000a). Family group decision-making and family violence. In G. Burford & J. Hudson (Eds.), *Family group conferencing: new directions in community-centered child and family practice* (pp. 171–185). New York: Aldine de Gruyter.

Pennell, J., & Burford, G. (2000b). Family group decision-making: protecting children and women. *Child Welfare, 79*(2), 131–158.

Pennell, J., & Burford, G. (2002). Feminist praxis: making family group conferencing work. In H. Strang & J. Braithwaite (Eds.), *Restorative justice and family violence* (pp. 108–127). Cambridge: Cambridge University Press.

Pennell, J., & Weil, M. (2000). Initiating conferencing. In G. Burford & J. Hudson (Eds.), *Family group conferencing: new directions in community-centered child and family practice* (pp. 253–261). New York: Aldine De Gruyter.

Peters, J. M., Dinsmore, J., & Toth, P. (1989). Why prosecute child abuse? *South Dakota Law Review, 34*, 649–659.

Petersilia, J. R. (2001). Crime victims with developmental disabilities. *Criminal Justice and Behavior, 28*(6), 655–694.

Petrucci, C. J. (2002). Apology in the criminal justice setting: evidence for including apology as an additional component in the legal system. *Behavioral Sciences and the Law, 20*, 337–362.

Pinheiro, P. S. (2006). *World report on violence against children*. United Nations Secretary-General's Study on Violence Against Children, Geneva.

Plotnikoff, J., & Woolfson, R. (2004). *In their own words: the experiences of 50 young witnesses in criminal proceedings, technical report*. London: NSPCC/Victim Support, London.

Poulson, B. (2003). A third voice: a review of empirical research on the psychological outcomes of restorative justice. *Utah Law Review, 2003*, 167–203.

Pranis, K. (2000). Conferencing and the community. In G. Burford & J. Hudson (Eds.), *Family group conferencing: new directions in community-centered child and family practice* (pp. 40–48). New York: Aldine De Gruyter.

Pranis, K. (2002). Restorative values and confronting family violence. In H. Strang & J. Braithwaite (Eds.), *Restorative justice and family violence* (pp. 23–41). Cambridge: Cambridge University Press.

Price-Cohen, C. (1992). The relevance of theories of natural law and legal positivism. In M. Freeman & P. Veerman (Eds.), *The ideologies of children's rights* (pp. 53–70). Dordrecht, the Netherlands: Kluwer Academic Publishers.

Prout, A. (2001). Representing children: reflections on the Children 5–16 Programme. *Children and Society, 15*, 193–201.

Ptacek, J. (2010). Re-imagining justice for crimes of violence against women. In J. Ptacek (Ed.), *Restorative justice and violence against women* (pp. 281–286). New York: Oxford University Press.

Quas, J. A., & McAuliff, B. D. (2009). Accommodating child witnesses in the criminal justice system: implications for death penalty cases. In R. Schopp, R. Wiener, B. Bornstein, & S. Wilborn (Eds.), *Mental disorder and criminal law: responsibility, punishment, and competence* (pp. 79–102). New York: Springer.

Rawls, J. (1999). *A theory of Justice* (revised ed). Cambridge: Harvard University Press.

Rayner, M. (2002). Why children's participation in decision-making is important. *International Association of Youth and Family Judges and Magistrates, XVI World Congress*, Melbourne.

Raz, J. (1986). *The morality of freedom*. Oxford: Clarendon Press.

Retzinger, S. M., & Scheff, T. J. (1996). Strategy for community conferences: emotions and social bonds. In B. Galaway & J. Hudson (Eds.), *Restorative justice: international perspectives* (pp. 315–336). Monsey, NY: Criminal Justice Press.

Riihelä, M. (2001). The storycrafting method. Available at: http://www.edu.helsinki.fi/lapsetkertovat/lapset/

Riihelä, M. (2002). Children's play is the origin of social activity. *European Early Childhood Education Research Journal, 10*(1), 39–53.

Roach, K. (1999). Four models of the criminal process. *Journal of Criminal Law and Criminology, 89*(2), 671–716.

Roberts, J. V., & Roach, K. (2003). Restorative justice in Canada: from sentencing circles to sentencing principles. In A. Von-Hirsch, J. V. Roberts, & A. Bottoms (Eds.), *Restorative justice and criminal justice: competing or reconcilable paradigms?* (pp. 237–256). Portland, OR: Hart Publications.

Robertson, J. (1996). Research on family group conferences in child welfare in New Zealand. In J. Hudson, A. Morris, G. Maxwell, & B. Galaway (Eds.), *Family group conferences: perspectives on policy and practice* (pp. 49–64). Leichhardt, NSW: The Federation Press; Criminal Justice Press.

Roche, D. (2003). *Accountability in restorative justice*. Clarendon Studies in Criminology. New York: Oxford University Press.

Roche, J. (1999). Children: rights, participation and citizenship. *Childhood, 6*, 475–493.

Rogehr, C., & Gutheil, T. (2002). Apology, justice and trauma recovery. *Journal of American Academy of Psychiatry and the Law, 30*(3), 425–430.

Rogers, C. M., & Wrightsman, L. S. (1978). Attitudes toward children's rights: nurturance or self-determination? *Journal of Social Issues, 34*, 59–68.

Ross, R. (1996). *Returning to the teachings: exploring Aboriginal justice*. Canada: Penguin Group.

Rubin, P. (2010). A community of one's own? When women speak to power about restorative justice. In J. Ptacek (Ed.), *Restorative justice and violence against women* (pp. 79–102). New York: Oxford University Press.

Runyan, D. K., Everson, M. D., Edelsohn, G. A., Hunter, W. M., & Coulter, M. L. (1988). Impact of legal intervention on sexually abused children. *Journal of Pediatrics, 113*(4), 647–653.

Russell, D. E. H. (1984). *Sexual exploitation: rape, child sexual abuse, and sexual harassment*. Beverly Hills, CA: Sage.

Saywitz, K. J., & Nathanson, R. (1993). Children's testimony and their perceptions of stress in and out of the courtroom. *Child Abuse and Neglect, 17*, 613–622.

Schechter, S., & Edleson, J. L. (1999). *Effective intervention in domestic violence and child maltreatment cases: guidelines for policy and practice, technical report*. Reno, NV: National Council of Juvenile and Family Court Judges.

Scheppele, K. L. (1989). Telling stories. *Michigan Law Review, 87*, 2073–2098.

Schiff, M. (2003). Models, challenges and the promise of restorative conferencing strategies. In A. Von Hirsh, J. V. Roberts, & A. Bottoms (Eds.), *Restorative justice and criminal justice: competing or reconcilable paradigms?* (pp. 315–338). Portland, OR: Hart Publications.

Seiffge-Krenke, I. (1995). *Stress, coping, and relationships in adolescence*. Mahwah, NJ: Lawrence Erlbaum Associates.

Selman, R. L. (1980). *The growth of interpersonal understanding: developmental and clinical analysis*. New York: Academic Press.

Shapland, J. (1984). Victims, the criminal justice system and compensation. *British Journal of Criminology, 24*, 131–149.

Shapland, J. (2003). Restorative justice and criminal justice: just responses to crime? In A. Von Hirsch, J. V. Roberts, & A. Bottoms (Eds.), *Restorative justice and criminal justice: competing or reconcilable paradigms?* (pp. 195–218). Portland, OR: Hart Publications.

Shapland, J. (2009). Victims and criminal justice in Europe. In S. G. Shoham, P. Knepper, & M. Kett (Eds.), *International handbook of victimology* (pp. 347–372). Boca Raton, FL: CRC Press.

Sherman, L., Strang, H., Angel, C., Woods, D., Barnes, G., Bennett, S., Inkpen, N., & Rossner, M. (2005). Effects of face-to-face restorative justice on victims of crime in four randomized, controlled trials. *Journal of Experimental Criminology, 1*, 367–395.

Sherman, L. W. (2000). Domestic violence and restorative justice: answering key questions. *Virginia Journal of Social Policy and the Law, 8*, 263–289.

Sherman, L. W., & Strang, H. (2004). *Restorative justice: what we know and how we know it, technical report 1*. Pennsylvania: Jerry Lee Program on Randomized Controlled Trials in Restorative Justice.

Sherman, L. W., & Strang, H. (2007). *Restorative justice: the evidence.* London: The Smith Institute.

Sherman, L. W., Strang, H., & Woods, D. J. (2000). *Recidivism patterns in the Canberra Reintegrative Shaming Experiments (RISE), technical report.* Canberra, ACT: Australian National University.

Sieppert, J. D., Hudson, J., & Unrau, Y. (2000). Family group conferencing in child welfare: lessons from a demonstration project. *Families in Society, 81*(4), 382–391.

Sinclair, R. (2004). Participation in practice: making it meaningful, effective and sustainable. *Children and Society, 18,* 106–118.

Small, M. A., & Limber, S. P. (2002). Advocacy for children's rights. In B. L. Bottoms, M. B. Kovera, & B. D. McAuliff (Eds.), *Children, social sciences and the law* (pp. 51–75). Cambridge: Cambridge University Press.

Smith, A. B. (2002). Interpreting and supporting participation rights: contributions from sociocultural theory. *International Journal of Children's Rights, 10,* 73–88.

Smith, P., Goggin, C., & Gendreau, P. (2002). *The effects of prison sentences and intermediate sanctions on recidivism: general effects and individual differences, technical report 2002–01.* Solicitor General, Canada.

Spender, Q., & John, A. (2001). Psychological and psychiatric perspectives. In J. Fionda (Ed.), *Legal concepts of childhood* (pp. 57–74). Portland, OR: Hart Publishing.

Stafford, A., Laybourn, A., & Hill, M. (2003). "Having a say": children and young people talk about consultation. *Children and Society, 17,* 361–373.

Strang, H. (2002). *Repair or revenge: victims and restorative justice.* Oxford: Clarendon Press.

Strang, H. (2009). Exploring the effects of restorative justice on crime victims for victims of conflict in transitional societies. In S. G. Shoham, P. Knepper, & M. Kett (Eds.), *International handbook of victimology* (pp. 537–555). Boca Raton, FL: CRC Press.

Strang, H., & Braithwaite, J. (Eds.) (2002). *Restorative justice and family violence.* Cambridge: Cambridge University Press.

Strang, H., Sherman, L., Angel, C., Woods, D., Bennett, S., Newbury-Birch, D., & Inkpen, N. (2006). Victim evaluations of face-to-face restorative justice conferences: a quasi-experimental analysis. *Journal of Social Issues, 62*(2), 281–306.

Strang, H., & Sherman, L. W. (2003). Repairing the harm: victims and restorative justice. *Utah Law Review, 2003,* 15–42.

Stubbs, J. (2002). Domestic violence and women's safety: feminist challenges to restorative justice. In H. Strang & J. Braithwaite (Eds.), *Restorative justice and family violence* (pp. 42–61). Cambridge: Cambridge University Press.

Stubbs, J. (2010). Restorative justice, gendered violence, and indigenous women. In J. Ptacek (Ed.), *Restorative justice and violence against women* (pp. 103–122). New York: Oxford University Press.

Sturgis, B. (2009). Protecting well-being while pursuing justice. In R. F. Schopp, R. L. Wiener, B. H. Bornstein, & S. L. Willborn (Eds.), *Mental disorder and criminal law: responsibility, punishment and competence* (pp. 103–115). New York: Springer.

Sunstein, C. (1995). Rights and their critics. *Notre Dame Law Review, 70*(4), 730–768.

Taft, L. (2000). Apology subverted: the commodification of apology. *Yale Law Journal, 109,* 1135–1160.

Taylor, S. C. (2004). *Court licensed abuse: patriarchal lore and the legal response to intrafamilial sexual abuse of children.* New York: Peter Lang Publishing.

Temkin, J. (1994). Disability, child abuse and criminal justice. *Modern Law Review, 57,* 402–418.

Thibaut, J., & Walker, L. (1975). *Procedural justice: a psychological analysis.* Hillsdale, NJ: Erlbaum.

Thomas, N. (2007). Towards a theory of children's participation. *International Journal of Children's Rights, 15,* 199–218.

Thomas, N., & O'Kane, C. (1998). When children's wishes and feelings clash with their "best interests." *International Journal of Children's Rights, 6,* 137–154.

Thurber, C. A., & Weisz, J. R. (1997). "You can try or you can just give up": the impact of perceived control and coping style on childhood homesickness. *Developmental Psychology, 33*(3), 508–517.

Tobolowsky, P. M. (1999). Victim participation in the criminal justice process: fifteen years after the President's Task Force on Victims of Crime. *Criminal and Civil Confinement, 25,* 21–105.

Todres, J. (1998). Emerging limitations on the rights of the child: the UN Convention on the Rights of the Child and its early case law. *Columbia Human Rights Law Review, 30,* 159–200.

Tyler, T. R. (1988). What is procedural justice: criteria used by citizens to assess the fairness of legal procedures. *Law and Society Review, 22*(1), 103–135.

Tyler, T. R. (1990). *Why people obey the law.* New Haven, CT: Yale University Press.

Umbreit, M. (1998). *Family group conferencing: implications for crime victims, technical report.* St. Paul, MN: Center for Restorative Justice and Peacemaking.

Umbreit, M. (1999). Avoiding marginalization and "McDonaldization" of victim–offender mediation: a case study in moving toward the mainstream. In G. Bazemore & L. Walgrave (Eds.), *Restorative juvenile justice: repairing the harm of youth crime* (pp. 213–234). Monsey, NY: Criminal Justice Press.

Umbreit, M., Coats, R. B., & Voss, B. (2001). The impact of victim–offender mediation: two decades of research. *Federal Probation, 65,* 29–35.

United Nations (1959). *Declaration of the Rights of the Child,* General Assembly Resolution 1386, UN Document a/4354 edn.

United Nations (1966a). *International Covenant on Civil and Political Rights,* 999 UNTS 171 edn.

United Nations (1966b). *International Covenant on Economic, Social and Cultural Rights,* 993 UNTS 3 edn.

UNODC and UNICEF (2009). *Justice in matters involving child victims and witnesses of crime: Model law and related commentary.*

Van Bueren, G. (1999a). Combating child poverty—human rights approaches. *Human Rights Quarterly, 21*(3), 680–706.

Van Bueren, G. (1999b). International perspectives on adolescents' competence and culpability: a curious case of isolationism: America and international child criminal justice. *Quinnipiac Law Review, 18*(3), 451–468.

Van Bueren, G., Capelaere, G., Morris, A., Skelton, A., & Nielsen, J. S. (1999). *United Nations and juvenile justice: a guide to international standards and best practice.* New York: United Nations.

Van Ness, D., & Strong, K. H. (1997). *Restoring justice.* Cincinnati, OH: Anderson Publishing Co.

Vig, S., & Kaminer, R. (2002). Maltreatment and developmental disabilities in children. *Journal of Development and Physical Disabilities, 14*(4), 371–386.

Wade, A. (2002). New measures and new challenges: children's experiences of the court process. In H. L. Westcott, G. M. Davies, & R. H. Bull (Eds.), *Children's testimony: a handbook of psychological research and forensic practice* (pp. 219–232). West Sussex: John Wiley and Sons.

Waldron, J. (2000). The role of rights in practical reasoning: "rights" versus "needs." *Journal of Ethics, 4,* 115–135.

Walker, N. E. (2002). Meaningful participation of minors with HIV/AIDS in decisions regarding medical treatment-balancing the rights of children, parents, and state. *International Journal of Law and Psychiatry, 25,* 271–297.

Weisz, J. R. (1986). Contingency and control beliefs as predictors of psychotherapy outcomes among children and adolescents. *Journal of Consulting and Clinical Psychology, 54*(6), 789–795.

Weisz, J. R., & Stipek, D. J. (1982). Competence, contingency, and the development of perceived control. *Human Development, 25,* 250–281.

Wemmers, J.-A. (1996). *Victims in the criminal justice system.* Amsterdam: Kugler Publications.

Wemmers, J.-A. (2004). Victims' perspectives on restorative justice: how much involvement are victims looking for? *International Review of Victimology, 11*(2/3), 259–274.

Wemmers, J.-A. (2005). Victim needs and conjugal violence: do victims want decision-making power? *Conflict Resolution Quarterly, 22*(4), 493–508.

Wemmers, J.-A. (2009). The meaning of justice for victims. In S. G. Shoham, P. Knepper, & M. Kett (Eds.), *International handbook of victimology* (pp. 27–42). Boca Raton, FL: CRC Press.

Whitcomb, D. (2003). Legal interventions for child victims. *Journal of Traumatic Stress, 16*(2), 149–157.

Wolfe, D. A., & Jaffe, P. G. (2001). Prevention of domestic violence: emerging initiatives. In S. Graham-Bermann & J. L. Edleson (Eds.), *Domestic violence in the lives of children: the future of research, intervention, and social policy* (pp. 283–298). Washington, DC: APA.

Wolfson, S. A. (1992). Children's rights: the theoretical underpinning of the "best interests of the child." In M. Freeman & P. Veerman (Eds.), *The ideologies of children's rights* (pp. 7–27). Dordrecht, the Netherlands: Kluwer Academic Publishers.

World Congress against Commercial Sexual Exploitation of Children (1996). *Declaration and Agenda for Action* (Stockholm, Sweden, 27–31 August).

Wundersitz, J., & Hetzel, S. (1996). Family conferencing for young offenders: the South Australian experience. In J. Hudson, A. Morris, G. Maxwell, & B. Galaway (Eds.), *Family group conferences: perspectives on policy and practice* (pp. 111–139). Leichhardt, NSW: The Federation Press; Criminal Justice Press.

Zedner, L. (2004). *Criminal justice.* Oxford: Oxford University Press.

Zehr, H. (1990). *Changing lenses: a new focus for criminal justice.* Scottsdale, PA: Herald Press.

Zehr, H. (2002). Journey to belonging. In E. G. M. Weitekamp & H.-J. Kerner (Eds.), *Restorative justice: theoretical foundations* (pp. 21–31). Cullompton, Devon: Willan Publishing.

Zolotor, A. J., Theodore, A. D., Coyne-Beasley, T., & Runyan, D. K. (2007). Intimate partner violence and child maltreatment: overlapping risk. *Brief Treatment and Crisis Intervention, 7*(4), 305–321.

INDEX